Anticapitalism and Culture

CULTURE MACHINE SERIES

Series Editor: Gary Hall

ISSN: 1743–6176

Commissioning Editors: Dave Boothroyd, Chris Hables Gray, Simon Morgan Wortham, Joanna Zylinska

International Consultant Editors: Simon Critchley, Lawrence Grossberg, Donna Haraway, Peggy Kamuf, Brian Massumi, Meaghan Morris, Paul Patton, Paul Rabinow, Kevin Robins, Avital Ronell

The position of cultural theory has radically shifted. What was once the engine of change across the Humanities and Social Sciences is now faced with a new 'post-theoretical' mood, a return to empiricism and to a more transparent politics. So what is the future for cultural theory? Addressing this question through the presentation of innovative, provocative and cutting-edge work, the *Culture Machine* series both repositions cultural theory and reaffirms its continuing intellectual and political importance.

Published books include

City of Panic Paul Virilio
Art, Time & Technology Charlie Gere
Knowledge Goes Pop: From Conspiracy Theory to Gossip Clare Birchall

Anticapitalism and Culture
Radical Theory and Popular Politics

Jeremy Gilbert

Oxford • New York

First published in 2008 by
Berg
Editorial offices:
1st Floor, Angel Court, 81 St Clements Street, Oxford, OX4 1AW, UK
175 Fifth Avenue, New York, NY 10010, USA

Berg is the imprint of Oxford International Publishers Ltd.

Library of Congress Cataloging-in-Publication Data

A catalogue record for this book is available from the Library of Congress.

Library of Congress Cataloging-in-Publication Data

Gilbert, Jeremy, 1971–
Anticapitalism and culture : radical theory and popular politics / Jeremy Gilbert.
p. cm.
Includes bibliographical references and index.
ISBN-13: 978-1-84520-229-3 (cloth)
ISBN-10: 1-84520-229-5 (cloth)
ISBN-13: 978-1-84520-230-9 (pbk.)
ISBN-10: 1-84520-230-9 (pbk.)
1. Anti-globalization movement.   2. Capitalism.   3. Globalization.
4. Liberalism.   5. Culture—Study and teaching.   I. Title.
JZ1318.G513 2008
303.48'2—dc22   2008017022

British Library Cataloging-in-Publication Data

A catalogue record for this book is available from the British Library.

ISBN 978 1 84520 229 3 (Cloth)
ISBN 978 1 84520 230 9 (Paper)

Typeset by Apex CoVantage
Printed in the United Kingdom by Biddles Ltd, King's Lynn

www.bergpublishers.com

Contents

Acknowledgments

This book was initially Gary Hall's idea, and without his patience and encouragement, and that of our editor at Berg, Tristan Palmer, it certainly wouldn't have happened. Some key issues were explored in my contribution to the book that Gary edited with Clare Birchall, *New Cultural Studies: Adventures in Theory* (Edinburgh University Press, 2007). A few pages of commentary on Žižek which appear in chapter 7 are reproduced from my contribution to Paul Bowman and Richard Stamp's collection *The Truth of Žižek* (Continuum, 2007). Some of the arguments made in this book were first aired, in a somewhat more polemical form, in Paul's collection *Interrogating Cultural Studies* (Pluto, 2003).

Without these guys, I would basically never write anything down.

The readers who read the first draft of the manuscript were all extremely helpful, making an excellent range of suggestions, all of which I've endeavoured to implement. Larry Grossberg in particular offered a very detailed and engaged reading of the first draft which had a dramatic impact on the final shape of the book.

Various friends and comrades from the 'anticapitalist' movement and from other strands of political activity have helped me with their friendship and inspiration in many different ways. A little bit of my commentary on Hardt & Negri first appeared in *Red Pepper* magazine, and I would particularly like to thank those friends who organised the 'radical theory forum' workshops with me at the European Social Forums in Paris and London: Jo Littler, Sian Sullivan, Steffen Bohm, and Oscar Reyes. Tiziana Terranova gave me a copy of *Empire* when it had just been published, which is still a treasured gift, and so is indirectly responsible for a good chunk of the book!

Several passages from the book initially appeared in articles in the journal *Soundings,* whose editors have all been friends, collaborators, and/or mentors for much longer than I've been working on this book, and have all contributed directly or indirectly to my attempts to think through the issues that it addresses.

Tony Bennett, Stuart Hall, Angela McRobbie, Mica Nava, and Alan O'Shea were kind enough to take part in a roundtable discussion on the relationship between cultural studies and wider political projects, which ended up having no issue beyond my somewhat improved understanding of that topic, but was extremely useful to that end; it was also an act of great kindness and generosity on all of their parts.

The first manifestation of the final chapter of the book was a paper I gave at the *Finding the Political* conference, Goldsmiths College, so I'd like to thank the organisers, Alan Finlayson and Jim Martin, for inviting me. Some other elements of it were aired at the *Democracy Beyond Democracy: Democratic Struggle in a Post-Democratic Age* symposium in Vienna, and I'd like to thank Rupert Weinzierl for inviting me to that, as well as my co-participants, Oliver Marchart (who was later also encouraging about a first draft of the first two chapters of this book), Simon Tormey, Chantal Mouffe, and Miguel Abensour. I was supposed to write it up into an article for the excellent *Social Movement Studies;* it was in the process of doing so that it took something like its current shape, so I'd like to thank one of the journal's founding editors, Tim Jordan, for his encouragement and then his forbearance when the article never appeared. I have also realised at the very late stage of proofreading the book that all references to Tim's *Activism!* have somehow been edited out—an embarrassing oversight on my part given the high value I accord to that work.

My colleagues and students at the University of East London are a never-ending source of inspiration and support. Ta for that.

Finally, I'd like to thank my Dad, for teaching me that there is nothing so practical as a good theory, and my Mum, for similarly helping me to see from a very early age just how much politics matters.

The book is a loving present for Jo Littler. Without her love and support it would have been very difficult. Without her inspiration, it could not have happened at all.

Introduction

This book tries to stage a dialogue between the histories, concerns and abstract ideas of cultural studies and of the anti-capitalist movement. By the anti-capitalist movement, I mean primarily the World Social Forum and the campaigns, projects, struggles and ideas connected to it.

There are good reasons for wanting to stage such a dialogue because cultural studies and the anti-capitalist movement have some deep affinities. The both have their intellectual and spiritual roots in the radical movements of the twentieth century, they both tend to be informed by egalitarian, pluralist and libertarian critiques of contemporary societies, and they are both interested in the multifarious forms of contemporary and historical power relationships.

Here is a brief outline of what follows.

The first two chapters of the book make up a partial, idiosyncratic, political history of cultural studies, whose argument runs something like this: cultural studies began life as a self-consciously radical discipline which was influenced by its proximity to, and its dynamic relationship with, the politics of the British labour movement. Cultural studies wasn't, in itself, a revolutionary political project or a substitute for any other kind of political activism, but it tried to look at issues like literature, social history, popular culture and political change as all connected to each other, and it attempted to look at them all from the point of view of an understanding of society and a set of values broadly derived from the traditions of the workers' movement. At the same time, it always sought to generate new insights into the present and historical workings of culture and power that might challenge or transform some of the received assumptions of the labour movement. In particular, cultural studies emerged from the concerns of one strand within that movement, the so-called New Left. As it evolved during the 1960s, 1970s and 1980s, most research in cultural studies continued to be engaged with those concerns. At the same time, the ideas and priorities of the New Left themselves also evolved. Most importantly, the emergence (or re-emergence) of movements such as feminism, anti-racism and gay liberation brought new sets of concerns and priorities. In particular, these movements brought to light new forms of power relationships which cultural studies scholars had to take into account in their various investigations, but they also brought new risks and problems for the political Left which many of those scholars sought to confront. These investigations within cultural studies intersected with a much wider theoretical interrogation of left thought, which the chapter outlines under the heading of the anti-essentialist turn.

Despite the intellectual richness of this moment, by the 1990s most of the organised Left—from the socialist and communist movements to the New Social Movements—had ceased to be viable as coherent, consistent projects for social transformation. The defeat of communism, the dispersal of the women's movement and the hegemony of neoliberalism all consolidated a situation in which there simply were no such radical movements for cultural studies to maintain such dialogues with. This has not prevented cultural studies from growing, proliferating and extending its project and its reach. Nor has it prevented the best work in the field from continuing to offer incisive analyses of contemporary culture in its many aspects. But it does mean that cultural studies has not had the benefit of that dynamic dialogue with radical political movements that was the source of some of its energy in the past. The second chapter therefore suggests that a dialogue between cultural studies and the anti-capitalist movement might be a good thing.

Chapter 3 outlines and reflects upon the emergence of this movement, which is sometimes called *anti-capitalist* or *anti-globalisation* or *global-justice* or *altermondialiste*. Since the early 1990s a range of projects and institutions have arisen around the world which try to challenge the global dominance of liberal capitalism, and which are informed by a set of libertarian and egalitarian values very similar to those which typified the New Left. This anti-capitalism is different from the traditional labour and socialist movements in ways which were to some extent prefigured and called for by the ideas of the New Left, and by the ideas of philosophers and theorists associated with the anti-essentialist turn. The chapter therefore argues that this movement can be said to be radical democratic in its aspirations, provided that we clear up some common confusions as to what the term *radical democracy* means. On the other hand, this movement is informed by, at best, some woefully simplistic ideas about culture and political strategy. It is precisely this poverty of thought which the best cultural studies work of the past has often tried to remedy in radical movements. As such, Chapter 3 contends that it is worth thinking through some issues about culture and political strategy from a position informed by the legacy of cultural studies and the concerns of anti-capitalism.

Chapter 4 considers a range of different ways of conceptualising the relationship between capitalism and culture, and it considers reasons as to why one might or might not want to take up a political or analytical position which is explicitly anti-capitalist. Although it rejects a classically Marxist anti-capitalism, it finds good reasons for taking up a position which sees capitalism in general—and neoliberalism in particular—as inimical to any democratic culture, and worth opposing on those terms. It concludes, however, that the anti-capitalism of the movement of movements might have to be mobilised under names less abstract than anti-capitalism if it is to prove politically effective in concrete contexts.

Chapter 5 tries to think about what would be involved in developing such a position, by comparing the theoretical ideas of a number of philosophers who have written in a spirit close to that of both New Left cultural studies and of the anti-capitalist movement. This chapter is unashamedly abstract in its approach because getting be-yond the kind of simplistic thinking about culture and politics which often typifies the anti-capitalist movement demands some rigourous abstract thought. The chapter expounds some of the ideas of Deleuze and Guattari, Laclau and Mouffe and Hardt and Negri in terms that will be comprehensible to a reader with no great prior famil-iarity with their work; the chapter also offers some rigourous comparison of those ideas. The chapter organises its discussion of these ideas partly in terms of a number of themes which are central to cultural studies—creativity, complexity, power and hegemony—because one of its aims is to think through what the use of those ideas might be for engaged cultural analysis. The chapter largely concludes that, despite the tendency of these writers and their supporters to polemicise against each other, their ideas can all be deployed very usefully in the attempt to think through what a contemporary, radical democratic, post-Marxism might be both for cultural studies and anti-capitalist politics.

Chapter 6 takes some of these ideas and tries to use them to make an analysis of key configurations of power in contemporary British culture. Ultimately, it asks what scope there might be for effective opposition to neoliberalism in the United Kingdom today, by looking at the ways in which neoliberalism is both implemented and destabi-lised in the current context. I would argue that it is this kind of so-called conjunctural analysis which is the core task of cultural studies, and that this is what cultural studies, at its best, can do for a radical movement such as anti-capitalism; to try to map its ter-rain and warn it of obstacles. I don't claim that such a task can be undertaken with any authority by one person in one chapter of a largely theoretical work such as this one. I would also argue that a great deal of current work going on in cultural studies *already does this*—although it may not be explicit or even conscious about for whom the work it being done. The point of the chapter in itself is therefore not to offer a definitive analysis, but to illustrate the kind of thing that cultural studies can do with the kinds of theories outlined in the previous chapter.

Chapter 7 continues the effort to think through the major obstacles to the success of any contemporary anti-capitalism, but it does so in a largely theoretical register. This chapter tries to deconstruct what it calls 'the activist imaginary'. Put simply, 'the activist imaginary' is an attitude which makes a fetish of the so-called outsider status of activists: this attitude prevents activists from really engaging in the kind of risky politics which might produce real change (because real change would ulti-mately threaten the outsider status of activists). The chapter discerns elements of this activist imaginary in elements of contemporary political theory and tries to decon-struct them on their own abstract terms, which takes a while, but is necessary. It ulti-mately argues for the importance of an anti-capitalist partisanship which is not tied to any political or social *identity,* and for a strategic orientation in radical-democratic thought and practice which is not tied to any singular homogenous strategy. Once again, it finds that the polemics between supporters of Deleuze and Guattari and Laclau and Mouffe tend to obscure important points of agreement between them, which might be better treated as opportunities for mutual-intensification as opposed to sterile sectarianism.

The conclusion offers a nice little polemic and is very short.

I am now going to offer some problematic clarifications of terms which I will be using, mainly in the first two chapters: the terms *cultural studies, cultural theory* and *politics*. Readers with strong opinions about the proper uses of these phrases should read this section carefully, lest they become annoyed by the way I use these words later. Readers who are indifferent to such issues, or find semantic quibbling frustrating, should probably just skip ahead to chapter one.

Some Terms of Reference

Although the overall aim of this work is to set up a dialogue between cultural studies and anti-capitalism, much of it is centrally concerned with questions of cultural and political theory. This is because theory is the zone in which ideas derived from apparently quite different sets of concerns and activities (for example, political activism and cultural analysis) can reach a level of abstraction at which they can be effectively compared and exchanged.

As such, much of the substance of this book is concerned with the relationship between cultural theory and politics. But the book is also concerned with the history and potential of cultural studies.

So it seems like a good idea to explore, very briefly, the relationships between these terms, before going any further.

Cultural Studies and Cultural Theory

Firstly, I want to clarify my understanding of the relationship between these two terms: *cultural studies* and *cultural theory*. Why do I want to do this? Simply because there is quite a widespread tendency today to regard these terms as interchangeable, and I don't want this book to contribute to that confusion.

So what is the relationship between cultural studies and cultural theory? These are themselves both quite loose terms, and I am not going to try to offer final definitions of them. But thinking about their relationship is important.

Cultural theory as the phrase has come to be used today is a capacious term which includes large chunks of what might otherwise be called philosophy, social theory, political theory, psychology, anthropology or linguistics, but it does not include everything in any of one those fields. Would it be possible to offer a coherent abstract definition of what it actually is and what it actually does? I don't think so: largely because within the field of cultural theory there is no agreement on what either culture, cultural or even theory necessarily mean. That doesn't mean that we can't recognise cultural theory when we see it. Rather cultural theory is defined by how it is used, by whom and for what. Put very simply, cultural theory is the set of theoretical tools—of abstract ideas and particular ways of deploying them—which is used within the discipline of cultural studies.

This produces a rather odd situation, in which we can say that the existence of cultural theory as a recognisable field is dependent on the existence of cultural studies as a discipline, even though, having identified it as such, we could say that cultural theory is actually much older than cultural studies. This is partly because cultural studies has always used ideas which pre-date its own formation as a distinct discipline, but also because, once the discipline of cultural studies emerged, it became possible to look back and see earlier thinkers as having been concerned with similar issues even though they could not have seen themselves as engaged in cultural studies or cultural theory because those terms were not in use. The result is that one could write a history of cultural theory which traces it back to the work of Vico (1999) or even Plato or Lao Tzu, but one could not begin a history of cultural studies as such any earlier than the 1950s, and it is only within this time frame that it can be strictly accurate to talk about cultural theory as a coherent field. In other words, many of the elements which make up cultural theory are much older than cultural studies, but their existence as part of a set of ideas and debates called *cultural theory* is a by-product of the emergence of cultural studies.

So what do we mean by *cultural studies*? Countless attempts have been made to offer a firm definition of cultural studies, and they not only disagree over what it is, but over what *kind* of thing it is. For some, cultural studies is simply a discipline concerned with the study of contemporary culture, whatever that might mean, and by whatever means a given researcher finds congenial. For others, cultural studies is a *disciplinary project* aiming to break down old disciplinary boundaries and perhaps to establish a whole new concept of useful knowledge. For some, cultural studies is particular *methodological approach* to the study of culture or its various manifestations which tends to stress the importance and relative autonomy of signifying practices and their inseparability from power relationships across a whole range of fields (from cinema to particle physics). For others, cultural studies is a straightforward *political project,* almost a movement in its own right, to further socialist, feminist and anti-racist ideas in universities and elsewhere.

In offering a partial history of cultural studies in Chapters 1 and 2, I am going to allow some credence to the first and simplest of these definitions, but I want to stress that it does not necessarily exclude any of the others. Commentators often object to calling cultural studies a discipline because this seems to overlook cultural studies' radically interdisciplinary character: that is, the fact that it has always borrowed from various disciplines in the social sciences and humanities rather than emerging from just one of them, and that it continues to do so rather than firmly distinguishing itself from other disciplines. However, my response to this is simply to point out that *all* disciplines have always existed in an unstable relationship with others: sociology could never be firmly separated from economics or history, or biology from physics and chemistry, for example. Disciplinarity is itself an inherently unstable condition. There is nothing particular to cultural studies in its instability. At the same time, any discipline, especially a relatively new one, will to some extent amount to a project simply insofar as the constitution and perpetuation of that discipline will require some active and ongoing intervention into the general field of academic knowledge and the institutions which legitimate it. Any new discipline has to be a project simply in order to emerge, carve out some space for itself, and survive. What's more, any discipline at given points in its history will have one or more prevailing methodological approaches, and there may be moments when one such approach is so dominant, so distinctive to the discipline in question, and so widely applicable that people come to think of the discipline and its prevailing methodology as identical; conceptually, however, they are not.

Finally, we come to one of the big questions for this book; the status of cultural studies as a project for the furtherance of left-wing political ideas. To a large extent this is what the first two chapters will be about. For now, however, let us be clear about the approach that I am going to take to this question, which is a resolutely historical one. Historically, cultural studies was pioneered and largely dominated by people who were themselves deeply committed to left politics in everything they did, including cultural studies. They wanted cultural studies to contribute as far as possible to the wider and deeper development of left politics, which is why although cultural studies has often been *critical* of received ideas and practices on the Left, it also helped to disseminate leftist ideas in the wider society. While the aim of their work was often to develop analyses of culture which were to some extent impartial and objective, those analyses were always being produced in the hope that they might ultimately be of use to particular political projects from the progressive Left. All of this does not mean that the very idea of cultural studies is inherently leftist, but it does mean that there is a very widespread identification of cultural studies as a whole with the political tradition to which most of its key contributors have belonged; the tradition of the New Left. However, we can only fully understand the political relationship between cultural studies and this tradition if we separate them conceptually, recognising that there is *nothing inevitable* about the association between cultural studies and left politics.

So that leaves us nicely back where we started: cultural studies is that discipline concerned with the study of contemporary culture, whatever that might mean, and by whatever means a given researcher finds congenial. As with any discipline the meanings of even its most fundamental terms (*culture,* for example) and the means appropriate to it are subjects for debate within it, but with that proviso, the definition of cultural studies as a discipline concerned with the study of contemporary culture can hold.

Or can it? The trouble with this definition is that it leaves us open to the situation in which cultural studies is more-or-less whatever anyone does who claims that they are doing cultural studies. Stuart Hall, for example, has argued that this very open definition allows people to claim to be practising cultural studies who have no interest at all in basic issues—such as the question of the imbrication of symbolic relationships with power relationships—which pioneers, such as Hall himself, have regarded as fundamental to their own researches (1997).

So now I want to do justice to Stuart Hall's repeated injunction that cultural studies shouldn't mean just anything, and I also want to do justice to a particular tradition of writing which has been at the heart of the cultural studies tradition. The work of figures such as Hall, Raymond Williams, Angela McRobbie, Paul Gilroy and Lawrence Grossberg has touched upon many areas: philosophy, political commentary, anthropology, art criticism and literary criticism, for example. Yet I would argue that there has generally been one objective, whether explicitly central or obliquely tangential, to whatever they were doing that might be called *cultural studies*. That objective is simply to make sense of the precise configurations of power which shape contemporary life, without prior assumptions as to the relative importance of economics, politics or the arts. It is this attempt to analyse conjunctures—complex configurations of power relationships—using whatever conceptual tools are necessary, which I think characterises the central project of cultural studies (Grossberg 1995). This should not be regarded as a prescriptive definition, however.

Many kinds of work today go on under the rubric of cultural studies, from phenomenological art criticism to ethnographies of the media industries to speculative philosophy and broad social commentary. Cultural analysis—the wide-ranging attempt to understand the power relations which organise contemporary life—is very far from being the only thing that goes on within this open field. But insofar as all of this work has anything to do with cultural studies *as such,* it at least has some possible use in the pursuit of such analysis. We might conclude then, that while cultural studies is a name for a very broad field of work in which elements of contemporary culture are studied, the core tradition of cultural studies is always concerned with the analysis of power relations within and through that culture.

The cultural studies which I am going to examine the history of in the two chapters that follow is therefore a field which is very broad and loosely defined—including cultural criticism, political sociology, various strands of philosophy, ethnography, social theory and psychology—but whose elements all interconnect and intermesh in various ways with this core tradition of conjunctural analysis, most strikingly represented by the work of Stuart Hall.

Politics and politics

The other key term to consider here is *politics.* Now, it is especially difficult to offer a concise definition of politics in this context, because one of the premises of almost all cultural studies to date has been the idea that the concept of politics needs to be expanded way beyond the traditional focus on contestation for state power between organised groups. Indeed, some might say that, along with the other definitions offered above, cultural studies simply *is* the result of a radical expansion of the concept of politics within the humanities and social sciences. This expanded conception regards politics as involving all those processes whereby power relationships are implemented, maintained, challenged, or altered in any sphere of activity whatsoever. Given that important traditions in philosophy and social science—which have both influenced cultural studies and been influenced by it—regard power relationships as infusing all aspects of human existence, and in some cases all aspects of all existence whatsoever (Nietzsche 1968: 297–300; 332–47), it seems like it might be possible to describe almost any situation in so-called political terms. This, in fact, is one of the great sources of anxiety within recent debates over the nature and practice of cultural studies: if everything is political, then does that mean that nothing is specifically political, as some commentators seem to fear (Eagleton 2000)? Is there any difference between offering a political analysis of a situation and a non-political one?

This, once again, is a highly controversial area to which several whole books could be devoted without exhausting the range of possible positions. However, it is also a debate within which this book will have to take a tentative position before it can proceed any further. For the sake of argument, then, I am going to propose a distinction between two levels of political engagement: the political and the micropolitical. With the phrase *micropolitical,* I am referring to that level of interaction at which all relationships (even those between non-human entities such as animals, plants or even, arguably, sub-atomic particles) might be described as political insofar as they can involve relative stabilisations, alterations, augmentations, diminutions or transfers of power. At the level of human culture, for example, even such a localised and historically insignificant incident as a university deciding not to offer a degree course in modern French might be understood as the outcome of micropolitical processes involving conflicts, disagreements and decisions over the allocation of resources, or the relative prestige attributed to different disciplines within the university, and so forth.

In the next two chapters, I am going to use the term *politics,* on the other hand, in the more widely understood sense of the general field of public contestation between identifiable and opposing sets of ideas about how social relationships should be ordered. Politics in this sense is the sphere in which social movements, political parties, large-scale ideologies and powerful institutions (such as governments and corporations) struggle to determine the outcomes of the big questions about what kind of societies we want to live in. In this sense, the struggle to keep open our university French department would only be political to the extent that it located itself in a wider context of struggles against public service cuts, 'dumbing down', xenophobia, or something beyond the immediate career concerns of its staff. I could use the term *macropolitics* for this level of engagement instead, and it might be more accurate, but it would sound clumsier and take up more space. Now, the relationship between these two levels is clearly unstable and at times conceptually problematic.

For example, if we take to extremes the molecular perspective associated with thinkers such as Gabrel Tarde, Michel Foucault and Félix Guattari, then we can argue that all political processes are simply the aggregate outcomes of micro-political ones—so, for example, elections which produce changes in government are only really the outcomes of millions of individual decisions over how to cast a vote—and as such it is micropolitics which is really important and really worth paying attention to. However, I don't think that any writer (certainly not these three) has ever actually taken such a simplistic view. Were they to do so, it would be possible to reply to them that it is only once certain micropolitical processes coagulate into political ones that they take on any wider historical importance (so, for example, no one cares how particular individuals voted and it doesn't matter: what matters is who got elected and what they will do).

Of course, in fact, the two perspectives are clearly not necessarily mutually exclusive. On the one hand, we can say that micropolitical processes are fundamentally constitutive of all social reality (and perhaps all material reality; Delanda 2006); on the other hand the (macro) political outcomes of those processes can go on to have real and concrete effects in their own rights and to condition the contexts within which further micropolitical processes take place: so while it is true that the outcome of the election is the result of millions of individual decisions, those decisions are taken in the context of the consequences of the policies pursued by the existing government, whose election was itself a macropolitical outcome of prior micropolitical processes, and so on, and so on ... Of course, there is nothing at all original in this understanding, which is arguably identical to Marx's famous assertion that people 'make their own history, but they do not make it ... under circumstances chosen by themselves' (Marx 1934, p. 10).

We will return to some of these issues later. For now, it is important to be clear that what we are going to be looking at in the first part of the book is the relationship between cultural studies and politics. I suggest that the core tradition of cultural studies has derived great dynamism from its relationship to wider political contests outside the academy; not merely from its micropolitical endeavours to open up new disciplinary spaces within the academy (as valuable as they may be in their own right) but from relationships to wider political contests.

I should be clear that I am not trying to establish a moral hierarchy between these different types of engagement, rather I would like to make a useful (if necessarily unstable) conceptual distinction. Effective micropolitical interventions are clearly more useful than empty political gestures. Finally, I would add that many of the types of engagement which I am here designating micropolitical might also be understood as not political but nonetheless *ethical* engagements. In this, I am perhaps in agreement with Joanna Zylinska's recent suggestion that much of cultural studies' practice has always been primarily ethical rather than political (Zylinska 2005). In another register, the level of analysis that I am designating 'micropolitical' might be called 'ecological' (Guattari 2000; Fuller 2005), insofar as it is often concerned with the symbiotic dynamics of relatively discrete systems. Such analysis is clearly extremely important, even where it has little to say about the relationship between those discrete systems and wider formations of power.

So I am not saying that politics is more important than micro-politics or ethics or ecology. I am not saying that any intellectual project that aspires to real radicalism has to engage with politics as conventionally understood. I am not saying that at all. My only contention is that the relationship between cultural studies and politics is worth thinking about.

Having thought through some of these preliminary terms, the next two chapters will look at the history of the relationship between cultural studies and politics. The story of cultural studies is very well known. Whether we think of it as an academic discipline, a looser tradition of ideas and texts, a particular methodology, a political project or movement, or a vague name for almost any kind of contemporary work in the humanities and social sciences, there already exist numerous accounts of its emergence and subsequent history. What is interesting is that the widespread shared account of cultural studies' emergence and development tends to stress the importance of the macro-political context and the political commitments of the key participants to the early formation of the discipline but tends to pay less and less attention to this set of issues as it brings its attention closer to the present. Cultural studies is generally seen as emerging from the context of the British labour movement and the New Left in the 1950s but tends to be depicted as evolving increasingly according to its own endogenous logic as it developed as a discipline, especially after the late 1970s (e.g. Lee 2003). The main purpose of the following two chapters is to correct this emphasis, examining the development of cultural studies up to the present in terms of the ongoing relationship between its disciplinary formation, the various micropolitical interventions which constituted it, and the political context in which they occurred.

A Political History of Cultural Studies, Part One: The Post-War Years
Cultural Studies and the Labour Movement

Cultural studies first emerged as a recognisable discipline in England at the end of the 1950s, with the publication of a number of key works. In their very different ways, these books were all concerned with questions of class, creativity, culture, history and power, and of the complicated relationships between different elements of social life. Richard Hoggart's *The Uses of Literacy* (1957) and Raymond Williams's *Culture and Society* (1958) were closely followed by Williams's *The Long Revolution* (1961) and E. P. Thompson's *The Making of the English Working Class* (1963). All of these emerged partly from the climate of discussion and commentary around journals such as *New Reasoner* and *Universities and Left Review* in the late 1950s.

This context was itself the product of a complex interaction between a number of different intellectual and political tendencies of the time. In particular it emerged out of the work of scholars, both as teachers and writers, who were working at the boundaries between formal higher education and institutions and organisations strongly associated with the British labour movement. Specifically, they were involved with the movement to provide education for working-class adults who had not had the opportunity to experience higher education, a phenomenon which was widely understood as one element of the broad project of the labour movement to establish institutions and forms of self-organisation which could improve the lives of working people, either through expanding public, state-funded institutions—the core elements of the so-called welfare state—or through forms of autonomous collective provision by working-class organisations. It's worth noting at this stage that the middle decades of the twentieth century saw a general tendency for working-class political movements—socialism, communism and their many variants—to move away from the tradition of autonomous self-organisation (that had produced institutions ranging from the cooperative retail societies of the United Kingdom to the workers' councils of revolutionary Russia), towards a strategy focussed on expanding centrally controlled universal state provision of a whole range of services, from education and health to transport and energy supply, and state control of a range of key industries. On a very small scale, cultural studies emerged in the space in between these two traditions of working-class political activity. On the one hand, many of its early practitioners were involved with the Workers Educational Association, a democratic organisation funded largely by trade unions and dedicated to providing a range of education to working-class people. On the other, many of them were involved with the extramural departments of leading universities; those departments set up in the late nineteenth and early twentieth centuries to meet the growing demand that people from outside the traditional professional and aristocratic elites be given access to some form of university education (Steele 1997).

Despite how politically different the Workers Educational Association and the extra-mural departments were from one another, they tended to be staffed by teachers motivated by similar political, ethical and pragmatic commitments. In fact many teachers worked for both groups. Their commitments involved not merely extending the opportunity for working people to access the same kinds of education as their more privileged peers but also developing new types of curriculum in the humanities which would be relevant to their experiences and which were informed by the socialist values which teachers and students in these contexts were presumed to share. This involved not only transferring the established university curriculum into new contexts but also interrogating the established boundaries and values of that curriculum. It has now become rather commonplace to observe that so-called humanities curricula have tended to promote the values and achievements of privileged elites down the ages (Williams 1977; Bourdieu 1986), but in the 1950s, when the received wisdom still held that the job of humanities scholars was to preserve a 'Great Tradition' (Leavis 1948) of 'the best that has been thought and said' (Arnold 1960), this itself was a highly subversive suggestion. The idea that, instead of simply reproducing the assumption that bourgeois high culture was self-evidently superior to the rest of the surrounding culture, and was inherently worthy of study for that reason, one might undertake a less hierarchical study of that culture as a whole or in different manifestations, a study which looked at the relationships between cultural, social and economic practices from a perspective informed by the egalitarian and collectivist values of the labour movement, emerged as a critique of those assumptions relevant this specific situation. It was this idea that eventually gave rise to cultural studies.

The point that I want to draw attention to here is that for all of its micro-political novelty and innovation, what marked cultural studies as different from other such interventions, and what has lent its story a certain heroic glamour ever since, was the fact that its disciplinary, pedagogic and intellectual innovations were all informed and motivated by a clear commitment to the political objectives of the British labour movement. Now, this on its own is a fairly uncontroversial statement. Things start to get more complicated, however, as soon as we have to address two facts. Firstly, there is the fact that the so-called British labour movement was never a singular homogenous entity, and it clearly never had a single coherent set of objectives. Secondly, there is the fact that most of the key figures responsible for the emergence of cultural studies were actually committed to one quite specific project *within* that movement. Let's try to deal with these one at a time.

Firstly, the British Labour movement. Of course, no movement is ever really homogenous, and movements of all kinds are often made up of a number of quite different and at times mutually antagonistic traditions and groupings bound together by diffuse and weakly defined goals. Comparatively speaking, the British Labour movement since the early twentieth century has been fairly easy to pin down as a recognisable entity with clearly defined parts, as British labour politics has been characterised by an unusually tight relationship between trade unions and a single political party. The Labour Party was created by the trade unions and a number of socialist societies during the first decade of the twentieth century and to this day has been the only political party which any major union has officially supported (apart from the National Union of Mineworkers, which briefly supported the Socialist Labour Party of Arthur Scargill), while continuing to rely on the trade unions for financial support. Of course, at any time during that period, there have been vast differences between the political and practical agendas and aims of different sections of the labour and socialist movements, and the official aims of the Labour Party have also changed drastically over time. For example, in 1983 its aim was to establish a socialist Britain, independent of the United States and Europe, in which a democratic state controlled the commanding heights of the industrial economy. By 2005 its aim was to equip Britain to face the rigours of global competition by subjecting as much as possible of social life to the competitive logic of market economics and by effectively dismantling the public sector altogether. Yet at each of these moments there were voices to be heard within the party supporting the agenda which dominated at the other moment. Despite these differences, at any given instance, the vast majority of socialists and trade unionists in Britain have been members of organisations which officially subscribed to the stated values and nominal objectives of the Labour Party at that time.

In the 1950s—although there was just as much fierce disagreement between different sections of the left as at any other time—it is worth bearing in mind that the vast majority of its partisans would have subscribed to a particular set of assumptions that today would be regarded as highly marginal, and extremely left-wing. Almost all of them would have agreed that capitalism is a social system with an inherent tendency to generate social instability and inequality which has to be reigned in by democratic institutions. Indeed, even many politicians of the mainstream right would have agreed with this view at the time. People of different political persuasions would have disagreed on the question of whether the regulation of capitalism by democratic institutions should mean simply regulation of certain key areas of industrial policy by civil servants, gradual extension of public ownership over more and more of areas of economic life, establishment of new kinds of cooperative control of core services such as housing and manufacturing (intended gradually to displace the old, hierarchical systems typical of industrial capitalism), or revolutionary overthrow of the bourgeois state and the creation of a soviet republic. While most would have agreed that capitalism was a great source of economic and technical progress and innovation, those who did not regard it as also, basically, a problem, to be dealt with by institutions composed of or representing the wider community, were at that time in a tiny minority. Thinkers like Hayek and Friedman who were to become so influential after the 1970s had no influence at all at this time. A powerful tradition within British conservatism had itself always been rather sceptical as to the value of unregulated capitalism, recognising the threat that it posed to social order, aristocratic privilege and the security of the poorest people. This tradition was represented in the twentieth century by those so-called One Nation Conservatives, who took the reforming Victorian prime minister, Benjamin Disraeli, as their model, and this strand was dominant within the Conservative party from the 1940s until the late 1970s. Mainstream sections of the Labour Party, therefore, were not considered terribly extreme when they expressed the firm conviction that the long-term goal of their movement was to replace capitalism altogether with a social system in which the means of production, distribution and exchange were collectively owned, as the constitution of the Labour Party continued to state until 1995, even though the right-wing of the party wanted to abandon this commitment from the 1950s onwards.

What all this means for us is that we can say with some confidence that as participants in the labour movement who were clearly not supporters of its extreme right wing, the pioneers of cultural studies all shared a very broad but very profound set of political beliefs and objectives which assumed the basically destructive, exploitative and undemocratic nature of capitalism, in particular its tendency to undermine all forms of community; and that the historic mission of the Labour movement was to replace it with a socialist democracy within which collectivist and democratic values would dictate the direction of future development. It was the desire to *work through* the implications of these assumptions for scholarly and pedagogic work in the humanities which was really the founding impulse of cultural studies, and which has had a profound influence on its development ever since.

Cultural Studies and the New Left

More than this, however, most of the early cultural studies writers were committed to a particular set of ideas about the direction which leftist politics in Britain and in the rest of the world ought to take and the values which ought to inform it. Indeed, several of these figures had a significant profile within the wider intellectual left which was by no means dependent upon their status as pioneers of cultural studies (which itself would not be fully recognised as such until at least the 1970s). It was as members of the so-called New Left, as much as innovators of a new field of scholarship, that figures such as Raymond Williams, Stuart Hall and E. P. Thompson would come to prominence. The stories of the New Left and of cultural studies are so intertwined that they are often thought to be just one story about one thing. My contention will be that they are not. In fact, we can only really understand the complex relationship between them, which was the defining relationship in shaping the political character of cultural studies until well into the 1990s, if we can conceptualise them as related but distinct entities.

So what was the New Left? Well, once again this is a term we have to be careful with, as it has been used in slightly different ways over time and rather differently in the United Kingdom and the United States. However, the first group to be identified with this label, the grouping that is now sometimes referred to as the *First New Left* (Kenny 1995), was a small number of intellectuals of two generations who coalesced around the journal *New Left Review,* founded in 1960 out of the merger of *New Reasoner* (edited by E. P. Thompson) and *Universities and Left Review* (of which Stuart Hall was one of the editors). Exactly how far these intellectuals represented anything but themselves and how far they were articulating the concerns and aspirations of a whole new generation of left-wing citizens is a matter for historical debate, which it is impossible for us to address with any authority, although we can say that at certain points in its history the New Left did seem to be broadly in tune with upcoming and influential strands of the wider political left. What is important for us at this stage is that they had a fairly specific and coherent set of ideas about what political course the organised left and its supporters should follow, and these ideas directly related to the values and priorities which they brought to the nascent discipline of cultural studies (Dworkin 1997). To understand these values and priorities, we have to understand the situation in which they emerged.

After the Russian revolution of 1917, the overriding fact shaping left politics across the world had been the existence of a nominal workers' state in the USSR, governed by a communist party supposedly committed to world-wide proletarian revolution; a party which also commanded the second most powerful military machine in the world. The USSR had suffered losses and hardships during the Second World War compared to which even the ordeal of the British people seemed mild, and the military organisation of the Red Army was without question one of the key factors in the global defeat of fascism. Despite this, both before and after the war, the USSR had been subject to ongoing pressure from the great capitalist powers such as the United Kingdom and the United States, pressures which included military intimidation, economic embargoes and the political harassment of communist sympathisers in those countries. It had always been claimed by anarchists, by followers of the exiled former Bolshevik leader Leon Trotsky, and by liberal and right-wing opponents of the USSR that Stalin had built a horrific totalitarian regime instead of a workers' paradise, but many dismissed this as propaganda. For many on the left, therefore some kind of loyalty to the USSR was a *sine qua non* of any effective radical politics. In countries like France, Italy, China and many others, the largest party of the left was the Communist Party, officially affiliated to the Communist Party of the Soviet Union. Even where the Communist Party was small, as in the United Kingdom, it was the natural home for many activists, trade-unionists and intellectuals who saw the more moderate socialist parties (such as the Labour Party) as too willing to compromise with capitalists, liberals, conservatives and US imperialism to be able to bring about lasting and far-reaching social change.

In the late 1950s a number of developments converged to change this situation. Most famously, in 1956, the USSR both officially admitted the extent of state terror under Stalin (who had died in 1953) and suppressed a democratic revolution in Hungary against single-party communist rule (a revolution supported by many Hungarian communists). These final proofs of the extent of Soviet militarism and authoritarianism permanently damaged the credibility of the communist movement in the West and led many to leave the communist parties. At the same time in Britain, a new kind of political movement was becoming the focus of activity for many middle-class activists and young people. Founded in 1958, the Campaign for Nuclear Disarmament was an organisation which attracted support from many sections of society and which sought to use peaceful but high-profile forms of protest to turn public opinion against the stationing of nuclear missiles in Britain; its supporters were not drawn from any one political party or social group. The Campaign for Nuclear Disarmament sought to withdraw Britain from the cold war military conflict between the United States and USSR, in which Britain was clearly on the side of the United States in allowing US military bases to be located on the British mainland, but it also opposed the militarism of both the US and Soviet states. In this, it was largely motivated by an ethical, humanist critique of both American-led industrial capitalism and Soviet authoritarianism (Taylor 1988).

Another great event of 1956 was the Suez crisis: the botched attempt by France, Israel and Britain to take control of the Suez canal, which had recently been nationalised by the left-leaning Egyptian government and was a strategically crucial route for shipping in the region. This is often remembered as the moment when the reality of post-Imperial geopolitics was brought home to the former Great Powers of Western Europe: France and Britain were thoroughly humiliated when it became apparent the United States would not back their plan and that as such it could not succeed. However, this was only one moment in the traumatic history of de-colonisation. The Algerian War was raging at this time: the experience of colonialism in Algeria and the French government's determined and bloody attempt to retain control of this colony would leave its mark on a generation of Parisian intellectuals (Foucault, Derrida, Lyotard, Bourdieu), not to mention Frantz Fanon, the godfather of postcolonial theory; all of whom would later become important influences within cultural studies. At the same time, the post-war period saw the first great wave of migration from the former colonies to the United Kingdom, bringing with it, amongst others, a young Stuart Hall from Jamaica to Oxford on a Rhodes scholarship. The questions of national identity, neo-colonial power and racism which the break-up of the old imperial system raised could not always be answered within the terms of traditional socialist thought, and this would provide a powerful impetus to the emergence of a new set of political sensibilities. At the same time as all this, the dynamics of class and culture within British culture were clearly changing in unexpected ways. The emergence of a consumer society and a comprehensive welfare state radically altered the condition of working-class people, changing the very meaning of *working class,* while the impact of American cinema, music, fashion and television on different sections of the population was provoking visible forms of cultural change which could not be easily dismissed as superficial or short-term.

This was the context which produced the New Left, which consciously sought to distance itself from both the communist tradition and the increasingly institutionalised and ineffectual mainstream labour tradition (the British Labour party, having won a historic victory in the 1945 general election which is still widely seen as having transformed Britain for good, had completely failed to build on this success, and was out of power for 13 years between 1951 and 1964). In particular this involved the investigation of socialist ideas from *outside* these traditions: the members of the New Left tried to break the hold which Soviet communism had had on the imagination of the radical left for decades by excavating the history of native radicalism in England, and by looking to the ideas of those communists who had been marginalised and suppressed by the dogma of Stalinism. Williams and Thompson both turned to the legacies of English radicalism—most notably the utopian, proto-ecological writings of the English socialist William Morris—for inspiration, and Hall and others would soon begin to take an interest in the writings of continental thinkers such as Gramsci, Lukacs, and Lucien Goldmann (Dworkin 1997). In many ways these twin impulses—to find elements of radicalism in one's own culture that could be built on in the future, and to discover those radical philosophers from other places and times who might have been neglected—have driven the development of cultural studies and cultural theory ever since.

Centre for Contemporary Cultural Studies

The first key institutional moment in the story of this development is the founding of the Centre for Contemporary Cultural Studies at the University of Birmingham in 1964. The fact that the centre was founded, and the term *cultural studies* was coined by Richard Hoggart, is significant for our story here. Hoggart is normally cited along with Williams and Thompson as one of the three founding figures of cultural studies. Hoggart was never clearly identified with the New Left—although it was he who employed Stuart Hall as a researcher in the new centre—and his classic work, *The Uses of Literacy,* was informed by a far more conservative concern to preserve elements of British working-class culture than was that of Williams and Thompson, with whom Hoggart shared a general identification with labour politics but not the intellectual and political ambition that was to characterise their interventions. Without Hoggart, there would have been no cultural studies, but his long-term influence on the discipline has been less than that of either Thompson or Williams, arguably because his influence was restricted to the micropolitical context of the university and had no substantial relationship to a wider political context. Incidentally, 1964 also saw an important publication by Stuart Hall and Paddy Whannel: *The Popular Arts* (Hall & Whannel 1964) was a ground-breaking study of the new popular culture which cinema, popular publishing, the recording industry and broadcast media had made possible. The study argued for educators to make discriminating but sympathetic forays onto the much-derided landscape of so-called mass culture.

The wider political context itself changed dramatically in 1964. Three years after the youthful liberal John F Kennedy was elected US president and the oral contraceptive pill was introduced, the first Labour government since 1951 was elected in the United Kingdom, the globalisation of Beatlemania occurred and a widespread expectation of further social and cultural liberalisation emerged (accompanied by a growing anxiety as to its degenerate and destabilising consequences). Prime Minister Harold Wilson was elected on a promise to modernise Britain rather than to implement democratic socialism, and while his government did introduce some lasting social reforms, it was a disappointment to the radical left before it had even been elected (Anderson 1964). Interestingly, Wilson himself was eventually to regard his own major achievement as having been the creation of the Open University, an innovative adult-education institution using broadcast media and distance learning to make formal university qualifications available to a similar constituency to that previously catered for by the Workers Educational Association and the extra-mural departments, which would become the intellectual home of cultural studies in the 1980s. The 1960s also saw a major expansion of ordinary university provision and the creation of a generation of new universities (such as the universities of Essex and Sussex), which would come to be key centres of intellectual influence for the New Left.

In the United States, the term *New Left* is generally used by historians today to refer to the student radical movement which emerged in the wake of the Civil Right campaigns in the mid-1960s (McMillan & Buhle 2003). Centred around organisations such as the Student Nonviolent Co-ordinating Committee and Students for a Democratic Society (Gitlin 1987) inspired by black struggles and increasingly appalled by America's sordid intervention in Vietnam, this New Left was, like its British namesake, mainly based around clubs and groups based at universities. Arguably it was better organised and more numerous than its British equivalent, but at the same time it never developed the distinctive programme of theoretical innovation and political analysis which characterised the New Left in the United Kingdom and which came to overlap so strongly with the emerging field of British cultural studies. However, what both versions of the New Left shared was a tendency to widen out the field of political analysis and intervention from localised issues (the failures of the British state's management of capitalism in the United Kingdom; the political marginalisation of black communities in the Southern states in the United States) to make broader critiques of systems of power, and a strong commitment to democracy against centralisation and hierarchy in their own organisations and in existing social institutions.

1968

Despite such reforms and some very significant measures to liberalise British culture, such as partially decriminalising both homosexuality and abortion, the Wilson government never initiated major changes to the socio-economic structure of British society, and to the dismay of that generation of activists motivated by Campaign for Nuclear Disarmament, it passively supported the US war in Vietnam. By 1968 it was clear that neither the New Left nor the emergent youthful counterculture was going to have any serious influence over its policies. Figures such as Williams were roundly ignored despite the wider impact of some of his publications. The new manifestations of youth culture were condemned and legislated against wherever they could not be directly co-opted. Wilson's government officially honoured the Beatles in 1965 and the premier was very happy to be photographed with them, but this didn't prevent the 1966 criminalisation of LSD or moves to shut down so-called pirate radio by the Labour government. In retrospect, then, it is perhaps no coincidence that the researchers at the Centre for Contemporary Cultural Studies began to take an interest in new forms of youth culture not long after the moment when the First New Left made one of its last coherent interventions into wider political debate. *The May Day Manifesto* (Williams 1968), published first in 1967 and updated in 1968, was essentially a long essay on the condition of the United Kingdom and the British left under Harold Wilson, edited by Raymond Williams and contributed to by figures such as E. P. Thompson, Stuart Hall and Terry Eagleton. Incidentally, this was not Williams's first foray into public politics. His book *Communications* (1966) concluded with a fascinating set or proposals for the reform and expansion of institutions which could make a critical public culture possible and healthy, although he obviously had no more idea as to how they might be implemented than to hope that maybe a benign government would undertake to carry out his plans.

While the world of corporatist capitalism that the *May Day Manifesto* describes may have largely disappeared, the frustration of its authors with a Labour government willing to deploy a hollow rhetoric of modernisation to justify abandoning egalitarian goals, and apparently serving the interests of capital unquestioningly, is depressingly familiar to anyone who lived through Tony Blair's premiership. Interestingly, however, the book is extremely vague about what the independent, vibrant, modern, democratic left that it would like to help will into existence might actually look like, and what tendencies in contemporary culture might feed and sustain it. The reader today comes away with little sense that the authors had a handle on the dramatic implications of the emerging trends of youth culture, the sexual revolution and the incipient crisis of post-war politics: it's intriguing to note that several of its authors would spend much of the subsequent decades addressing these issues, one way or another, and that cultural studies as we know it would be the result.

The relationship between the *May Day Manifesto* and the more famous events of May 1968 is instructive. 1968 saw an international wave of often violent rebellions against many elements of the prevailing order—from US imperialism to conservative university curricula—the most famous of which involved a national wave of strikes, factory occupations and protests against de Gaulle's presidency and the entire regime of corporatist capitalism in France in May of that year. While it was only in France that the famous events seemed to bring the country close to revolution, radical students in Germany, the United States, Italy, Mexico, Argentina and many other places engaged in sustained militant activity, sometimes in alliance with radical sections of the labour movement. In the United States, many felt anger and frustration at the assassinations of radical leaders such as Martin Luther King Jr and at the imperialist war in Vietnam, famously culminating in the riots which accompanied the Democratic national convention in Chicago. Even in prosperous and relatively sedate Britain, the wave of student protests against the authoritarianism of universities which had been building since 1966 took on new momentum, and the protests against the Vietnam war—most famously at the US embassy in Grosvenor Square, London—attracted tens of thousands. The authors of the *May Day Manifesto,* however, didn't see this coming at all; in the words of Hall and Michael Rustin (two of its key authors): 'It completely blew us away' (Bird & Jordan 1999: 213).

Determining just what the significance of 1968 was for global left politics and for the New Left and cultural studies is not a simple task, but there is no question that a great number of different histories converged to make that year into a symbolic landmark of immense importance. In the United States, this was the year when King's assassination convinced many in the Afro-American community that there was no future for peaceful politics, leading to the intensification of black militancy represented by the emergence of groups such as the Black Panthers. At the same time it was the year of the emergence of the women's liberation movement in the United States and the historic strike by women working at Ford's Dagenham plant in East London that demanded equal pay with men. It was the year when those elements of youth culture which caught the media's attention were not the peace-loving dropouts of Haight-Ashbury or the fashion-butterflies of Carnaby Street but the revolutionary militants occupying the London School of Economics and protesting at the Miss America pageant. At the same time, however, it also was the year when the clearest signs of another new political force began to be seen in those countries. This was the year when the British Conservative politician Enoch Powell gave his notorious 'rivers of blood' speech, arguing that urban unrest could be the only result of black and white people living side-by-side in English towns. It was the year when Richard Nixon was elected to the US presidency on a promise to represent the 'silent majority' who supported the war, despised protestors and hippies alike, and espoused the 'traditional' values of American suburbia. In France, the revolution stalled and petered out, having been actively opposed by the Communist Party, who distrusted its anarchistic tone and the refusal of its partisans in the factories to submit to union discipline. In Prague, soviet tanks rolled in to crush a move towards democratisation, which had been led by the Czech communist leadership itself, in an awful repetition of the events of 1956.

This convergence of events and their long-term consequences can be understood in a number of different ways, and any such assessment must look at 1968 from the perspective of what we know now about subsequent history. On the one hand, we can see at this moment the first major manifestations of a range of political movements and projects which would have serious impacts on global society in the decades to come. Clearly, the opportunities which women and young people, and in many cases non-white people, have today for education on their own terms, for self-expression in many spheres of life, for different kinds of creative and fulfilling work, would have been almost unimaginable in 1965, except to a few socialist visionaries, and many of these gains could not have been made without the utopian militancy for which the term *1968* has become a by-word. On the other hand, these things have not been won in anything like the way that the radicals of 1968 expected nor have they been won without considerable costs. Gains in opportunities for all have nor come about through a radical democratisation of the social democratic gains made in the middle of the twentieth century, and they have certainly not come about through the aboli-tion of capitalist social relations. Instead, on the whole, they have come about in the context of a world-wide shift in the structures and patterns of capitalism itself, which has enabled people to live in far more diverse and fluid ways than at any time in the past. This has produced a situation in which people increasingly relate to themselves, to each other and to all social institutions solely as autonomous individuals rather than as members of communities, families, identity-groups, national groups, classes, unions, genders, or anything else. In the process, many of the gains which the labour movement made in the middle of the twentieth century have actually been lost. It is often forgotten now, but the right to a steady job with predictable working patterns and a guaranteed income, which would enable someone to plan a family and to plan the course of their life, was one of the great prizes which working people fought for during this time and for a hundred years previously. The promise of the welfare state to eradicate poverty and insecurity for all citizens has been withdrawn in most advanced societies today. The very existence of a public sector and a public sphere not governed by the logic of the market in the media, in education, in the areas of healthcare and other types of social provision is under serious threat. The freedom which students demanded in May 1968 may have been won, but it often seems to have been won at the expense of any hope of a society based on values of social solidarity, equality and democracy.

It is clearly no coincidence that these changes have been accompanied by massive declines in trade-union membership, as industrial manufacturing has been largely relocated to those parts of the world where labour organisation is low, and so labour is cheap; by the collapse of Soviet socialism; and by a general decline of mass par-ticipation in the political process, either through membership of political parties or through simply voting in elections (Crouch 2004). For many Marxists, the decline of social democracy and the wider crisis of democracy as such is a direct result of the defeat of the organised working-class in the developed world in the 1970s and

1980s. At its most pessimistic, this view can give rise to the observation that perhaps the Communist Party was right to oppose the students in France in 1968: for in the end, what did the radicals achieve in France or the United States or even the United Kingdom but to frighten the majority of people into support for the nascent New Right, paving the way for the eventual victories of Thatcher and Reagan, and the all-out assault on the left that they would make? From this perspective, the so-called 68-ers may have temporarily believed themselves to be anti-capitalists revolutionaries, but in fact they were merely the harbingers of a more advanced form of unregulated, consumer-led capitalism in which every demand for diversion and self-gratification could be met (many of the slogans of the French students demanded 'fun' and opposed 'boredom'), but in which the poor—a group which does not include very many university graduates—would still suffer as they always had.

A completely opposed view of the historic relationship between *1968* and the new form of capitalism which would emerge in subsequent decades is that associated with the Italian autonomist school of Marxists, the most famous of whom today is Antonio Negri. Negri's perspective is no doubt influenced by the fact that Italy was arguably one of the places where sustained militant activity by both students and workers had a long-lasting impact on political culture, unlike France or Britain, but his perspective is not a merely national one. For Negri, it is certainly true that a new, dynamic, innovative, flexible form of capitalism emerged in the wake of 1968, but that does not mean that the militancy of that year was merely a harbinger of that new capitalism. Rather, it demonstrates that the *success* of 1968 was to *force* capital to change its modes of operation in order to meet the demands of students, women, and so forth; demands which the so-called official labour movement and the communist parties were incapable of representing, incarnating, or making effective (see Negri 1988: 235. I heard Negri make this case at its most forceful when he spoke at the 2004 European Social Forum in Paris). In many ways this view is endorsed by the detailed researches of Boltanski and Chiapello (2005).

However, while this view is opposed to the preceding one in terms of its understanding of historical causality—of whether 1968 was the cause or the effect of a new kind of capitalism emerging—even Negri (who was eventually forced into exile by the right-wing administration which took power in Italy in the 1970s) would not argue that the period following 1968 was one of unqualified success for progressive forces. To take such a view, one would have to take up a position which was not allied in any way to the historic socialist project of the labour movement. Only an anarcho-capitalist, right-wing libertarian (e.g. Hoppe 1989) who cares nothing for issues such as equality, social solidarity, or the protection of the environment, could take such a position. There are people who do take such a position, drawing on rather perverse readings of philosophers such as Gilles Deleuze to support their case (e.g. Land 1992: 13), but they have nothing but antipathy for the New Left, the Old Left or any kind of cultural studies. At the same time, one can only regard 1968 as an unqualified disaster if one takes a socially conservative view, be it from the right or the left, which regards the advances made by women and young people since 1968, the proliferation of new cultural forms and experiments in lifestyle and social being, as damaging and destructive; either breaking down the traditional fabric of society or dissolving the solidarity and political discipline of the organised working class. Again, there are people who do take such views—many on the right, and a dwindling number in traditional communist organisations—but they have had no influence at all on cultural studies.

Taking neither of these positions, the politics which has informed different strands of cultural studies has all, one or way or another, had to deal with the fact that 1968 represented both success and failure. It was a success in that it saw the emergence of a whole new set of democratic demands and utopian possibilities into the public sphere which were never to go away and which were to have profound and worldwide social effects. What's more, it is worth bearing in mind that the tone of these demands—which sought to escape from the formality and hierarchy of official socialism and soviet communism—was very much in keeping with the tone of Williams's and Thompson's advocacy of a bottom-up view of history, in which change can only occur under a radically democratic form of socialism rooted in the working-class traditions of co-operation and community organisation and a utopian vision of a future of creative fulfilment for all. However, it was arguably a moment of failure in two ways. For the traditional left it was a disaster which arguably demonstrated the redundancy of traditional Marxist politics and priorities: the official Left had opposed the students and done little for the women's movement, and had advanced into no new ground of its own as a result. The Soviet suppression of the Prague Spring was for many the final confirmation that the Russian Revolution had in fact ended in a totalitarian nightmare worse than the most brutal forms of capitalism. But it was also a moment of failure from the point of view of the emergent counterculture of hippies and radicals. A radical Democrat was not elected President of the United States: Richard Nixon was. In Britain, dock workers (thought to be in the vanguard of proletarian consciousness since the great London dock strike of 1889) demonstrated in favour of Enoch Powell's racist anti-immigration policies, and the Ford women did not win equal pay. There was no revolution in France: the fragile alliance of workers and students did not last into the summer, and the Gaullist right won the national elections later that year. In the several years that followed, the Vietnam war would continue, right-wing juntas would stage a wave of successful coups in South America, and the Italian left would be completely destabilised by a campaign of intimidation and harassment from the state and paramilitary forces, with left-wing leaders imprisoned or effectively exiled. None of this would have been possible if the new radicals had succeeded in winning over those sections of the populace who did not spontaneously share their view of the world. They did not, and more importantly, from a historical vantage point there does not seem to be much evidence that they tried. Instead, they simply asserted their 'new' vision loudly and proudly, at best hoping to unite different marginal strands of the culture, and they were met with incomprehension, hostility and often violence by the state and the 'silent majority'.

What did come out of this moment was a much more widespread identification with a politics akin to that of the New Left than had been visible before. Indeed, the term *New Left* came to be used in the United States to refer to the whole swathe of so-called new social and political movements—such as Women's Liberation and in particular the radical student movement—and has been described persuasively by Katsiaficas as a 'World-Historic movement' in the period from 1968 to 1970 (Katsiaficas 1987: 17–27). Ironically, just as this was happening, internal disputes at the house journal of the British New Left, *New Left Review,* led to a marked split between Williams and Thompson and a younger coterie of writers such as Tom Nairn and Perry Anderson who were more directly influenced by the austere philosophical rigour of French Marxist theorist Louis Althusser than by the English tradition of Romantic Humanism—a split which was severe enough for this younger group to come to be referred to as the second New Left. To make matters more confusing, the term *New New Left* is sometimes used for this group of intellectuals and is sometimes used to refer to the entire generation of radicals who came of age in the later 1960s, especially in the United States. There is a considerable literature on these different developments, and the historical details need not trouble us too much now. From a wider historical perspective, I would argue that what the New, Old, First, Second, British and American New Lefts had in common was immeasurably greater than what divided them. They were all committed to radical social transformation informed by values that were at the same time libertarian and egalitarian, collectivist and pluralist. For all of these groups the idea of democracy as a key value and one which should be expanded and promoted in the social, economic and cultural spheres as well as the conventional field of politics was axiomatic (Williams 1961: 332–43; Miller 1987: 23). They all defined themselves against the authoritarian collectivism of the Old Left and its tendency to place issues of economic equality above all others, against the social conservatism of the political right and the traditional left, and against the possessive individualism of the classical liberal tradition. As such, we can talk about the New Left as a discursive formation, or, in Williams's terms a 'structure of feeling' (Williams 1977), which was first given public expression in the English-speaking world by Williams, Hall et al but which had an implicit resonance with much wider tendencies in the societies of the Western world. This resonance, however, did not form the basis for any real political victory.

The Left in Retreat

Despite its widespread resonances with various constituencies, the New Left never emerged as a coherent political movement, and historians only tend to designate it as such during the brief period of Campaign for Nuclear Disarmament's public prominence in the United Kingdom at the end of the 1950s (Dworkin 1997: 45–78), or during the period of international activism around 1968 to 1972 (Katsiaficas 1987). In some countries, actual political parties informed by the politics of the New Left emerged to play a role in public politics; most notably the German Green party. In small countries with long liberal and egalitarian traditions like the Netherlands and Denmark or in isolated politically advanced municipalities in the United States and the United Kingdom (such as London in the early 1980s; see Hall & Jacques 1989), the politics of the New Left had a clear impact on areas of public policy. For the most part, however, the New Left had little immediate impact on the sphere within which the political life of most people was shaped and lived; that of electoral politics, state institutions, national and international corporations and large-scale collective actors (unions, political parties, the mass media, etc.). As Katsiaficas writes 'the New Left proved itself incapable of consolidating a popular base'. Instead, the counterculture's challenge to accepted norms contributed to a general sense of public disquiet emerging from the end of the historic post-war consumer boom, the first rises in unemployment in the United States and United Kingdom since the 1930s, and a wave of anxieties over the urban politics of race in both of those countries (Hall, Critcher, Jefferson & Clarke 1978: 247–0). The result was not the realisation of utopia, but the widespread victory of the right in the early 1970s, a victory that would be consolidated at the end of that decade with the elections of Ronald Reagan and Margaret Thatcher. There was a brief radical upsurge around 1973–4, when a wave of trade union militancy brought down the conservative UK government and the United States was finally forced to withdraw from Vietnam, but the broad trend was inexorably to the right.

This is the context in which cultural studies developed, during its most famous period of institutional consolidation and intellectual innovation; the period of Stuart Hall's leadership of the Centre for Contemporary Cultural Studies in the 1970s. This story is normally told in terms of the internal development of the Centre for Contemporary Cultural Studies's theoretical understanding of culture and ideology via the engagements of Hall and others with the work of Gramsci, Althusser and Poulantzas, and the break between the culturalist humanism of Raymond Williams and the structuralism of the Centre for Contemporary Cultural Studies (e.g. Lee 2003: 73–107). However, looking at this work and its most potent results from a historical vantage point, the work of the Centre for Contemporary Cultural Studies now looks like a logical response to the historic failure of the New Left(s) to win the wider public battle of ideas, despite some spectacular short-term achievements. For it was at just this moment that intellectuals of the New Left seem to have been looking back to that other great moment of left-wing defeat, the 1930s. The Western Marxist tradition had produced its first great theorisations of ideology and culture at that time, in the wake of the defeat of the communist movement by fascism in much of Western Europe. It was in exile from Hitler's Germany and in an Italian fascist prison cell that Adorno and Gramsci respectively developed the first fully developed bodies of work on the politics of culture written from a socialist perspective. Despite their very different conclusions, both were to some extent motivated by the same question: how had the barbaric forces of fascism won the battle for hearts and minds and why had the communists lost it? Whether or not they were conscious of any such motivation, it seems logical now to conclude that at some level, it was the defeat of the radical promise of the 1960s which was motivating some of the most creative minds of the British left to reactivate this tradition in the 1970s, translating Gramsci into English for the first time (some short texts had been translated in the 1960s) and engaging with those more contemporary continental thinkers who seemed to be in the same tradition, such as Louis Althusser.

To understand the relationship between this political context and the internal evolution of cultural studies, it is worth reflecting on how widespread the turn to Gramsci was in the 1970s. The English edition of Gramsci's *Prison Notebooks* was published by the Communist Party of Great Britain's house publisher, Lawrence and Wishart, at a time when the political influence of the Communist Party of Great Britain within the labour movement was considerable (Andrews 2005: 105–77). Gramsci was widely read by large sections of the left and the labour movement at this time, and his influence was sufficient that the man who came to lead the Labour Party between 1983 and 1992, Neil Kinnock, would routinely cite Antonio Gramsci, an Italian communist who died before he was born, as the greatest influence on his political thought. Gramsci did not only shape cultural studies; his thought influenced an entire generation of the British left in the 1970s and 1980s.

For the pioneers of cultural studies, Gramsci was pivotal to their evolving project to generate a new discipline for the study of contemporary culture. The ideas set out so allusively and often incoherently in his prison notebooks seemed at once to offer a more satisfactory theoretical framework for *doing* cultural studies than had been available before, and to offer justification for the importance of cultural studies' intellectual project to the wider left. Gramsci had worked as a journalist and newspaper editor as well as a full-time political organiser, and in his notebooks he wrote explicitly about the value of undertaking a systematic study of contemporary popular culture with the aim of better understanding the political terrain of mass democratic politics and intervening in it more effectively. He argued that this was an important task for the left because it was only by winning the struggle to persuade large and various sections of the population to accept at least partially its view of the world that any political group could win enough support to effect social change. Gramsci's description of the 'war of position', the metaphorical trench warfare which socialists would have to wage in advanced democracies, sounds rather like the battle between the counterculture of the 1960s, with its sympathisers in the media and educational institutions, and the conservative forces of the right. The observation that any group which hoped to win such a battle would not just have to create its own autonomous culture, but would also have to work on the terrain of popular culture as it already existed, must have seemed timely indeed in the mid-1970s, as the counterculture spun out into ever more extreme experiments in alternative living while fascists began to attract significant votes in local elections in Britain for the first time since the 1930s. (For a detailed if strangely grumpy account of the story of Gramsci's reception within cultural studies, see Harris 1992).

Of course, Gramsci was not the only thing happening to cultural studies in the early and mid 1970s. The discipline was developing creatively in a number of directions, marked by several key publications. Stan Cohen's *Folk Devils and Moral Panics* (1972) was a pioneering work which prefigured many of the later concerns of cultural studies across a number of different areas. In the long term, its influence was felt most by those researchers who tended more towards critical media studies than towards ethnography and social anthropology. Its suggestion that the mods and rockers—youth subcultural groups who were the object of considerable press attention in the mid 1960s—were largely media fictions has remained a touchstone for this current of thought. The collection edited by Stuart Hall and Tony Jefferson *Resistance Through Rituals* (1976) was an innovative collection of work which also investigated the emergent phenomenon of youth subcultures, this time from a more anthropological standpoint. Contrary to the caricature which some later critics of this work were to draw, the books' authors never did romanticise youth subcultures as forms of resistance to the dominant culture, but offered a very complex account of the structural dynamics and contradictions shaping the contexts into which subcultures emerged and to which they constituted responses. If anything, they were, by contemporary standards, excessively sceptical about the value of working-class or middle-class youth subcultures, operating as they were within a framework which still implicitly judged the value of such formations in terms of their potential contribution to the long-term project of working-class revolution. Having said this, they rejected any simplistic account even of the middle-class counterculture which merely condemned it for its complicity with emergent trends in capitalism (even while they recognised that complicity), acknowledging the problems which it—like working-class youth cultures—could pose for the dominant culture. *Paper Voices* (Smith 1975) was a detailed textual study of *The Mirror* and *The Express* newspapers over several decades of the twentieth century, analysing the consistent assumptions about the readership which shaped the tone of both papers. Paul Willis's *Learning to Labour* (1977) was a classic piece of detailed ethnography, examining the lives and attitudes of a group of working-class boys in their last years of school and considering the extent to which their values and expectations were conditioned to prepare them for lives as manual workers. Between them, these works demonstrated the wide range of methodologies and topical concerns which was to characterise cultural studies in the future.

The Structuralist Turn

At the same time, work at the Centre for Contemporary Cultural Studies was profoundly influenced by the widespread interest in structuralism. Broadly speaking, this was a movement in thought which started from the work of the Swiss linguist Ferdinand de Saussure (1916), and from his observation that linguistics itself could in the future come to be seen as merely one element of a wider science of signs, or *semiotics*. Saussure had revolutionised linguistics for many by arguing against the importance traditionally accorded to philology, and for an approach to languages which studied them synchronically, as they functioned at one given moment rather than as they changed over time. Saussure's attention to the underlying structures of languages as sign-systems, and his insistence that the relationship between signs (e.g. words) and their meanings was entirely arbitrary, with no natural 'motivation', had a profound influence on many thinkers during the twentieth century, especially in France. In the 1960s and 1970s these ideas came to have a powerful influence on several strands of work in the Anglophone humanities and social sciences. In particular, they made it possible to study a range of cultural phenomena—from novels to advertisements to clothes—as 'texts', objects which were understood to be meaningful because they deployed particular systems of signs, while also insisting that the meanings of those texts were entirely a function of their location in a wider system of social meanings. In one stroke, this made it possible to analyse a vast range of cultural phenomena in useful ways, and it also broke with the assumption that the meanings of texts were simply an expression of the intentions of their authors. Structuralism also often seemed to authorise a kind of relativism which made it necessary to accept that social differences were socially and linguistically constructed, although the ethical dilemmas raised by that observation have never ceased to bedevil cultural studies ever since. Structuralism was influential way beyond the Centre for Contemporary Cultural Studies, and it is important to remember that some of the most important works to appear at this time and were later to influence cultural studies were produced by writers not connected to the Centre. For example, Judith Williamson's *Decoding Advertisements* (1978) combined structuralist semiotics with Althusserian and Lacanian theory to offer detailed analyses of particular adverts and adverts in general. Williamson produced the book at Berkley, a long way from Birmingham, but was clearly working to a very similar agenda as the Centre for Contemporary Cultural Studies researchers. The structuralist psychoanalysis of Jacques Lacan was central to the wider emergence of feminist cultural theory: Laura Mulvey's seminal essay 'Visual Pleasure and Narrative Cinema' first appeared in the journal *Screen* in 1975 (Mulvey 1989), offering a sophisticated theorisation of the place of women in the erotic economy of Hollywood film. Like Juliet Mitchell's *Psychoanalysis and Feminism* (1974), published the previous year, it proposed that Freudian ideas could be of great value to feminist analysis, contrary to the views of those feminists who saw in Freud only a patriarchal ideologue.

By the early 1970s, the generation of French radical thinkers who have come to be central to the development of Anglophone cultural theory (Derrida, Deleuze, Guattari, Kristeva, de Certeau, etc.) were mostly reacting *against* some of the problems generated by post-war structuralism, and so these writers came later to be known in English-speaking world as post-structuralists. Several of the most important thinkers of this period (Lacan, Foucault, Barthes) themselves moved away from the structuralism of their own work of the 1950s and 1960s. However, at institutions like the Centre for Contemporary Cultural Studies, both structuralist and post-structuralist ideas were being absorbed at much the same time, and what emerged was really something in between, influenced both by the structuralist Marxism of Althusser and the structuralist semiotics of the early Roland Barthes and by the post-structuralist semiotics of the later Barthes and Julia Kristeva. In his accounts of the take-up of these ideas, Stuart Hall has stressed the issue of what it was that the Centre for Contemporary Cultural Studies researchers wanted to *do* with them. In particular, he has emphasised the importance for them of the idea of culture as a field of 'signifying practices' which had some autonomy from each other and from the social and economic processes of the wider society. Signifying practices are activities by which groups and individuals make meaning, using whatever tools are available to them. So, for example, while the earlier work on youth subcultures at the Centre for Contemporary Cultural Studies tended to see the emergence of groups like the skinheads as a social but unconscious reaction to wider social changes, by the end of the 1970s Dick Hebdige (1979) was stressing the idea of style as a deliberate signifying practice whereby youth groups more-or-less consciously *intervened* in the social world of cultural signs. Hall has remarked on the difference between this approach and that found in the work of Raymond Williams, in which all aspects of a culture and a society are seen as related to all other aspects, to the extent that it becomes difficult to differentiate meaningfully between different elements of the social totality, or to locate sites of agency for specific groups or individuals (Hall 1997). However, the idea that this should mean a move away from considering the interconnected nature of cultural, social, political and economic phenomena was never part of Hall's agenda. Indeed, as we shall see, the struggle to hang on to the idea that all such phenomena are *connected,* without reproducing a simplistic notion of totality, was to become one of the key tasks of cultural theory and cultural studies.

This is a crucial point for understanding the evolution of cultural theory. Consider Hall's stress on the importance of according some autonomy to 'signifying practices', as compared to Williams's emphasis on social processes as constituting 'expressive totalities' and belief that modernity could be understood as a coherent and broadly progressive 'long revolution'. We can see a parallel here between Hall's theoretical move and a growing political emphasis on the fact that social change often happens in complex, piecemeal, ambivalent and unpredictable ways. Such an approach required the refinement of analytical tools which understand the relationships between different elements of a culture as complex and unpredictable. I think that, consciously or otherwise, it was this realisation that was driving many of the theoretical innovations and appropriations of the Centre for Contemporary Cultural Studies in the 1970s, just as it was to drive the major theoretical innovations of related theorists such as Lalcau and Mouffe in the 1980s. Most importantly, I think we should stress one point here. Once we come to see history and politics as complex and unpredictable, whatever side we think we're on, it becomes very important to be able to think *strategically* about the nature of power relationships in any given situation and the possibilities for intervening in them. Broadly speaking, I would contend that most of the radical innovations in cultural and political theory which we will look at in this book, including the Centre for Contemporary Cultural Studies's move away from Williams, have been driven by the need for democratic, egalitarian and libertarian forces to formulate new kinds of political strategy in the wake of the failures of communism and social democracy and the emergence of new forms of capitalism, new ways of living, new political antagonisms and new potential solidarities.

New Movements, New Capitalism, New Right

Given this level of intellectual innovation, we can't say that the New Left was entirely in retreat during this period. At the same time as the right was in the ascendant politically, the very continued existence of cultural studies in a publicly funded institution was testament to the localised successes of the New Left. Many believed that the 'war of position' against capitalist hegemony would necessarily entail a 'long march through the institutions'[1] as more and more of the influential organs of civil society came under the influence of the Left. As such, bringing leftist perspectives to bear on scholarly work within the institutions was seen as in itself a contribution to this struggle, a struggle which the New Left saw as slowly bearing fruit as the agendas of some of the new social movements began to influence public opinion. By the end of the 1970s, for example, legislation outlawing discrimination on the basis of gender or ethnicity had been passed in the United Kingdom and in many countries around the world, which was clearly a great political victory in many ways.

Furthermore, the concerns and practices of cultural studies itself were radically transformed by the impact of the new social movements. Feminism, anti-racism and the public visibility of nominally political strands of youth culture brought a concern with power structures and social divisions other than those of class and political objectives other than those of simple social democracy to cultural studies. The key figures to emerge from the Centre for Contemporary Cultural Studies in the 1970s—such as Angela McRobbie, Paul Gilroy, Lawrence Gossberg and Dick Hebdige—all made their names taking up perspectives informed by feminism, by a concern with the politics of race and by an interest in the radical potential of youth culture, and much of the work done at the centre was informed by such concerns. For example, *Women Take Issue* (Centre for Contemporary Cultural Studies Women's Studies Group 1978) was a ground-breaking collection which included theoretical, historical, literary, media-studies and ethnographic essays from a feminist perspective, although it also illustrates the theoretical dependence of the Centre for Contemporary Cultural Studies on a broadly Althusserian framework at that time. The evolution of this perspective is well illustrated by the career of Janice Winship, whose Centre for Contemporary Cultural Studies occasional stencilled paper 'Woman becomes an individual' (1981) takes a mainly Althusserian approach to the ideological function of women's magazines. By 1987 her book *Inside Women's Magazines* adopted a more historical and reflexive approach while retaining a strong critique of the competitive individualism exemplified by magazines such as *Cosmopolitan*. The politics of anti-racism also had a clear impact. *The Empire Strikes Back* (Centre for Contemporary Cultural Studies Race and Politics Group 1982) was a collection of essays deepening or inspired by the analysis of the popular racism pioneered in the earlier study *Policing the Crisis* (discussed in detail below). From a historical vantage point, however, perhaps the most significant contribution to the multi-authored volume was one which made no reference at all to that analysis. Hazel Carby's 'White Woman Listen! Black Feminism and the Boundaries of Sisterhood' raised an explosive set of questions over the relationships between feminism, anti-racism and class politics which would set the tone for many debates over identity politics, the nature of political solidarity, and the problem of essentialism for much of the subsequent decade. Hebdige's *Subculture: The Meaning of Style* (1979) was innovative in many ways, but most notably for its investigation of the importance of complex *interactions* between so-called black and white youth cultures in the post-war period, a harbinger of later anti-essentialist work on race and ethnicity. Overall, issues which had first been raised publicly by the new social movements had become central to the work of cultural studies.

It's important to note here that most people studying and practising cultural studies at this time would probably have regarded themselves as socialists and would have seen the limited social, cultural and politics gains made by women, non-white peoples and youth at this time as unlikely to be extended very far without major changes to the economic organisation of the society they inhabited. In this, they were descendants of the 1968 generation, as well as of the longer radical tradition which had fed into that moment. One of the animating beliefs was the assumption that the mono-cultural tedium, the gendered power relations and the marginality of non-white people in post-war culture could only really be challenged by the overthrow of existing relations of production. The choice between taking up a liberal position which condemned all sexism and racism without challenging such economic structures, and a socialist position which argued for their necessary transformation, would probably not have seemed a very meaningful one to them.

In many ways, these assumptions were correct. Capitalism as it existed in the middle decades of the twentieth century could not deliver the opportunities for personal fulfilment and public recognition that women and many other groups demanded. However, those who believed that an attack on the so-called traditional nuclear family, or the racist hierarchies of Western culture, was therefore also an attack on capitalism as such (and vice-versa) have turned out to have been deeply mistaken. In fact it was only the very specific form of 'Fordist' capitalism (Gramsci 1971) which had been in place during the middle decades of the twentieth century which generated such a hierarchical and conformist culture, and it was about to be displaced. The transformation of global capitalism in the 1970s, 1980s and 1990s has created a world of fast-moving, highly differentiated markets and systems of production which can accommodate a vast range of cultural differences and individual lifestyles, which the slow-moving corporations of the post-war economy, heavily dependent on national state institutions and typically centralised and hierarchical in structure, could not. The idea that serious inroads can be made against sexism or institutional racism in a society which is still resolutely capitalist is one which most post-war radicals, including the 1968 generation, largely discounted, but it is an idea which is today indisputable. Capitalism has shown that it can accommodate itself to the demands of women, non-white people, youth and so forth, by transforming its institutional and technological apparatuses but without altering its most basic patterns of exploitation. The problem of coming to terms with this fact has turned out to be one of the great theoretical and political problems for the left (new or otherwise) since the 1970s. In many ways, in fact, cultural studies has always been nothing more or less than the attempt to come to terms with it (Grossberg et al. 1992: 277–86).

The other such problem has been its obverse: the rise of new forms of politics which are inherently hostile to the traditional aims of the left, be they communitarian or libertarian, but which do not look or behave like the traditional forms of conservatism. We can broadly understand these in terms of two main developments. On the one hand, the decades since 1970 have witnessed the apparently inexorable rise of neoliberalism, a set of political ideas and practices which revives the core assumptions of nineteenth-century liberalism: that the individual in competition with other individuals for resources is the irreducible unit of human experience; that the first purpose of politics is to protect the autonomy of the private individual; that the right to accumulate, possess and dispose of property at will is the most fundamental right of such individuals; that the role of the state is therefore to ensure that nothing interferes with the capacity of private individuals to accumulate and enjoy property (Harvey 2005). The political implications of this philosophy are far-reaching and include, for example: the assumption that governments should work to lower taxes wherever possible, even if that means cutting forms of welfare provision that promote social cohesion; the idea that high levels of public spending are justified on institutions like the police and the military which may be required to protect the capacity of individuals to enjoy their property unmolested; the idea that corporations (which should be recognised either as individuals or as temporary contractual collaborations between individuals) should be largely free to behave as they like; the assumption that trade unions should be severely restricted in the types of activity in which they are permitted to engage, none of which should infringe the aforementioned rights of property owners or corporations. At the international level, the implications of a highly developed neoliberal agenda have come to include the assumption that international law should prevent national governments from interfering with the rights of corporations to pursue profit within their own borders by such unfair means as maintaining a state monopoly over the provision of essential services like education and water supply (Whitfield 2001). It is these ideas and policies which have been relentlessly pursued by successive US administrations and their allies at every level of government around the world, from small municipalities to the leadership of the World Bank.

The other key development has been the rise of new forms of authoritarian collectivism, which have tried to promote one particular way of life to the exclusion of others. These so-called fundamentalisms include the right-wing Christian conservatism which has grown into a major political force in the United States (Grossberg 2005), the militant Islamism which now appears to pose the most immediate threat to peace and security in the West, the militarist Zionism which convinces millions of Israelis and their supporters around the world that they are justified in their decades of oppression of the Palestinian people because God said that the land between the Nile and the Euphrates was theirs; the new forms of ethnic nationalism which tore apart central Europe in the 1990s; and the rise of Hindu nationalism in India. In many cases these tendencies derive in part from older traditions of social conservatism and authoritarian populism, traditions which have undergone a parallel renewal in countries like the United Kingdom and France where, in particular, hostility to cultural change has crystallised around hostility to immigration. In other cases there are almost entirely unprecedented developments, as in the revolutionary Islam of Ayatollah Khomeini and his followers.

At first glance these two set of developments might seem to be logically contradictory. On the one hand, neoliberalism tends to promote a general deregulation of most areas of social and personal life, the better to enable capital to pursue the invention of new commodities and new sources of profit. The immediate policy goal of neoliberalism is generally the spread of market relations to as many spheres of human activity as possible, by modelling many kinds of social relations (such as those between workers and employers, between teachers and students, even those between members of families) on the relations between customers, traders and competitors in an open marketplace. Neither ancient traditions nor modern egalitarian ideals are of much use in encouraging the spread of market relations beyond the limited spheres in which they been have historically obtained. For example, immigration from poor countries to rich ones is a phenomenon which is directly encouraged by the global deregulation of both travel and labour markets, and will tend to produce the effect of both raising the real wages of immigrants while lowering the general cost of labour in the host countries. For neoliberal economists this is an all-round win-win situation. Conservative resistance to immigration is therefore not to be encouraged from such a perspective. Conversely, there is no reason for social conservatives to support an overall economic programme which, like that of neoliberalism, tends to disrupt the coherence of established communities. Nonetheless, in many cases since the early 1970s, they have done just that. In some contexts, such as Iran, social conservatism has been linked to more predictable policies of state regulation of the economic as well as the social and cultural spheres. At the same time in the West there has always existed a small minority of right-wing libertarian thinkers and politicians who have advocated free markets, low taxation and privatisation of public services along with such policies as the decriminalisation of drugs, the removal of restrictions on same-sex relationships and the complete abandonment of all state censorship. However, the political force which emerged in the 1970s and which was to re-shape both national and world politics from its bases in the United States and the United Kingdom was one which combined social conservatism—using the machinery of the state to try to enforce social norms and police marginal communities (such as ethnic and sexual minorities)—with economic liberalism: slashing taxes and public-spending, deregulating financial markets and restricting the activities of trade unions in a general effort to lower labour costs for business (Grossberg 2005: 111–55).

Why these different policy agendas should have been brought together is an interesting question. The perspective of classical Marxism is clearly useful in helping us to understand the neoliberal agenda, which represents on all points the traditional effort of the capitalist class to restrict wages and protect profits and property (Harvey 2005). From a simple Marxist perspective, however, there is really no good reason for capital or its political representatives to advocate any kind of social conservatism. Such social changes as the entry of women into the labour market or the public recognition of same-sex relationships do nothing to reduce profits and in many cases help to generate them, by expanding the pool of workers competing for jobs and thus driving down wage bills, and by expanding the range of specialist services and consumer goods which can be marketed to specific social groups (from child-care services to gay-friendly taxi companies). Something more is therefore needed to explain the politics of the New Right than a simple idea of class interests. The most straightforward explanation is to follow the Marxist assumption that the political right, as it always has done, represents the interests of the powerful, and therefore to infer that the ruling groups in society must have something to gain from the promotion of social conservatism above and beyond the simple accumulation of profit.

This sounds simple, but its implications for radical theory in the 1970s and 1980s were profound. As soon as we acknowledge that power relationships in modern societies are not simply a matter of the class struggle between workers who want to maximise their wages and overall standard of living and capitalists who want to minimise wages and maximise profits, but involve other types of conflict and antagonism as well, then our picture of those societies threatens to become vastly more complicated, and a whole set of new questions arise. Which power relationships are the really important ones? What are the relationships between different types of power? Is there any overall set of power relationships shaping society as a whole? These are the questions which radical political theory, inside cultural studies and beyond it, has been trying to address since the 1970s.

To understand the significance of these questions, we have to understand the reliance of much radical thought on a general Marxist frame of reference during the twentieth century. Only the crudest and most dogmatic of so-called Marxists ever thought that the struggle between labour and capital was the only one that mattered. It was clear from the late nineteenth century that the struggles of women and of colonised peoples and oppressed nations around the world could not be ignored or reduced simply to aspects of the class struggle. Nonetheless, a great deal of Marxist and neo-Marxist theory in the twentieth century argued that prevalent forms of sexism, racism and homophobia were inextricably tied to the capitalist mode of production. Hence, to struggle against these phenomena effectively it was necessary to join the class struggle on the side of the workers (possibly through allying oneself to communism) and, conversely, any real progress against these different forms of oppression had to be seen implicitly as progress by the working class itself. The exclusive attention to class, at the expense of other dimensions of social experience, in Marxist political theory until well into the 1970s effectively implied that all significant social antagonisms could be reduced to facets of the class struggle. This was encouraged by a very strong tendency amongst social theorists of most political persuasions during the middle decades of the twentieth century to assume that the highly organised form of capitalism which emerged during that time was the logical form of advanced capitalism as such, an idea greatly influenced by Max Weber's argument that bureaucratic rationality was, in effect, the dominant organisational paradigm of Western modernity (Weber 1947: 328–41). Together, these intellectual tendencies converged upon the assumption that advanced capitalism was a total system that could only produce a stultifying and hierarchical culture and that any attack on any element of that culture was therefore an attack on capitalism itself. As we have already discussed, this set of assumptions could not survive the radical changes in the nature of how capitalism was practiced in the 1970s and 1980s, and it was in trying to make sense of the emergent politics of the New Right that the Centre for Contemporary Cultural Studies writers made some of the most significant headway in grasping the nature of these changes.

The Emergence of Thatcherism

Arguably the most significant piece of cultural studies ever produced was a book published by Centre for Contemporary Cultural Studies researchers in 1978. *Policing the Crisis*—a volume co-written by Hall, Chas Critcher, Tony Jefferson, John Clarke and Brian Roberts—remains a remarkable work. It begins as a study of the moral panic over mugging in the British press in the 1970s, observing that statistically, violent street robbery perpetrated by young black men against white victims had not undergone any kind of increase during this period, although the press were going to some lengths to create the impression that it had. Their attempts to explain why this should be the case lead the authors to offer an overall analysis of the crisis of the British state in the 1970s and the emergence of a political solution to this crisis from the right. Put very simply, the argument runs as follows. In the post-war period countries like Britain arrived at a social settlement according to which labour militancy never escalated to the point of posing a serious threat to capitalism as such, in return for which labour was accorded major concessions: full employment, a welfare state, rising standards of living, and governments broadly committed to pursuing social justice and prosperity for all, whatever their nominal political character. However, that settlement was dependent upon very high profit levels and relatively stable and predictable markets enabling such prosperity to be pursued without incurring major risks for capital. For a number of reasons (and economists are still debating exactly what they were: e.g. Brenner 2005) the profitability of both British and American firms began to decline during the 1960s, and by the 1970s unemployment in those countries was rising for the first time since World War II, as the traditional imperative of capital to lower labour costs was asserted.

The cumulative effect of this shift and the general decline of consensus as to what kind of society people wanted to live in amounted to a full-scale crisis for the post-war settlement, a crisis whose outcome would be decided by political struggles between different political tendencies and class fractions to create large-scale coalitions of interests committed to implementing some particular new settlement. From this perspective, the greatest danger to capital and its profits was posed by the possibility that a configuration of forces including the newly radicalised groups (women, youth, students, black people, gay people) and a well-organised labour movement would succeed in demanding a settlement which permanently weakened the power of capital to maxmise profits and suppress wages, probably through the further socialisation of large parts of the economy. Conversely, the great opportunity for capital was that it might be able to shed the constraints of the post-war settlement, to pursue its goals more effectively. In order to achieve this aim, it was necessary for a configuration of social forces to emerge which included at least some of the elements which were in danger of being radicalised in the new political context, and which bound them to the new project of capital. It was therefore necessary for capital and its allies in the press and politics to try to win support from those sections of the working classes who had not already been radicalised by the new wave of trade union militancy to a view of the situation which would ensure that they were not so radicalised and would oppose the policies of those who were. That support was won by the invention and popularisation of a public narrative about what the nature of the crisis was and how it could be solved. Essentially, this narrative maintained that the crisis should be understood as a 'breakdown of law and order' provoked by uncontrolled immigration by so-called alien elements, excessive 'permissiveness' towards minority and youth cultures on the part of parents and the state, and irresponsible militancy on the part of trade unionists and radical political groupings, all of whom represented either narrow sectional interests or more sinister conspiracies to destabilise the social order (either in the name of sheer anarchy or in alliance with international communism). The creation of a panic around mugging—supposedly a sure sign of this social breakdown—was just one element of this emergent project.

What Hall and his colleagues saw emerging, then, was a whole new political configuration, within which a large section of the left's traditional constituency— so-called ordinary working class people—would be persuaded to back a political agenda which included, amongst other things, the heavy use of the state's repressive apparatus against their traditional representatives, the trade unions. This constituency had gained relatively little from the social liberalisation of the 1960s, most of the gains of which were being enjoyed by that new cohort of educated liberal professionals which the 1968 generation had grown into. Many working-class people were experiencing the cultural upheavals which such liberalisation had produced, along with the effects of waves of non-white immigration and the loss of so-called traditional manufacturing jobs, as impositions which they had never asked for. At the same time, the broad economic context was one of clearly visible economic stagnation throughout the 1970s, something for which the press and the political right were keen to blame the 'greedy' and 'uncooperative' trade unions, whose militancy was presented as a key cause of British industrial decline. This was the context in which Thatcher and Reagan came to power, and the means by which they put together a new social coalition to support them. Promising to restore a sense of national purpose, attacking trade-unionists at home and communists abroad, promising to limit immigration, restore traditional social values and lower taxes and public spending, this was a new political programme. In the United Kingdom, at least, the Centre for Contemporary Cultural Studies writers were among the first on the left really to see what was happening, and they did it with a study that began by looking at a short-lived moral panic in British newspapers: a phenomenal achievement for cultural studies.

Importantly, it was the analytical framework offered by Antonio Gramsci which really allowed them to make the analysis that they did, and in the long term it was the success and prescience of that analysis which was one of the major reasons for the prestige which Gramsci would acquire on the anglophone left in the 1980s. Unlike most mid-century Marxists, Gramsci did not argue that the highly organised capitalism which he saw emerging in the 1930s was the only form that advanced capitalism could take. Rather, in his famous essay 'Americanism and Fordism', he analysed the social system being built in America as one very specific form of capitalism. Gramsci's understanding of modern politics as characterised not simply by the class struggle, but by the struggle for hegemony (social leadership) between different class fractions and political groupings, enabled the Centre for Contemporary Cultural Studies writers to grasp the complexity of the crisis of the 1970s. It also gave them a keener sense than many of the scale of the task which would face the left if it wanted to defeat the New Right in a struggle for hegemony. It would be a long time before most of the British left woke up to just what that task would have involved. In Britain, very few on the left in 1978 realised just how bad the coming decade would be for them, and virtually none were prepared for the wholesale victory of the right when it came. When the Labour government was defeated by Thatcher in 1979 following a disastrous wave of pay disputes with public-sector unions, many believed that it was that government's capitulation to pressure from business, the press and international finance to implement major cuts in public spending which was to blame. The Labour party therefore proceeded to elect the most radical and the least charismatic leader in its history, Michael Foot, and for the only time in Labour Party history, it went into the 1983 general election with a manifesto promising to implement a radical socialist programme. In the process it provoked the biggest internal split in its history, and performed so poorly at the ballot box that it seemed unlikely that there could ever be a Labour government again. The left had temporarily won control of the party, but they had failed dismally to win over the country, and indeed they appeared to have lost sight of that objective altogether.

The disastrous consequences of this strategy were brought home a year later when the National Union of Mineworkers went on strike in protest against government plans effectively to run down the British coal industry. This resulted in the longest industrial dispute in British history. Armies of massed pickets clashed with police at coal mine pits for much of the year. While the right-wing press demonised the miners and their leader, Arthur Scargill, media celebrities, pop stars, intellectuals and thousands of ordinary people rallied to the miners' cause, donating money and time to the infrastructure of the strike: a considerable achievement considering that up and down the country, miners' families were without any regular income for much of the year. In the end, however, it was not enough. Support for the strike was far from unanimous and unequivocal, even from unions members and the Labour leadership, sections of the National Union of Mineworkers broke away from the unions, and eventually the strike was defeated: the miners returned to work without concessions from government. One of the obstacles to more widespread and intense support for the strike was Scargill's outright refusal to hold a ballot of members to legitimate the strike, despite the fact that such a ballot would certainly have been won by supporters of the strike. A highly orthodox Marxist–Leninist, Scargill regarded such an exercise as a distraction, an unacceptable concession to liberal notions of democracy at a time when revolutionary discipline demanded that the authority of the workers' leaders be respected. Scargill's determination to maintain the proletarian purity of the miners' struggle, untainted by bourgeois ideals of democracy, did not win much support outside the ranks of the so-called hard left. Thus, in the wake of Thatcher's 1979 and 1983 election victories, the British left did not pursue a hegemonic project to win over new constituencies to its cause at all: instead it took the opposite line of asserting a political identity characterised by working-class militancy and radical socialism at a time when fewer and fewer members of the public had any concrete reason to identify themselves in such terms. It has simply never recovered from the comprehensive defeat that ensued.

Perhaps things could have been different had more attention been paid at that point to Stuart Hall and his colleagues. By the end of the 1970s he was refining his account of the emergent politics of the New Right into an analysis of the phenomenon which he was the first to name *Thatcherism*. Hall was one of a number of voices

at that time, in various countries, arguing that the broad social changes accompany-
ing the decline of industrial manufacturing and the consequent erosion of support for
the unions would permanently weaken the traditional labour movement. Along with
such figures as the great communist historian Eric Hobsbawm and the political scien-
tist Andrew Gamble, Hall became at this time one of a group of writers contributing
to the magazine *Marxism Today*. Technically the house journal of the Communist
Party of Great Britain, *Marxism Today* came under the sway of that section of the
party most influenced by Eurocommunism, a tendency in western European communist parties to reject Leninist orthodoxy and embrace more democratic and pluralistic
forms of politics, partly under the influence of the so-called new social movements.
A kind of belated rapprochement with the politics of 1968, Eurocommunism was
closely associated with the policies of the Italian Communist Party and with the
thought of its greatest icon, Gramsci (Andrews 2003). Under the editorship of Martin
Jacques, *Marxism Today* came to be the most influential organ of ideas on the British
left, with a readership that went well beyond the ranks of the Communist Party. It
was a conduit for new thinking across a range of fields, from economics to cultural
theory, but one overriding question informed the debates which it hosted: how could
the left understand the defeat it had suffered since the 1970s, and what lessons could
be learned from that defeat? The potential answers explored were various and often
deliberately extreme, and in some cases amounted to a simple concession that the
socialist project was redundant, but this was never the line pursed by Hall. It was
through *Marxism Today* that Hall and some of his colleagues in cultural studies came
to the attention of a much wider audience than radical sociologists and humanities
scholars or readers of *New Left Review*, and Hall used that position to argue consistently for a radical left politics which would try to engage with the broader sphere
of popular culture, making alliances and connections between a range of existing
constituencies and at time shedding its own shibboleths in order to acquire new support, making itself relevant to the new situation of post-industrial Britain. This was
the politics of New Left cultural studies writ large. The best record of this moment
is Stuart Hall's collection of essays *The Hard Road to Renewal* (1988)—his only
single-authored volume, intriguingly—which was mainly a set of political writings
drawn from his contributions to *Marxism Today* and *New Socialist* magazines. It is a
fascinating document of British left politics in the 1980s, as well as a unique collection of exemplary political analyses.

But what was happening to cultural studies itself at this time? As the decade
turned, Birmingham remained a centre of innovation. David Morley's *The Nation-
wide Audience* (1980) was a ground-breaking study of differential responses to a key
TV news programme which was already clearly informed by a nascent post-Marxist
perspective, stressing the importance of the political discourse in which particular social groups participated as conditioning their responses more dramatically than their
class location understood in any simple terms. *Culture Media Language* (Hall, Hobson, Lowe & Willis 1980) was a diverse collection which demonstrated the growing

theoretical, topical and methodological scope of cultural studies, covering work on media, literature, linguistics ethnography and audience-studies. Interestingly, while the book contains reflections on the changing institutional context of cultural studies and on the latest theoretical debates, it contains no reference to the broader political context or to the current state of those political and social movements which are the source of many of those ideas. As we have just seen, figures such as Hall, the editor of the volume, were to continue to focus their attentions on issues of immediate political concern: but the relationship between those and the wider work of cultural studies was changing as the left went further into retreat.

Note

1. This phrase is usually attributed to Rudi Dutschke, one of the leaders of the West German radical student movement in 1968 and one of the founders of the West German Green Party in the 1970s.

–2–

A Political History of Cultural Studies, Part Two: The Politics of Defeat

Into the 80s …

It was at this time that Stuart Hall himself left the Centre for Contemporary Cultural Studies to work at the Open University, which in the 1980s became the key site for innovation and consolidation in the field. The powerful cocktail of structuralist semiotics and Gramscian theory which the Centre for Contemporary Cultural Studies had mixed in the 1970s became the key paradigm for work across a range of fields at the Open University (e.g. Middleton 1990) while Centre for Contemporary Cultural Studies graduates began to staff new programmes in cultural studies at institutions such as Portsmouth and North-East London Polytechnics. At the same time, the political crisis of the left, the politics of the social movements, and the long-term influence of 1968 all impacted on the methods of cultural studies and its choice of objects for study.

To get to grips with the nature of these changes, it is necessary to understand still further the broader conjuncture in which they took place. While the right seemed absolutely hegemonic in political and economic terms, so-called mass culture in the early 1980s looked in many ways like a site of progressive change. In the United Kingdom, Thatcher may have won elections, but the pop charts were topped by gay singers who publicly supported the striking miners while the fashion and advertising industries promoted the pro-feminist 'New Man' as the ideal model of masculinity (Nixon 1996). The fourth national television network, Channel Four, started broadcasting in 1982 with an explicit remit to represent minority interests, and for much of the decade did indeed offer programs catering explicitly to feminist, gay and ethnic minority interests. The channel even made a minor celebrity of Marxist historian Gwyn Williams (a lifelong friend of Raymond Williams). Pop culture must have looked to many at this moment like a more promising site of struggle than the picket line or the polling booth. At the same time, importantly, the mainstream political left had never embraced the libertarianism of the 1960s with any enthusiasm, and this was a growing problem in terms of its ability to reach new constituencies.

Throughout the developed world, the generation who had grown up in the 1950s and 1960s included many people who wanted to enjoy the freedoms of the new liberal consumer society but had no investment in preserving the social gains of the post-war period now that they felt prosperous enough not to have to rely on the state, the unions or their local community for support in hard times. By the end of the 1970s there were many such citizens working in new and expanding economic sectors—most notably the service industries, media and communications, and information technology—who had no interest in radical politics and no reason to identify with the labour movement, with its firm historical base in manufacturing industries. In many metropolitan and suburban areas, such people were a crucial addition to the coalition supporting the New Right, whose rhetoric promised to encourage free enterprise and release the spending power of the overtaxed consumer even while it promised to curb immigration and union power. The dream of 1968 had always been that the hedonism that the new consumer society made possible, and the right to self-expression, which was one of the demands of the new social movements, need not lead only to such a selfish individualism. Indeed, the utopian tradition of romantic socialism which had inspired Williams and Thompson (like the anarchist tradition which they tended to ignore) had itself always asserted that capitalism could not ultimately contain a demand for true autonomy and creative fulfilment on the part of all citizens. However, the mainstream communist and socialist left had been barely touched by this sensibility in the twentieth century, and had tended to appeal to ideals of class or national solidarity rather than to any kind of hedonistic imperative amongst its possible constituencies. Indeed, both the communist tradition and the mainstream socialist tradition (which, according to Harold Wilson, 'owed more to Methodism than to Marxism') tended to adopt a rather censorious stance towards the new pleasures which consumer culture made available. By the 1980s it had become clear that this was an approach which could never win support in relatively prosperous countries. Since the 1950s, one of the appeals which the New Left had made to the Labour mainstream was to take seriously the challenge posed by the enthusiastic embrace of consumer culture on the part of young people, women and conservative politicians, and this was clearly one of the motivations behind the initial project of cultural studies itself. Now both the urgency of this task and the opportunities it seemed to represent were greatly enhanced.

This was the context for the moment of cultural populism. This term was used to describe the way in which nominally leftist commentators working in or influenced by cultural studies began to embrace elements of contemporary popular culture for their potential radicalism and to denigrate as elitist and exclusionary cultural forms or theoretical positions informed by any kind of avant-gardism. The cultural populism of the 1980s was a recognisable and coherent body of attitudes and approaches, but it did not amount to a consistent and homogenous political perspective. Instead, it is better understood as a continuum of opinion which ranged from the democratic, libertarian Marxism of E. P. Thompson to the perspectives of those who argued that the defeat of socialism was so complete that nihilistic or celebratory abandonment to the postmodern world of hyper-capitalism was the only reasonable response (Baudrillard 1988a). In the specific context of British left politics in the 1980s, all of these positions found common ground in their resistance to that so-called old left conservatism, which insisted that the basic features of the classic struggle had not changed and that political tactics appropriate to the beginning of the twentieth century remained appropriate at the end of it. Critics of Stuart Hall and other cultural populists of the 1980s have consistently refused to address this aspect of the political context in which they were operating, asserting without any substantive argument that the political implications of all elements of the cultural populist continuum were effectively identical (e.g. Žižek 2001, Frank 2002). As we will see, subsequent history comprehensively undermined this assumption: whereas one section of the left was to embrace the corporate populism of Blair and Clinton in the 1990s, New Left cultural studies figures such as Hall and McRobbie did not.

Cultural populism was exemplified by some of the key cultural studies works of the period. Ien Ang's *Watching Dallas* (1985) offered a fascinating description of the range of responses to the popular TV show amongst members of the Dutch audience and identified a tension between the dominant ideology of mass culture and a populist aesthetic which opposed it. While the study raised some important questions about the complex relationships *and non-relationships* between quotidian pleasures, private fantasies and modes of political identification, its failure to offer answers to any of those questions and its lack of any coherent theoretical framework left it open to charges of simplistic populism (charges which the book itself explicitly denied, but without offering any coherent alternative conclusion to be drawn from its own critiques of anti-populist positions). John Fiske's *Television Culture* (1987), a now notorious classic of 1980s cultural populism, envisages contemporary culture as a 'semiotic democracy' in which audiences are free to make their own meanings from the various materials of media culture. Fiske's work has been widely seen as absurdly optimistic, effectively denying that either the specific content of media outputs, the economics of media ownership, or the power differentials between different components of media networks are of any real political importance. However, is it easy to caricature Fiske, who was in many ways working in the same spirit as E. P. Thompson in his efforts to record the history of English working-class agency. Fiske saw himself as asserting the capacities of ordinary people against the elitism and fatalism of certain strands of ideology critique and the naïve moralism of much mainstream commentary on media culture. However, as much as one would like to defend Fiske against his legions of critics, it is undeniable that his work inspired a wave of commentary which seemed to assume that anything that was popular was thereby inherently radical, democratic and good. By no means all cultural studies of this moment was so naïve, however. Coming at the end of this phase, Mica Nava's *Changing Cultures: Feminism, Youth and Consumerism* (1992) brought together a number of essays which exemplified the new emphasis on consumer agency in novel and useful ways, emphasising the unpredictable creativity of consumers, especially young ones. Angela McRobbie remained at the forefront of this kind of research, looking for signs of democratisation in the culture wherever they might be found, but without succumbing to naïve populism at any stage: *Feminism and Youth Culture: from 'Jackie' to 'Just Seventeen'* (1990) is a collection of McRobbie's important writings and remains exemplary of its kind.

Marxism Today and the New Times

At this stage of the argument, it is important to grasp the extent to which the old left continued to dominate radical political discourse in the Britain of the 1980s. Still by far the most visible and well-organised groupings to the left of the Labour leadership at this time were neo-Trotskyists such as the Socialist Workers Party and the notorious Militant Tendency: an entryist faction whose express aim was to destroy the 'bourgeois socialist' Labour Party from within, but whose members and supporters were nonetheless indignant at being hounded out of the party by the Labour leadership in the latter part of the decade. All of these groups were explicitly opposed to those so-called revisionists who, following Gramsci, argued that the tactics and forms of political organisation which had worked in Russia in 1917 might not be effective in the world of mass democracy, consumerism and globalised capitalism. They also tended to regard it as their revolutionary duty to impose their view wherever they had any influence (in local government, trade unions and Labour Party branches), by means of physical intimidation if necessary. At the same time, despite the government actually being voted for by a minority of the electorate, a divided mainstream opposition was allowing the Thatcher government to implement the most right-wing political agenda of any since the advent of mass democracy. It is easy to understand how intelligent socialists like Stuart Hall, searching for alternatives that might have a wider popular appeal, could make common cause with writers from the left such as Charles Leadbeater and Geoff Mulgan, even if those particular figures were in the process of abandoning socialism altogether. *Marxism Today* was where that common cause was made (Hall & Jacques 1989).

What that cause amounted to was never a coherent political programme, but an attempt by a number of writers and analysts to paint a broad picture of what was happening to the economics, culture and politics of the advanced capitalist democracies at the time, and in particular to think about what that meant for the future of British left politics, broadly defined. This project to map the 'New Times' gained further impetus from the collapse of soviet communism at the end of the decade, especially given that *Marxism Today* was still ostensibly a communist magazine. However, in retrospect, we would have to say that even this cataclysm was, like Thatcherism, only one localised symptom of a global process. As we have seen, since the early 1970s international capitalism had gone through a process of wholesale restructuring which had increased and intensified global flows of money, goods, ideas and people. New technologies in the fields of communications, electronics and robotics enabled manufacturers to dispense with large parts of their workforce permanently and to move production from one region, country or even continent to another in search of lower labour costs. The deregulation of international finance markets enabled investors and speculators for the first time to move capital in and out of a country almost at will. As fashion cycles, changing tastes and intensified competition made consumer markets ever-more unpredictable, the mid-century model of the mighty vertically integrated firm—the total corporation with its own market research, research and design, manufacturing, distribution and marketing divisions—gave way to the ideal of the lean corporation, specialising in a narrow range of tasks and entering into a range of flexible short-term contractual relationships with other small specialised firms. Naturally, such corporations wanted that kind of flexibility in their relationships with their employees, and rising unemployment meant that they could demand it, despite the protests of trade-unionists who had spent the past 150 years struggling to achieve security and stability for ordinary workers. The system of production and general social organisation described by Gramsci as 'Fordist' (because he associated it with the Henry Ford's innovative policy of paying his workers a high wage for deeply unrewarding work on assembly lines while imposing stringent conditions of 'respectability' on their personal lives) was giving way to a new 'post-Fordist' world of 'disorganised capitalism' (Lash & Urry 1987), unashamed consumer hedonism, an ever-proliferating array of lifestyles and an ever-shrinking degree of social cohesion.

The winners from this shift towards consumer hedonism were those capitalists who could adapt to it and those consumers who could afford to benefit from the vast new range of choices available to them. The losers were all those groups, individuals and institutions whose habitual ways of dealing with the world assumed the relatively stable, predictable and ordered world of Fordist capitalism or pre-modern traditions. National governments quickly found that they could not maintain high levels of taxation without driving capital out of the country, and so could not afford to maintain expansive and generous social programmes or to invest heavily in economic infrastructure. Those firms which depended heavily on state protection, regulation, or provision of infrastructure (such as transport networks) could not survive. The Soviet economies, entirely controlled by and dependent on national governments, were simply unable to compete under these conditions: they could not deliver consumer satisfaction or generate sufficient productivity to support the Soviet Union's ever more costly arms race with the United States. In 1989, under pressure from mass protests, Soviet leaderships more or less abandoned the attempt to maintain a non-capitalist economic model in Eastern Europe. In the meantime, the 1980s had seen nominally socialist governments in places as far apart as France and Australia implement neoliberal economic policies, cutting taxes and public spending while privatising publicly owned services and enterprises. It is often forgotten in Britain that the neoliberal programme of governmental cost-cutting was begun by the Labour government in 1976, under enormous pressure from the International Monetary Fund, not by Thatcher in 1979.

The essays brought together in the Hall and Jacques volume *New Times* (1989) charts the importance of new kinds of political mobilisation (such as *Live Aid* and consumer boycotts) in a heavily mediated culture and the weakness of forms such as traditional trade-unionism. Published at the very moment of the Soviet system's collapse, the book could not have been more prescient. But the political conclusions to be drawn from its analyses were by no means clear, even to the volume's own editors. Could post-Fordist capitalism be the context for new, more democratic forms of labour organisation to emerge? Could the new political antagonisms around questions of sexual identity or the politics of ecology form the basis for a new radical politics? Or was socialism completely finished? Was politics itself now just a nostalgic game for those unwilling to accommodate to the new world of consumer capitalism? While one section of the left influenced by the *New Times* analysis, represented by writers like Mulgan and Hall, would ultimately advocate the abandonment of anything like the traditional goals of socialism, this would never be the route taken by those more closely associated with cultural studies and the New Left. What exactly those writers *would* advocate would be increasingly unclear as the years went by, however. It is one of this book's contentions that the politics of contemporary anti-capitalism represents at least a possible answer to that question. For the moment, however, we should focus on the fact that the New Times charted by Hall and colleagues were characterised by a few interesting democratic possibilities, but also marked the consequences of the left's defeat, at home and abroad.

Culture Wars

In the United States, the left was similarly marginalised, although the scale and complexity of American politics cannot be easily compared to the United Kingdom's highly centralised political system, in which the leader of the parliamentary majority can effectively govern the entire country by diktat. While still influential in Congress and at a local and state level in many areas, the Democrats were out of the White House throughout the 1980s. More importantly, the public backlash against left-wing ideas went much further than in the United Kingdom. Both the legacy of the New Deal—the historic social settlement implemented in the 1930s which remained the basis for the American welfare state—and the achievements of the new social movements came under savage attack from the newly politicised Christian right and a strain of anti-federalist libertarianism with deep roots in American political culture. Politically, the anti-communism of the 1950s had created a long-term context in the United States whereby it was virtually impossible for any national politician to admit to sympathy for even moderate kinds of socialism or social democracy. Even in the late 1960s, only the most radical sections of the counterculture or the new social movements had publicly allied their cause to any kind of serious economically egalitarian agenda. As such, the New Left in the United States came largely to concern itself with cultural politics, and in particular the struggles of women, gay people, non-whites and other minorities to be protected from discrimination and enabled to participate in public and private life on equal individual terms with straight white men, although this in turn often involved demands for local, state of federal government support for programmes to combat the social and institutional effects of entrenched traditions of discrimination against such groups.

It was in this context that *liberalism* acquired a new meaning in the American political vocabulary. The very movement which had culminated in the American Revolution and the constitution of the Republic had been one informed by the principles of classical liberalism. In practice, however, the rights to free speech and equality before the law supposedly enjoyed by all citizens of a liberal polity had never been extended to groups such as southern black voters, who had been customarily disenfranchised for generations before the Civil Rights movement succeeded in criminalising such practices in the 1950s, just as in earlier times both women and all propertyless people had been excluded from the franchise. In both Europe and the United States, the left had often been divided between those who saw liberalism as an ideological mask for entrenched inequalities of class, race and gender and those who saw the language of individual rights as providing the basis from which to attack those inequalities. During this period, it was largely the latter tendency which prevailed. Elements of the new social movements often tried to model themselves on the Civil Rights campaign, demanding access for all to the political privileges of liberalism. In many cases, however, this implied a radicalisation of the liberal tradition to the point where it threatened to transform all kinds of existing power relationships. As such, the term *liberalism* came to be associated with those who made these new demands, rather than with the political tradition of classical liberalism which had informed the whole of US constitutional law up to that point. At the same time, *liberal* had been acquiring a further slightly different meaning since the advent of the New Deal in the 1930s, in this case referring to an attitude towards government spending which was liberal in its generosity, as opposed to one advocating fiscal conservatism. During the 1970s, these terms and meanings crystallised what became the definitive fault line in American politics; that between liberals, who sought to use the power of government to break down old hierarchies, either through the promotion of equal rights agenda for women and minorities or through the extension of welfare programmes and wealth redistribution, and conservatives, who were committed to low government spending, low taxation and so-called traditional family values, and who were opposed to any legislation which seemed to threaten the latter (Grossberg 2005: 160–4). This conservative sensibility was to prove far more robust in the United States than in Europe.

In Western Europe, those demands and gains of the social movements which could easily be accommodated by a liberal (but not socialist) politics were largely absorbed into everyday political common sense, such that by the 1990s no mainstream politician could publicly espouse racist views or defend the traditional limitation of women to the domestic sphere. In the United States, by contrast, the so-called moral majority campaigned hard for such policies as the full-scale recriminalisation of abortion (which even Ireland legalised in the 1990s and which there has been no significant move to re-criminalise in any European country). At the same time, the centrality of the liberal tradition to American politics and American constitutional law meant that campaigners for minority rights and other elements of the New Left agenda had in many cases far more powerful resources to draw on than their European counterparts: the rights to free speech, freedom of conscience and equality before the law set out in the US constitution and the Declaration of Independence had no real equivalent in much of Europe (even in France, where no constitution had held for more than a few decades since the revolution of 1789), and they were often powerful weapons in the hands of campaigners. For example, many of the major gains of the civil rights movement—such as the right to abortion for women and the rights of black voters in the south—were technically won by demonstrating legally that any infringement of those rights by local or state institutions was *and always had been* constitutionally illegal. On the other hand, the tradition which sees the United States as a fundamentally Christian country, a republic of the Godly, has arguably even older roots, stretching back to the Puritanism of the first English and Dutch colonists in New England. The Christian right has called on this tradition to argue that almost any practice which they regard as unbiblical falls outside the protection of the constitution (or even, at their most extreme, to argue for the modification of the constitution itself). For example, the debate over whether individuals of the same sex should have the right to marry has seen both the letter and spirit of the constitution invoked by both sides of the argument and has seen Republicans agitate for a national constitutional amendment outlawing gay marriage.

In this situation, the success of these competing agendas—radical liberalism and hardline conservatism—has largely depended upon local conditions in the United States. In institutions or geographical areas where conservative Christianity constitutes the basic cultural frame of reference, the conservative agenda has prevailed, and the reverse has applied in those contexts characterised by a liberal culture. In situations where no one of these formations is clearly prevalent, bitter clashes have occurred, and in the 1980s and 1990s the so-called culture wars (Gitlin 1995) constituted much of the substance of meaningful political debate. One product of this conflict was the emergence of the discourse of political correctness in the 1980s. According to conservative commentators, liberal cultural mediators (including journalists, editors, teachers and academics) were engaged in a conspiracy to silence and censor the views of their political opponents, practising a kind of diffuse Stalinism with their insistence that racism, sexism and homophobia be excluded from public discourse. The term *politically correct*—not one that liberals or leftists would ever have used, unless ironically—was mobilised with remarkable skill by conservative mediators in order to characterise almost *any* attempt to problematise the ways in which conventional institutional and linguistic practices work to reinforce traditional social hierarchies as inherently authoritarian and anti-pluralist. At the same time, during the 1980s and early 1990s, those fragments of the New Left which were especially influential in academic debates within the humanities and student campus politics did exhibit a tendency to concentrate on cultural issues and identity politics (concerned with asserting the right to public recognition of various marginal social identities, from women to people with disabilities) to the virtual exclusion of more traditional left concerns like economic inequality and expansive collectivism. At the same time, many felt that the waning prestige of Marxism as a general analytical framework for critical work in the humanities and social sciences at this time was not accompanied by the emergence of any coherent alternative which could engage with such issues. As such, identity politics and even the hypothetical political correctness were eventually to come under attack from critics on the left as well as the right in the 1990s (e.g. Klein 2000).

The main concern for the British left at this moment, in the mid to late 1980s, was the persistent hegemony of Thatcherism. In the United States, at the same time, the Reagan administration pursued a similar agenda. It was easy, at this moment, to see the New Right and its success as the main political problem facing the left. So relatively few commentators in the United States and the United Kingdom were paying attention to the fact that neoliberal economic policies were already being pursued by nominally socialist governments in France and Australia, a fact which suggests that the long-term strength of neoliberalism was a different issue from the short-term success of the New Right in the 1980s. Instead, many radical thinkers and activists understandably focussed on the most immediately objectionable elements of the New Right programme; its conservative hostility to feminism, gay liberation and anti-racist politics. This focus on cultural issues chimed well with cultural studies' long-term assertion that issues of culture and identity should be considered as properly political questions, not as merely superficial issues compared with the 'real stuff' of class struggle and economics, and this created a context, especially in US universities, for a massive expansion of interest in cultural studies (Grossberg, Nelson & Treichler 1992). However, this development, combined with the visible populism of some strands of cultural studies at that moment, created a situation in which many commentators outside cultural studies, and even some inside it, came to see cultural studies as naturally antagonistic to more traditional leftist agendas, quite contrary to the intentions of the discipline's key figures and those practitioners closest to its sources.

The Anti-Essentialist Turn

It is at this moment that the history of cultural studies as such intersects with that of a much broader turn towards new forms of theoretical thinking across disciplines in the anglophone world, to which cultural studies contributed and by which it was itself affected. The rise of film and literary theory to central rather than marginal positions in their respective fields, the theoretical development of feminist cultural theory beyond the often rather simplistic positions of the 1970s, and the emergence of postcolonial and queer theories as orienting positions within an expanded field of cultural criticism, are all developments which cannot be conflated with the rise of cultural studies as such, although they are often elided in casual commentary. Indeed, the term 'cultural studies' is today often used to refer to almost any intellectual approach which makes reference to French philosophy of the past four decades. While this conflation is entirely inaccurate, it is understandable, given the extent to which cultural studies proper was a key site at which issues in cultural theory were debated and discussed. What follows now then is not merely an account of the development of cultural studies, but of the broad field of post-structuralist political philosophy, cultural criticism and cultural theory, with which cultural studies has intersected since the 1980s.

Despite the relative political paralysis of the left, the mid-late 1980s did see some very important developments in radical theory. Although all of these were later to be parodied by critics as over-intellectual, idealist tendencies which ignored the continuing reality of class inequality under capitalism, the key developments of this period were all one way or another trying to meet the challenge posed by the new social movements, the legacy of 1968, the worldwide defeat of socialism and communism, and the rise of the new right. The emergent developments of particular significance to us here are postcolonial theory, queer theory and post-Marxism. Significantly, all of the most influential representatives of these tendencies were heavily influenced by the wave of French post-structuralist philosophers who came to prominence in the late 1960s and 1970s, in the wake of 1968. However oblique the relationship of thinkers such as Derrida, the later Foucault, the later Lacan, Deleuze, Guattari, Irigaray, Kristeva, Lyotard, and so forth may have been to the events of 1968, their thought in the ensuing period clearly shared much of the spirit of that moment. Specifically, they were inspired by and refined the perceived challenge of 1968 to the orthodox Marxism of the French Communist Party and the highly theorised structuralist Marxism of loyal French Communist Party members such as Louis Althusser. This is a very crude summary, but put simply, we can see a parallel between the refusal of the French Communist Party to seize the moment of 1968 and the inability of high structuralism to grasp the potential contingency of social relations and hence the unpredictable possibilities for transformation which new and unexpected historical conjunctures might throw up. The structuralism of Althusser, Levis-Strauss and the early Foucault, like the historiography of their contemporary, Fernand Braudel, found it notoriously difficult to imagine human agency as having any real role in history at all, instead seeing social life in terms of deep and largely immovable structures determining and limiting the entire field of human action. This way of thinking lent itself very well to a highly orthodox form of Marxism which assumed that it understood the iron laws of history and that those laws decreed only the industrial proletariat led by the communist vanguard to be capable of effecting revolutionary change. One of the most memorable slogans of 1968 had been a deliberate rejection of this view: 'Structures don't march in the street!'

In many ways the theoretical legacy of 1968 is still being worked through in anglophone cultural theory. Of all the theoretical works to have been directly influenced and inspired by the spirit of that moment, the most lastingly important is almost certainly Deleuze and Guattari's *Anti-Oedipus,* a monumental critique of the authoritarianism implicit in much structuralist and psychoanalytic thinking and of an entire philosophical frame-of-reference which sustains it. Outside of the pioneering work of Lawrence Grossberg, Deleuze and Guattari's critique had relatively little direct impact on either cultural studies or critical thought up until the end of the 1990s. Much more significant for this broad area in the 1980s was the intervention of Ernesto Laclau and Chantal Mouffe in their 1985 breakthrough volume *Hegemony and Socialist Strategy.* This remarkable piece of work offered a historical genealogy of the concept of hegemony in the Marxist literature of the early-twentieth century from a perspective informed by the key philosophical developments coming from France since the later 1960s. At this point, many on the anglophone left had already been influenced by the post-structuralist thought of Michel Foucault and Jacques Lacan. However, Jacques Derrida's deconstruction and the postmodern philosophy of Jean-François Lyotard had been widely misunderstood as advocating a nihilistic epistemological relativism which simply undermined the possibility of any effective politics (which is how ignorant commentators such as Terry Eagleton and Thomas Frank continue to refer to postmodernism to this day), although in emergent fields such as postcolonial studies, the political value of Derrida's writings had already long been recognised.

Hegemony and Socialist Strategy was the first major work of anglophone political theory to be fully informed by these developments and it sought to bring their insights to bear on the problems facing the left in the increasingly complex and fluid societies which advanced capitalism was producing. Perhaps the key position which this work popularised was anti-essentialism; a position which refuses to acknowledge any essential absolute, final, objective reality to social and political identities, instead seeing them as the always contingent outcome of political struggles and negotiations. Within this frame of reference, identities which had been fundamental to left politics—such as worker or woman—came to be seen as merely contingent positions within discourse whose meaning could be changed at any time by virtue of their shifting relationships with other identities in the wider social field. While for many this was a radically destabilising position, cutting the very ground from underneath progressive movements, for others it provided the only framework with which to confront the destabilisation of political identities which had ensued in the years since 1968.

Laclau and Mouffe argued, in effect, that almost any social, cultural or political identity could be 'articulated' (connected) to any other if the political circumstances were right. So there was nothing inevitable or even probable about workers linking their struggles to those of women or black people, for example: instead, if such struggles were to be connected, then connecting them would require a great deal of political work, and the elaboration of a common frame of reference which was not dependent upon one or the other of those identities taking precedence over the other. Feminism could no longer be expected to be connected to socialism either by women accepting that their struggle was subordinate to the struggle of all workers or by asserting the overriding importance of opposition to patriarchy as the basic form and source of all oppression. Instead, Laclau and Mouffe argued that the progressive movements could be linked together by virtue of a shared commitment to deepening and expanding the democratic revolution of modernity, thereby extending the progress that had been made in the extension of liberal democracy to include all citizens of advanced countries through furthering other forms of social, economic, political and cultural democracy.

Laclau and Mouffe's advocacy of radical democracy as a new positive political position was persuasive and inspiring, even while it was never fully elaborated as a coherent ethical and political programme and the definitions of radical democracy which they offered tended to change over time. What is perhaps most important to realise about Laclau and Mouffe's work for our purposes here is that, on the one hand, it corresponded on an abstract theoretical level to currents within the post-1968 social and political movements which also sought to reject the authoritarianism, centralism and homogeneity of earlier forms of left politics, while on the other hand it emerged from exactly the same intellectual and political milieu as British cultural studies. Strands of the feminist and Green movements had been practising and advocating something very like radical democracy in their non-hierarchal, leaderless networks for some time, while the American politics of the rainbow coalition, aiming to create a diverse political alliance of various socially marginalised groups (McKelvey 1994: 258–69), looked rather like that advocated in *Hegemony and Socialist Strategy*—and the loose coalitions of radicals which would emerge in the anti-capitalist movement of the 1990s would look even more so. Yet Laclau and Mouffe's work was emerging from a direct conversation that was taking place between them and figures such as Stuart Hall, both in person and on the pages of *New Left Review* and *Marxism Today*. Laclau and Mouffe's work is therefore a key reference point for us, and it is one to which we will return in detail.

A similar and parallel theoretical shift was effected in a number of quarters by both the wider critique of Althusserian Marxism and the growing influence of the ideas of Michel Foucault. Perhaps the most significant moment in the history of British Althusserianism was the publication of Barry Hindess and Paul Hirst's *Mode of Production and Social Formation* (1977). A dense, fascinating little work, this book was an explicit critique of the authors' own previous work, *Pre-Capitalist Modes of Production.* In short, the authors conclude that they, like their mentor Althusser, have simply not gone far enough in abandoning essentialism and economism, and that the only way this can be done is to jettison the key concept of Marxist historical analysis mode of production, replacing it with a commitment to the study of 'definite social formations'. This was a conceptual gesture very close to the neo-Gramscian insistence on attending to the specificities of 'the conjuncture', the complex set of power relations obtaining at a particular historical moment—which had such an influence on Williams and Hall, and which would lead both Hindess and Hirst away from the Marxist tradition altogether. Hirst in particular would go on to mine an interesting if idiosyncratic vein as a political theorist of 'associational democracy', drawing on an English socialist tradition with its roots not in revolutionary party communism but in the co-operative movement and traditions of local democracy and self-organisation.

Similarly to the post-Althusserians, the French thinker Michel Foucault—already a well known figure to anglophone readers by the mid-1970s—was continuing his long-term project to find ways of describing the relationship between forms of knowledge and forms of power which did not make the kind of crude assumptions associated with conventional Marxism. Foucault became an increasingly influential force within cultural studies and literary history as his own approach became more dynamic and sophisticated during the course of the decade and the early years of the 1980s. From his early emphasis on 'discursive formations' (systems of ideas about topics such as medicine or madness) as relatively autonomous from each other and from wider social forces (Foucault 1961; 1972), Foucault developed a much more political approach informed by the ideas of Friedrich Nietzsche, which stressed the extent to which knowledge only ever emerges in a field of conflict and contestation (Foucault 1979). Although often seen as some kind of enemy of all Marxism (Foucault 1981), at key points in his work Foucault deployed a vocabulary and explanatory approach very close to Gramscian Marxism, stressing the centrality of class struggle to shifting ideas and assumptions about the world (Foucault 1979: 115–31).

A friend and associate of Gilles Deleuze, Foucault was the subject of a full study by Deleuze, and there are clear points of convergence between their ideas. Deleuze and Guattari's concept of 'assemblage' (*agencement* in French) was closely related to Foucault's notion of 'apparatus' (*dispositif*) (Deleuze 1995: 196), which more-or-less replaced his notion of 'discursive formation', and both were clearly also close to Hindess and Hirst's use of the term 'social formation' (Hindess & Hirst 1977: 46–62). In all of these cases, a very loose general term is deployed in place of some more definite alternative: *social formation* instead of *mode of production; discursive formation* instead of *ideology,* and so forth. The reason is that theorists using these concepts wanted to get away from the assumptions built into some of these earlier terms. Using these more open concepts freed them up to analyse the *specific* mechanisms of power operating in particular social, historical and cultural contexts—in which the relationships between economic, symbolic and political power might operate very differently—rather than assuming in advance that those relationships must follow set patterns. Broadly speaking, this was what anti-essentialism initially meant at the level of abstract social analysis. In addition, however, all of these strands of thought tended towards a position which recognised the identity of social *beings* as constituted entirely by the specific sets of relationships into which they are inserted, rather than seeing them as the expression of some underlying essence. As such, the term *anti-essentialism* also came to designate a resistance to any idea of *identity* as fixed and inherent rather than malleable and relational.

While Laclau and Mouffe were largely concerned with offering a critique of class essentialism, other theorists in the 1980s were concerned with applying similar critiques of essentialism in thinking about gendered, ethnic and sexual identities. Under the influence of Laclau and Mouffe themselves and of similar sources in French post-structuralist philosophy to those inspiring Laclau and Mouffe, a generation of thinkers were opposing any notions of such identities as fixed or natural. Again, although this point is rarely made, we can see this development in part as a response to the breakdown of many of the assumptions of radicals which had obtained since the nineteenth century, through the experience of 1968 and its aftermath, up until the 1980s. The realisation that it was possible actively to pursue and in many cases to achieve goals such as the decriminalisation and normalisation of same-sex relations without engaging with any other political agenda was surely one of the factors problematising essentialist notions of identity, as many had previously assumed that there was something essentially revolutionary about, for example, asserting a public gay identity (D'Emilio 1992). While less militant gay campaigners had always believed in the possibility of a gay-tolerant liberal capitalist society, most who identified with the radical tradition had believed that capitalism—and perhaps all ordered, hierarchical society—relied upon the heterosexual nuclear family as its basic unit of socialisation. So it was thought by commentators on both the left and the right that anything that undermined the sanctity of this social model—such as the assertion that gay sex is not sinful and should not be illegal—constituted an implicit threat to the existing social order, and hence to capitalism as such. The fact that assumptions such as this turned out to have been mistaken, with the dissolution of the normative family model and the decriminalisation of homosexuality having no impact at all on the prevalence of capitalist social relations, was surely one of the historical impetuses behind the rise of anti-essentialism.

Another such impetus was the inherent political problems caused by the forms of oppositional politics which were emerging as alternatives to traditional socialism. The legacy of the new social movements led many activists towards forms of political and intellectual engagement which sought only to assert the validity of one particular social group, understood in terms of its key shared feature. Identity politics concerned itself with the rights of women, gay people, non-white people, disabled people, and so forth, to participate fully in the life of the community (whatever that was taken to mean). Identity politics tended to oppose any perceived attempt to subjugate such demands to any wider, more universalistic project for human emancipation.

Identity politics of this nature was something which tended to emerge in practice but was often difficult to justify in theory, because any abstract reflection on its implications makes quite clear what its problems are. On the one hand, how can such a politics cope with the fact that individuals might belong to more than one group from which they can derive an identity? On the other hand, how can any politics grounded in a single identity aspire to move beyond the rather limited ambition of protecting the rights of the members of a certain group to participate in the liberal polity on the same terms as other individuals? The critique of essentialism was in part motivated by both of these questions, and it sought to stake out a position which argued that because no identity was fixed and homogenous, identity as such could not be the basis for any effective politics, and that every community was an imaginary, contingent construct (Laclau & Mouffe 1985: 85–134; Anderson 1983; Miami Theory Collective 1991). To put this another way, what emerged in the work of writers such as Laclau and Mouffe was a view according to which all politics was, and always had been, about the shifting and overlapping meanings attributed to certain identities and the various struggles to define them. From this point of view, the discourse of the class struggle was just one particularly ambitious attempt to assert the validity of a particular identity (e.g. worker) and to persuade large numbers of people to identify themselves with it and act accordingly, at the expense of any contrary identification (as, for example, English, or Polish, or Christian) which would lead them to behave differently (by voting for nationalist political parties, for example). As such, the idea of a specific identity politics was foolish, given that *all* politics is to some extent identity politics.

At the level of cultural theory, these insights had the greatest impact in the emerging fields of queer and postcolonial theory. *Queer* was a homophobic term of abuse deliberately adopted by militant gay activists, especially in response to the AIDS crisis, in the 1980s (Shepard & Hayduk 2002). Queer politics and queer theory took on rather different meanings in different contexts (Morton 1996). In some cases, especially within activist culture, queer designated a militant position which refused any liberal notion of assimilation, rejecting the political objective of simply winning the same rights for same-sex couples as heterosexual couples enjoyed and asserting the subversive nature of non-straight sexuality. In practice this type of militancy often took on a decidedly essentialist character, asserting an authentic queer radicalism as preferable to the half-hearted, subservient liberalism of respectable gay people. The body of work which came to be known as queer theory—most notably the work of Judith Butler—took on a quite different character, however. Inspired and informed by deconstruction, postmodernism, post-structuralism and post-Marxism, queer theory tended to assert the instability and contingency of all sexual and gendered identity, just as anti-essentialist feminists were increasingly tending to do. From this point of view, the key to a progressive sexual politics was to move away from any fixed notions of masculinity, femininity, homosexuality or heterosexuality. Significantly, this echoed the views already expressed on this matter in the writings of Michel Foucault, Jacques Derrida and Deleuze and Guattari (Derrida 1991; Foucault 1979; Deleuze & Guattari 1988: 278).

Judith Butler's *Gender Trouble* (1990) remains the paradigmatic statement of queer theory and anti-essentialist feminism, deploying all of the theoretical resources which had come into the North American academy via the fascination with French post-structuralist philosophy in literature departments to promote the view that all gendered and sexed identity was socially constructed and as such at least potentially open to challenge and transformation. The book reads now as dated, uneven and flawed, but its historic importance is unquestionable. It was to prove a crucial resource for cultural studies as much as anything because it marked the maturation of anglophone post-structuralism into something more than a school of literary criticism lacking the intellectual ambition of its French sources. Along with Laclau and Mouffe's work, it suggested the possibility of a sophisticated political position deriving from the most radical currents of the French philosophical stream from which cultural studies had been drinking, albeit sporadically, for so long. Donna Harraway's 'Cyborg Manifesto' (1991), appearing only a year after *Gender Trouble,* further consolidated the emergence of a distinctively post-structuralist, anti-essentialist, but clearly leftist position in feminist theory. Arguing against the primitivist tendencies of certain strands of goddess-worshipping ecofeminism, Harraway effectively launched a whole sub-genre of cultural studies concerned with assessing the impacts and possibilities of emergent communication technologies.

Closely allied to queer theory was the emergent field of postcolonial theory; a body of work which emerged from the encounter between anglophone literary-critics with third world affiliations and the writings of Foucault and Derrida, but whose roots go back further, most notably to the work of the Martiniquan psychoanalyst and partisan of the Algerian anti-colonial struggle, Frantz Fanon. Stuart Hall, amongst others, also became heavily involved in this body of work, which is far too rich and detailed to chart in detail here (Morley & Chen 1996). What is significant for us is that this body of work, much like the queer theory of Judith Butler and the post-Marxism of Laclau and Mouffe, stressed the extent to which all social identities are partial, contingent and temporary outcomes of a variety of interacting power-struggles, and as such no single form of power—whether, for example, classed power or gendered power—can be seen as the source of all others: no aspect of a person's identity is necessarily more or less political, or politically important, than any other. The postcolonial theorists tended to stress the hybrid nature of all identities as a way of overcoming any essentialist understanding of race, ethnicity or nationality. (e.g. Bhabha 1994).

To this day, many commentators assume that writers in these fields believe that identity is just a kind of fiction, that there is no such thing as truth, that there are no values which we can appeal to against cruelty and injustice of all kinds, and that there is no point engaging in active politics. Nothing could be further from the truth. In fact, all of these writers have been implicitly motivated by an understanding that precisely *because* no identity, and indeed no social situation, is fixed forever, then many kinds of political activity are possible and many more kinds may be useful than were envisaged by the revolutionaries of the past. Perhaps most importantly, these writers have been motivated by the recognition that all successful political projects are carried out by *coalitions* of diverse and often very different groups and individuals, and that such coalitions are always unstable, and as such, they require ongoing political work to maintain them. Indeed, these writers point out that every individual is a kind of microscopic coalition, constituted as they are by multiple and sometime competing sets of loyalties. This is the real meaning of the anti-essentialist turn. As we will see, in many ways this is a philosophical attitude which prefigured the anti-capitalist movement's stress on 'unity-in-difference' and its refusal ever to let one single organisation speak for the 'movement of movements'.

Back to Cultural Studies

Within the mainstream of British cultural studies, it was Angela McRobbie once again who engaged most directly with some of these developments. Her *Postmodernism and Popular Culture* (1994) was a significant collection of essays that linked the pluralist politics of the New Left and the women's movement with the philosophical and cultural trends which variously went under the name of postmodernism. Her 1992 essay 'Post-Marxism and Cultural Studies' marked a key moment of engagement between the two fields and was presented as the concluding essay to the massive *Cultural Studies* (Grossberg, Nelson, & Treichler 1992) which remains the most ambitious of its kind to date. The anti-essentialist moment in cultural studies was also represented by Kobena Mercer in his 1994 volume *Welcome to the Jungle,* which opens with Mercer's famous celebration of Michael Jackson's *Thriller* video. Mercer argues that the video is a deliberate experiment with androgyny and parody, refusing any number of clichés about the authentic nature of the black male body:

> What was important and empowering about the redefinition of black identity in British society in the 1980s was that it showed that identities are not found but *made;* that they are not just there, waiting to be discovered in the vocabulary of nature, but have to be culturally and politically *constructed* through political antagonism and cultural struggle.

> (Mercer 1994. 292).

Mercer's book represents arguably the most coherent and explicit deployment of Laclau and Mouffe's work in the mainstream of cultural studies, offering in its later chapters a brilliant analysis of the shifting parameters of black cultural politics in the post-war era. At the same time, these chapters reveal a real frustration with the apparent failure of the plural, radial democratic left envisaged in their work (and, for that matter, by the New Left in the 1960s) to emerge in the postmodern context. Intriguingly, the book concludes with a rather vague critique of the historic failures of the left and the New Left, but without making at all clear what Mercer thinks the alternative political formation could look like. It's worth reflecting that the book appeared in the same year that the Zapatista uprising began.

However, most of the key figures of mainstream cultural studies were never really caught up in this wider post-structuralist moment. The previous year, Paul Gilroy had published his seminal study *The Black Atlantic* (1993), which posited black culture as a geo-historical continuity inseparable from the experience of slavery and its aftermath, but he argues that black culture should not be understood simply as an expression for some essential African identity. Gilroy's *There Ain't No Black in the Union Jack: The Politics of Race and Nation* (1987) had already proved highly significant in putting issues of race at the heart of the cultural studies agenda, and *The Black Atlantic* did much to open up cultural studies to an approach less fixated on national cultural contexts than it had previously been. Hall had been an admirer of Laclau's earlier work towards an anti-essentialist theory of politics (Chen & Morley 1996: 146), and he had influenced the broader anti-essentialist turn, but he vocally declined to follow Laclau and Mouffe down the path they had taken in *Hegemony and Socialist Strategy*. Hall, like many others, thought that this book ended up with a problematic position which ignored the material constraints on political struggles. Laclau and Mouffe themselves offered perhaps their most brilliant work in responding to such charges, providing a sophisticated defence of their own materialism in the essay 'Post-Marxism Without Apologies' (Laclau 1990: 97–132), but neither their critics nor they themselves showed much interest in pursuing the resultant line of enquiry into the 1990s. Hall, in the meantime, continued to work in a number of veins. He was instrumental in developing a tremendously sophisticated model of the relationship between race and class which was to influence an entire generation, inspiring a generation of young artists and film-makers to explore complex questions of identity, belonging and exclusion, and re-shaping the ways in which British intellectuals understood the postcolonial status of their own culture (Chen & Morley 1996: 411–503). He was influential in shifting the focus of cultural history and cultural studies away from apocalyptic pronouncements about the end of history or narrowly economistic accounts of late capitalism, focussing attention instead on the historical specificity of emergent and residual forms of modernity (Hall 1992). Perhaps most importantly, he remained a key voice on the left arguing for the possibility of a populist, democratic, inclusive vision of an alternative modernity to that proposed by Thatcher and Reagan (Hall 1988).

Raymond Williams, who died in 1988, had never been enamoured of structuralism or post-structuralism and had continued to try to develop his Gramscian cultural materialism up until his death. Lawrence Grossberg, who emerged as the key figure in North American cultural studies, was a former student of Hall's who had also never pursued the post-structuralist line, having argued very early indeed for the effective inclusion of Deleuze and Guattari in the cultural studies canon of theorists (Grossberg 1982). Grossberg's 1992 volume *We Gotta Get Out of This Place* was an ambitious attempt at the kind of conjunctural analysis which cultural studies had produced little of after *Policing the Crisis*. Offering an original synthesis of Gramsci, Foucault and Deleuze and Guattari, it set out to map the emergence of a conservative structure of feeling in American popular culture which paid particular attention to the affective power of popular music. Whereas Hall remained closer to post-structuralism in his reliance on Saussurian semiotics and post-Lacanian psychoanalytic theory, Grossberg's approach in some ways revived Williams's scepticism towards both psychoanalysis and the consequences of 'the linguistic turn' (Gilbert 2004b). It seems surprising, looked at from one angle, that *We Gotta Get Out of This Place* is not cited more often in the wider field of cultural studies, as its explicitly Deleuzian materialism is very much in line with current fashion, and it also represents one of the singular attempts to pursue cultural studies' central vocation: rigourous conjunctural analysis of the intersecting power relationships shaping, and shaped by, contemporary culture. Nevertheless, the moment of its publication was clearly one characterised by a new level of intellectual ambition and institutional and geographical reach for the young discipline of cultural studies, as well as a new prominence in international cultural studies for Grossberg. A large conference which had been held at University of Illinois in April 1990 marked cultural studies' full emergence on the North American scene, and the 788-page volume *Cultural Studies* (1992), which Grossberg edited with Carry Nelson and Paula Treichler, remains to this day the most ambitious snapshot of the discipline at any one moment in its history, featuring as it did a vast range of contributors from the United States, Australia, and the United Kingdom. Unfortunately, the degree to which the political tradition which had given birth to cultural studies had been defeated was only just beginning to become clear.

Cultural Studies after Communism

At the close of the 1980s, as we have seen, the broader political context underwent arguably its greatest transformation since the end of the second world war. The collapse of the soviet system in 1989 marked the final victory of the United States and its allies in the Cold War, and the emergence of the unipolar world in which American economic and military power would meet with no serious political opposition outside of the Islamic enclaves. The initial response to this event on the part of those strands of the left associated with the New Left and *Marxism Today* was almost celebratory[1]. This was hardly surprising. These tendencies had long defined themselves in terms of their opposition to Stalinism and its undemocratic legacy. The sight of the massed citizenry of Eastern European countries taking to the streets to demand, and win, a complete transformation of their social system could not fail to warm the hearts of any revolutionary. In the medium term, however, the consequences of the collapse of communism were to prove far more ambivalent. For most people in Eastern Europe, the result was not simply their accession to the Western European world of prosperity and democracy. Instead, across much of the former Soviet Union, the collapse and rapid privatisation of state industries resulted in massive unemployment, almost total social breakdown and a drop in average life expectancy for nearly 2 decades. On a global level, the United States quickly set to work on two grand projects which we must assume it would have engaged in much earlier had the power of the Soviet Union not presented them with such an obstacle: the imposition of neoliberalism on the rest of the world and the military subjugation of the oil-rich Middle East.

It was apparent by the early 1990s that this situation posed a grave problem for the very existence of the political left in the Western world. On a local level, the Communist Party of Great Britain, like many of its European counterparts, tried ineffectually to reinvent itself before effectively ceasing to exist. *Marxism Today* (which, it was revealed—much to the chagrin of its unknowing staff—had always been secretly subsidised by the Soviet Union) folded, and the British left never again had an equivalent space within which to debate new ideas. Perhaps more significantly, the democratic left now no longer represented a third way between the two great competing systems of centralised socialism and liberal-democratic capitalism. Instead it represented only an abstract and practically impotent set of critiques of the one dominant social model: liberal capitalism. However, the full extent of this crisis was not to be felt until the 1990s were well under way, because the continued electoral success of the Conservatives and the Republicans allowed many to continue to hope that Democrat or Labour administrations would resume the twin projects of social liberalisation and social democratic reform. Many people optimistically assumed that these projects had merely been interrupted by the hegemony of the New Right.

The vanity and futility of such hopes may be apparent with hindsight, but in practice there were good reasons for people in the tradition of the New Left to entertain them. Both Clinton and Blair belonged to the generation that came of age in the late 1960s and early 1970s. What's more, the ideas of the New Left were well-known to have been directly influential on key figures in both administrations. Blair had written for *Marxism Today,* and one of its key writers in the period immediately preceding its closure, Geoff Mulgan, was to become his policy chief when he took power in 1997. In the US, figures like Robert Reich, Clinton's secretary of state for labor, were generally seen as typical of the New Left generation in their combined commitments to egalitarianism, social liberalism and feminism. During the course of the 1990s, however, it became apparent that both the constraints of the unipolar world order and their own political predilections were driving these politicians and their advisors in quite different directions to those aimed at by the New Left or even by mainstream supporters of the welfare state. Mulgan, for example, showed no commitment to the democratising traditions of the Labour movement, and came instead to exemplify a new generation of elite technocrats who were attracted to postmodernism's rejection of utopian thinking but unmoved by its implicit critique of all notions of expertise. Loathing political activists, the key generation of young politicians and advisers around Blair were nonetheless confident of their own ability to solve social problems from the centre.

Where both the Clinton and Blair administrations were to fulfil some of the hopes of the New Left was in their genuine commitment to social liberalisation, making significant moves towards the full normalisation of same-sex relationships, encouraging mothers to work, and actively encouraging the development of multicultural societies. This wasn't particularly difficult. Arguably the key reason as to why both the Republicans and Conservatives lost power in the 1990s was that their brand of nationalistic social conservatism came to seem increasingly anachronistic in the individualised world of highly mobile, consumer-focussed advanced capitalism. The libertarian values which had once been the preserve of the 1968 generation sat perfectly with the new world of diverse and ever-proliferating forms of pleasure, and the New Right's articulation of neoliberal economics with social conservatism no longer made political sense in this context. The real political achievement of Clinton and Blair was to re-articulate the neoliberal economic agenda to a liberal social agenda. By making a few concessions to their traditional supporters (raising public sector pay in the United Kingdom, for example), each managed hold together a coalition of traditional left-wing constituencies and aspiring, prosperous consumers who no longer felt the need to be reassured by the conservative platitudes of a Reagan or a Thatcher. In the United States, in contrast to most European countries, this coalition has been flanked to the right by a religiously motivated constituency, whose concerns can be articulated to those of a much wider public at times of perceived cultural, economic or military crisis, securing support for a conservative regime such as that of George W Bush.

Of course, their precarious dependence upon affluent centre voters who did not want to see tax rises of any kind led Clinton and Blair to do very little to extend the post-war social democratic project. Blair's New Labour government, having flirted with variants of communitarian philosophy in the late 1990s, actually took on the task of continuing to dismantle the remnants of the welfare state. New Labour became wholly committed to the neoliberal project of extending competition, individualism and market relations into every area of social life, whether the public wanted it or not (Leys 2001). The bitter disappointment of the survivors of the New Left was palpable. *Marxism Today* was revived for one special issue in 1998 merely so that a collection of its contributors from the 1980s could denounce Blair and his betrayal of the left tradition, its cover emblazoned with one word: 'Wrong'. However, from a more detached perspective, we have to ask if such a response was ever fully justified. In the broad context of a unipolar world and an in increasingly interconnected global economy, it is not at all clear that Blair or Clinton could have behaved in any other way. Their electoral success was not accompanied by any large-scale upsurge in political activism amongst a wider public: there were no demonstrations in the streets of British or American cities welcoming the dawn of a new era of social democracy.

This might sound like just a humorous image, but it is not intended as such, because arguably it just such scenes which would have to have been witnessed if Clinton and Blair were ever going to have had a real chance of renewing the social democratic project. The pressure on both governments from institutions committed to neoliberalism—all major corporations, the financial markets, the US Federal Reserve, the European central banks, the International Monetary Fund, the World Bank, the newly formed World Trade Organisation and the conservative media, especially the vast empire of Rupert Murdoch—was immense. Without countervailing pressure from organised labour, mass-membership political parties on the left, and a heavily armed block of nominally socialist countries in Eastern Europe and beyond, it is hard to see how such pressure could ever have been resisted. From this point of view, the complete marginality of the New Left to mainstream politics in the United States and the United Kingdom only became fully apparent in the late 1990s, but it had been a historical fact since the defeat of the miners strike in the United Kingdom and Jesse Jackson's rainbow coalition in the United States in the early 1980s (indeed, much of the American left had given up on the Democratic Party when it failed effectively to lead opposition to the Vietnam War, at the end of the 1960s). Panitch and Leys, in their detailed study of the historical marginalisation of the Left in the Labour Party, have argued persuasively that it was naïve for anyone to believe that the Labour leadership was likely to pursue a New Left agenda after 1983/4, but they point out that many *did* believe in the likelihood of such an outcome (Panitch & Leys 2001: 211). It was this belief, however mistaken, which continued to inform the political imaginary of mainstream cultural studies, until it became fully clear under Blair that there was no way this would happen.

The political tradition informing mainstream cultural studies had therefore been becoming increasingly detached from any real-world political movements for nearly 20 years, but the extent of this detachment only became clear in the first years of the new millennium. It is ironic then, that the 1990s saw cultural studies sweep through the anglophone academy. By the end of the decade, what had been a fashionably cutting-edge but institutionally marginal discipline in the late 1980s had been fully established as a recognised field in institutions throughout the English-speaking world, taught at every level in its own right, with its own apparatus of journals and international conferences, but also informing the mainstream of new research and teaching in fields as various as sociology, literature, history and fine art. Why did this happen? Why, at the very moment when the New Left project effectively ended in the ignominy of Clinton's and Blair's complete capitulation to neoliberalism, did cultural studies as practised by Stuart Hall emerge as arguably the leading paradigm in the humanities and social sciences?

Any number of answers to this question have been offered, any number could be invented, and none will ever be fully definitive. The most pessimistic accounts see the two developments as wholly interdependent. Some actually see the radical left as having been lured into complicity with neoliberal hegemony by the offer of an amusing life of intellectual dilettantism: why bother organising the workers when you can be paid a good salary teaching ideology-critique to intelligent and personable students? (Frank 2002) Others point to the fact that the politics of cultural studies shifted subtly just as the politics of the New Left did when it was modulated into the ideas and practice of Clinton's New Democrats and Blair's New Labour: in both cases, traditional commitments to the goals of the labour movement were dropped in favour of a banal liberalism. Certainly some work in cultural studies has followed this trajectory, simply criticising racism or sexism from a liberal perspective, and therefore finding itself with no reason to criticise anything of consequence in the world of twenty-first-century liberal capitalism, where George W. Bush appeals to feminism as justification for attacking the Taliban and neoliberal governments encourage the growth of cosmopolitan culture because higher rates of immigration lower the overall price of labour. But this is a relatively small tendency in work published as cultural studies, most of which is still written from a perspective which is well aware of the legacy of egalitarian critiques of capitalism, even if it has no great interest in them; so the foregoing is only a partial explanation as to how the institutionalisation of cultural studies managed to happen at the same time as the marginalisation of the New Left.

Another explanation is to look at these two related phenomena from a slightly different angle. The so-called institutionalisation of cultural studies has to be understood as in part a result of its massive popularity amongst scholars working in the humanities and social sciences: this isn't simply a matter of cultural studies becoming institutionalised but also of institutions changing under the impact of cultural studies' programme. One way in which we might explain this popularity is to look at the global context in which such scholars now find themselves. From a sociological perspective, university teachers and researchers belong to a particular social group: public-sector professionals. This group was virtually brought into existence by the post-war expansion of the welfare state and has a natural inclination to support social democratic policies: it is, after all, only taxes and government spending on public services which pays the salaries of teachers, professors, lecturers, social-workers, local government officers and (in countries with a socialised health service) health professionals. The neoliberal era has seen savage cuts in public spending compared to the post-war period, even while the demands of the knowledge economy have seen a massive growth in higher education throughout the developed world. The result is that for decades now university teachers have seen their relative salaries cut, their social status downgraded and their workloads increased, as have most workers in education and in similar service sectors such as public health. At the same time, the social composition of many of these professions has changed in recent decades, such that they are no longer dominated by white males educated at elite educational institutions, as they once were. Consequently, it should be no surprise to find that a generation of workers in this sector should be far less inclined than their predecessors to act as agents for the transmission of mainstream social values and far more likely to adopt positions which are critical of the general norms and direction of the culture they inhabit. In this sense, the discontented radical attitudes of the New Left and 1968 were only the forerunners of a far wider sense of disaffection and marginalisation amongst university teachers in the neoliberal world, a disaffection which has encouraged workers in those sectors to look around for more radical perspectives, perspectives which some found in New Left–inspired cultural studies. At the same time, the fact that these professions attracted many of the most militant members of the post-1968 generation is no surprise: even radicals have to make a living, and if they want to do it working in the public services rather than in the profit-oriented private sector, then this is hardly surprising as it does not compromise the authenticity of their politics.

The reality is that the situation is complex. No doubt some liberal versions of cultural studies merely reflect the ideological norms of neoliberal culture, as Marxist critics of cultural studies often assert (e.g. Žižek 2001). No doubt it is also true that the absence of any strong organised opposition to neoliberalism drove some radicals into safe academic careers as opposed to full-time political militancy. Overall, however, the rise and institutional success of cultural studies is a consequence of the convergence between the ideas and attitudes of the New Left and the attitudes of those many university teachers and students whose social situation and political background have tended to drive them to the left over the past thirty years. It is interesting to note, then, that university teachers and other public service professionals are not the only group of people whose political attitudes have come to resemble closely those which took shape amongst the New Left after 1956. The anti-capitalist movement which has emerged since the 1990s has also been informed by a very similar set of attitudes and approaches.

The implicit affinities between some strands of cultural studies and the emergent anti-capitalist movement have at times been quite striking. Angela McRobbie's *British Fashion Design: Rag Trade or Image Industry* (1998) marked a turn away from the consumption-oriented studies of fashion and other aspects of contemporary culture with which much feminist cultural studies had come to be associated, examining in detail the production practices and working conditions in the industry and the ideological mechanisms which legitimated them. The book appeared less than a year after Andrew Ross (ed.) *No Sweat: Fashion, Free Trade and the Rights of Garment Workers* (1997), and two years before the publication of Naomi Klein's *No Logo*, much of which shared the concerns of these two books. Perhaps the most significant observation to make for our purposes here, however, is that while being in itself an extremely substantial piece of work of great topical relevance, McRobbie's book makes no reference to the emergent political movement against sweated labour and the commercial exploitation of popular culture documented in Ross's and Klein's books. The organisational divergence between New Left cultural studies and those wider political movements which continue to share its concerns is surely well illustrated here.

In fact, if we were to look at a broad sample of work in cultural studies from, say, the mid-1990s to the present, then we would see something of a change in the way in which new themes and issues have emerged into cultural studies from that which marked the earlier phases. Broadly speaking, this shift has to do with the way in which cultural studies researchers chose their objects and approaches, and it involves a shift from a situation in which explicitly political motives are driving those choices to one in which a more diffuse project of generally expanding the range of cultural studies' possible objects, and responding to changes in the larger world and in the wider intellectual environment, is the driving force. So it is not the concerns of new or even existing political movements which is represented by such work, but a general effort to map the emerging contours of the present. The rise of digital culture, the globalisation of world culture, issues raised by the urbanisation of life on earth, multiculturalism, cosmopolitanism and their consequences, the emergence of new trends in music or fashion, and so on; these have been the types of new objects and issues to preoccupy cultural studies over the past decade or so. At the same time the massive institutional success of cultural studies has involved not just an expansion of the discipline itself, but a great deal of exchange between cultural studies and contiguous disciplines which have borrowed from it: media studies, geography and sociology, for example, have all taken on board many of cultural studies' concerns and approaches such that there is not much discernible difference now between much work in those areas and specialist branches of cultural studies. Cultural studies since the 1970s has drawn on continental philosophy for the formulation of its basic theoretical concepts, and the continuing exploration of different strands of philosophy, especially recent French philosophy, has become an autonomous project within cultural studies that is more-or-less devoid of explicit political motivation. In addition, since the early 1990s there has been a steady stream of work reflecting on cultural studies' history and the politics of its competing paradigms, both consolidating earlier work and reflecting upon some of the discipline's implicit assumptions (e.g. Harris 1992; McGuigan 1992; Frow 1995; McRobbie 2005). The collection of essays by and about Hall edited by David Morley and Kuan-Hsing Chen under the title *Critical Dialogues in Cultural Studies* (1996) is the only volume to offer anything like a representative selection of Hall's contributions to cultural studies and cultural theory, and as such represents something of a coming-of-age for the discipline. More recently, works such as Byrne and McQuillan's *Deconstructing Disney* (1998) and Gary Hall's *Culture in Bits* (2002) arguably marked the emergence of a new generation of cultural studies writers who had been as influenced by the impact of post-structuralism on literary studies as by the legacy of the New Left and the Centre for Contemporary Cultural Studies, explicitly deploying tropes and techniques borrowed from Derridean deconstruction in order to question some of the received assumptions of the discipline. Similarly, Joanna Zylinska's *The Ethics of Cultural Studies* (2005) consolidated this trend, while Paul Bowman's *Post-Marxism Vs. Cultural Studies* (2007) marks an important intervention, arguing for a deep affinity between deconstruction and the persistent self-interrogation of Hall's form of cultural studies. At the same time, writers working within a more sociological tradition have opened up new areas of inquiry at the borders between cultural studies, political economy, anthropology and social psychology (e.g. Couldry 1999; Hesmondhalgh 2002; Hills 2002), and in particular, these writers have worked to chart the increasing integration of the capitalist economy with all forms of culture. In addition to all this, the full impact of post-1968 French philosophy has arguably only begun to be felt recently. Since the publication of Brian Massumi's seminal *A User's Guide to Capitalism and Schizophrenia* (1992), young scholars with a particular interest in possible relationships between new science and cultural theory have ploughed a radical Deleuzian furrow at the very edge of the cultural studies field (e.g. Parisi 2004; Fuller 2005). What is remarkable is that there has been as yet virtually no exchange between this strand and work more directly committed to radical political analysis.

Now, this can create an impression, to anyone who does not bother to read the work in question, that cultural studies has abandoned its political project and simply become a part of the culture it once criticised. Cultural studies is accused of having been reduced to the status of a kind of journalism which simply reports on the superficially changing world but does not show any desire to critique its fundamental structures of power. In some cases this is true, but in most cases of work that gets published under the heading of cultural studies it is not. Any study of the works just mentioned, or any survey of the contents of journals like *Cultural Studies* or *New Formations* over the past 12 years will reveal that most of the conceptual, political and ethical assumptions of such work are clearly inherited from the legacy of cultural studies' evolution through the 1970s and 1980s. Most of this work is clearly informed by a broadly egalitarian and libertarian politics and seeks to understand new cultural phenomena, or to use new philosophical ideas, from the point of view of such a politics. What happens much more rarely than in the past, however, is any attempt to specify the theoretical and political coordinates of the work being done and their relationship to any wider political configurations or projects. Theoretical tools and approaches are simply deployed much as they have been for some time. The consequence of this is that cultural studies today tends to work with a set of political and intellectual reflexes inherited from key moments in the past, be it the Marxism of the 1970s, the voluntarism of the cultural populist 1980s or the under-theorised libertarianism of the anti-essentialist moment. None of these perspectives are currently useless or irrelevant, and it is surely laudable that most of the actual work that gets done in cultural studies is still informed by a resolutely political critique of capitalism, individualism, patriarchy, colonialism and hierarchy in general. More than this, a good deal of work in the field continues to undertake the discipline's core task of mapping the emergent conjuncture from the perspective of an egalitarian politics. Figures such as Lawrence Grossberg, Andrew Ross and Henry Giroux, or the British social policy expert John Clarke (one of the co-authors of *Policing the Crisis*), still strive to map the coordinates of power which shape neoliberal culture using the analytical methods of cultural studies. It is therefore difficult to see how commentators such as Frank, Klein and Žižek could continue to parody cultural studies as a wholly institutionalised form of cultural liberalism, if they actually bothered to survey the field in any detail. However, there is one possible reason why commentators such as this do not feel inclined to undertake such surveys. For although such work clearly shares the concerns of the new movements against neoliberalism, very little of it tries to engage with them directly. It is this situation which following chapters of this volume will seek to address.

We can, however, point to one rather different example of the institutionalisation of cultural studies, wherein its political character did seem to change in response to the needs of state institutions. In Australia in the 1990s, cultural studies was actively supported by a Labor government which was committed to the implementation of multiculturalism as a broad programme, encouraging positive attitudes to cultural diversity across a range of spheres, from education to arts policy to broadcasting to local government. Cultural studies, partly insofar as it was understood to be a discipline in which the challenges faced by a multicultural society could be addressed head-on—but also insofar as it was seen to be informed largely by a set of attitudes which were amenable to the priorities of official multiculturalism—was viewed by the government as something to be encouraged. In this context, a number of cultural studies writers became interested in making a direct engagement with debates in cultural policy (a rather amorphous category including arts policy, some aspects of heritage and education policy, etc.), and a school of writers quickly emerged, central to which was the British veteran of the Open University, Tony Bennett. Theoretically, these writers were heavily influenced by a particular reading of the work of Michel Foucault which tended to stress its anti-utopian dimension as opposed to its anarchistic appeals to the politics of 'bodies and pleasures'. Broadly speaking, these writers accused the mainstream of cultural studies of a naïve romanticism, which manifested itself in the humanistic attitudes of the early Raymond Williams as well as the utopian politics of the later New Left and writers such as Stuart Hall. Instead of allying itself to progressive social movements, figures such as Bennett have argued that cultural studies would do better to accept that *all* pedagogic practices are forms of disciplinary practice (and as such are not necessarily malevolent) and that cultural studies can be of most use when it allies itself to specific fields of cultural policy practice rather than vainly dreaming of social revolution and counter-hegemonic wars of position.

The trouble with this work—of which the exemplary case is Bennett's book *Culture: A Reformer's Science*—is that it invariably fails to specify the ethical or political position from which it proposes to engage in specific, discrete, non-utopian forms of government. This work deploys a rhetoric which seeks to distance itself from any naïve revolutionary pretensions, for example, in Bennett's titular appeal to reform (the traditionally conceived opposite of revolution, and a word with a long and honourable legacy in British political history, evoking memories of the pragmatic, piecemeal, but ultimately effective programmes for social change enacted by various local and national governments in the nineteenth and twentieth centuries). The question is: reform of what, for what, by whom? Bennett never even addresses these questions, and in the process takes a position which is in fact precisely analogous to that of Geoff Mulgan and other proponents of the Third Way (the name given to the mixture of mild technocratic reformism and social liberalism typical of the Blair and Clinton administrations: see Giddens 1998). Claiming to have outgrown the childish vestments of political ideology, such figures present themselves as carefully, pragmatically solving social problems one at a time as they arise, unencumbered by any overarching vision or grand analysis. Such writing remains apparently oblivious to its own ideological status. Put very crudely, the most basic concept of ideology to be derived from the Marxist tradition understands ideology as a world-view which expresses the particular interests of a specific social group as if it was universal truth. In this case, it could hardly be clearer that the privileged technocrats of the Third Way or Australian Cultural Policy Studies had a great deal to gain by popularising the idea that social problems could be solved by experts in specific fields of knowledge without any need for recourse to old-fashioned utopian ideas like justice or democracy. Whether the people who put forward such ideas are truly unaware of their obviously self-promoting, ideological status is unclear: ideology which really wants to persuade people to believe in it never advertises itself as ideology and always tries to pass itself of as common sense (Gramsci 1971; Barthes 1972).

Even on their own terms, the Cultural Policy writers never address the question which becomes immediately apparent as soon as one moves out of the local (and now historically superseded) context of Australia in the 1990s: what do you do, as a Cultural Policy Studies scholar, if you don't have a sympathetic government keen to implement your policies? Under these conditions—which have obtained throughout the English-speaking world, including Australia, for most of the past 40 years–the pragmatism of the reformers comes to seem even more naïve than that utopianism of the revolutionaries. For what use is a mild-mannered technocrat whose policy suggestions are entirely ignored by government? These writers are not stupid, however. In practice, it seems clear that they do not trouble themselves greatly over this issue because in fact the politics which informs their perspectives *is* largely hegemonic in the developed world. Although it is never specified, what is clearly implicit in the priorities and attitudes of the Cultural Policy scholars is that their politics is more-or-less that of the Third Way. That is to say; promoting a liberal cultural and social politics, and a range of state interventions which seek to mitigate the worst social effects of neoliberalism, without challenging its fundamental premises, is in fact the implicit goal of their proposals. As such, it is these so-called Cultural Policy Reformers far more than the reviled cultural populists of the 1980s who actively promote a version of cultural studies which would put it fully at the service of current ruling elites and their political projects.

However, the defenders of this position have a very powerful response to make to such criticisms, and it is simply this: what is the alternative? In the early 1980s, when the Soviet Union still existed, and many hoped that it would undergo democratic reform without capitulating to capitalism, when the first wave of neoliberalism in the developed world was provoking fierce resistance and the election of radical socialist governments in countries such as France and Nicaragua, it might have made sense to ally oneself to the labour movement and the socialist tradition. Theoretically, it made good sense to ally one's work to Marxism when Marxism was still the philosophy nominally informing some of the most powerful political institutions in the world, institutions with whom one broadly wished to take side against American imperialism and capitalist exploitation. Today however, the real political struggle in the developed world is not between capitalism and socialism (which has been comprehensively defeated, however much we may regret the fact) but between the socially liberal, forward-looking, mildly egalitarian administration of capitalism by figures such as Clinton, Blair (and Mulgan, and Bennett) and the violent, nationalistic, fundamentalist politics of the American religious right, the European far right, Zionism, Islamism and Hindutva. In this context, what does it mean to ally oneself with a political perspective more radical than the socially liberal egalitarian mode of capitalism, except to indulge in meaningless and impotent abstractions?

This is not an argument made explicitly by such writers, or by those celebrants of popular culture and consumer agency (e.g. Mort 1996; Hermes 1996) whose work implicitly endorses the hegemonic norms of neoliberal culture, but it is one implicit in the positions that they take, and it must in turn be taken seriously. For the situation which these writers have really responded to is simply the end of that political project which gave a coherent political identity to the mainstream of cultural studies for forty years: the New Left. The inaugural moments of the Clinton and Blair administrations represented the last times when anybody entertained serious hopes that the ideas of the New Left would have any real impact, however indirect and diluted, on mainstream politics, and those hopes have been comprehensively crushed. While the egalitarian, collectivist aspects of New Left thinking have been wholly marginalised, its libertarianism and social liberalism have been largely incorporated into the hegemonic common sense of our times. Today, no serious candidate for political office in Britain could publicly espouse the view that people of different ethnicities cannot live together peacefully, that homosexuality is a perversion and a natural crime, or that women with children should not work; and amongst the advanced capitalist societies it is only in the United States that such views still have any currency in the political mainstream. It is true that the global social dislocation produced by neoliberalism is now provoking a range of authoritarian state measures on the part of government in the United States, the United Kingdom and Australia—measures which, in targeting terrorists, immigrants and asylum seekers, are all aimed at regulating the mobility of the poor—but opposition to these measures comes from the libertarian right and the liberal tradition more than from the tradition of the political left.

The New Left can be seen as having achieved some partial victories. For example, it helped popularise a critique of racism in institutions such as the police force, which has become part of official discourse in the United Kingdom (Marlow & Loveday 2000), and it transformed university curricula through the success of cultural studies. But in broader political terms, its project appears to be finished. In the United Kingdom, the great task it had set itself had been the modernisation and democratisation of the labour movement and its political institutions. In the late 1980s it had seemed conceivable that this goal might actually be achieved. Instead, Blair's so-called reforms of the 1990s saw the Labour party modernised so as to make it a compliant agent of neoliberal governance, with almost all power to participate in the administration and decision-making of the party removed from ordinary members, and a commitment to the full neoliberal programme at the heart of the Labour government's agenda. The direct conclusion drawn by Angela McRobbie is that 'left-academic endeavours, like cultural studies, must rely more on the academic environment and the university for their continued existence ... Voices like that of Hall now have to function as "productive singularities", and there is a certain loneliness in such distinctiveness' (McRobbie 2005: 38). Does this mean that those writers and scholars who have worked in the mainstream of cultural studies from a perspective directly informed by the agendas of the New Left are now entirely isolated, forced to chose between a pragmatic accommodation to liberal capitalism or complete political irrelevance?

Not necessarily. For while they may yet have had little impact on electoral politics in the developed world, the years since the end of the cold war have seen the emergence of a range of political tendencies informed by just the same values and ideas as the New Left. Perhaps most striking has been the emergence of the Green movement, and in particular the Green parties of Western Europe. It's striking that in the United Kingdom, for example, the Green Party's programme and organisational procedures are directly informed by New Left thinking, unlike any other large membership organisation in the country. Although there are strong conservative strands within the environmentalist movement, including both authoritarian traditions and attitudes rooted in the largely anti-political tradition of conservative scepticism, Green politics is dominated by attitudes and priorities which in, many cases, derive directly from the experiences of the New Lefts and 1968 (for example, Daniel Cohn-Bendit, the most famous spokesman for the Paris Students in May 1968, eventually became a Green MP). The Greens' deep questioning of the fundamental values and orientations of contemporary culture and their typical commitment to a politics which connects libertarianism with egalitarianism and communitarianism all point to a strong affinity with the politics of the New Left, as does the historic Green commitment to feminism. At the same time, key figures in the evolution of Cultural Theory have written on ecological themes, most notably Raymond Williams and Félix Guattari (Williams 1973; Guattari 1989). Despite all this, there has been little significant engagement between the remnants of the New Left, key figures in cultural studies, and green politics, despite some notable exceptions (e.g. Wheeler 2006). In the United Kingdom, there has been a gradual influx of left-wing activists from the Labour party into the Green party, but joining the Greens has only been a minority response even from disaffected leftists, amongst whom a general sense of despondent disengagement is a much more typical response—a response that has effectively typified the political current most associated with cultural studies. At the same time, the lack of any apparent resonance between Green politics and its countercultural attitudes and the attitudes of the vast majority of the public cannot leave anyone trained in the Gramscian tradition with much hope as to its capacity to build the kinds of coalition needed for radical social change.

The Green parties, however, are only one manifestation of a far wider environmental movement which to some extent includes everybody who has ever recycled some paper or cycled to work. At the same time, the more militant sections this wider environmental movement intersects with a range of political movements which have emerged since the early 1990s to challenge or protest the unmitigated hegemony of corporate power in the era of neoliberalism. From the new forms of democratic socialism which have emerged in Latin America to the radical environmentalism of the British anti-roads movement of the 1990s, from the actions which shut down the World Trade Organization meeting at Seattle in 1999 to the World Social Forum, a range of movements and activities has emerged which is not bound together by a single ideology or vision of the future but by a rejection of neoliberal hegemony. Although much is often made of the diversity and incoherence of these movements, of the absence of any single ideology unifiying them, this is clearly a somewhat disingenuous claim on the part of both supporters and critics of the 'movement of movements'. The fact is that all of the many diverse and discontinuous movements and projects participating in the World Social Forum, for example, are informed by a broad set of shared values, without which it would be impossible for them to join in rejecting not just neoliberalism but all of the authoritarian and conservative alternatives to it. These values may be loose and general, but, crucially, they involve the combined commitment to egalitarianism, libertarianism, feminism, democracy and communitarianism which has been absolutely typical of the New Lefts.

We can recognise this convergence even more clearly if we consider the programmatic commitments of cultural studies set out in one of the most thoughtful considerations of the discipline to have appeared in recent years. In *Inside Culture,* Nick Couldry (2000) proposes the following five principles as informing all work in the cultural studies tradition (which, I would stress, we should specify as the New Left cultural studies tradition):

The first principle involves valuing what *all* members of a 'culture'—any culture—have to say, in their own voice and not as spoken for by others (p. 37).

Cultural studies has to be a space for both speaking and listening (p. 38).
    Cultural studies, however, should involve not only dialogue, but *reflexivity* ... including reflection about the means through which all the voices in the dialogue have been formed, and the conditions which underlie the production of the space of cultural studies itself (p. 38).

In looking at how voices and cultures are formed, it must adopt a *materialist* perspective (p. 39).

Cultural studies must be an *empowering* practice, a practice which acts directly upon the conditions of culture to change them (p. 39).

The overlap between these principles and those embodied in the founding charter of the World Social Forum (set out in the following chapter) is striking.

The survivors, legatees and descendants of the New Lefts do then find themselves today with a choice. They can accept a position of lonely isolation, or they can ally themselves to the neoliberal project of cultural liberalisation. But a third option is available: to explore the extensive common ground between the intellectual legacy of the New Left and the aims and values of the emergent anti-capitalist movement. It is this third option which the rest of this book is going to explore in detail. However, undertaking such a task is not so simple as it might initially sound. On the one hand, it is not at all clear what the anti-capitalist movement is, or even if it really exists outside of the imagination of journalists and a tiny number of activists. If it does exist, then the fact that it has largely only been participated in consciously by activists raises all kinds of questions about how people engaged in other lines of activity—cultural theorists and cultural studies scholars, for example—might ally themselves to it. Certainly not just by dogmatically declaring themselves its partisans: as we have seen already, cultural studies has always been in relations of critical dialogue with the political movements it has been related to. As I will discuss later on, any political movement which is made up only of its activists has a problem—as without a large number of passive but committed supporters, no movement has ever changed anything—and one of the great problems for anti-capitalism today is finding meaningful points of connection with supporters who are not full-time activists. This also brings us to around to another question: are there any reasons for supporters and activists within the anti-capitalist movement to be interested in the legacy of cultural studies? I think so. On the one hand the sheer richness of the intellectual legacy of the New Left and the several decades of political experience which have informed it means that this is a resource which anti-capitalists would do well to draw on, given that the values and aims informing it have always been absolutely compatible with those of contemporary anti-capitalism. On the other hand, cultural studies has had a historically unique relationship to radical social movements, insofar as it has always been concerned with the question of what it might mean to think about everyday life and the whole complex tapestry of contemporary culture from the point of view of the values and aims of such movements, and anti-capitalism today is badly in need of some serious reflection on this set of issues. The rest of this book will ultimately be concerned with exploring this set of possibilities: asking what it might involve to deploy a position in contemporary cultural theory which activates some of the values and priorities of the anti-capitalist movement in the way that cultural studies has historically activated the concerns of the New Left and the movements associated with it; asking also what the potential strengths and weaknesses of the anti-capitalist movement might be from the point of view of the New Left tradition; and above all seeing how far cultural studies can be used to usefully map the terrain on which the anti-capitalist movement must fight. To begin that task, we have to ask in some detail what the anti-capitalist movement actually is.

Note

1. See, for example (Laclau 1990: xi–xvi) or (Bobbio 1989). It is important to note that many such writers, such as Laclau, have themselves subsequently criticised the celebratory tone of this moment.

–3–

Another World is Possible:
The Anti-Capitalist Movement

Anti-Capitalism?

Since the mid-1990s opposition to the global hegemony of neoliberal institutions and the corporate interests which they serve has grown immensely. This movement is often called anticapitalism, anti-capitalism or the anti-capitalist movement. The name *anti-capitalism* is a problematic name for several reasons; however, it is the name that I am going to use, and whose implications we are going to explore, for the simple reason that it is the name used by the most comprehensive and articulate works to document this movement in any coherent way (i.e. Tormey 2005; Notes from Nowhere 2003; etc.). This chapter will not try to offer an exhaustive documentary account of the movement—partly because these works have done that job better than I could—although it will delineate what I think to be its most novel and notable features.

Not much can be said with any certainty about this movement. Indeed, the very existence of a coherent anti-capitalist movement is not something that all commentators would assent to. For example it is doubtful that any rigourous investigation of the term *movement,* such as one would find in the academic field of social movement studies, would be able to discern a coherent anti-capitalist movement in the United Kingdom[1]. Since the mid-1990s, a number of political formations have arisen around the world which seek to oppose the imposition of neoliberal policies such as the World Trade Organisation and the North American Free Trade Agreement. The World Social Forum has come to be widely recognised as a point where these oppositional formations converge. How far these formations have anything in common, how far they represent a set of new developments rather than continuations and survivals from the past, and how far they can be said to cohere sufficiently in their objectives and priorities to be described accurately as a movement, is not at all certain (Tormey 2005: 38–70; Starr 2000).

A variety of terms have been used to describe this possibly hypothetical movement. The first name to be widely circulated in the press was the *anti-globalisation movement,* because it was seen as specifically opposing the globalisation agenda of the World Trade Organisation, which has been characterised by the drive to liberalise world trade at every level, irrespective of the local social consequences. The term *anti-globalisation movement* led many observers and commentators to assume that protestors against the World Trade Organisation and enforced neoliberalism were opposed to the intermixing and hybridisation of local cultures, the erosion of state control over borders and the mobility of people, and the generally cosmopolitan and internationalist outlook which are all associated with globalisation. While this may be true of some elements of the movement, it is clearly not typical of the vast majority of participants, who see themselves as opposed not to the general principle of international exchange and a weakening of national borders, but to the situation in which these processes are driven solely by and for corporate interests. In its place, some activists have sought to assert their own internationalism by arguing that theirs is a movement for 'globalisation from below' or an 'alternative globalisation'. In France, in particular, the terms *altermondialisme* (literally 'alter-globalism') and *mouvement altermondialiste* ('alter-globalist movement') have come into widespread use. Others have argued, less influentially, that the movement cannot be simply a movement *against* something; alternative names such as *global justice movement* or the *pro-democracy movement* have been suggested. Such titles recognise two key facts: that the movement shares a common goal of defending the capacity of people collectivity to determine their own destinies in the face of threats to that capacity from concentrations of corporate power; and that there are many groups broadly opposed to capitalism (e.g. Moslem Jihadists) who are not part of the movement and share none of its goals.

In subsequent chapters we will explore in more depth some of the issues raised here, but we cannot entirely overlook them for now. Firstly, we have the problem of defining exactly what it means to be anti-capitalist. This is a particularly tricky issue, as some may regard anti-capitalism as involving the wholesale rejection of the existing social order and a determination to replace it with a wholly different one, while others may see anti-capitalism simply as a matter of limiting corporate power or opposing the implementation of the neoliberal programme for capitalist governance, which imposes market relations even where they are not wanted. The potential constituency for the anti-capitalist movement can be seen as much bigger or much smaller depending on which of these definitions of anti-capitalism we accept. At the same time, the general reluctance to make any attempt to unite the movement behind a common programme belies the extent to which it is clearly united by some consistently shared values. Probably the most authoritative statement of these values is the Charter of Principles of the World Social Forum, which makes clear that, at the very least, a commitment to democracy and a certain egalitarianism is central to the philosophy which informs it (World Social Forum 2002). In its commitment to these values, the anti-capitalist movement is clearly distinguishable from the other major forms of opposition to global neoliberal hegemony: nationalism and religious fundamentalism.

At this stage it's worth reflecting that the term *capitalism* does not necessarily mean the same thing to all people, and as such, neither does the term *anti-capitalism*. Broadly speaking, we can distinguish between an understanding of capitalism as a particular set of socio-economic *practices* and the social relations which they engender, reproduce, and come to depend on, and an understanding of capitalism as a total social, cultural, economic and political system to which those practices are central but which cannot be reduced to them. The political implications of this distinction are profound. From the second point of view, to oppose capitalism must mean to oppose an entire social system and to seek to replace it with an alternative: this is the view associated with the tradition of revolutionary communism derived from the ideas of Marx, to which Leninism was so central in the twentieth century, and there certainly are remnants of the Leninist left who now seek to attach themselves to the anti-capitalist movement (e.g. Callinicos 2003). From the first point of view, on the other hand, to be anti-capitalist might simply be to be opposed to the hegemony of capitalist practises—buying, selling, commodification, investment for profit—within all areas of social life. Now, within the revolutionary tradition, this attitude is associated with reformism: political beliefs and projects which seek to ameliorate the worst effects of capitalism on the society and the environment but without transforming the fundamental social relations of capitalism. From the alternative perspective, however, it is not necessary to accept the distinction between revolutionary and reformist politics. Instead it is at least theoretically possible to take up a position which might or might not advocate the abolition of capitalist institutions and their substitution with alternatives, depending on what is feasible at a given juncture. If contemporary anti-capitalism has a novel feature, then it is the tendency and the potential within the movement to take up positions which are militant in their opposition to specific institutions (e.g. the World Trade Organisation), policies (e.g. the privatisation of public services) and projects (the General Agreement on Trade in Services, for example). Although contemporary anti-capitalist groups are often prepared to fight institutions by any means necessary, but they are not committed to the arguably impossible goal of overturning all existing social relations and are not committed to a singular vision of an alternative. This positions is well summed up by the Brazilian social theorist Robert Unger, when he writes that

> To be progressive today is to insist upon crossing the boundaries of the established institutional settlement in a democratising direction. Anyone who accepts the established institutional framework as the horizon within which interests and ideals—including egalitarian ideals—must be pursued is not a progressive. The European social democratic parties are not progressive. A pessimistic, socially concerned, but institutionally conservative reformism is not progressive. The error lies in believing that the alternative to resignation is the total substitution of one "system" by another. (Unger 1998: 295)

This is certainly the politics which seems to typify the participants in and the founding principles of the World Social Forum. Another writer who in recent times has tried to map out ways in which it might be possible to move beyond the institutional limitations of neoliberal capitalism and liberal democracy is Michael Albert. He proposes replacing the institutions of liberal capitalism with institutions which would enable the emergence of a participatory economy in which key economic decisions were the outcome of egalitarian processes of collective decision-making, involving

- social rather than private ownership
- nested worker and consumer councils and balanced job complexes rather than corporate workplace organisation
- remuneration for effort and sacrifice rather than for property, power, or output.
- participatory planning rather than markets or central planning
- and participatory self-management rather than class rule. (Albert 2003: 84)

Again, what is distinctive about Albert's position is that it effectively abjures the distinction between revolutionary and reformist approaches which was typical of twentieth-century radicalism, in its pursuit of a radically democratic socialism. It's this willingness to push back the boundaries of democracy without insisting on a singular imagined future which most strikingly characterises the politics of the World Social Forum.

From Chiapas to Seattle

The World Social Forum is probably the phenomenon which best justifies any reference to anti-capitalism as a coherent movement; it is the place where the 'movement of movements' comes together (Sen, Anand, Escober & Waterman 2003). To understand how this has come about, however, we have to understand something of the history of its constituent elements. The most commonly cited starting point for this process of resistance and convergence was the first day of the Zapatista insurgency in Chiapas, Mexico, 1 January 1994. The Zapatistas, who take their name from the Mexican revolutionary hero Emiliano Zapata (1879–1919) remain in many ways the ideal symbol of everything that is distinctive about the anti-capitalist movement. They are a radical movement based amongst the indigenous Mayan community of rural Chiapas, principally concerned with defending a traditional way of life. They are clear and explicit that what threatens the traditional way of life is the neoliberal programme embodied in the North American Free Trade Agreement. They argue for the right of communities to self-determination, the right to practice rigourously participative forms of democracy, the right to defend a largely communalist way of life and the right explicitly to reject the vanguardism of the revolutionary communist tradition. So the Zapatistas are clearly and indefatigably anti-capitalist and pro-democracy, yet they actively reject much of the revolutionary tradition, with its insistence on class as the only basis for a meaningful political identity and its tendency towards centralising and authoritarian political methods.

For all these reasons, the Zapatistas almost seem to have sprung from the pages of post-structuralist and postmodernist political theory: as we will see, the resonances between Zapatista practice and radical democratic theory are at times uncanny. But there is still more. The Zapatistas main spokesperson is the mysterious and beguiling

Subcomandante Marcos, a former Marxist revolutionary whose true identity is not known with absolute certainty (although it is no longer regarded as much of a secret), partly thanks to the balaclava which he never removes in public. Marcos's deliberate anonymity and his adoption of a different moniker (delegado Zero) in the Zapatista tour of Mexico which paralleled the 2006 general election are all seen as gestures designed deliberately to deflect the possibility of any kind of personality cult developing around Marcos, and as a consequent rejection of any hierarchical or individualist value system. The content of Marcos's public pronouncements and writings, while rarely ambiguous in their meanings ('I shit on all the revolutionary vanguards of this planet' being a typical opening line) are deliberately evocative and poetic in character. Marcos himself has spoken ironically of his thinking as having been 'thoroughly spoilt by literature; its irony and humour' (Mertes 2003 14) before he ever got around to reading Marx and Engels, in a manner decidedly reminiscent of Jacques Derrida's persistent problematisation of the boundaries between philosophy and literature, or the revolutionary poetics of the Russian Formalists and Julia Kristeva (Derrida 1982; Kristeva 1984; Bennett 1979). Most importantly, his writings are obviously the product of an encounter between modern leftist thought and the traditional beliefs and practices of the Mayans which refuses the modern imperative to assume the superiority of the former or any primitivist reverence for the latter. The impact of the new social movements is very clear on Marcos, who has spoken more than once, for example, of the need to reject the traditional homophobia of the Latin American left. In his most famous statement, Marcos declared that

> Marcos is gay in San Francisco, black in South Africa, an Asian in Europe, a Chicano in San Ysidro, an anarchist in Spain, a Palestinian in Israel, a Mayan Indian in the streets of San Cristobal, a gang member in Neza, a rocker in the National University, a Jew in Nazi Germany, an ombudsman in the Defense Ministry, a communist in the post-Cold War era, an artist without gallery or portfolio. ... A pacifist in Bosnia, a housewife alone on Saturday night in any neighborhood in any city in Mexico, a striker in the CTM, a reporter writing filler stories for the back pages, a single woman on the subway at 10 pm, a peasant without land, an unemployed worker ... an unhappy student, a dissident amid free market economics, a writer without books or readers, and, of course, a Zapatista in the mountains of southeast Mexico. So Marcos is a human being, any human being, in this world. Marcos is all the exploited, marginalised and oppressed minorities, resisting and saying, 'Enough'!

> (qtd. in Mertes 2003: 3–16)

At the same time, the Zapatistas explicitly reject any claim to be able to speak *on behalf* of any other group of individual. According to their own view, the Zapatistas do not *represent* the oppressed and marginalised of the globe, but they are in some sense in *solidarity* and in common cause with them, insofar as they are victims of neoliberalism or any other anti-democratic project for the perpetuation or implementation of hierarchical power relationships. The relative success of the Zapatistas in maintaining the autonomy of the region under their control has been an inspiration to the many sympathisers around the world who have been following the course of their campaign via the internet since they began to use it to publicize their cause in the 1990s (Burbach, Robinson & Jeffries 2001).

It is easy enough to see the Zapatistas as the first manifestation of a new, post–Cold War, postmodern type of anti-capitalist politics. However, there are clearly many antecedents to Zapatista thought and practice, not least in the tradition of the New Lefts and the various strands of the 1968 generation. The complex relationships (actual and imaginary, practical and theoretical) between the Anglo-American New Lefts and Latin American socialist movements would warrant a whole book of their own, and we won't have space to investigate them here (see, for example, Raby 2006). More important for us to note here is the fact that several strands of contemporary anti-capitalism have a clear line of continuity stretching back from the 1990s to the 1960s and even earlier.

To some extent, the Zapatistas belong to a current of resistant movements which have emerged in the post-colonial context of recent decades: the movements of so-called indigenous peoples. This is a loose and problematic term, but broadly it refers to the movements of those peoples living in pre-modern village or tribal communities who have been displaced, marginalised or threatened by colonialism and its consequences. For example, the struggle of the Native American peoples to defend their culture and their land began almost with the first European colonisations. What has changed since the global wave of decolonisation of the mid-twentieth century is that there has been a much wider recognition within hegemonic cultures of the justice of such people's claims. Consider that even until the early 1960s, it was routine for Hollywood to depict Native Americans as the savage enemies of heroic white settlers on the Western frontier: a depiction which at best would not be taken seriously today, and at worst would provoke outraged condemnation. The worldwide process of decolonisation and anti-colonial struggle, the civil rights and anti-racist movements which have re-shaped attitudes in many countries since the 1960s (but which interestingly have very few links with the anti-capitalist movement at the present time), and even the influence of cultural studies and other strands of radical thought have all played their part in changing this situation. At the same time the awful legacy of the Holocaust and the experience of fascism still stand as memorials to what can happen when one culture determines another to be inherently inferior to it. More broadly, we can say that this change is one of the key indexes of the postmodern sensibility: privileged Westerners no longer feel confident that the way of life typical of capitalist modernity is inherently superior to all others and so are no longer likely to regard cultural genocide as a progressive project. Now, this is not to say that things have greatly improved for many indigenous peoples or that they do not continue to suffer terribly from both the legacy of colonialism and from capital's continued drive for new sources of profit (natural resources, cheap labour, captive markets). In some countries (Canada, New Zealand) there have been some very real gains made, but in many there have not. The great importance of the Zapatistas is that they have taken a militant stand against the forces which oppress them, without appealing to an imagined neutral standard of justice and human rights within a specific national-legal framework. They fight in explicit solidarity with all those whose opportunities to live as they wish are threatened by neoliberalism, but without any attempt to subsume all of those resistant groups into a single common identity. It is this defense of a radical cultural *pluralism* which characterizes the contemporary indigenous movement, and it is one of the most characteristic features of twenty-first-century anti-capitalism. Whereas the communist and socialist traditions generally saw the preservation of traditional communities as an obstacle to their modernising goals, these movements— more in the tradition of Gandhi than Lenin—do not necessarily argue for the mere *conservation* of traditional ways of life, but for the right to follow their own distinctive paths, in solidarity with other groups wishing to do the same.

One such is the peasants' movement which unites small farmers and the so-called landless, who include those from subsistence-farming cultures who have been deprived of land, from southern France to Brazil (Bové & Dufour 2001). What all of these movements have in common is that despite their pluralism, and to some extent their particularism, they must oppose themselves to fundamental features of the way in which capitalism is currently organised. For not only does the capitalist accumulation process threaten their immediate way of life, its incessant destruction of natural resources puts the very land on which they depend in danger (Shiva 1997). It is for this reason that they cannot be considered as merely particularistic movements, latter-day nationalisms, and it is for this same reason that they must be understood to share a fundamental affinity with another key strand of contemporary anti-capitalism: the environmental movement. This is a strand which is often relatively overlooked in accounts such as this one, in part because it does not have clear roots in the socialist and anarchist traditions of the nineteenth century, despite sharing certain affinities with elements of them. Concern with the preservation of the natural environment has a long history, notably in the conservation movement of the nineteenth century, which amongst other achievements gave rise to the institution of the great National Parks in the United States. However, organised green politics really emerged for the first time in the early 1970s, first in Australia, Canada and New Zealand and then in Western Europe. While organisations such as the British Ecology Party—later to become the Green Party—seem to have been motivated by an agenda which was purely environmentalist, other green parties were more clearly influenced by New Left thinking, as the UK Green Party was itself to become. It's surely no coincidence that all of these organisations came into existence in the wake of the wholesale questioning of established Western values which was embodied in 1968 and the spread of the counterculture of the 1960s. At the same time, non-party environmentalist activist organisations such as Greenpeace and Friends of the Earth, both formed between 1969 and 1971, emerged at precisely the same moment, sharing a commitment to campaign for an agenda which was more radical in its opposition to growth-led economic policies in general than conservationist organisations had been up to that point. Greenpeace in particular pioneered a new style of political activism which grew out of some of the methods of the 1960s while eschewing any pretense to mass participation: funding missions by skilled cadres of professional activists to disrupt military tests and the operations of polluting corporations, drawing the attention of the world's media to issues of concern, with resources provided by an otherwise largely passive membership. This emphasis on direct action is something which the early green movement shared with certain strands of anarchist thinking, and which both would bequeath to the contemporary anti-capitalist movement, with all of its ambiguities as to what direct action actually constitutes and how it connects with any kind of democratic practice (Doyle & McEachern 1998).

In the early 1990s, in the United Kingdom and North America, probably the most prominent elements of what would come to be called anti-capitalism were groups of militant environmentalists situating themselves to the left of organisations like Friends of the Earth, and skeptical about the value of party politics even as practiced by the radical 'deep' greens of the various green parties. Those parties were by this time clearly divided between deep radicals and more moderate elements who sought less radical transformations of the social order, looking for an ecologically regulated form of capitalism rather than a complete end to the consumption-oriented society. In the United States, members of the *Earth First* network had throughout the 1980s deployed a range of confrontational tactics to challenge any ecological threat, in particular damming and logging projects. *Earth First*'s eschewal of any form of structure or formal organisation in favour of a decentralised pattern of wholly autonomous and self-directed cells was to prove highly influential on sections of the anti-capitalist movement, although its biocentric philosophy (rejecting humanism and instead regarding all life as of equal value) was to prove less so. In the United Kingdom the early 1990s saw a wave of organised protests against road projects through ancient woodlands which captured the imaginations of large sections of the public, tapping into a deep vein of English pastoral sentimentalism as well offering a political outlet for many disaffected citizens of John Major's Britain. These protests drew in part on the communities of cultural dissidents which had grown up in the 1970s and 1980s: the squatters of London and other big cities and the nomadic travelers who spent their summers traveling between campsites and free festivals (McKay 1996). While in rural areas these protests were more-or-less directly derived from *Earth First!* practice and were concerned exclusively with defending woodlands, in East London the campaign against a major road project (the so-called M11 Link Road) was also a campaign to save the hundreds of homes that would be destroyed in this traditional working-class community inhabited by large numbers of young squatters as well as many elderly folk who had lived in the area for decades. The result was a sustained mass campaign which was concerned with far more than rural conservation, developing a critique of the extent to which a policy agenda dictated by the motoring lobby was at odds with social justice in areas such as housing and local democracy (local government bodies having long opposed the building plans). Energised by those sections of the free rave movement who were fighting their own battles against criminalisation, the Reclaim the Streets project which emerged from the M11 campaign staged a series of innovative street protests against car culture around London which involved occupying large sections of urban road for an afternoon and using them to hold a rave. Reclaim the Streets, for all of the limitations of its tactics and agenda, was to prove a lasting inspiration to campaigners around the world and was to become the point at which British radicals made the most direct contact with a wider international anti-capitalist movement (Mckay 1998: 100–51).

The broad-based British anti-roads movement of the 1990s was actually a remarkably successful coalition of interests, bringing together anarchists, travelers, squatters, conservationists, moderate greens and sympathizers from across the political spectrum. Although it did not succeed in preventing the completion of any of the road projects to which it turned its attention, few had expected it to do so: rather, the aim had always been to raise the profile of the government's extensive road-building program while adding to its costs, by requiring massive expenditures on security to remove and keep out protesters from road-building sites. The effect was, temporarily, remarkable, as by 1996 the Conservative government had been forced temporarily to shelve all of its programs for major road-building (Wall 1999: 187–90; see also the archive of the British *Earth First!*–sympathising publication *Do or Die* at http://www.eco-action.org/dod/). This effect was not to last, however.

The direction taken by London Reclaim the Streets in the late 1990s remains one of the most instructive instances from recent British history of the paradoxes of radical politics. Buoyed up by the success of the anti-roads campaign, many in the group, whose principle organizers had always been anarchist-inspired militants, wanted to make more direct connections with the international tendencies such as the Zapatistas and the movement against the World Trade Organisation which was to come to global attention in Seattle in November 1999. Five months prior to the Seattle events, on 18 June 1999, the London Reclaim the Streets group organised a so-called Carnival against Capitalism in the London financial district which was timed to coincide with similar protests in cities around the world and attracted thousands of protesters and some terrified press (footage of a branch of McDonalds, that notorious symbol of US imperialism, being vandalised, was widely circulated). While this may have created international connections with anti-capitalists elsewhere and helped to provide inspiration for the Seattle events later that year, it did not succeed in carrying many of the elements of the anti-roads coalition towards a full-scale critique of capitalism. By this time, Tony Blair's New Labour government was already in the process of fully reinstating the postponed road-building plan, and the anti-capitalist movement in Britain did not expand after the so-called J18 protests: instead its events dwindled in size over the course of a couple of years until completely disappearing from the political scene. Some spectacular connections with an international movement had been made, but at home, the few political gains made in the 1990s had been lost in the process.

This story illustrates many of the ongoing problems inherent in the relationship between anti-capitalism and campaigns for limited but achievable social objectives. If we believe that the entire social system generated by capitalist social relations is inherently destructive of the environment, or inevitably produces unacceptable levels of poverty, or invariably undermines democratic institutions, then at some point we have to tackle the very existence of capitalism. Or do we? By the same token, we might argue that if this is the case, then attacking any of the symptoms of capitalism will inevitably lead us to attack the whole basis of the social system eventually, and as such there is no need to make any direct assault on abstractions such as capitalism. On the other hand, if we assume that capitalism is not *inevitably* destructive of the environment, but we nonetheless have particular problems with the ways in which capitalist institutions work, or with the imposition of market relations on particular areas of social life (such as education), then anti-capitalism becomes necessary as a specific political critique of specific institutions and their policies, rather than as a general systemic critique of contemporary society as a whole. However, in that case we might still want to *forge* connections between anti-capitalist activity and activity in defence of the environment or social justice. In any of these cases, effective political action is going to depend upon making a calculation as to what course of action is going to have the desired effect, whether that be to mobilise a mass struggle against capitalism as such, or to create connections between different political campaigns including campaigns against the hegemony of capitalist interests. On any of these counts, the course followed by Reclaim the Streets at the end of the 1990s was not successful: no effective challenge to neoliberal hegemony emerged, no alternative to capitalism was brought onto the political agenda, no lasting connections were made between the anti-roads movement and international anti-capitalism, and no lasting affect was felt on UK transport policy. It is not obvious from this account just what course of action would have had some lasting success, but it is clear that simply failing to think through the paradoxes and complexities of a shift from the environmental reformism of the anti-roads movement to revolutionary anti-capitalism was a disastrous mistake from which a once-potent strand of British radicalism has never recovered.

From a global perspective, however, this was a shift which always made some sense. A movement to draw attention to and challenge the agenda of the World Trade Organisation had been growing since that institution's inception in 1995, and the intervening period has seen a number of significant gatherings of activists at meetings of the World Trade Organisation and the G8 (Canada, France, Germany, Italy, Japan, the United Kingdom, the United States and Russia), some of which have led to major confrontations with police: it's understandable that militants of a group like Reclaim the Streets should want to direct their energies to contributing to this movement. The summit protest is one of the most distinctive features of contemporary anti-capitalism. These often quite large gatherings are generally not coordinated by any single organisation or institution, but come into existence by way of activists dis-cussing plans and communicating intentions through email lists, online forums and word of mouth. Various organisations may assist their members and sympathisers in attending, but there is rarely if ever any centralised system. The classic (although not the first) summit protest which did so much to fix the idea of an anti-globalisation movement in the mediated public imagination was the November 1999 protest against the World Trade Organisation meeting in Seattle, at which a coalition of radical trade unionists, anarchists, economic justice campaigners and environmentalists caused such disruption to the city with their imaginative tactics and highly devolved forms of self-organisation that they succeeded in preventing the World Trade Organisa-tion delegates from concluding their business (Yuen, Katsiaficas & Rose, 2002). The symbolic impact of this success was huge, inspiring waves of local activism across the globe. At my own institution, the University of East London, it inspired a wave of student militancy which managed to put a halt to compulsory staff redundancies and unseat an incompetent and unpopular management in a way which decades of conventional trade union lobbying had not managed to do. This was only one of the many ripples sent out by this extraordinary event, and it should remind us of just how incalculable and unforeseeable the results of such action can be.

Are We All Anti-Capitalists Nowadays?

The heyday of the summit protests is now sometimes thought to have passed, with the largest gatherings and most spectacular confrontation with authority having taken place at Seattle in 1999, Prague in 2000 and, perhaps most notoriously (because of the murder by Italian riot police of activist Carlo Giuliani), Genoa in 2001. However, 2005 saw a novel configuration of forces around the G8 summit at Gleneagles, Scot-land. Although the presence of militant activists at the summit was relatively small, the real political focus was on a massive demonstration held in Edinburgh the previ-ous weekend. The culmination of the Make Poverty History campaign to pressure G8 leaders into cancelling third-world debts and reforming trade practices which discriminate against poor countries (the perpetuation of which is arguably the main geopolitical function of the European Union, for all of its free-market rhetoric), the demonstration was supported by a range of political groupings led by major NGOs (non-governmental organisations) such as Oxfam. Make Poverty History had been a very broad-based campaign which even the UK finance minister Gordon Brown had been obliged to put his name to, and which had involved tens of thousands of citizens and celebrities wearing the campaign's trademark white wrist-bands. How far the campaign's political goals were understood, beyond general approbation for the notion of abolishing poverty, is a moot point. Still more so is the question of how far any of the reforms it proposed were feasible without mass political mobilisation against key capitalist and neoliberal institutions, given that most of them involved major costs for such institutions in terms of profits and power. Still more populist and less focused was the Live 8 concert organised by British impresario, social entrepreneur and sometime rock musician Bob Geldof, in a reprise of the epochal Live Aid concert of 1985. The political aims of Live 8 never even claimed to be more specific than to draw the attention of the G8 leaders to the fact that a large public was aware of their activities. Unsurprisingly to partisans of militant anti-capitalism, the campaign achieved very little indeed, with figures such as Brown and Geldof presenting minor progress on debt-relief as major political victories and all but the most institutionalised and politically conservative NGOs expressing great disappointment at the failure of the summit to push through major reforms to the international trade and finance regime.

This event tells us a great deal—almost everything—about contemporary anti-capitalism in the global north. On the one hand, a broad range of policy objectives which, if implemented, would involve more-or-less reversing the entire neoliberal programme and greatly weakening the power and profitability of finance capital and institutions like the World Trade Organisation, has support from huge sections of the public: probably a clear majority throughout Europe, for example. On the other hand, the organisations which lobby for these policies in the political mainstream—from NGOs to trade unions to social democratic political parties—continue to address their arguments to political and institutional leaders or to a public to whom they are *assumed* to be accountable, on the implicit assumption that the fundamental role of these institutions is to implement the policy preferences of those publics and to protect the general welfare of the world's people.

But this latter point, as any Marxist or any stockbroker could tell you, contains an absurd assumption: because the function of all of these institutions (including democratic governments) is, and has been for several hundred years, to maintain the profitability of the corporations, financial institutions and wealthy individuals whose interests they represent. Certainly there are many occasions on which such aims happen to coincide with the promotion of the well-being of large publics, especially when the profitability of corporations happens to depend on the spending-power of those publics. But broadly speaking, Western governments and powerful institutions have *never* enacted major policy initiatives simply because their citizenry wanted them to or because it was the moral thing to do. Why they should start doing so now—when the lack of engagement of most people with electoral politics and the lack of radical alternatives in the political mainstream means that there is no real danger even to elected representatives in simply ignoring public pleas for reform—is quite unclear. The radical anti-capitalist critique of this perspective is therefore not dogmatic but pragmatic: what, it asks, are we going to do when we realise that banks, governments and supra-national bodies such as the European Union are simply *not* going to implement the reforms we desire just because we, the people, keep asking them to? The problem is similar at the level of national politics. In the United Kingdom, for example, governments since 1977 have implemented a programme of privatisations of national utilities and public services which has effectively dismantled most of the public sector as it existed in the 1970s. This programme has never been supported by a majority of the electorate, and opinion polls have shown consistent opposition to it throughout that time. Nonetheless, mainstream opposition to this programme, to this day, tends to be framed in terms which imply that it could be easily reversed if only a change of attitudes or personnel amongst key government ministers were forthcoming. The fact that this programme has been consistently implemented by range of ministers from both of the main parties since the late 1970s seems to have little impact on this discourse and those who perpetuate it. The anti-capitalist critique of this type of reformism is initially just an observation that it clearly is not getting anywhere, and that as such some other type of politics might be necessary in order to implement even its more modest goals.

Now, it would be far too simplistic to proceed from this observation to the conclusion that electoral politics is a waste of time. History suggests that in a country like the United Kingdom, only government institutions can enable or implement the kinds of reforms that are being sought here, and this will remain the case unless the country enters some unprecedented political crisis. However, history also suggests that the Labour leadership will only challenge capital when it is forced to do so by an organised body of public opinion pushing it to the left. It is not a question of making a distinction between electoral and other kinds of politics, but rather of recognising the sheer unpredictable complexity of relationships between state institutions, capital, and various publics. In these terms, the challenge is to engage directly with the state while fully recognising its limitations; not ignoring it, but pushing its democratic capacities past breaking point. The important point for the moment, however, is that political leaderships in the capitalist democracies will never offer any challenge to the neoliberal agenda until some groundswell of popular energy demands that it do so.

From this point of view, we might say that the major NGOs and the social democratic political parties occupy a fundamentally similar political position. While divided between wings which are reconciled to the neoliberal paradigm (much of Oxfam, the right-wing of the British Labour party, the Democrats) and those which are not (the World Development Movement, which campaigns strongly against policy initiative such as the General Agreement on Trade in Services in the United Kingdom, the left wing of the German SPD and of the French Socialists, the Green party and the radical left of the Democrats in the United States), they generally find their powers limited to those of a weak lobby to be set against the enormous power wielded by those lobbies which can call on the full reserves of wealth and influence possessed by great corporate institutions. In the absence of effective democratic institutions and movements, all that they can do is to carry on asking state and corporate bodies to implement reforms but with no means of forcing them to do so. The response of the anti-capitalist movement to this situation has been broadly to propose that new forms of democratic power be constituted which might be able to do this, and we will discuss this in more detail shortly. However, it is worth considering at this stage just how far bodies such as the NGOs and the social democratic parties are themselves part of this movement. Clearly, some sections of both see themselves as such, and other sections do not. Perhaps more interestingly, even the more moderate of these bodies represent large sections of public opinion which broadly oppose the entire thrust of neoliberalism. This raises the question of how far we can think of the anti-capitalist movement as extending: in some senses, a majority of opinion in Europe, for example, supports policies which are effectively anti-capitalist in nature. What then is specific about the agenda of the anti-capitalist movement which distinguishes it from mainstream political opinion?

An answer which could be given to this question would be that anti-capitalism belongs to the revolutionary tradition while these other tendencies are reformist, committed to the gradual improvement of social conditions without any fundamental attack on the overall social system. This, however, would be an old-fashioned and unhelpful way of formulating the distinction. In fact it would be more accurate to say that the contemporary anti-capitalist argument is that *even* the type of minimal reforms being proposed by the moderates cannot be implemented under the current political conditions obtaining in those countries, in which government is largely the preserve of a technocratic elite and the public to whom they are nominally answerable plays a very small role in influencing the formation of fundamental policy agendas, and exercises an often ineffective veto. Only a shift in power towards new or renewed institutions of popular power could now make such reforms possible, and only a mass movement could bring such institutions into existence or radicalise existing ones sufficiently. Of course, even this is a position which the more radical sections of the NGOs and social democracy have always supported, and as such it is unsurprising that, for example, the World Development Movement in the United Kingdom and sections of the French socialist party have been associated with anti-capitalist campaigns.

A number of European organisations occupy novel places in this landscape. For example, in France the campaigning organisation ATTAC (Association for the Taxation of Financial Transactions for the Aid of Citizens: see http://www.attac.org/), which campaigns for a so-called Tobin tax (a tax on speculative currency trading, first proposed by the economist James Tobin), which would limit the power of financial institutions and the proceeds of which would be used to alleviate third-world poverty; ATTAC is both a lobby group and a 30,000 strong membership organisation with affiliated organisations in 40 countries, which campaigns across a range of issues concerned with the neoliberal assault on the public sphere and the public sector (Cassen 2004). One of the key leaders of French ATTAC is the American-born activist and writer Susan George, whose book *Another World is Possible If...* (2004) is one of the most thoughtful documents so far to reflect upon the experience of the movement to date and draw lessons for a possible future. We should also mention here another organisation with which George is associated: the Amsterdam-based Transnational Institute (http://www.tni.org/), which is the nearest thing to an international anti-capitalist think tank.

While several small far-left parties across Europe see themselves as sympathetic to the anti-capitalist movement (even constituting a relatively informal bloc—The European Anti-Capitalist Left), Italy's *Communista Rifondazione* (Refoundation Communist) party is perhaps unique as a party which actually has played a significant role in government, being part of the national governing coalition elected in 2006, and which is explicitly affiliated to the anti-capitalist movement (Andrews 2005: 91–106). Originally a splinter from the dissolution of the Italian Communist Party in the early 1990s which was opposed to the reformist social democratic turn taken by the largest section, *Rifondazione* has taken on many of the critiques of traditional party structures typical of the anti-capitalist movement; they encourage the spread of social forums which are not dominated by the party or any other political party, and they practise open and participatory democracy within its own structures. In this it has been itself influenced by the example of the Brazilian Workers' Party, which has worked to bring together radical trade-unionists, socialists, social movements and landless peasants with great success in recent decades (Branford & Kucinski 2003). Apart from *Rifondazione* and a handful of far-left parties of no electoral significance, it is actually the Greens, of all the various European parties, which today tend to have a political analysis and approach closest to that of the anti-capitalist movement. The story of the rise of eco-socialism as the dominant strand of European Green politics would require a book in its own right, but it would be fair to say that, for example, the British Green Party today stands on a platform which is clearly derived from the political tradition of the New Left and is sympathetic to the goals of the anti-capitalist movement. However, these parties are small and possess little influence, especially at a national level. In effect, then, anti-capitalism has had a negligible impact on national electoral politics, apart from the instance of Ralph Nader's strategically disastrous bid for the US presidency in 2000 (which clearly helped Bush to secure the White House). In France in 2005 the opposition of ATTAC and the anti-capitalist left to the proposed European Constitution contributed to the success of the "No" campaign leading up the referendum on its ratification, but this did not prevent the election of the aggressively neoliberal Nicolas Sarkozy as president in the election of 2007. In that election, anti-capitalist hero José Bové, a leader of the international peasants' movement and friend of Subcomandante Marcos (Bové & Dufour 2001), received a pitiful 1.5 per cent of the vote. European electorates seem to dislike neoliberalism, but they are not yet convinced of the need for, or the feasibility of, radical democratic alternatives.

Hope Rising in the South: Latin American Socialism and the World Social Forum

In Latin America, things have been quite different. Recent years have seen a now very widely documented shift to the left in South American electoral politics. In Brazil, 2003 saw the election of anti-capitalist icon Lula (Luiz Inácio Lula da Silva) to the presidency. In Argentina, the complete melt-down of the national economy

in 2002 saw the emergence of a whole mass movement for local participatory democracy and the large-scale occupation of factories, land and buildings, in direct
opposition to the international neoliberal programme which was blamed (rightly) for
the bankruptcy of the country. The consequence was the eventual election of a left-
wing, Peronist Néstor Kirchner, as president. In Venezuela, significantly one of the
world's great oil-producers, the election of outspoken militant socialist Hugo Chavez
provoked an attempted coup, supported if not backed by the US administration and
significant corporate interests. The coup failed owing to the massive popularity of
Chavez and his explicitly anti-capitalist, anti-neoliberal administration. The failure
of Chavez's recent attempt to concentrate executive power with a national referendum is an ambivalent moment in this process, possibly marking the limit point of
Chavez's so-called Bolivarian Revolution, possibly marking the welcome deflection
of that revolution away from a path towards tyranny. In Bolivia the election of Evo
Morales as President in 2005, following several years of campaigns against foreign
corporate control of local water supplies, led to the rapid nationalisation of industries
such as gas extraction and water supply. At the time of writing the long-term global
consequences of this constellation of developments are not clear. What is clear is
that the US administration is not currently equipped to put down this uprising to its
South as it has done in the past (with its ruthless backing for the military opposition
to the elected government of Nicaragua in the 1980s, for example). Bogged down
in costly and unpopular wars in the Middle East, facing a serious challenge to its
economic supremacy in the shape of emergent China, and unable to prevent the
new socialist governments profiting from the very high prices which their mineral
reserves currently command on the world markets, America's outraged opposition
to these governments has so far proved quite ineffectual. Whether their example is
taken up in other parts of the world probably depends on how far the anti-capitalist
movement is able to create connections between mainstream socialists and social
democrats and other strands of radicalism at home, and how far it is able to cement
international solidarities within and across these movements. If it is able to do this
at all, then the spread of the social forums will certainly be one of the key means by
which it does it.

The election of Lula as President of Brazil was the culmination of a quarter century of campaigning at local, regional and national level by the *Partido dos Trabal-
hadores* (Workers' Party, PT; Genosko 2003). Although Lula disappointed many in
office with his apparent willingness to accommodate to neoliberalism, it is not at all
clear that political or economic circumstances at that moment left him with much
choice, and it is certainly the case that the PT has over the years innovated many new
and important forms of political organisation. Perhaps the most famous of these was
the implementation of the participatory budget process by the municipal government
of Porto Alegre. This radical departure in local governance involved much of the
local community in setting the city's annual budget, by way of a year-long round
of open public meetings and forums that attracted attention from around the world

(Wainwright 2003: 42–69). It was for this reason that when ATTAC and the editors of the radical journal which founded it, *Le Monde Diplomatiqe,* were looking for partners in a new political initiative, it was to the PT government of Porto Alegre that they turned. This initiative was for a parallel summit to the annual World Economic Forum at Davos, a meeting of banks and other powerful institutions and finance ministers from the wealthiest countries. The World Social Forum was to be a meeting place for all of the organisations and individuals involved in the struggle against neo-liberalism, without the control of any one governmental institution and without the participation of sectarian organisations (so political parties as such were not allowed to participate, although their members were free to do so). The forum held in 2001 attracted 12,000 delegates and was regarded as a landmark event simply in taking place at all. The forum became an annual event, growing rapidly in size and moving from Porto Alegre to Mumbai in 2004, where it attracted over 100,000 participants. Returning to Porto Alegre in 2005, over 155,000 registered for the forum, and in 2006 it was decided to make the forum polycentric, taking place simultaneously at a number of locations around the world. During this period, local social forums sprang up in cities around the world, most notably in Italian cities with the encouragement of *Rifondazione,* and regional social forums such as the European Social Forum also started to appear. All of these forums see themselves as autonomous nodes in an international network, and all adhere to the principles of the World Social Forum, adopted by the organisers of the first forum in 2001:

1. The World Social Forum is an open meeting place for reflective thinking, demo-cratic debate of ideas, formulation of proposals, free exchange of experiences and interlinking for effective action, by groups and movements of civil society that are opposed to neoliberalism and to domination of the world by capital and any form of imperialism, and are committed to building a planetary society directed towards fruitful relationships among Humankind and between it and the Earth.
2. The World Social Forum at Porto Alegre was an event localised in time and place. From now on, in the certainty proclaimed at Porto Alegre that "another world is possible", it becomes a permanent process of seeking and building alternatives, which cannot be reduced to the events supporting it.
3. The World Social Forum is a world process. All the meetings that are held as part of this process have an international dimension.
4. The alternatives proposed at the World Social Forum stand in opposition to a process of globalisation commanded by the large multinational corporations and by the governments and international institutions at the service of those corporations interests, with the complicity of national governments. They are designed to ensure that globalisation in solidarity will prevail as a new stage in world history. This will respect universal human rights, and those of all citizens—men and women—of all nations and the environment and will rest on democratic international systems and institutions at the service of social justice, equality and the sovereignty of peoples.

5. The World Social Forum brings together and interlinks only organisations and movements of civil society from all the countries in the world, but intends neither to be a body representing world civil society.

6. The meetings of the World Social Forum do not deliberate on behalf of the World Social Forum as a body. No-one, therefore, will be authorised, on behalf of any of the editions of the Forum, to express positions claiming to be those of all its participants. The participants in the Forum shall not be called on to take decisions as a body, whether by vote or acclamation, on declarations or proposals for action that would commit all, or the majority, of them and that propose to be taken as establishing positions of the Forum as a body. It thus does not constitute a locus of power to be disputed by the participants in its meetings, nor does it intend to constitute the only option for interrelation and action by the organisations and movements that participate in it.

7. Nonetheless, organisations or groups of organisations that participate in the Forums meetings must be assured the right, during such meetings, to deliberate on declarations or actions they may decide on, whether singly or in coordination with other participants. The World Social Forum undertakes to circulate such decisions widely by the means at its disposal, without directing, hierarchising, censuring or restricting them, but as deliberations of the organisations or groups of organisations that made the decisions.

8. The World Social Forum is a plural, diversified, non-confessional, non-governmental and non-party context that, in a decentralised fashion, interrelates organisations and movements engaged in concrete action at levels from the local to the international to built another world.

9. The World Social Forum will always be a forum open to pluralism and to the diversity of activities and ways of engaging of the organisations and movements that decide to participate in it, as well as the diversity of genders, ethnicities, cultures, generations and physical capacities, providing they abide by this Charter of Principles. Neither party representations nor military organisations shall participate in the Forum. Government leaders and members of legislatures who accept the commitments of this Charter may be invited to participate in a personal capacity.

10. The World Social Forum is opposed to all totalitarian and reductionist views of economy, development and history and to the use of violence as a means of social control by the State. It upholds respect for Human Rights, the practices of real democracy, participatory democracy, peaceful relations, in equality and solidarity, among people, ethnicities, genders and peoples, and condemns all forms of domination and all subjection of one person by another.

11. As a forum for debate, the World Social Forum is a movement of ideas that prompts reflection, and the transparent circulation of the results of that reflection, on the mechanisms and instruments of domination by capital, on means and actions to resist and overcome that domination, and on the alternatives proposed to solve the problems of exclusion and social inequality that the process of capitalist globalisation with its racist, sexist and environmentally destructive dimensions is creating internationally and within countries.

12. As a framework for the exchange of experiences, the World Social Forum encourages understanding and mutual recognition among its participant organisations and movements, and places special value on the exchange among them, particularly on all that society is building to centre economic activity and political action on meeting the needs of people and respecting nature, in the present and for future generations.

13. As a context for interrelations, the World Social Forum seeks to strengthen and create new national and international links among organisations and movements of society, that—in both public and private life—will increase the capacity for non-violent social resistance to the process of dehumanisation the world is undergoing and to the violence used by the State, and reinforce the humanising measures being taken by the action of these movements and organisations.

14. The World Social Forum is a process that encourages its participant organisations and movements to situate their actions, from the local level to the national level and seeking active participation in international contexts, as issues of planetary citizenship, and to introduce onto the global agenda the change-inducing practices that they are experimenting in building a new world in solidarity.

> Approved and adopted in São Paulo, on April 9, 2001, by the organisations that make up the World Social Forum Organising Committee, approved with modifications by the World Social Forum International Council on June 10, 2001. (World Social Forum 2002)

In practice, most Social Forum events are huge conferences, with large-scale plenaries featuring speakers from social and political movements, trade unions, political parties and even governments and smaller-scale seminars and workshops organised by myriad groups on every imaginable theme, from abstract philosophical issues to entirely concrete and localised political campaigns. Their significance lies in the fact that there simply is no precedent for this global exercise in mass deliberation. While many criticise the social forums for their failure to constitute real decision-making bodies for the anti-capitalist movement, their supporters point out that the mere maintenance of open, deliberative public spaces is a crucial element of the struggle against neoliberalism, and that any attempt to force the forum to take public positions on issues would compromise its status as such a space. Whether the forums will prove to have been the forerunners of new, dynamic and participative forms of popular democratic institution able to challenge the neoliberal assault on democracy, as many hope, is impossible to predict. What can be said with some confidence is that even if they do, one could not have expected them to have had more impact in the first five years of their existence than they have had to date. And if they do not, even if they decline and disappear in the near future (as is perfectly possible), they will continue to represent an important point of reference for twenty-first-century radicalism, just as the uprisings of 1848 and the experience of the Paris Commune were key points of reference for the generations of communists and socialists who followed them.

The location of the fourth World Social Forum and the sixth (spread between Venezuela, Mali and Pakistan) indicates another important aspect of the anti-capitalist movement: its vital presence across the global South, not limited to Latin America. Indeed, many governments of so-called developing countries, as victims of the international financial system which keeps them crippled by debt and forces them to implement neoliberal policies against the wishes and interests of their own publics, may be considered natural supporters of the movement, along with the entire populations that they represent. In India, notably, the left of centre United Progressive Alliance, a coalition of parties including the Indian National Congress, is supported by the Left Front, which is powerful in some regions and sympathetic to the movement. Across India and Asia mass movements organise workers, landless peasants, women, environmentalists and poor farmers (some of whom are connected to small farmers in the North via the *Via Campesina* organisation, which includes the French anti-capitalist farmer José Bové) in struggles that are in many ways far more urgent and intense than those experienced by anti-capitalists in the North. Unfortunately, it will be outside the scope of this book to dwell on these, as the book is of necessity limited to a northern, and indeed an Anglo-Saxon perspective, except where (as in the case of the Zapatistas), developments in the south have had a real impact on anti-capitalist thinking in the north. But their presence cannot be forgotten.

Radical Democracy and Minor Politics

At this point, it seems reasonable to think about how the distinctive politics of the anti-capitalist movement might be conceptualised. We have surveyed several different manifestations of that movement, and so we should now ask what it is, at a more abstract level, that the various movements have in common with each other, and what makes them different from other forms of resistance to hegemonic formations, neoliberalism, or capitalist social relations. Here, two features are most striking. Firstly, we can note the refusal to subsume multifarious struggles into one overarching identity. Secondly, we can identify the demand for concentrations of power (both State power and corporate power) to be broken down by the proliferation of sites for participative decision-making. On the one hand, we have a radical pluralism, and on the other hand, a pursuit of democratisation as a radical process of participation. Following these two lines of thought, we can conceptualise this politics in terms of some key bodies of philosophical work which we will examine in much more detail in subsequent chapters, but which it will be useful to consider here briefly.

Firstly, radical pluralism and refusal of identity bring to mind Gilles Deleuze and Félix Guattari's famous celebration of the *minor* (Deleuze & Guattari 1988: 291–3). Deleuze and Guattari make a fascinating distinction between majorities and minorities which has nothing to do with numerical discrepancies. *Majorities* are those identities, those modes of being, which occupy the powerful position of the *norm* within any given culture. They are always resistant to possibilities of change, always defined by their position of dominance over the not-norm. So woman is always a minor position in a patriarchal culture, even if there are more women than men (hence it is still common for histories of democracy to treat women's suffrage as a relatively unimportant issue, or to ignore the fact that Athens, the supposed cradle of democracy, was a slave society in which a tiny proportion of the actual population were allowed to vote). Following this logic, a minoritarian politics could not be one which aspired merely to occupy the position of majority, but which sought to free all minorities and all fixed majorities from their static conditions. Now, crucially, this is not a matter of identity politics promoting a rainbow coalition of oppressed groups, each defending its pure status as woman, or black, or gay. Rather it is a matter of seeking the destabilisation of all such fixed positions: 'only a minority is capable of serving as the active medium of a becoming, but under such conditions that it ceases to be a definable aggregate in relation to the majority' (Deleuze & Guattari 1988: 291)'

From this point of view, the so-called movement of movements might be conceived as a loose assemblage of minorities, waging war against all majority. So does this mean that it would have to be conceived as opposed to all democracy as such?

Well, that depends how we conceptualise democracy. If we imagine that democracy means simply majority rule, then of course Deleuze and Guattari could have no truck with it. But what if we conceptualise it differently?

> the notion of radical and plural democracy ... will be central to our argument from this point on ... Pluralism is radical only to the extent that each term of the plurality of identities finds within itself the principle of its own validity, without this having to be sought in a transcendent or underlying positive ground for the hierarchy of meaning of them all and the source and guarantee of their legitimacy. And this radical pluralism is democratic to the extent that the autoconstitutivity of each one of its terms is the result of displacements of the egalitarian imaginary. Hence, the project for plural and radical democracy is nothing other than the struggle for the maximum autonomisation of spheres (Laclau & Mouffe 1985: 167).

Ernesto Laclau and Chantal Mouffe here offer an account of radical democracy which is entirely compatible with the minoritarian perspective. From this point of view, radical democracy does not imply the tyranny of the majority, but an ongoing effort to *maximise autonomy* for groups and individuals, against the rule of either capital or state institutions. It therefore seems hard not to argue that the anti-capitalist movement is, as much as anything, a movement for *radical democracy.*

Here is one point to keep in mind. Whichever vocabulary we choose, this minoritarian radical democratic perspective depends on one thing. It depends on a rejection of *all* old-fashioned ways of thinking about politics which see society as a single coherent thing with a centre, or a top, a singular locus of power, which a radical movement must seek to occupy and control. Neither government, nor control of the means of production, nor anything else, can be seen as the one source of power and the one objective of struggle. In other words, although we may continue to regard all the elements of world culture as *connected* and *related* in complex ways, we can no longer think of society, or capitalism, or anything else, as simple *totalities*. This will prove to be a very important point later in the book. For now though, let's move on from this assessment of the abstract politics of radical democratic anti-capitalism, to look briefly at the ways in which the movement thinks and acts in regard to one of this book's key issues: culture itself.

Anti-Capitalist Culture?

Along with the social forums, one of the great achievements of the anti-capitalist movement has been the creation of an alternative media infrastructure, particularly through the internet. Even before the globalisation of the Web, media activists such as *Undercurrents* (http://www.undercurrents.org/), who specialise in cheap activist-produced investigative documentaries, had done much to offer a model in miniature of what a democratic public sphere could look like. In recent years the *Indymedia* network of Web sites has emerged to provide open access news reporting on a range of issues, from local campaigns to global politics (www.indymedia.org; Kidd 2003). Anyone can post to these sites, which are maintained to a high standard by committed teams of programmers and which often feature blow-by-blow real-time reports from major events such as summit protests. However one of the notable features of this new media form is its tendency to concentrate very much on events and concrete political actions. One rarely finds discussions of wider issues of political strategy on *Indymedia* sites, never mind any engagement with issues around contemporary culture, lifestyle, philosophy or ethics. In this, *Indymedia* tends to reproduce a notion of politics which is in fact incredibly narrow, focussed on events and campaigns rather than the complex interactions of work, leisure, politics and economics. To be fair, many of these issues are themselves addressed by the types of campaign supported by *Indymedia* and other sections of the anti-capitalist movement, particularly in North America, where anti-capitalism operates as much as anything as a consumer movement concerned with the ethical and political implications of particular lifestyle choices. At the same time, a network of more conventional media institutions across the world remains committed to the movement and its goals and analyses: these include *Le Monde Diplomatique; Z Magazine* in the United States (whose Web site http://www.zmag.org/is a fantastic resource); *Red Pepper* and *New Internationalist* in the United Kingdom; and the radical French philosophical journal *Multitudes*.

Another key element of the anti-capitalist media is the strand of so-called culture jamming associated most closely with *Adbusters* magazine (Lasn 1999). Culture jamming is a generic name given to a range of activities which seek to re-work and re-contextualise elements from mainstream culture in order to make some kind satirical comment on their contents. While the term is usually credited to the band Negativland, pioneers of a kind of satirical sonic collage which does for sound what the radical artist John Heartfield did for visual media, the most characteristic form of culture jamming is probably the work of the Billboard Liberation Front (http://www.billboardliberation.com/) who have been disseminating the practice of deliberate alteration of commercial billboards—transforming advertising and political messages into radical anti-capitalist ones—for 30 years. *Adbusters,* under its founder and editor Kalle Lasn, has more-or-less elevated culture jamming into an entire political philosophy, albeit a decidedly incoherent one. Highly critical of all mainstream politics and commercial culture, and of most of the organised left, *Adbusters* and its contributors tend to seem very convinced of the radicalism of their own practices and are decidedly dismissive of anyone they consider less authentic in their anti-capitalism, although it is never at all clear from what political or ethical perspective they actually make these judgements or what positive politics they would like to pursue (see, for example, Littler 2005). As such, the *Adbusters* activists are often typical subjects of what I will call in following chapters the activist imaginary. This is hardly surprising given that their main theoretical and practical point of reference is the work of Guy Debord and the Situationist International (which we will also discuss shortly).

One of the key objects of *Adbusters* critique has been, for many years, the culture and practice of branding. This critique was brought to a much wider public with the publication and enormous success of Naomi Klein's *No Logo* in 2000. This work's critique of the emergence and costs of brand culture was intellectually problematic to say the least—theoretically weak, frequently unoriginal, and politically inconsistent—but it was a passionate work by a committed journalist exploring a complex set of interrelated phenomena: corporate strategy, cultural change, fundamental shifts in capitalist organisation, contemporary politics. Perhaps more importantly, the book tried to document not just the emergence of the brand as the key meta-commodity of late capitalism, but the emergence of a movement against those key brand-based companies—most notably Nike—who relied on extremely cheap labour in China and the South. The anti-sweatshop movement, which began on US campuses in the 1990s, with students campaigning against companies relying on workers with few rights and poor pay and living conditions and against universities involvement with them, has had a major impact on the behaviour of key corporations, and it is itself a key component of the anti-capitalist movement in the north. But it is questionable whether it would have become so important without the intervention of *No Logo* in documenting it, celebrating it, theorising it (however clumsily) and disseminating it. Here we have an excellent example of the significance of culture for political intervention. Klein's singular cultural intervention amplified the anti-sweatshop movement in a way which nothing else could have done.

No Logo was only the first of a new wave of popular books and films to make a direct critique of contemporary capitalism, or some manifestation thereof. The writings and films of socialist Michael Moore—whose first film, about the social consequences of de-industrialisation in Michigan, appeared in 1989—have had a major impact, constituting in themselves a whole sub-genre of popular anti-capitalist critique, tackling subjects from gun control to racism. Morgan Spurlock's anti-McDonalds propaganda piece *Supersize Me* (2004) was a major hit, despite the vacuity of its political message (elite metropolitan health food good, junk food bad) and Robert Greenwald's *Wal-Mart: The High Cost of Low Price* (2005) achieved success through a network of home-viewing parties organised over the internet. Taking all of this into account, it would perhaps be fair to say that in the United States, anti-capitalism is essentially a media phenomenon. This, however, is not to devalue it in any way: the creation of a non-corporate media infrastructure is without question a major political achievement, and the value of the interventions made by figures such as Klein can be registered in the enormous attention paid subsequently to many of the issues that she raised.

What is interesting about this situation, however, is that almost all of this cultural anti-capitalism operates in a documentary mode. It's about uncovering, discovering and detailing the iniquitous and unsavoury activities of major corporations. Only Moore's work ever goes much further, actually reflecting on some of the wider problems faced by any movement to organise against corporate power: for example suggesting, in a classically Gramscian vein, ways in which a radical might 'Talk to Your Conservative Brother-in-Law' (Moore 2003: 183–201). What anti-capitalist culture does not engage with to any significant degree is the world of sport, entertainment, popular fiction (cinematic, televisual and literary), music and the other arts which so preoccupies much of the world's population: in other words, popular culture. One rarely finds a record review on *Indymedia*. There is little sense of what an anti-capitalist movie that was not a documentary might look like. Explicitly anti-capitalist musicians usually restrict their politics to the *content* of their productions (such as lyrics or album packaging), or else assume that an austere avant-gardism is the appropriate correlate to an anti-capitalist politics. For example, America's Rage Against the Machine spent much of the 1990s combining earnest and articulate anti-capitalist rap with a heavy rock soundtrack, the overall effect of which was to generate an extremely macho sound which had little appeal beyond heavy rock's usual constituency of straight white young men. While there have been works of fictions (such as Rob Newman's 2003 *The Fountain at the Centre of the World*) set around the movement, there's little discussion as to what a critical perspective on literary production an anti-capitalist perspective might entail: Marcos's generic adoration of literature as such hardly amounts to a critical perspective, and his favourite author is Cervantes, the most predictably canonical author in the Spanish language.

This is all woeful. One of the strengths of the movement of movements is that it focuses on specific sets of issues upon which many of its constituent elements can agree at a given moment, without dogmatically expecting them to sign up to a single coherent world view. However, if this is the case then it ought to be able to constitute spaces for critical debate on a wide range of issues. More than this, perhaps, any social or political movement which hopes to achieve real change must seek to extend itself beyond the cadres of its committed activists, developing both a language and a set of shared experiences for relatively inactive supporters of the movement and some rigourous philosophical concepts of its own. One of the great paradoxes of current northern anti-capitalism is that it is a movement whose self-identified partisans are almost all committed activists, and yet it espouses aims and values which are not in conflict with the aspirations of vast sections of the public. In other words, it does not have many passive supporters amongst the public at large, even though it shares the views of many. What's more, the emphatic belief of those activists in the importance of direct participation in politics, action, democracy and life in general would tend to imply that this divide between committed activists and the general public is actually a good thing. I want to suggest that in fact this is a mistaken view. While any democratic movement must to seek to enthuse its members to participate in politics as actively as possible, at the same time any movement which cannot inspire sympathy and support amongst those large numbers of people who will never have the time or skills or energy or inclination to do so is not going to achieve much. The absence of any sense of what it would mean to be an anti-capitalist when engaged in any other activity than attending a summit demonstration or planning to do so is a great handicap for the movement in the United States and the United Kingdom, in particular. This is not simply a question of developing an anti-capitalist identity, however (in fact I will suggest later that this would not necessarily be a helpful thing to develop). Rather, it is a question of how it might be possible to create common ground between the self-conscious anti-capitalism and that popular anti-capitalism which is expressed in, for example, the popularity of Michael Moore and the unpopularity of privatisation programmes in the United Kingdom. It is worth considering, then, that one of the aims of New Left cultural studies was always to find ways to explore the territory between the implicitly progressive elements of popular culture and the explicit political projects of the socialist, feminist and other movements. However, that tradition has been sadly neglected by partisans of the anti-capitalist movement to date.

So what ideas about culture and its politics *have* actually been influential within that context? In many cases, the only thing that amounts to a theory of culture in contemporary anti-capitalist thought is some very crude applications of Marxist or anarchist jargon to random social or cultural issues. However, we can pick out two strands of thought which have been used to elaborate more sophisticated approaches within certain strands of the global justice movement and have influenced practices such as culture jamming: Situationism and social ecology.

Situationism

Situationism is a body of ideas and practices with roots in the inter-war avant-gardes of the early-twentieth century. The Situationist International was a group of artists and intellectuals which emerged in the 1950s from some fragments of the Surrealist movement and which to some extent followed the Surrealist model of combining avant-garde art practice with leftist political theory. They were active until the early 1970s and were to prove both prescient and influential in much of their thinking and aesthetic practice, influencing radical students in 1968, punks in the 1970s and anti-capitalist culture jammers in the 1990s. It has been argued that their thinking in many ways prefigured the post-Marxist radicalism of figures such as Deleuze and Lyotard, although perhaps more persuasively links have been made between their thought and the postmodern political pessimism of Jean Baudrillard (Baudrillard 1988b; Plant 1992). Their name, rather obscurely, derived from their professed determination to create 'situations'—moments of shared authentic experience for small groups—which they saw as a tactic for challenging the forced inauthenticity of life in modern culture. Not that they saw this as a sufficient measure for challenging the social basis of that culture: the Situationists were committed political revolutionaries after all, not just artistic pranksters. Perhaps their most famous and typical aesthetic practice was their *'détournement'* (Debord 1959)—deliberate alteration or re-contextualisation—of existing art objects or cultural commodities, such as in the case of André Bertrand's polemical collage comic-poster, *The Return of the Durutti Column* (Ford 2005: 114–5). But their lasting legacy was not artwork of any kind, but a set of theoretical concepts and analyses and a generic attitude of guerilla utopianism which was to have enduring appeal for political and cultural activists.

To some extent however, there was always a contradiction between these two aspects of the Situationist project, and it is a contradiction which a great deal of anti-capitalist thought and practice has inherited. On the one hand, their activities amounted to a piecemeal tactical warfare against the tedium and passivity of life in the consumer society. On the other hand, their theoretical framework amounted to a wholesale denunciation of that society which leaves little scope for imagining any kind of political progress without some impossible moment of absolute transformation, a revolution more complete than any previously seen in human history. This framework emerges in the two principle texts of the Situationist International: their leader Guy Debord's *The Society of the Spectacle* (1994) and Raoul Vaneigem's *The Revolution of Everyday Life* (1983). Although subtly different in emphasis and political implications, these two books propose and assume a common central concept: the *spectacle*. The continued importance of this concept is attested by its recent use by the radical collective Retort in their widely read account of contemporary geopolitics, *Afflicted Powers* (Retort 2005), and it has proved to be a persistently suggestive, but also persistently problematic, term since the 1960s. The term is used most famously by Debord to designate the accumulation of images which characterises the sensory environment of advanced capitalist societies and which in some senses constitutes the alienated reality of those societies, rendering all life within them a process of passive contemplation (Debord 1994: 12–15). The Spectacle is understood as at once the site and the most developed and integrated form of ideology, the concrete manifestation of 'false consciousness' and the most powerful agency of exploitation. Debord writes that 'The Spectacle is not a collection of images; rather it is social a relationship between people that is mediated by images' (1994: 12).

Essentially, the concept of Spectacle is the culmination of two related traditions of philosophical thought: the Marxist humanist tradition which regards alienation and reification as the key features of modern (or post-modern) life and that long tradition which, going back to Plato, mistrusts the visual in general (Debord 1994: 17) and suspects the world of appearances of superficiality and falsehood. From this point of view, capitalism is characterised by its tendency to separate people from each other and from the products of their labour, and to mask social relationships by giving objects and institutions (from commodities to the institutions of the state) the appearance of real things with a life and agency of their own. This is certainly a valid observation about the social dynamic of capitalism: what is much more problematic is the implicit assertion made by commentators such as Debord that it defines the totality of social relations in advanced capitalist societies. Under this rubric it comes to be very unclear how we can imagine any real resistance to capitalism manifesting itself. In fact, the range of responses to this problem imagined by such thinkers is instructive. They tend implicitly or explicitly, to identify only fleeting and momentary or entirely isolated forms of resistance—school students truanting, lovers momentarily freed from alienation by their passion, city-dwellers rioting, radical philosophers denouncing the inauthenticity of modern life—as having any real validity, while looking to some future moment of full-scale proletarian revolution as the only possible source of permanent change. Every other form of apparent resistance is regarded as always-already recuperated by the institutions of capitalism. From this point of view, for example, the apparent achievements of Social Democracy—from the New Deal in the United States to the establishment of more-or-less extensive welfare states in the Northern European democracies—were not real victories for the working classes at all. Instead their purpose was merely to enable the citizens of those countries to function more effectively as (healthier, better educated, so more efficient) workers and, crucially, as consumers.

The problems with this perspective are well-documented. To put it simply, it is a view which tends implicitly to assume that the prejudices and priorities of artists and intellectuals are of universal value: anyone who doesn't want to be a fully active, creatively vibrant, original, but ultimately rather ascetic participant in the endless construction and re-construction of their world is clearly a hopeless slave to capitalism and its ideologies. The idea that, given the choice, most people might choose freely to be well-fed, well-housed, secure and rather lazy is not on the agenda here, despite the anti-work rhetoric of some Situationist writings. However, there is a more fundamental problem with this whole way of conceptualising social relations, which brings us to one of the key points of difference between the thinkers who are closer to the tradition of New Left cultural studies. While there are many differences between them, writers such Deleuze and Guattari, Foucault, Lyotard and Laclau and Mouffe share one important tendency. They all move decisively away from any notion of society as a totality. They reject any view which would conceptualise social relations within a given context as constituting a singular whole governed by an overarching force, principle or historical destiny. Instead they see social formations as constituted by complex and contingent configurations of elements. By contrast, we can compare the Situationist position to that of two theorists who have been very popular with anti-capitalist activists in recent years: Michael Hardt and Tony Negri. Hardt and Negri locate a singular formation—'Empire'—as the dominant force in the world today. Now, although they understand that formation as a complex network—a 'rhizome', almost—and insist that it has no centre, they nonetheless insist on both its singularity and its ubiquity to an extent which has serious political consequences. Most obviously, their claim that an attack on any part of Empire is equal to an attack on any other leads directly to a refusal of any attempt to build lateral connections between different elements of the struggle against neoliberal hegemony: in other words, to a refusal of politics as such. In fact, given their rejection of such strategic politics, we can read Hardt and Negri as endorsing the kinds of low-level tactical innovation typical of the anarchist and Situationist strands of the anti-capitalist movements which have so singularly failed to have any significant political effects. What we are left with, in this case and in the case of Situationism, is a position which implicitly endorses isolated acts of creative, symbolic or theoretical resistance and some future revolution which would completely transform all social relations, but which maintains an austere distance from any other kinds of political activity. We can see this in the rhetoric of those culture jammers who seek to elevate their activities well beyond their warranted status as interesting but minor interventions against corporate hegemony (www.adbusters.org) and in the carnivalesque activities of those activists—such as radical clowns (http://www.clownarmy.org/), who dress up as clowns and taunt the police on anti-capitalist demonstrations, and so-called space hijackers (http://www.spacehijackers.co.uk/clp3/) who organise spontaneous urban gatherings—and whose antics and messages are often simply indistinguishable to the wider public from the activities of viral marketers and cutting-edge corporate publicists.

Perhaps surprisingly for a work written in explicit sympathy with anti-capitalism, this book takes the view that this is an approach whose political futility is both logically apparent and historically incontestable. Real alternatives to the hegemony of capitalism and its institutions have only ever been built by complex social coalitions willing to experiment with a range of institutional and democratic innovations: from squatters building alternative communities with the tacit support of local government to the coalitions of workers, bureaucrats and professionals who built the institutions of the welfare state in the twentieth century. Sitting around and waiting for the revolution or making radical statements which only our friends understand has never achieved anything. However, accepting such a view need not imply that the innovative tactics of jammers and clown are simply without value: nor need it entail abandoning the utopian impulse to remake the world and to remain constantly dissatisfied with imbalances of power. The challenge for anti-capitalism today is to bring together such exciting and innovative tactics into new formations of political possibility: that is, to assemble them into potentially effective *strategies*. Realising such potential means having to accept the irreducible and ever-intensifying complexity of social life and the messy, always compromised nature of politics, without simply abandoning ourselves to the rule of neoliberalism. Believing in simplistic fairy-tales like the Spectacle just leaves us spitting in the wind.

Social Ecology

The formation of complex strategies may be the great political challenge facing anti-capitalism, but it is not the primary one facing humanity as a whole today. Without doubt, the major obstacle facing us in the early years of the twenty-first century is the ecological crisis which threatens to render life on Earth impossible for many species, including our own. For this reason alone, the next thinker for us to consider must be regarded as a significant contributor to contemporary thought. The so-called ecological anarchist Murray Bookchin ploughed a consistent but often lonely intellectual furrow through much of the latter half of the twentieth century, being one of the first writers and activists to emerge from the Marxist tradition with a clear theoretical commitment to what would eventually come to be known as green politics. Of course, Bookchin was not alone in treating ecological themes—of the writers mentioned so far in this book, Williams (1973), Guattari (2000) and Vaneigem (2003) have all written on these issues at different times—but he was unique in placing them at the centre of his thought from the early 1950s onwards, and as such he is one of the venerable figures of the green movement, and one who has been widely read and discussed within this important strand of anti-capitalism. Given that this great figure of the American left died such a short time before writing—in 2006—it is rather sad that my main purpose in this short commentary will be to draw attention to the limitations of Bookchin's thought, limitations typical of much thinking within the anti-capitalist movement.

Bookchin was no doubt, in his own way, an erudite scholar and a highly original thinker. As with the work of many autodidacts, however, his idiosyncratic scholarship generated as many misconceptions and glaring absences in his work as it did original insights. His most famous work, and in his own view his greatest, *The Ecology of Freedom* (Bookchin 1991), offers a complete theory of humanity's relationship to nature which is grounded in a specific history of the socio-technological evolution of human civilisation. In this it bears an interesting resemblance to Deleuze and Guattari's *Anti-Oedipus,* and it is also close in spirit to the work of materialist historians such as Braudel, Mumford and Wallerstein. Bookchin takes a position which is largely informed by the same Hegelian humanism as inspired the early Marx, and which draws on the mainstream Western philosophical tradition as mediated by the classics of Western Anarchism and early Marxism. In setting out the terms for his philosophy of social ecology, Bookchin makes some remarkably advanced arguments concerning the inseparability of humanity from nature (1991: 1–42), which in spirit brings him close to the Spinozan materialism of Deleuze or Negri, and this resonance can be seen all the more strongly in Bookchin's sympathy for certain radical mystical and Gnostic traditions (despite his rejection of contemporary mystical or quasi-religious approaches to ecology). Bookchin's interest in the radical implications of early Christianity—despite his own background in Jewish socialism—prefigures the later argument of Alain Badiou that Pauline Christianity is the foundation of all later philosophies of universal human emancipation (Badiou 2003). His insistence on the continuity of human and natural processes, of the social and the ecological, brings him close to those contemporary thinkers drawing on complexity theory to understand the similarities between natural and social processes. His emphasis on the inherent productivity of matter has strong resonances with Deleuze and Guattari's machinic materialism and with the thought of Luce Irigaray, who identifies a tendency to regard matter as inert substance within the 'phallogocentric' economy of patriarchal thought. His rejection of primitivism and biocentrism combine with a belief in the democratic, communal and human-centred nature of 'organic' societies (pre-industrial, only primitively agricultural) to create an account of human history which is idiosyncratic in places, but largely mirrors Marx and Engels's account, whereby the aim of political struggle is to recover a lost communality, while preserving the vast expansion of human capacities which modernisation has entailed (a conception which is actually supported by much contemporary anthropology; Bookchin 1991).

However, Bookchin's thought reveals its limitations whenever it encounters a view which does not sit with his precise formulation of social ecology. His emphasis on the irreducible value of wholeness—both in human societies and in their relationship to nature—is decidedly problematic in the light of a perspective which rejects the idea of society as a coherent totality. For example, the psychoanalytically inflected ideas of Ernesto Laclau stress the extent to which wholeness is always a fantasy, a thing that we (as groups or individuals) always wrongly imagine ourselves to have lost and to have a chance of recovering (1990), while Deleuze and Guattari would see this fantasy as the direct production of Oedipal culture (1983). According to this view, no human society has been or *could be* without conflict, and no person is ever fully at one with their social and physical environment: nor could they be while retaining the status of a functioning human subject rather than a mere passive block of matter. This is a perspective which Bookchin simply ignores, while dismissing psychoanalysis out of hand (1991: 112–18). In much the same way, Bookchin's Hegelian neo-Marxist account of human history as a process of progressive alienation from nature through the division of labour now seems quite archaic compared with those theoretical approaches to human history which stress the contingency and complex interdependence of material and social processes, and which emphasise even the historicity of matter itself (Prigogene & Stengers 1984: 208; Delanda 1997; Delanda 2002). Where these various approaches coincide with the post-Marxism of Laclau and Mouffe is precisely in their implicit or explicit rejection of the Hegelian idea of totality to which Bookchin remains attached and which constitutes the greatest limitation of his thought.

Bookchin's attitude to much of the important intellectual work of recent times was frankly reactionary. The introduction to the 1991 edition of the book simply dismisses postmodernism, deconstruction and cultural studies entirely out of hand, while demonstrating no apparent awareness of their relationship to political traditions very close to Bookchin's. Given the apolitical and nihilistic image of these currents of thought in the United States at the time, this is not entirely surprising, but it is telling that Bookchin seemed to be entirely unaware of the ecological socialism of writers such as Raymond Williams and Félix Guattari. Ultimately, his thought raised some of the most important questions of recent times, in terms which were way ahead of their time, but in cutting himself off from the most relevant developments in radical thought, Bookchin severely limited the long-term usefulness of his thought.

Perhaps one illustration of this is his attitude to other strands of the Green movement which he (almost always rightly) condemned for a lack of rigourous theoretical thinking. Bookchin alienated many with his efforts to distance himself from the mystifications of quasi-spiritual or biocentric green thought, an effort which was motivated by a wholly appropriate suspicion of any religious or supernatural beliefs or any beliefs which implied a lack of concern for other human beings. He was understandably appalled, for example, by the attitudes of prominent *Earth First!* activists who viewed third-world famine as a positive way of reducing the human burden on the Earth's ecosystem (Bookchin 1991: xxxi; Bookchin 1988). However, his attitude to a wide range of such views was so thoroughly dismissive that he seemed incapable of grasping the nature of their persuasive power for many people. For example, Spinoza's work and the subsequent history of its reception makes clear how difficult it can be to draw a line between rationalist materialism and pantheist mysticism, a line which Bookchin tends to assume that he can stay on the rationalist side of even while asserting the inherently non-parsimonious character of nature. This is a problematic assertion and, some might argue, an unnecessary one. Biocentrism may be an extreme view to many, but it raises profound questions as to the bases of our ethical judgements (just why *should* we place highest value on human life?), which cannot be waved away as easily as Bookchin would like (see http://raforum.info/article.php3?id_article=1761).

There is no question that both Bookchin and the Situationists offer profound insights into the workings of capitalist culture and the nature of possible opposition to it. Ultimately, however, neither of these bodies of work makes much attempt to engage with the full range of ideas which can inform radical theory at the beginning of the twenty-first century. In particular, we have seen that there is an interesting fault line between these thinkers (and we could add to their list the kinds of dogmatic

Marxist still typical of small Western European revolutionary organisations such as the British Socialist Workers Party) and the anti-essentialists, Deleuze and Guattari and Laclau and Mouffe. While the former tend to see capitalist society as a totality of which contemporary culture is one integral element, the latter see social and cultural formations as the outcome of relatively contingent processes of 'articulation' (Slack 1996) and 'assemblage' (DeLanda 2006). The implicit differences between these two sets of positions are profound, because it is really only in the latter group that there is any scope for understanding *politics* as playing a significant role in the world. Indeed, at the present time, when neoliberal capitalism has established itself as, in the words of Perry Anderson, 'the most successful ideology in world history' (2000), it is not clear why believers in totality who are opposed to capitalism should do anything today but despair. If there is to be any scope for politics at all, then we surely need more complex and fluid accounts of the relationship between culture and capitalism than these.

Note

1. For a relevant study of green political activists in London, see Saunders (2007). On the persuasive criteria used by Saunders, there would be no question of designating the disparate fragments of contemporary British anti-capitalism a 'movement'.

–4–

(Anti)Capitalism and Culture

In some ways, the very modern idea of culture emerged as a critique of capitalism. If culture is always a collective endeavour, then both conservative and radical traditions of critique have tended to see capitalism as inimical to it (Williams 1982, 1961; Mulhern 2000). If we think of culture as the expressive arts, then there is a long tradition which assumes that commercial motives must always corrupt aesthetic activity. If we think of culture in anthropological terms as a way of life, then there is still a long history of commentary which believes that capitalism necessarily distorts, preys on or corrupts traditional ways of life or the self-organised activity of innovating groups. On the other hand, there are good reasons for arguing that any attempt to conceptually separate culture and capitalism is simply ridiculous. From this point of view, capitalism is not something that happens *to* culture. Rather, capitalism *is* a culture, a way of life, a set of practices and institutions which cannot be separated from the wider formations in which they emerge (Foucault 2004: 169–71). Both of these perspectives have some validity, insofar as capitalism is never *lived* as an abstraction, and yet it must be possible to identify its 'singularity' (Foucault 2004: 170) to be able to say anything about it at all. In this chapter we will consider different ways of conceptualising the relationship between capitalism and culture, and their consequences for thinking about the politics of the anti-capitalist movement in various manifestations.

Capitalism, Creativity and Conservatism

Ideas about the cultural effects of capitalism are themselves dependent upon more fundamental sets of ideas about what capitalism is and what it does, ideas such as those discussed at the beginning of the last chapter. Nonetheless, we can identify a fairly consistent set of themes as being shared by commentators from a number of often mutually hostile political traditions. As Marx showed (Marx & Engels 1998; Marx 1992), what drives capitalism as a social process is the constant invention of new commodities and the search for new markets to sell them in. Those commodities might be actual new things, or minor modifications of existing things, or various types of service or intangible goods; and those new markets might actually be new groups of people or they might be existing groups who have been persuaded to buy new things in new ways; but overall the logic is the same. For centuries, commentators have variously praised or condemned the social and cultural consequences of this process, although there has often been a good deal of agreement about what those consequences actually are. Conservative commentators have bemoaned the fact that the restless innovations of a society bent on inventing new things and new ways of doing things must inevitably undermine traditional beliefs, communities and social relations. Others have seen exactly the same process as benign and welcome. In the late-eighteenth century, Adam Smith was already extolling the civilising virtues of commerce and trade, and indeed Marx was to echo this view, describing the emergence of a globally integrated economy as a force for bringing the world together and for modernising the less developed parts of the world (Marx & Engels 1998). Throughout this period there were voices questioning the destruction of traditional ways of life in the colonised world that this process involved, but they were seldom heard (James 1989: 4). There were many negative responses in their times to the social consequences of industrialisation and the capitalisation of agriculture, from street riots to poetry, and today the destructive social consequences of globalisation are one of the main reasons for the existence of the anti-capitalist movement but also one of the main causes provoking the rise of new forms of national, religious and ethnic fundamentalism. Every time a conservative commentator complains about the social consequences of drug abuse, hip-hop, pornography or TV, they are in effect decrying the cultural effects of certain relatively new types of commodity (drugs, music recordings, TV-shows, various forms of porn) being in circulation.

This is only one half of the capitalist story, however. Capitalism is not merely to be defined by processes of commodification, because it is perfectly possible to have a market economy without having capitalism. Rather, what defines capitalism is the rule of capital: of that special kind of wealth that can be used to generate more wealth, and of those who control it. The characteristic features of a capitalist society include the concentration of productive wealth in the hands of an oligarchical elite and the tendency for their drive for capital accumulation—profit—to organise all of the activities of that society, as well as the prevalence of wage labour throughout the economy. In fact, this will often involve processes which are quite opposite to the profligate inventiveness of an ideal free market. In order to secure profits, and to maintain their position of privilege against potential rivals, capitalists (both individuals and institutions) will frequently work to secure monopoly control of particular economic sectors, limiting invention and production within those sectors. In addition, capitalists engaged in commodity-production will tend, where possible, to try to take advantage of possible economies of scale by producing and selling identical commodities to large markets. This will tend to encourage the standardisation of commodities, and as such will give capitalists a direct interest in encouraging a standardisation of tastes amongst consumers. Both monopolisation and standardisation can be understood as different aspects of what Manuel Delanda (following Fernand Braudel) calls 'antimarkets' (Delanda 1996).

Antimarkets are organisational strategies which seek to stabilise, limit and contain the free production and exchange of commodities. So we can see that capitalism is not merely about the invention and distribution of commodities through market relations; it is also sustained by the strategic deployment of antimarkets[1]. Which of these components is the more powerful in any given context will depend upon a range of circumstances: technological limitations, the balance of forces within and between different social groups, and so forth. For example, so-called monopoly capitalism, characterised by a high level of cooperation between capitalists, will tend to limit innovation and creativity. Conversely, high levels of competition between capitalists will tend to lessen their ability to resort to the construction of antimarkets, as they are forced to innovate and to encourage wider innovation in the search for new products and production methods which can help them compete with their rivals.

In fact, following a line of argument that runs from Marx through to Negri, it is possible to claim that the creativity which gives rise to such new inventions—artistic, scientific, or utilitarian—is never really engendered directly by capital at all but is always the result of human interaction outside of the circuits of capital accumulation. Capital, from this perspective, must always feed on this creativity and work to transform its products into profitable commodities, but it is never the source of new value in itself. This is why capital must locate itself near great centres of collective exchange and creativity (Paris and London in the nineteenth century, New York and California in the twentieth) and must to some extent allow those zones to exist. The great bohemian centres are always in close proximity to financial centres, because capital needs their innovative energy, although it can never fully control it, however hard it tries. This is why the ideas, practices and social innovations of radical forces are often so superficially similar to those of leading-edge capitalism (the Bay-area counterculture and Silicon Valley; The Loft and Studio 54). Capitalism needs to allow these great laboratories of change to thrive, and it cannot always direct and capture what comes out of them, although it will try. When it cannot, when they become connected to other forces, progressive social changes can ensue.

Consider, for example, what happened when the technology of oral contraception emerged in 1960s Britain: its wide availability was a product of the interaction between elements of the welfare state and decades of feminist campaigning for women's contraception, led by the legendary Marie Stopes. The potential for liberation of women from the housewife role was initially captured by the promotion of the Dolly Bird as the new feminine ideal: sexualised, but ultimately even more powerless and passive than the housewife, her role limited to that of a consumer of cosmetics and an object in turn of male consumption. It took the strategic coordination of the women's liberation movement to recapture this potential and amplify it in democratic directions. There was a very fine line, but all the difference in the world, between the liberated woman of 1964 and the liberated woman of 1972, and the difference was entirely a function of capital's relative ability to capture and direct the creativity of this new technology against the strategic capacity of women to do the same. This kind of democratic change is always a risk inherent in the kinds of new technology which capitalism must permit and encourage if it is to keep moving forward profitably.

This is why a wholly negative response to the social consequences of capitalism as such has generally been the preserve of traditionalist conservatives. Logically, to oppose capitalism as such, *except in the name of some imagined future alternative* would be to defend the society and culture which it has displaced; and by definition those who have sought to defend, say, the feudal order of medieval Europe or Japan, or the society and values of the Ottoman empire, or even the patriarchal customs of earlier capitalist moments, have not been on the left. Even where traditional, non-Western values have been articulated to anti-imperialist projects, as with the evolution of Indian nationalism in the early twentieth-century, only the most reactionary variants have actually wanted to revert to some simply pre-modern, pre-capitalist state. Historically, certain currents within the left have idealised a romantic vision of some aspects of medieval or pre-medieval life or culture, and most historians agree that standards of living deteriorated for most people in the early stages of the industrial revolution, but the Enlightenment ideal of a future that would be better than the past was fundamental to the emergence of most of the political traditions—socialist, anarchist, social democratic, communist, liberal—that emerged in the wake of the industrial revolution and which contribute to contemporary anti-capitalism.

As such, radicals have generally tended to see the process whereby traditional social structures—and the cultures which sustained them—are displaced as either benign in itself or as the necessary precondition for any truly democratic social change. In the most general terms, this is the process which sociologists refer to as *detraditionalisation:* a process whereby traditional patterns of belief and behaviour are dismantled and displaced. Interestingly, two of the key theoretical perspectives that we are concerned with in this book have produced their own terminologies for describing such a process. Deleuze and Guattari's 'deterritorialisation' is just such a term and evocatively alludes to the ways in which the destabilisation of routinised patterns is almost always bound up with a re-ordering of spatial relationships (so the break-up of so-called traditional rural ways of life in many parts of the world today is bound up with the depopulation and re-ordering of the countryside and the migration of populations to new urban centres). Much the same emphasis is given by Laclau's concept of 'dislocation', which designates both the process by which established forms of social life are disrupted, and also the inherently unstable dimension of any social identity or structure, however apparently fixed it may be. Laclau sums up a great deal of democratic thought on the social effects of capitalist modernisation when he writes:

> Let us consider the dislocatory effects of emerging capitalism on the lives of workers. They are well known: the destruction of traditional communities, the brutal and exhausting discipline of the factory, low wages and insecurity of work. But this is only one side

of the effects, for the workers' response to the dislocation of their lives by capitalism was not to submit passively, but to break machines, organize trade unions, and go on strike. In this process new skills and abilities were inevitably born, which might not have been the case otherwise. (Laclau 1990: 39)

Dislocation, deterritorialisation and detraditionalisation are by no means exclusively effects of capitalism and its spread. They can be the consequences of quite different changes to the social order (consider, for example, the destruction of peasant communities by Stalin in the 1930s or the Chinese Cultural Revolution of the 1960s). They can be the consequence of ecological shifts which undermine the material infrastructure of an earlier way of life—drought, famine and plague can force a change in traditional patterns of behaviour just as effectively as socio-political changes—or of technological innovations such as those which made the English master weavers redundant within a generation in the early nineteenth-century. In the latter two instances, however, it is worth reflecting that capitalism's tendency to technological innovation and to the intensive exploitation of natural resources has generated the most intense and the most rapid ecological and technological transformations in human history since the beginning of the modern period.

Having said this, we should note that progressive anti-capitalism has rarely been informed by a purely modernistic or futurist sensibility which is simply dismissive of the past in its entirety. Even where it has rejected the hierarchy and squalor which characterised previous social orders, progressive anti-capitalist thought has identified a tendency in capitalism to undermine certain practices and values which are typical of most human cultures and whose loss they regret: even while they may have no nostalgia for feudal hierarchy, for example, socialists have tended to regret the passing of a sense of mutual responsibility which seems to have informed much of pre-industrial European society (Polanyi 1944: 165–77) and indeed most other human societies. This conservative element has historically been a minor strand of radical thought. Today, however, when neoliberalism seeks to impose capitalist relations on those modern collectivist institutions—in particular the institutions of the welfare state—which were partially built by the working classes and their representatives for their own protection, then it is much easier for those in the radical tradition to take a wholly conservative position, concerned only with defending the achievements of twentieth-century social democracy. This is a notoriously problematic position for anyone on the radical left to take: those institutions were never perfect, and in the United Kingdom, for example, were never very democratic. However, it is hard to deny that central to the neoliberal project is the attempt to turn those vast collective resources into objects of primitive accumulation, in a process widely seen as analogous to the enclosure of common land in eighteenth-century England (Hardt & Negri 2004: 186; Retort 2005; de Angelis 2001). In this context, even those who regard the institutions of the welfare state as unwieldy, undemocratic and outdated are forced into a defensive position to the extent that they have any desire to retain their status as common resources under some kind of democratic control. This is what makes possible a certain continuity between the aims of even the most moderate social democrats and more radical sections of the anti-capitalist movement, even those who share little of the radical tradition's faith in the progressive potential of capitalist modernisation.

One such is the strand of Green primitivism represented by some members of groups such as *Earth First!* Even here, however, it is worth nothing that the primitive state to which Green primitivism would like to return is not one which is simply pre-capitalist, but one which long pre-dates feudalism and even any highly developed form of agriculture. This connects it with another important strand of contemporary anti-capitalism, the campaigns by indigenous peoples against the dislocatory effects of capitalist primitive accumulation. Most famous of these is, as we have seen, the Zapatista movement, which has absolutely no desire to see any form of industrial modernisation imposed on Chiapas and finds in native Mayan traditions a way of life which is simply more democratic and more ethically, politically and ecologically desirable than any which capitalism could make possible. The Zapatistas are not simply defenders of tradition: their commitment to principles such as gender equality and sexual freedom has no particular basis in traditional Mayan attitudes to these issues, which are much more conservative. However, like many twentieth-century radicals who rejected the classical Marxist idea that only the industrial working class can lead a socialist revolution, they seek to implement democratic values in a social, economic and material context not wholly disfigured by capitalist social relations.

We can see then that a defensive resistance to neoliberalism and a commitment to democratising existing social relations and institutions without subjecting them to the logic of the market is what ties together the apparently disparate strands of contemporary anti-capitalism. The question which remains for us to examine in detail is what the cultural effects of capitalism are which critics in this tradition have objected to, and what might be the correlate of contemporary anti-capitalism in thinking about culture in general.

Creative Destruction

Capitalism has tended to produce a general set of social and cultural effects which has caused anxiety even amongst those commentators who, like Marx, have been relatively gung-ho about the modernising benefits of capitalism. As Marx himself observed, capitalism's basic function is to generate commodities. For commentators such as Marx and Schumpeter, capitalism is at once and in equal parts fantastically creative and fantastically destructive. We can see these dual aspects of capitalism just by examining the basic process of producing a commodity. Any commodity is ultimately produced by a process of appropriation and creative destruction. For example, chopping down a tree and turning it into a table involves someone appropriating the tree, destroying it and creating something new. Arguably this is what capitalist social relations do to everything, in trying to make everything (from food to clothes to education) into commodities. The process by which resources which were once owned in common by a community, or by no one, are appropriated by groups or individuals, is called by Marx 'primitive accumulation', and the process by which those resources are transformed into commodities—units of exchange with a currency value—is called *commodification*. At the heart of the Marxian tradition of social criticism is the observation that capitalism as a social system tends to apply these processes not only to previously unexploited natural resources but also to resources which communities rely on for survival as well as to many other things.

For example, the changing relationship between artists and their publics in the centuries following the Renaissance can be understood in terms of the transformation of music, visual art objects and literary works into things which could be bought and sold on the open market. It is interesting to reflect that this was in many ways not a bad thing: the fine arts had up to this point been largely the preserve of the aristocratic elite who could afford to retain the services of artists who were essentially specialist servants. But the consequences of marketisation are not always so benign. At the present time, the efforts of institutions like the British government to transform public services such as education and health provision into units of service which can be bought and sold competitively is a perfect example of this process being actively enforced against the wishes of most concerned groups. While most professionals working in those fields and most users of those services do not want to reduce their relationships to buyer–seller transactions, such a transformation of those relationships is necessary if private corporations are to be enabled to provide such services for a profit and to compete with each other to do so. In this context, the social resources built up by the welfare state in the post-war period are treated as objects of primitive accumulation and subject to processes of commodification, even against the wishes of a majority of people concerned. So whereas most people would regard healthcare and education as collaborative enterprises— requiring a high level of cooperation between carers and patients, educators and students—neoliberal policy insists that the interests of both service users and service providers, and of different groups of providers, be seen as antagonistic in just the same way as the interests of buyers and sellers of commodities are (buyers wanting lower prices, sellers wanting higher prices). This set of relationships is enforced, entrenched and institutionalised by policies designed to re-organise service provision into competing units, setting schools and hospitals in competition with each other and forcing parents, students and patients to treat them as competing commodity producers: for example, by removing local democratic control over such institutions, leaving service users with no way of exercising power over them except by choosing to use some services and institutions rather than others. This exemplifies the process whereby commodification leads to a reduction of almost *all* human relationships to buyer–seller transactions.

What are the cultural effects of this process? This is not a matter on which there is absolute agreement, so let us consider a number of views here. The most famous commentator on this issue in the Marxist tradition is Theodor Adorno (1903–1969), who argued that the conditions of production of artistic commodities for a mass market led to a generalised homogenisation or standardisation of the output of the culture industry: such as similar-sounding records, clichéd movies and identikit detective stories or romance novels. This is a common complaint about commercial culture to this day, and it clearly has a good deal of validity. However, we should consider in more detail just what this account assumes and implies. For one thing, it is not at all clear that such cultural standardisation can be blamed entirely on capitalism, because, to put it bluntly, most human communities have displayed fairly conservative cultural tastes, capitalist or not. Most communities, even relatively non-hierarchical ones have maintained traditional forms and themes in story-telling, poetry, music and art, and it's by no means clear why an anti-capitalist critic should be as wedded to the classically bourgeois values of individuality and originality as Adorno is (values which he never defends as such, but simply assumes to be self-evident). Having said this however, there is a strong socialist tradition, not least that informing the first phase of British cultural studies (e.g. Hoggart 1957), which makes a clear distinction between such organic traditions and the output of the culture industry, which is characterised by a far more passive relationship between the consumers of culture and the culture they consume.

This is an important point, because Adorno's view is part of his much wider account of capitalist society in the middle decades of the twentieth century which would similarly support the distinction between an industrialised, passive culture and a more participatory and active one. Adorno's account of capitalist culture, which arguably owes more to Weber than to Marx (Weber 1968: 1156), stresses the growth of administration: the centralised, bureaucratic regulation of social, cultural and personal life by powerful institutions (Adorno & Horkheimer 1997: 131). It was an extremely widespread assumption at that time that this was the inevitable destiny of capitalist modernity, and probably of 'actually existing socialism' too. This is understandable, given that this is the era when centralised economic planning became popular with governments of all political persuasions throughout the industrial world, and when the new advances in mechanisation—the culmination of the so-called second industrial revolution—made it possible to manufacture all kinds of goods (from cars and radios to foodstuffs and textiles, not to mention books, magazines and records) cheaply according to vast economies of scale. It was Henry Ford who summed up the aesthetic of the new consumerism when he said of his famous Model T (the first mass market motor car) that it would be available in 'any colour so long as it's black' (Jardim 1970: 83), and it was Antonio Gramsci who named this new type of regulated and administered capitalism 'Fordism' (Gramsci 1971: 279–318). The great era of mass culture, when economies of scale found millions of people consuming similar products, watching the same movies and reading the same newspapers must have looked like one in which standardisation had indeed become the normal mode in which capitalist commodity-production would work.

Of course, even Adorno had to recognise a potential problem with such an account. As is quite obvious, and Marx was certainly aware, capitalist ideology *claims* that capitalism offers consumers an ever-widening choice of commodities of all types. Adorno argues that in fact this is a lie: the products of the culture industry are only superficially different from one another, characterised by the pseudo-individualism of purely cosmetic differences. This is an argument which is many ways very close to the later ideas of the Situationists, who also claim that, in effect, capitalist commodity culture creates a feeling of freedom and widening-choice for its inhabitants which is simply illusory, a screen for their complete lack of real agency or authenticity.

Now, there are several major problems with this line of argument. One is that the critic who pursues this line of argument must claim the authority to determine what constitutes real differences between objects and what differences are merely superficial. Adorno's most famous writings on these topics relate to music, and Adorno was notoriously narrow and elitist in his views as to what characterised good music, having no time for anything outside the tradition of Austro-German orchestral music and maintaining a rather narrow view even of composers that properly belonged to that tradition. As many commentators have since pointed out (Middleton 1990), Adorno's criteria are not only explicitly elitist, they are also wholly ethnocentric. In musical traditions in which formal innovation of certain given musical structures is less highly valued than re-interpretation of other musical parameters his criteria would simply have no purchase: in house music, for example, where a minor timbral contribution—an unusual sound, an unexpected filter effect—to a standard track might be heard by connoisseurs as a significant innovation. In broader terms, the dismissal of consumer culture by commentators such as Adorno and Debord often seems to proceed from the austere hauteur of intellectuals for whom the material fabric of everyday life has just never been much of an issue: for most of the human race through most of its history, by contrast, the difference between one cloth and another, one cheese and another, and so forth, has been the stuff that cultures, identities and lives have been built from (Miller 1987: 189–96; Slater 1997).

However, it would be too simplistic to conclude that Adorno and company are simply wrong. Capitalism may encourage the development of real and powerful new objects, both in producing new types of commodities and in continually innovating existing ones, but, importantly, it is never capital that does the inventing. Even new kinds of soap-powder are produced in the collective space of the laboratory, rather than in the boardroom or on the trading-floor. In these terms, the chemical research lab is a precise analogy to the artistic bohemias mentioned earlier—both are protected zones of experimentation which capital must keep close to itself if it is to find new resources for accumulation.

This view has a particular relevance today, in the era of so-called post-Fordist capitalism (Amin 1994). One of the characteristic features of post-Fordism is that manufacturing systems have become so sophisticated and so powerfully integrated with both retail and with research and design that it is in effect possible for manufacturers and retailers to dispense with economies of scale while still servicing a mass consumer market. One of the classic features of post-Fordism is the prevalence of just-in-time ordering systems in industries such as food or fashion. Supermarkets or fashion stores today will typically only carry a small quantity of any one item. Sophisticated computing and communication technologies make it possible for suppliers to be notified every time a single item is sold and to supply a replacement immediately. In some sectors, products can even be slightly modified in accordance with emergent trends in demand on a weekly basis (so one week more red scarves can be produced, but if blue scarves start to sell faster then more of them can be produced). Overall, this allows manufacturers, suppliers and retailers to compete more effectively to meet precise consumer demands, so enhancing profitability. The consequences of this shift are enormous. Capitalist culture in this context has a much weaker interest in promoting conformity than it did when it was trying to sell vast numbers of identical objects to consumers. The era of mass culture is over, and it is now clear that it was only ever typical of one specific form of industrial capitalism, adapted to the technological capacities and limitations of the early-twentieth century. We can see this just by turning on our TV sets or scanning the internet for online radio stations: there really is a vast range of cultural output now available to us, and even if we don't think any of it has much value, it is hard to argue that the differences which characterise it are merely superficial.

This is not to say that we should celebrate the commodification of everything that advanced post-Fordist capitalism entails, but it does draw attention to the fact that it is difficult to explain what is actually wrong with it in terms drawn exclusively from Adorno, or similar commentators like Debord. Even from a Marxist perspective, it's possible to argue that Adorno's implicit celebration of real individualism is itself inherently bourgeois: often the terms in which Adorno criticises the culture industry seem drawn more from Romanticism than from the socialist tradition. But does this mean that we should simply dismiss commentators such as Debord and Adorno altogether? It does not. There remains a certain powerful truth to their views if we come back to the basic question of the socio-cultural effects of widespread commodification. For while commodification may generate a situation in which very real differences between *commodities* are actually produced, it nonetheless serves to homogenise *social relations* by reducing them all to buyer–seller transactions. Marx described the process whereby commodification comes to mask the real social relations which make the production of commodities possible as commodity fetishism, and in such instances we can see the logic of commodity fetishism extending into new domains of culture. The result is a kind of flattening out of social and cultural experience whereby we are able to chose from a vast range of possible lifestyle-elements and experiences, but the nature of our relationships to all of those things will be identical. From university courses to shoes to restaurant meals to holidays to dates with potential partners: everything will become, in effect, something we buy. This is the anxiety which Adorno and Debord so eloquently express, and the contemporary cultural scene—in which the broadcast and print media obsess about celebrity lifestyles while entirely failing to report the fact that the welfare state is effectively being dismantled, against the express wishes of the public—seems to bear out their fears more than a little.

No Logo: In the Empire of the Commodity

The most celebrated strands of contemporary anti-capitalist thought to have something like a theory of culture are heavily preoccupied with the issue of commodification. Most notably Naomi Klein's *No Logo,* the publication and success of which was itself, as we have seen, a major factor in popularising the notion of an anti-capitalist movement, takes contemporary processes of commodification as its central theme through its concern with the apparent triumph of branding in contemporary culture and its relationship with global patterns of exploitation. For all its strengths, the book is intellectually weakened by Klein's apparent unfamiliarity with the tradition of Marxist and post-Marxist thought: nothing in the book is inaccurate from the point of view of this tradition, but its claims to originality are highly problematic. In effect, Klein simply repeats a point already made many times by commentators going back to Marx, which is that the extreme effect of commodity fetishism is to mask the reality of social relations, alienating workers from each other and from the products of their labour, and so alienating consumers from workers and from the material world in general. Even her casual claim that the triumph of brands as the key commodities of our time marks some decisive new era of capitalism is wholly unoriginal, echoing both the Situationists and the work of thinkers such as Lyotard and Baudrillard who have analysed far more carefully the processes whereby images and units of information become commodities in highly advanced capitalist economies. However, Klein, who is by profession a journalist, and one of the most important of our time, can hardly be blamed for not being an expert on political and cultural theory. It would be absurd for us to attack her for these shortcomings: instead it is the job of a book like this one to try to fill in some of these gaps.

So let's look at a range of more theoretical writers who have in relatively recent times considered the cultural consequences of what we might call deep commodification. At their most extreme, the views of such thinkers would tend to imply that there is simply no point in trying to maintain a perspective which is in any way anticapitalist. Jean Baudrillard is one example. In his early work, Baudrillard argues that in an advanced capitalist society, commodity exchange is always an exchange of meaningful signs. He argues that the notion important to Marx, of a commodity having 'use value' (it's real value) as distinct from its 'exchange value' (it's market price), is a false one: uses are always socially imagined and as such it is only its location in a system of meanings which constitutes any object as in any way useful; therefore, all value is exchange value (Baudrillard 1988b: 57–97). Baudrillard, quite logically, moved from this perspective to argue that in contemporary culture, all of our experience is mediated by the exchange of signs which have no direct correspondence to any material reality. In fact, he argues, we can no longer speak of 'signs' but only of 'simulacra' (images and representations which have no referents in a real world) as constituting the totality of contemporary experience. Baudrillard therefore argues that reality as such has been overwhelmed by the 'hyperreality' of absolute commodification. In a nutshell, Baudrillard carries the pessimism of Adorno and Debord to its logical conclusion, arguing that once commodification has reached a certain level of intensity, any struggle for authenticity is futile: the game is now up (Baudrillard 1988b: 166–84).

A rather different view would be implied by the ideas of Jean-François Lyotard. Lyotard also considers that commodification has had a dramatic effect on the status of truth, but he reasons along different lines. In his most famous work *The Postmodern Condition* (1984), Lyotard argues that knowledge has become a commodity today. Just consider the fact that Bill Gates has become the world's richest man by selling, not physical goods, but pieces of knowledge—most notably the Windows operating system—and you can see the truth of this. In fact since Lyotard wrote this amazingly prophetic account in 1979, the idea that we now live in a 'knowledge economy' (Rutherford 2003) has become a truism of government policy and mainstream economics. Lyotard points out that this implies not only a change in the nature of the global economy but a change in the social status of knowledge, also. Whereas in the past, knowledge has been judged in terms of how it fits into traditional pictures of the world or into 'Big Stories' about the purpose of human history, it now comes to be judged solely in terms of its functionality. Lyotard points out, very interestingly, that this is already, in effect, how science values knowledge: the development of theoretical physics since the late-nineteenth century, for example, has shown that science can tolerate quite incompatible theoretical paradigms as long as they continue to generate respective experimental and practical results. Incidentally, Lyotard's approach is in a certain sense the opposite of Baudrillard's. Where Baudrillard collapses the distinction between use value and exchange value by arguing that all values are exchange values, Lyotard implicitly collapses the distinction by arguing that all values are use values: so even the symbolic value of commodities exists only because of the social uses to which those symbols can be put. (This reading would tie in interestingly with the ideas of Pierre Bourdieu (1986), who argues that symbolic commodities are largely used as deliberate markers of social differentiation). In subsequent work, Lyotard develops a rather obscure philosophical response to this situation which we have no space to try to summarise here. To put it very crudely, however, he argues that the proper ethical response to this situation must be to refuse any 'totalitarian' attempt to impose a single system of meanings and values on the world (Lyotard 1984, 1988). We now inhabit a world in which no Big Story (or 'grand narrative', as the term is usually translated) can contain and legitimate all knowledge, and so we must learn to live with the co-existence of incommensurable systems and types of knowledge. In fact, what Lyotard proposes is very close to the terms in which sections of the anti-capitalist movement, such as the Zapatistas, frame their opposition to neoliberalism today.

A different perspective again is offered by those Marxist commentators who take a less apocalyptic view of matters than Adorno or Debord. In the English-speaking world, critics such as Frederic Jameson (1991), David Harvey (1989; 2005) and Paul Smith (1997) have offered compelling accounts of the relationship between advanced capitalism and various types of social and cultural change. These writers tend to stress the importance of understanding shifts in the technical, material and geographical organisation of capitalism for understanding that range of recent cultural changes which are sometimes collectively understood in terms of a transition to a new postmodern era. Unlike the key figures of cultural studies, these writers tend to see nothing at all to be happy about in recent times and very little to be optimistic about without some return to fairly traditional forms of labour movement politics. As such, they tend to offer a simpler critique of contemporary capitalist culture than the mainstream of cultural studies or the anti-capitalist movement, and they tend to have little interest in the latter as a potential vehicle for opposition to neoliberalism. We should also include in this category Slavoj Žižek, who is perhaps the most vociferously anti-capitalist of contemporary cultural theorists, but who is contemptuously dismissive of both the anti-capitalist movement and cultural studies (Žižek 2002: 170–1, 273).

What are the actual features of contemporary culture of which these critics are critical? Well, it is interesting to note that in some senses the key features which they identify as typical of the current era are not so different from those identified by commentators with slightly different political emphases. Sociologists such as Zygmunt Bauman (who might be described as a maverick Marxist), Ulrich Beck and Anthony Giddens (who are certainly not Marxists) and the team of Scott Lash and John Urry (whose complex post-Marxism is more-or-less analogous to Stuart Hall's), all see the general process of detraditionalisation as generating a culture which is pluralistic and individualistic, in which the logic of commodification is extended across a wide range of social fields and in which the nineteenth- and twentieth-century institutions of social solidarity dissolve (e.g. Beck, Giddens & Lash 1994; Bauman 2001). However, these sociologists tend to a more complex view of the losses and gains arising from such a situation than do the followers of classical Marxism. What distinguishes the more nuanced views of this group of sociologists from those of these Marxist commentators is really a matter of how they value these changes, and how far they regard them as reversible or inevitable. For Žižek, for example, the commodification of all culture is neither inevitable nor desirable but can probably only be confronted by a full-scale revolutionary assault on capitalism as such. For Harvey, the answer would seem to be a resumption of the social democratic or revolutionary communist projects of the mid-twentieth century: Harvey does not make this explicit, but his generalised condemnation of most cultural change since the end of that moment seems to imply this (Harvey 1989: 284–307; Harvey 2005). Jameson is always unclear as to what the solution should be, but given his terms of reference, it must presumably be proletarian revolution. My own view of these Marxist commentators is that they offer brilliant and entirely accurate *descriptions* of contemporary capitalist culture, but that they do so from a perspective which has become incapable of generating effective political *responses* to the situation they describe. For now, let's consider some aspects of these descriptions in a little more detail.

For the Situationist Raoul Vaneigem the basic logic of capitalism is 'separation' (1983: 87)). This is a suggestive phrase. Recall my account of the logic of commodification above: the process by which the tree is turned into the table is clearly a process whereby some wood is *separated* from the tree, the tree is separated from the ground, the ground in question is probably, in some way, separated from the common ground of which it was once part. What's more, separation is also something that appears to happen to people in capitalist societies, as traditional forms of community are dissolved and people come increasingly to see themselves as isolated individuals, separate from and largely in competition with all other individuals, rather than as members of any kind of group (be it tribe, nation, family, neighbourhood, party, union, or class). This is the process which other commentators have named 'individualisation' (Beck & Beck-Gernsheim 2001), and it is arguably the key socio-cultural tendency of the precise form of neoliberal capitalism which has been hegemonic in the West since the 1970s (although there are powerful countervailing tendencies, as we will see in later chapters). Even more than this, the traditional Marxian critique of alienation sees separation as part of the process whereby people lost sight of the fact that the material world they inhabit—a world of commodities—is in fact entirely the product of collective human labour.

Separation, individualisation, alienation: in different terms these all describe aspects of a process which is endemic to unregulated, unopposed capitalism, and which has manifested itself in many different ways throughout the history of capitalist modernity. At the present moment, however, it appears to be particularly effective. Rising crime, an obsession with celebrities, a decline in political participation: these are all, arguably, symptoms of this dissolution of the social and of any generalised sense of human solidarity. Carried to its logical conclusion, this process would undermine the very idea of the human being as a *social* animal at all. If anything more substantial than the struggle for autonomy binds together the disparate elements of the contemporary anti-capitalism, it is an antipathy for this process. In the United Kingdom, as discussed in the previous chapter, one of the key moments in the emergence of the movement was the Reclaim the Streets project of the 1990s, which took as its main object of attack the car culture which was prepared to see both ancient woodlands and affordable urban housing stock decimated by massive road-building plans. Inspired in part by Situationist theory, this antipathy to cars was informed not just by environmentalist concerns but by a political critique of the socio-aesthetic function of the motor car. Cars in many ways embody the cultural logic of separation, alienation and individualisation. They enable private individuals, with or without select groups of acquaintances, to travel wherever and whenever they like. As such, at a purely individual level, they are hugely liberating. But they form part of a general system of transport (Urry 2004) which is extraordinarily dangerous—millions of people running around in metal boxes that travel at lethal speeds with no effective system of coordination—and hugely damaging to the environment, both through carbon emissions and the heavy demands which tarmac roads put on finite stocks of land. They protect their users from any form of direct human contact, and from any participation in public space at all: going from home to work by car can save the suburban commuter from even having to walk down the street. To oppose the ubiquity of the motor car in our society is one way to attack the whole culture of alienation and individualisation which dominates it.

We can see, then, a clear continuity between the approach of the anti-capitalist movement, and that of various critics in the Marxist tradition who identify and criticise the dominant cultural tendencies of advanced capitalism. We might ask, then, just why we would need anything more than this in order to generate a position in cultural theory which is generally usable by that movement or its sympathisers. I will try to deal with that question now.

For one thing, it is important to remember that these Marxist writers are generally either indifferent or mildly hostile to the anti-capitalist movement, which they see as no good substitute for the great projects of communism and social democracy. Now, in one sense this is quite justified. After all, what has this movement actually achieved, especially when compared with the colossal achievements of the labour movement in the twentieth century? Absolutely nothing worth mentioning, in truth. However, there seems very little reason to believe that a return to the tactics of the twentieth-century labour movement is going to achieve anything in the future, given that that movement was so comprehensively defeated in the last decades of that century. More than this, however, I am going to argue that there is something problematic about both the attitudes of these scholars *and* certain prevalent attitudes within the anti-capitalist movement itself which point to a problem with the very idea of anti-capitalism. However, before we can get into this issue, we are going to have to pull back a moment and think a bit further in abstract terms.

Most Marxist cultural criticism takes as its object of attack the basic cultural effects of capitalism, which are usually understood in terms of the logic and consequences of commodification. Put very simply, however, my argument is that it is very difficult to sustain a position which is opposed to *all* commodification *as such.* There are some contexts in which commodification is not a bad thing. Let us take as an example the general field of the production and distribution of music. This is a good example because Adorno, the great critic of commodification, was particularly interested in music and particularly clear about the implications of his position for thinking about it. Now there are a number of perspectives, including Adorno's, according to which it is possible to argue that commodification as such is bad for music. If one believes that commodity-production necessarily implies standardisa-tion, or if one believes a particular tradition (or several co-existing traditions) to be the sole repository of great music, then commodification will be a bad thing. In the first case this will be because standardisation *as such* can be argued to be clearly a bad thing: even where musical traditions are relatively conservative, conservatism is not exactly the same thing as the enforced and mechanical conformism of industrial standardisation, which, in itself, no one is going to defend. In the second case it will be because commodification necessarily implies a process whereby the integrity of a tradition is compromised: music is taken out of its intended context to be sold else-where (as sheet music or recordings) and as such much of its impact is lost and it is not properly understood by its performers or its listeners.

However, none of these propositions stand up if one accepts that the field of popular music since the early days of recording has been characterised by a great deal of welcome innovation, experiment and progressive practice. For the very exis-tence of popular music as we know it depends entirely on a material, economic and technical framework of commodification. There was no jazz, no rock, no hip-hop, no soul, no funk, no disco, no house that ever really existed outside of a framework of commodity-circulation. The very cultures into which these musics emerged existed primarily through the material medium of the exchange of commodities: records, radio broadcasts and sheet music. Indeed, for that matter, Adorno's hero Beethoven also relied on a certain types of commodification (selling sheet music and tickets to public concerts rather than being employed by wealthy patrons as previous genera-tions of composers had been) to give him the independence to be able to revolutionise European orchestral music. In the case of popular musics, this is clearly something more than a case of creativity surviving *despite* the culture industry. Many of these musics could never have achieved the impact or the levels of creative innovation that they have done without the capacity to cross borders (between places, times, com-munities and generations) that is the unique capacity of the deterritorialised com-modity (Gilbert 1999). Of course, these are remarks that Marx himself, praising the civilising virtues of trade, would certainly have gone along with.

This discussion brings us back to the overall anti-capitalist position outlined at the beginning of this chapter. There are two key points to emphasise here. One is that, as we saw earlier, commodification is very far from being the whole story of what capitalism does and how it works. On this point there are several more things to say. One is that while Marx *begins* his great analysis of capitalism by examining the nature of the commodity, he ultimately argues that the real truth of capitalism lies in its status as a system of production. What is fundamentally wrong with capitalism, from the point of view of Marx's model, is not the proliferation of commodities, but the exploitation of workers by capitalists. More recently, various commentators with an ambivalent or hostile attitude to capitalism have argued that what is wrong with capitalism is not trading in free markets or private ownership, but the concentration of power in the hands of small numbers of unaccountable institutions and individuals which capitalism as a social system involves (Kingsnorth 2003: 278–311). Fernand Braudel, the greatest historian of capitalism, includes in the conclusion to his monumental survey of capitalism's global history the observation that 'neither the little workshops of Prato nor the small printers of New York can be regarded as examples of true capitalism. … This is enough to make one think again before assuming that our societies are organised from top to bottom in a "capitalist system". On the contrary, putting it briefly, there is a dialectic very much alive between capitalism on the one hand and its antithesis, the non-capitalism of the 'lower level' [of small-scale trade, manufacture and the informal economy] on the other.' (1984: 630). In the case of the music industry, this line of argument would tend to the view that as long commodity production and distribution is in the hands of musicians or a diversity of small companies, then the situation can be regarded as healthy. Now, of course, working for such a situation may involve all kinds of political and legal battles—to change copyright laws or to provide access to recording facilities for poor musicians, for example—but they do not necessarily have to involve an opposition to all market relations. Anti-capitalism in this context may mean a determined but ultimately localised resistance to corporate monopoly rather than opposition to commodification as such.

However, from the anti-capitalist perspective that we are developing here, there may still be something unwelcome about contemporary processes of commodification in music. It is one thing to commodify, say, tea: it is another to force every possible element of human existence into the mould of the bought and sold commodity. Music-making is by nature an inherently social, collaborative process (Toynbee 2000). However, a wholly commodified music culture tends to mask this fact. Artists must, as far as possible, present their work as entirely their own (without, frequently, acknowledging the input of session musicians, music-software designers, engineers, other musicians who may have influenced them, etc.) in order to maximise returns from it in the market place, and consequently the media tend to focus on musicians as personalities rather than as participants in a collaborative process when reporting on music and contributing to music culture. Music culture therefore increasingly comes to be presented as a kind of narrative drama about competing personalities rather than as a scene of collective creativity (just consider the roles of Amy Winehouse and Peter Doherty in the UK press; these aren't artists, but characters in a soap opera). Music culture is thus subjected to individualisation and becomes a site for the propagation of *individualism,* that ideology which maintains that individualisation is merely a process by which we come to realise the essential truth of the human condition, rather than a process by which the real nature of human interrelationship is masked. This masking is in part what is described by the key twentieth-century Marxist concept of *reification* (a term which might literally be translated as 'thingification'): the transformation of relationships and processes into fixed and static objects, at least in appearance (Bewes 2002). If anti-capitalist cultural criticism has a job in this context, it is first and foremost to expose the extent to which individualism is a falsifying reification and music-making is a collaborative process. If anti-capitalist cultural activism has a job, then it will be to defend and extend sites at which the collaborative production, distribution and consumption of music can take place without the maximisation of corporate profits being the overriding objective, or even any objective at all.

No Logo, No Choice? Democracy vs. the Market

So far we have discussed the politics of commodification in a specific context—contemporary popular music culture—which has to some extent only ever existed in the medium of the commodity. This is quite different from considering the consequences of commodification in those contexts which have been shaped in other ways, particularly contexts which have previously been thought of, or been actively constructed as, sites protected from the market logic of commodity exchange. In the attempt to privatise large sections of the public sector which characterises the current global project of neoliberalism, we see not an organic process of ground-up production and circulation, but the violent imposition of a particular set of social relations from outside and above with the ultimate aim of enabling capitalists to profit from provision of services that were once provided collectively on a non-profit basis. One consequence of this is to deprive communities of access to common goods (from education to water supplies) or 'commons' (de Angelis 2007) and to force them to access those resources only as individual consumers. In cases such as the so-called reform of healthcare in the United Kingdom, this project is justified by government in terms of a rhetoric of consumer choice, explicitly promoting the ideology of individualism which denies the existence of any real commonality of interests between either service users and providers, or between different consumers except insofar as they share the limited and short-term interests of buyers in a market place. In this context, individualism is clearly promoted as an ideological justification for the transformation of common resources into sites of accumulation, and individualisation is actively enforced. This is a very important point to note: in instances such as this one, which have been replicated the world over since the 1970s (Harvey 2005), the commodification of once-common goods involves the violent imposition of market relations, the enforcement of individualisation and the promotion of individualist ideology. None of these are organic or spontaneous developments.

Following these observations, we can argue that what is wrong with commodification is not commodification per se. Rather, there emerge two distinct problems with it, especially as it tends to occur today. Firstly, there is the exercise of power by capitalists and institutions which support their agendas to ensure that commodification takes place even where it is unwanted and to limit its benefits to themselves. Secondly, there is the tendency of market relations in general to promote an individualist mis-conception of social reality and the deliberate promotion of this ideology by institu-tions trying to enforce and normalise processes of commodification. So far, there seems to be no reason not conclude from this that the entire Marxist legacy is still valid: aren't we just saying that it is the 'class power' (Harvey 2005) of capital which has to be challenged by some radical alternative? This is fair enough. But the Marxist tradition goes much further than simply recommending that the excessive power of capital be challenged and curbed. Historically, this tradition tends to assert that such a challenge can only be made by virtue of a direct challenge to the existing relations of production, conceived of as the basis for a social totality, and, crucially, that it can only be made by the proletariat, politically mobilised as a 'Class for Itself' (Lukacs 1971). In concrete terms, this means that only the labour movement, being organised and mobilised on the basis of its class identity and demanding the socialisation of the means of production, can mount such a challenge.

Post-Marxism

This is where I, and the anti-capitalist movement, part company with classical Marx-ism, for a very simple reasons: there are simply any number of possible reasons for people working together to oppose the concentrated power of capital, and any number of political identities which might be mobilised or might be brought into existence, or deliberately deterritorialised, in the process of doing so. People *might* mobilise on the basis of their shared identity as workers, they might understand the excessive power of capital primarily in terms of its tendency to extract surplus value from their collec-tive labour, and they *might* therefore demand the socialisation of the means of produc-tion so as to ensure this outcome. But they might equally well mobilise as, say, public service-users and simply demand the protection of public services from privatisation. They might mobilise as democrats and demand the extension of democratic control over commercial institutions by means of legal supervision and regulation. They might mobilise as members of a national community and demand an end to foreign control of key assets, but without such control necessarily being handed over to anyone but more localised elites. They might mobilise as the poor and demand better access to key resources, again without necessarily following the classic socialist programme. Broadly speaking, the anti-capitalist movement is united by a common desire to assert some kind of democratic control over the deployment of material resources and to resist the imposition of market relations where they are not wanted, without appealing to nationalist or fundamentalist religious identities, but only one narrow section of the movement argues for this on the basis of a hypothetical class identity.

If there exists a coherent theoretical framework for such a break with Marxism, then it is to be found in the post-Marxism of Ernesto Laclau. Laclau argues persua-sively that the Marxist tradition has been mistaken in assuming that there is an inher-ent tendency in the social relations of capitalism for political identities to constitute themselves along class lines. Simplifying his argument considerably, we can say that while it is true that, insofar as they are economic actors in a marketplace, workers and capitalists will have certain tendential interests which are necessarily in conflict with each other—namely, their respective desires to raise or lower wages—there is no guarantee that this will lead to workers constituting a collective political identity as workers. The relationship between workers and capitalists is competitive, but it does not involve the very identity of one party being threatened in the way that, say, a putative national invasion in time of war might do. We might reflect here that the bitterest industrial dispute in British history was not a conflict over wages or working conditions, but over the threat of Thatcher government effectively to wind up the British coal industry, thereby threatening the social identities of whole communities who had defined themselves in terms of their place in it (Laclau 1990: 3–41)[2]. Of course, Laclau's insight, in practical terms, is not new: it was Lenin himself who famously concluded that without specific political leadership, the working classes would never develop a fully self-conscious political identity but would remain forever at the level of 'trade-union consciousness', simply organising opportunistically to maintain or raise their real wages rather than challenging their very place in the social order. We can interpret Laclau here as arguing that it is not, as Lenin and his followers believed, because the working classes fail to recognise their true historical destiny, but because Marxist theory is wrong to suppose that it is necessarily the historical destiny of workers qua workers to become revolutionary socialists.

This is not to say that anything in Laclau's theory or the ideas and practice of the anti-capitalist movement necessarily *precludes* traditional or new forms of labour organisation in the pursuit of socialism. It is rather to argue against the imposition of any particular model of who will engage in democratic struggle against corporate power and how they will do it. Once again, we come to the fact that the anti-capitalist movement is characterised by a certain pluralism, an unwillingness to impose any one model of social organisation, and a refusal of neoliberal hegemony not on the basis of a single class identity or even a single universal human identity, but precisely on the basis of a defence of such pluralism against neoliberalism's tyrannical monomania. In understanding this, it is important to reiterate that one of the most striking features of this movement is its refusal of a monolithic concept of socio-economic development and its consequent defence of the rights of indigenous and third-world peoples to relative self-determination. In this, the attitudes of the movement are very close to those informing another branch of recent thought with strong links to cultural studies and to the work of thinkers like Laclau. Post-colonial theory is a vast body of work taking in many differing political and philosophical perspectives, which we will not have time to address in detail in this book. However, it is very important to note the extent to which it shares some features with aspects of contemporary anti-capitalism. Post-colonial theory has its roots in the anti-colonial struggles of the 1950s (particularly against French imperialism) and has been characterised by some very original engagements between Marxism, psychoanalysis and various strands of continental philosophy from that point until the present. Much of this work may be regarded as post-Marxist in a sense rather similar to Laclau. While it does not deny the validity of the Marxists critique of capitalism or the usefulness of Lenin's understanding of imperialism (as a highly developed form of capitalism which exports capital, and hence exploitation, to non-Western countries and therefore reduces political tensions at home: see Lenin 1975 84–118), it is concerned with identifying the specific mechanisms and effects of colonialism and its aftermath on people in colonised countries, on the colonising culture, and on the relationships between the two, and in doing so from a point of view which does not automatically assume the superiority of Western culture and ideas to those from other parts of the world.

How far this marks an *elaboration* of a Marxist approach and how far it marks a *break* with it is a matter of intense debate within the field, and it is not one that we have space to dwell on here. What is important to note is that this perspective has introduced a powerful non-Western perspective into contemporary cultural studies, as key figures such as Stuart Hall and Paul Gilroy have been heavily involved with its development, whereas critics associated more with literary postcolonial studies have been heavily engaged with cultural studies on the one hand, with the intellectual sources of Laclau's post-Marxism on the other (Bhabha 1994). If a single thread runs through much of this work, it is a concern with the tendency of the West to marginalise, suppress or occlude cultural difference, assuming that that which does not fit the normative models of European culture is by that token inherently inferior, whether the case in point be notions of beauty, ideas of democracy, or the whole concept of social and scientific progress (Hall 1992). In some cases the work inspired by this observation is motivated to sustain the well-established critique of 'cultural imperialism' (Gopal & Lazarus 2006), while in other cases it involves more oblique attempts to problematise any notion of national or ethnic identity as fixed and stable (Bhabha 1994; Mercer 1994), but in all cases what is always at stake is a resistance to any *imposition* of identity. It is worth reflecting that in his later work, Theodor Adorno himself came to understand the suppression of difference and the imposition of identity on heterogeneous objects as the fundamental mode of oppression (Adorno 1973).

Within this whole spectrum of post-Marxist thought, then, we find a perspective which is very close to that of the anti-capitalist movement in its refusal of neoliberalism's impositions and its rejection of classical Marxist modes of engagement. To flesh out and illustrate some of these points, it might be worth finally considering some actual interventions from the movement in the light of the foregoing remarks. Firstly, let us actually return to Naomi Klein's *No Logo*. For all of the reasons offered above, this book presents an undoubtedly simplistic and largely unoriginal account of the contemporary forms of commodity fetishism. However, the book should not be judged as a work of cultural theory. Rather, it is an attempt at a particular kind of intervention, trying both to report upon and to amplify an existing set of movements against corporate hegemony with a particular focus on sweated third world labour and the cultural ubiquity of processes of branding. Now the type of campaigning work of which *No Logo* is an example and on which it reports can be seen as superficial in many ways. It has little to say about the systemic nature of capitalism or even about the extent to which neoliberalism is a sustained and coherent political programme which might require something more than isolated campaigns to challenge it. However, the book's sheer commercial success suggests that it spoke to a new public in ways which traditional leftist thought does not, and it is not hard to see why. For in attacking the ubiquity of branding and the specific issue of sweated labour, Klein succeeded in making a connection between elements of lived experience in the Northern hemisphere which are widely and intuitively experienced as distasteful—the invasion of public spaces of all kinds, and even of human bodies, by corporate branding, and the extension of marketing practices to all sites of social discourse (from the promotion of university courses to the campaigning of political parties)—and forms of labour exploitation so intense that one hardly need be a revolutionary Marxist to find them appalling. From the point of view of readers in the North, this helped to make branding and its practices a visible point of conflict between a broadly shared set of public values and the actual practice of neoliberal capitalism. The effects have been limited, but nonetheless striking, as a large market in unbranded, fairly traded and ethically produced clothing and other produce has opened up in the affluent world, bringing tangible benefits to many poor communities. Now this may not be the kind of revolutionary transformation which Marxist critics would prefer, but it is a more successful mobilisation than the socialist and communist movements have managed for some considerable time.

Let's consider another example, revisiting a story that I began to tell in the previous chapter. Reclaim the Streets, the group who organised a series of pioneering protests against car culture in the 1990s, was born out of a broad-based local campaign to save affordable housing stock and ancient woodland in a mainly working-class area of East London, and in the first few years of its existence it was associated with its trademark practice, the staging of noisy street parties—complete with truck-driven sound systems blaring out rave music—in locations designed to cause maximum disruption to traffic and attract maximum publicity. This deliberately playful policy won a large degree of public sympathy, especially amongst the young, although it antagonised the authorities from very early on. At this moment the British anti-roads movement comprised not only Reclaim the Streets but also a range of other protest groups around the country, all of whom used various types of non-violent direct action—from occupying tree-tops to digging tunnels underneath the trees—to disrupt road-building projects, drawing attention to the ecological issues and adding massively to the security costs incurred by such projects (Mckay 1998: 100–51). The social coalitions involved in the defence of some ancient countryside, such as Twyford Down and woodlands near Newbury, were very wide, including conservative middle-class conservationists as well as anarchists and Earth-Firsters. On a national level, a high level of public sympathy for the campaign and the extravagant costs being generated by it led government to shelve significant road-building plans and to reduce the overall road-building budget each year through most of the mid 1990s: a real victory for the movement (Wall 1999: 187–90; see also http://www.eco-ac tion.org/dod/no7/1–4.html for a snapshot of the movement's thinking at this time). All this changed in the month that Tony Blair was elected Prime Minister, ending eighteen years of Conservative Party rule. May 1997 saw the culmination of the Re- claim the Future project to build an alliance between the new direct-action politics and radical trade unionists supporting Liverpool dock workers who had been fired for trade-union activism. The result was an enormous (by the standards of the time) demonstration to Trafalgar Square on 1 May 1997, involving for the first time both significant numbers of activists associated with projects like Reclaim the Streets and masses of trade unionists from around the country. In many ways this was Reclaim the Streets's finest moment: the group that pioneered the street party as a form of non-violent political protest managed to get a sound system into the road outside the National Gallery, filling its famous steps with dancers. The combined event became a mixture of free rave and traditional rally—trade unionists and Trotskyists listened to speakers from the conventional left, while many of the young ravers joined them as others danced in the sunshine. The potential for an alliance between the new poli- tics and the old felt palpable.

Or at least, it did for the first couple of hours. But once the rally had ended, and the many ravers and eco-protesters who had listened patiently to a tediously predict- able set of speeches in support of the dockers went to join the dancing throng, some- thing both disappointing and profoundly symbolic happened. The trade unionists, with a few bewildered and occasionally disgusted backward glances at the frivolity on the National Gallery steps, started to leave. Within an hour or so most of them had gone home. The momentary alliance had lasted for as long as the kids and 'crusties' were prepared to participate on their terms, but the idea that any significant number of the leftists might join this particular kind of party was simply not on the agenda. Those left behind felt suddenly isolated, and they were. Immediately the trade union contingents had vacated the square, it was sealed off by police who began a hos- tile set of manoeuvres intended exclusively to antagonise, intimidate and provoke the remaining protesters. The result: for the first time, Reclaim the Streets saw its name connected with a violent affray between protesters and police, rather than with the creative non-violence which had been its trademark up to that point. It's worth remembering this moment, because just there and then, it was the traditional left who were not interested in working creatively with this new political-expressive force. If they had to dance, it wasn't their revolution.

It was immediately after this that Reclaim the Streets and the wider, diffuse pro- test movement to which it had become unwittingly central shifted attention from the local, popular and winnable goal of forcing a change in the direction of UK trans- port policy, to, as we have seen, the much more abstract objective of confronting capitalism itself. Although this move did enable some of the activists of the 1990s protest movement to forge real and important connections with the wider emergent anti-capitalist movement, at just the time that the Seattle events and the success of *No Logo* were turning it into an international *cause celebre,* the British sections of that movement have subsequently made very little contribution to its progress on a global or European level. By 2005, it was left almost entirely to the NGOs to organise the major protests against the G8 summit in Gleneagles, Scotland, and the 2004 European Social Forum in London was dominated by the moribund politics of a Leninist sect, the Socialist Workers Party.

Precisely what the movement lacked at that crucial moment in 1997 was any sense of the texture, the limitations and the potential of what Gramsci famously calls the 'national-popular': the site at which, within the socio-cultural context of the nation state, on the terrain of its everyday life, hearts and minds are won and lost. What most of the labour movement lacked was the strategic imagination to reach out to this new phenomenon, mesmerised as it was by the prospect of a Labour government. So substituting a language which had no resonance with the lives of most British people (the rhetoric of anti-globalisation) for one which had united sentiments from Glasgow to Middle England (the utopian environmentalism of the anti-car movement), Reclaim the Streets lost what little ground they had won in their war of position, and they were forced back into an isolated trench, the political ghetto of hardcore anti-capitalist anarchism. The trade unions soon learned what New Labour government would mean: a few minor reforms which would still leave British workers with the poorest working conditions in Western Europe, and a wholesale intensification of the Thatcherite programme of public-service privatisation. What's interesting to observe from our point of view is that key figures in the history of cultural studies have always seen its role precisely in terms of its attempt to generate just that sense of the political possibilities of culture which was lacking on both sides of this tragic equation. Radical movements are too often willing to ignore the pragmatic limitations set by the cultural contexts in which they operate. The mainstream left is almost always too slow to realise the radical potential in emergent cultural tendencies. At its best, cultural studies has tried to address both these problems and to understand the connections between them. There is no reason why it should not carry on trying to do so.

Beyond Anti-Capitalism?

So am I arguing that Reclaim the Streets was only interesting when it was deliberately limited and constricted in its aims, pulling back from direct confrontation with capital? Not exactly. From my perspective, the explicitly utopian dimension of the Reclaim the Streets project was absolutely integral to its success. Without its creative re-imagining of urban space (which included laying turf in the road outside the houses of parliament in 2000: see http://www.primalseeds.org/mayslides.htm), it would never have inspired so many people, giving rise to hundreds of local Reclaim the Streets groups in cities around the world, as it did. Reclaim the Streets's Situationist-inspired challenge to the whole culture of alienation, individualism and environmental destruction was brilliantly encapsulated in its opposition to the car and provided a concrete glimpse of what a challenge to that culture might look like in practice and why it might actually generate something *more pleasurable* than what it challenged. This was an intervention that was effective aesthetically and pragmatically, rather than just ideologically, but it was effective because it successfully made connections between a whole set of issues and constituencies which might otherwise have remained separated. But this is a point on which a classical Marxist would probably concur.

What would be different would be the ways in which we might conceptualise the situation. From the point of view of the revolutionary Marxist, an anti-car campaign is only really valuable to the extent that the car is a profound symbol of capitalism, and an attack on cars must lead implicitly to an attack on capitalism as such. From the point of view which I am trying to develop here, the attack on cars is effective precisely because it *could* lead to an attack on capitalism as such, but it doesn't *have to* in order to be effective. If it doesn't, then reducing car use, or raising questions about the consequences of individualisation and individualism, or promoting public transport and a general defence of public space, are all goods in and of themselves that might lead to positive social change even if they do not lead to the revolutionary overthrow of capitalism as such.

What are the implications of these reflections? One might be that anti-capitalism is just not a very good name for the movement which bears that name. If its most vibrant and politically successful manifestations are projects which do not explicitly oppose themselves to capitalism as such in toto, then should it be called something else? Perhaps, although I would argue that actually anti-capitalism is a good name for a movement bound together by no single positive project but by common resistance to neoliberalism.

Are there better names available? Anti-neoliberalism might be more accurate but that may be just too ugly a phrase to use. Perhaps the French term *altermondialisation* sums up best the position of looking for some alternative to the neoliberal model of globalisation. *Alterglobalism* is an Anglicised version which is popular in some circles, and which I personally like, but which does not yet have very wide currency. Perhaps the most popular name for the movement in English at the time of writing is the global justice movement, and it's a useful label in some contexts, because it sounds unthreatening and uncontroversial. In deference to its current popularity, I have used it on occasion throughout this work. However, to my mind this is actually an appalling label, implying a detached appeal to some imagined standard of morality, rather than a defiant challenge to neoliberal power. That name has become popular as issues of trade justice and third world debt have come to the fore (as they did during the build-up to the 2005 G8 summit), but it is unlikely to have much resonance in wider contexts. International solidarity against neoliberalism is only likely to be possible when citizens of the prosperous West recognise the extent to which their own interests are threatened by the neoliberal agenda, rather than simply being outraged at the injustices perpetrated on the South. From a rigourous analytical perspective, anti-capitalism must remain a key element of the critique of both global poverty and the international drive to privatise public services, because it remains crucial to bear in mind that neoliberalism and the neoliberal project for globalisation are not historical accidents, nor are they entirely contingent and self-constituting assemblages of strategies, techniques, institutions and practices (as suggested in Barry, Osborne & Rose 1996: 12–16). They are deliberate projects, and they are designed primarily to consolidate and extend the power of those social groups and institutions which have a vested interest in the maximisation of profit and the relative suppression of wage levels. In other words, neoliberalism is a capitalist project, and to deny this or seek to obfuscate it is to go further than is reasonable in breaking with a classical Marxist analysis. The post-Marxist anti-capitalist position may differ from classical Marxism in its understanding of what we can *do* about capitalism and who the *we* might be that can do anything, but it retains the insight that capital is the primary source of the reigning political projects of our age, and that any denial or occlusion of this fact suppresses the possibility of meaningful politics in the twenty-first century.

Lawrence Grossberg, the leading figure in US cultural studies, has recently written

> I do not believe that many people will be persuaded to join a movement defined by its opposition to capitalism. Those same people, however, may be convinced—intellectually and affectively—to join a struggle to transform society according to a vision that would make it a more liveable environment for the majority of people. The centre can be won by a vision that seeks a new 'planetary humanism', that refuses to give up either the project of universality or the recognition of singularity, that offers new forms of affiliation, and new structures of commonality. But the centre can be moved only by engaging it, by entering into a conversation with it. We need a conversation that moves between imagination and strategy. (Grossberg 2005: 320)

Grossberg may well be right. As should be clear from the preceding argument, I share his scepticism that anything as totalising or abstract as opposition to capitalism understood as a total social system can be an effective basis for a popular movement, except under very exceptional circumstances. At the same time, however, I have tried to argue that a certain attitude of anti-capitalism is indispensable for any current perspective which recognises what it is that stands in the way of 'a more liveable environment for the majority of people'. What Grossberg draws our attention to—and this is a point to which we will return in Chapter 6—is the fact that any movement which organises itself on the explicit basis of its anti-capitalism is unlikely to achieve much in the West today, precisely because capitalism is too abstract a process for many people to define themselves in opposition to it.

I think that the story of Reclaim the Streets clearly shows that Grossberg is correct, and that even while a certain self-conscious anti-capitalism is a necessary element binding the international movement against neoliberalism, anti-capitalism is not much use as an explicit label to be deployed in campaigning contexts such as the United Kingdom and the United States. Another way of putting this, in a post-Deleuzian register, might be to posit anti-capitalism as the 'fractal attractor' which pulls the diverse elements of the 'movement of movements' into a virtual 'plane of consistency' (Massumi 1992: 67), uniting them at the level of a certain shared immanent potential. The successful actualisation of that potential in particular contexts will require many different and unpredictable acts of naming and of carefully calculated intervention, which only detailed analysis of specific conjunctures can make possible. We can see then, that Grossberg is here raising a much bigger set of questions than those implied by a semantic quibble. In particular he is raising the question of what might be involved—for those of us who share an anti-capitalist analysis—in actually bringing together those many people who aspire to create a more livable environment, but who will not necessarily identify themselves with any self-titled anti-capitalist movement. How do we actualise the shared anti-capitalist potential of those who will never call themselves anti-capitalists? This is a question which cannot be ignored, because it is arguably the constitutive question of all politics: the question of *strategy* (which is also to say, the question of *actualisation*). We will return to it in some detail in the chapters that follow.

Notes

1. The concept of the antimarket is clearly related to Deleuze and Guattari's concept of 'antiproduction': see Deleuze and Guattari (1983).
2. We could actually relate Laclau's position here to Deleuze and Guattari's claim in *Anti-Oedipus* that capital derives surplus value not from the direct exploitation of labour power but only from the differential between variable and fixed capital. In both cases, the claim that exploitation can be located in a simple way at the point of production is problematised.

–5–

Ideas in Action: Rhizomatics[1], Radical Democracy and the Power of the Multitude

Do not forget that ideas are also weapons.

Subcomandante Marcos (Hayden 2001: 315)

There is nothing more practical than a good theory.

James Clerk Maxwell (attributed)

As we can see from previous chapters, the ideas that inform both cultural studies and the anti-capitalist movement come from a wide range of sources and take a variety of forms. This chapter is concerned with one particular point of interface between these sets of ideas: in particular, with those areas of recent political thought which constitute points of overlap between the concepts of the movement and key trends within cultural studies and cultural theory. In recent decades, similar circumstances, histories, goals and concerns have influenced the anti-capitalist movement, anglophone cultural theory, and several strands of political philosophy. In fact, as should be clear from the history related in Chapters 1 and 2, the main components of cultural theory have *always* been formulated in relation to wider political changes and projects, to the extent that one might even say that the distinction between cultural theory and radical political theory is often impossible to draw. This suggests an important axiom for both cultural studies and radical politics: those conceptual resources which are most useful for analysing power relationships in culture should also be of potential use in orienting political action, and *vice versa*. Every one of the writers whose ideas we will consider in this chapter has formulated their ideas with direct reference, or in direct response to, particular political problems, events and projects, and in the process has produced conceptual tools which are of great value for the analysis of power relationships in culture. In particular we will consider here the work of three pairs of writers who have written their most celebrated works as teams: Deleuze and Guattari; Hardt and Negri; Laclau and Mouffe. However, before addressing their ideas in detail, I want to consider a number of key concepts which are central to any attempt to think through the relationship between culture and politics. These are power, complexity, hegemony and creativity.

Power

As Mark Gibson shows (2007), *power* is really the central concept of cultural studies—which assumes that power infuses all social relations—and probably the most influential account of power within the field is that developed in the later work of Michel Foucault[2]. For Foucault, particularly in Volume One of *The History of Sexuality,* power must be thought of differently from the ways in which Western political thought has usually conceived it. In his account, power is not something that happens *to* social relations, distorting and transforming them, but is something which only exists *through* social relations, and which is therefore immanent to them. On this model, power does not only negate or suppress; it also produces, acting upon the world inventively. Power relations are always a complex configuration of differentials in which there is no one party who simply has power.

> –Power is not something that is acquired, seised or shared, something that one holds onto or allows to slip away; power is exercised from innumerable points, in the interplay of non egalitarian and mobile relations.
> –Relations of power are not in a position of exteriority with respect to other types of relationships (economic processes, knowledge relationships, sexual relations), but are immanent in the latter; they are the immediate effects of the divisions, inequalities and disequilibriums which occur in the latter, and conversely are the internal conditions of these differentiations; relations of power are not in superstructural positions, with merely a role of prohibition or accompaniment; they have a directly productive role, wherever they come into play.
> –Power comes from below; that is, there is no binary and all-encompassing opposition between rulers and ruled at the root of power relations, and serving as a general matrix—no such duality extending from the top down and reacting on more and more limited groups to the very depths of the social body. One must suppose rather that the manifold relationships of force that take shape and come into play in the machinery of production, in families, limited groups and institutions, are the basis for wide-ranging effects of cleavage that run through the social body as a whole. These then form a general line of force that traverses the local oppositions and links them together; to be sure, they also bring about redistributions, realignments, homogenisations, serial arrangements, and convergences of the force relations. Major dominations are the hegemonic effects that are sustained by all these confrontations.

(Foucault 1979: 94)

Foucault goes some way towards answering the question of what power actually *is* in his mobilisation of the term *power-knowledge*. What this term is used to imply is that there is simply no effective distinction to be drawn between power and the capacity to define a situation. *Power* and *knowledge* are merely two sides of the same coin. It is not the case that having power (military, economic or political) confers the ability to exercise cultural authority on certain groups and individuals who have it, or that *acquiring* specific kinds of knowledge *confers* particular kinds of power; it is rather that *what power is* is precisely the capacity to set the terms of reference in any given situation, defining what is to be accepted, implicitly or explicitly, as truth and normality. The capacity of the medical profession to designate certain conditions (homosexuality, for instance) as normal or pathological is one example. Another might be the capacity to designate a range of unruly behaviours in children as 'attention deficit disorder', rather than 'naughtiness' or 'high spirits' (Grossberg 2005: 32–6).

The importance of such a conception of power to cultural studies can hardly be overstated, and it is widely accepted that almost all cultural studies accedes to and shares Foucault's account. Foucault's studies of different forms of modern power— some of which are only recently coming to light (e.g. Foucault 2004)—continue to be a major source of inspiration. Foucault's approach is also an analytical tool of great use to any present or future anti-capitalist politics, because as we saw in different ways in the previous two chapters, anti-capitalist theory and practice has a tendency to oversimplify its understanding of the cultural logics of power to the point where its capacity to offer effective resistance is severely limited.

At the theoretical level, this oversimplifying tendency is most clearly illustrated by John Holloway's influential book *Change the World Without Taking Power* (2002). While in many ways this work is to be welcomed for its creative development of a twenty-first-century Marxism, it's deliberate simplification of the political universe into blocs of 'power' and 'anti-power' is an explicit example of this tendency. We can see the problem with it at exactly the moment when Holloway tries to discuss the ideas of Michel Foucault. Holloway argues that

> [Foucault's perspective] allows him to elucidate the enormous richness and complexity of power relations in contemporary society and, more important from our perspective, the richness and complexity of resistance to power. However, the richness and complexity are the richness and complexity of a photograph, or of a painting ... Thus in Foucault's analysis there are a whole host of resistances which are integral to power, but there is no possibility of emancipation. The only possibility is of an endlessly shifting constellation of power-and-resistance. (Holloway 2002: 39–40)

Holloway's argument only works by virtue of a dichotomy, which Foucault refuses, between endless amorphous adjustments to power relationships and absolute emancipation. In fact Foucault writes: 'Are there no great radical ruptures, massive binary divisions, then? Occasionally, yes. But more often one is dealing with mobile and transitory points of resistance' (Foucault 1979: 96).

Clearly, Holloway's understanding simply cannot accommodate the actuality of Foucault's position: of course there are real revolutionary ruptures in politics *sometimes,* but these are not the normative paradigm by which we should understand political antagonisms. Politics happens, change happens and revolutions happen: they are just far more complex phenomena than Holloway wants to imagine. This brings us to the second key term, *complexity.*

Complexity

One reason that Foucault's account proved so attractive within cultural studies almost from the moment of its publication is that it emphasises, as cultural studies always has done, the sheer *complexity* of power relationships. The unwillingness to oversimplify, to assume that power relationships operate across simple binary divides or that social change is the outcome of Manichean conflicts, has always been one of the hallmarks of cultural studies. We can see from this and from examples in earlier chapters that an attentiveness to complexity is an important dimension of any effective political analysis. We will keep this in mind over the course of this chapter. But how do we bring this together with our first key concept, *power*? How is power exercised in complex situations? In fact, this is precisely the question engaged by the thematics of *hegemony*.

Hegemony

Considering the issues of power and complexity brings to mind this third key theme: *hegemony*. There are different ways to conceptualise hegemony, which we will discuss in more detail below, but what the various conceptions developed within cultural studies and post-Gramscian political theory have in common is that they see hegemony as a condition in which complex and unpredictable sets of power relationships are temporarily stabilised, while something like power-knowledge is effectively deployed by a hegemonic group, institution, individual or idea. The question of hegemony is always the question of strategy. As Foucault writes

> Just as the network of power relations ends by forming a dense web that passes through apparatuses and institutions, without being exactly localised in them, so too the swarm of points of resistance traverses social stratifications and individual unities. And it is doubtless the strategic codification of these points of resistance that makes a revolution possible, somewhat similar to the way in which the state relies on the institutional integration of power relationships. (Foucault 1979: 96)

This is, in fact, almost a precise summary of the neo-Gramscian concept of hegemony proposed by Laclau and Mouffe, as we shall see. But now for our fourth and final key concept, *creativity*.

Creativity

Creativity is another key issue for any attempt to theorise politics and culture. The issue of creativity—what it is, what are its conditions of possibility, to what extent it is a social or an individual phenomenon—was central to the very first work in cultural studies: implicitly in Hoggart's *The Uses of Literacy* (1957) and Williams's *Culture and Society* (1958), and very explicitly in Williams's *The Long Revolution* (1961). One might follow Gibson's argument (2007) by suggesting that the issue of power has since come to occlude this equally fundamental one in some cases, but one might equally argue that Foucault's emphasis on power's productivity is itself a complex way of thinking creativity: certainly Nietzsche, one of Foucault's great inspirations, at times promoted the idea of creativity as the ultimate expression of will-to-power (Nietzsche 1968: 272). The anti-capitalist position developed in the previous chapter is predicated in part on a distinction between the creativity of innovative groups and capital's attempt to limit, codify, contain and commodify that creativity. The possibility of radical democratic alternatives to neoliberalism is clearly, in part, dependent upon the possibility of new modes of collective self-invention being made possible by various social groups and communities. In fact, one might go so far as to say that if the entire project of cultural studies has just one key message it is this: contrary to the assumptions of bourgeois ideology, all creativity is inherently *social* in character. This question of creativity will be another key issue to consider, then.

Bearing these themes in mind—power, complexity, hegemony, creativity—let's begin our survey of three pairs of radical theorists: Deleuze and Guattari; Hardt and Negri; Laclau and Mouffe. Any attempt to summarise the views and ideas of such complicated thinkers as these is bound to fail to some extent, so perhaps all that we can hope for here is to get a sense of the contexts in which they have emerged and into which they have intervened, and the overall nature of their projects. In fact, we can situate the emergence of each of these bodies of work at one of the crucial junctures outlined in Chapters 1 and 2. Gilles Deleuze and Félix Guattari's first major collaboration, the monumental *Anti-Oedipus* (1983), is widely regarded as being one of the major intellectual products of the 1968 moment in Paris. Ernesto Laclau and Chantal Mouffe's *Hegemony and Socialist Strategy* appeared in the United Kingdom in 1985, the year after the defeat of the miners' strike had marked the effective end of the socialist labour movement in Britain. Although this book was partly inspired by the crisis of traditional left politics at that time, it also implicitly took 1968 as one of its key imaginative points of reference. Michael Hardt and Antonio Negri's major recent works *Empire* (2000) and *Multitude* (2004) are widely seen as the first great intellectual interventions to be inspired by the experience and historical novelty of the international anti-capitalist movement and the global neoliberal hegemony to which it is a response, writing in the wake of the 1999 Seattle protests, but both books are also explicitly in the tradition of 1968.

It would be a mistake to see any of these works merely as products of or responses to the historical events in question: each of them is also the outcome of rigourous attempts to work through a pressing set of political and conceptual problems within and beyond the terms of a particular philosophical tradition. At the same time, the relevance of each of these works is absolutely contemporary. The importance of Deleuze and Guattari for a growing number of commentators and practitioners within both the anti-capitalist movement and cultural studies, and their closeness to the concerns and traditions of key parts of the movement, means that it is very important to engage with their ideas. Hardt and Negri, who see themselves as followers of Deleuze, are simply as close as anyone apart from Subcomandante Marcos to being the official philosophers of the movement, but the status of their ideas as cultural theory, interestingly, has really not been explored. Of the three pairs, it is actually Laclau and Mouffe who are the least widely read and least understood within the anti-capitalist movement and cultural studies, although their work has considerable relevance, as we will see. In this chapter, we will try to engage with a range of ideas from these authors, with a concentration on those ideas that illuminate the themes of creativity, hegemony, complexity, power and with an eye to how these ideas might be useful for generating political analyses of contemporary culture, in broad sympathy with anti-capitalist aims. The discussion here should not by any means be regarded as an adequate summary of the totality of these writers' works, excellent introductions to all of which are in print, and of course, there is never any substitute for reading philosophical texts for oneself.

Deleuze and Guattari

When Gilles Deleuze and Félix Guattari published their first collaboration, *Anti-Oedipus,* in 1972, each was already a well established figure in his own field. Deleuze was a philosopher who had produced a number of influential commentaries on key thinkers such as Nietzsche, Bergson and Spinoza, along with his major works *Difference and Repetition* (1994) and *The Logic of Sense* (1990). Guattari had been active as a political militant, personally involved in the events of May 1968 and the wave of student militancy that had preceded it, and was working as an experimental psychotherapist at the celebrated Le Borde clinic.

Anti-Oedipus is a sustained engagement with themes that emerged from both of these sets of preoccupations, and it is one of a wave of important works published by key French thinkers in the wake of 1968. This moment in French radical thought is perhaps characterised by two sets of concerns. On the one hand, there was a widespread questioning of the ways in which a previous generation of thinkers had deployed Marxism and psychoanalysis within a broadly structuralist intellectual framework to produce rather totalising and rigid accounts of human culture. Marx and Freud had enjoyed immense prestige amongst French intellectuals in the post-war period, but by the end of the 1960s both Marxism and psychoanalysis had come to feel to some like stifling orthodoxies rather than philosophies of liberation. The structuralist emphasis on understanding deep, static patterns to human culture seemed to offer no scope for understanding what made social or personal change possible, even in the work of supposed revolutionaries such as communist loyalist Louis Althusser (1971). On the other hand, there was a reaction against the perceived authoritarianism of psychoanalytic institutions, academic institutions and the political institutions of both the state and the organised left. The antipathy of the Communist Party for the student movement and the libertarian counter-culture of the late 1960s—and the contempt of psychoanalysts for both, as well as for the nascent feminist and gay liberation movements—provoked understandable hostility on the part of militants and radicals.

This was also the high water-mark of the international anti-psychiatry movement, most famously represented in the anglophone world by the Scottish therapist and philosopher, R. D. Laing. The anti-psychiatrists argued, rather as Michel Foucault implied in his *History of Madness* (2005), that psychiatric treatment caused mental illness more than it cured it, by defining a range of emotional states and behaviour as pathological which had no need to be so defined, and by refusing to recognise the social causes of those illnesses which did clearly cause great distress to those suffering from them. Practices such as institutionalisation, pharmacological treatments and conventional Freudian analysis (especially the so-called ego psychology championed by Sigmund Freud's daughter Anna in the United States) were all seen as attempts to force individuals to behave and even think in particular ways, and to punish and constrain those who would not do so. For these thinkers, there was no great difference between psychiatric practice in the West and in the Soviet Union, where political dissidents were routinely institutionalised for their 'insane' opposition to official doctrine. Influenced by the revolutionary tradition and its contemporary representatives such as Herbert Marcuse, they argued that the inability of the so-called mad to adapt to contemporary social norms was not something to be discouraged when the norms were those of a violent, militaristic and fundamentally exploitative society. This was taking place at a time when the ideologues of the counter-culture were declaring all forms of sexual repression to be not, as Freud had argued, the necessary price to be paid for a civilised life, but the most pathological and destructive features of modern societies, as the surrealist idea that to release the unconscious might be a politically revolutionary gesture resurfaced with great vigour.

In this context, many former communists were to produce works arguing for some more fundamentally libertarian politics than that envisaged by the previous generation of Freudo-Marxists. Figures such as Roland Barthes and Jean-François Lyotard (who were both to prove influential within anglophone cultural theory) rejected much of their more orthodox leftist past (Barthes 1990; Lyotard 2004). The ideas of Friedrich Nietzsche, previously suspect because of the Nazis' unfortunate and misinformed appropriation of them, were mobilised as the basis for an *anti-fascist* philosophy (Foucault 1983). Arising from such a general atmosphere of revolt, but also from a very serious philosophical collaboration, *Anti-Oedipus* (Deleuze & Guattari 1983) was the most lastingly influential product of this ferment. It presents itself on first reading as a critique of psychoanalysis and its apparent complicity with bourgeois culture, but it is far more than this. Indeed, the book is arguably not a *critique* of psychoanalysis as such at all, but an attempt to push the radical implications of Freud's findings further than he or most of his followers had ever been willing to go. To put it very crudely: Freud had shown that the modern Western assumption that we are all rational, self-controlled individuals is false, but psychoanalysis had merely provided tools to enable individuals to get that bit closer to being rational, self-controlled individuals. But what if this was the wrong approach? What if the problem was not the inability of some individuals to fit that mould, but the mould itself? What if there was something wrong with the whole culture that tried to force all of the marvellous, multifarious possibilities of material experience into boxes like 'I', 'you', 'man', 'woman', 'humanity', 'nature', 'animals', etc.? Several whole histories of radical thought, from socialists, anarchists, feminists, philosophers, mystics, hippies, bohemians, artists, Buddhists, Taoists, thinkers such as Marx or Nietzsche or even ancients such as Lucretius and Democritus, all seemed to imply that there was something wrong with this kind of categorization of self. What if we needed a whole way of thinking about the world that could allow us to step outside of these categories and act in a very different way?

Anti-Oedipus is actually the first half of a larger work titled *Capitalism and Schizophrenia,* which attempts nothing less than such a new way of thinking. The title of this work is important to understand, as is the name which Deleuze and Guattari give to their overall project: 'schizoanalysis'. There is nowhere any clear indication of how schizoanalysis might manifest itself as concrete therapeutic practice, even though we know that it was in fact closely related to Guattari's therapeutic work at Le Borde. Rather, it is presented as a position from which to understand the world rather as psychoanalysis can provide the basis for cultural, social and even political theory, a position which takes seriously the 'schizzes': the fragmentary elements of code and experience which are contingently assembled into subjects (Deleuze & Guattari 1983: 39). In part the term *schizoanalysis* marks an affinity with the radical psychoanalytic aspiration to find a non-medical treatment for the psychoses (Lacan 1977: 179–225), but it also indicates Deleuze and Guattari's identification of schizophrenia as a concrete manifestation of some important dimensions of human experience. Put very simply, Deleuze and Guattari see schizophrenia as a condition of radical, uncontrolled creativity which is defined as pathological by a culture which can only sustain itself by limiting and containing creativity at every level of experience. Crucial here is Deleuze and Guattari's novel conception of *desire.* For Deleuze and Guattari, desire or 'desiring-production' is understood as a positive, productive, creative, inventive engagement with the world. This is very different from the psychoanalytic conception of desire as *lack:* where for psychoanalysis, all desire is symptomatic of our endless search for something we can never have (the perfect contentment which was lost to us the moment we had to leave our mother's breast and go out into the cold, cruel world alone), Deleuze and Guattari conceptualise desire as the force which makes everything happen in the world.

For Deleuze and Guattari, psychoanalysis belongs to a philosophical tradition which has always been obsessed with the idea that what is real is what is unchanging, static and self-enclosed and which can only conceptualise anything which is not in negative terms. The psychoanalytic account of the human condition is essentially tragic: human beings are doomed to a life of relative dissatisfaction, ultimately governed by desires which can never be satisfied partly because of social constraints on their full satisfaction, partly because it is in their very nature to remain always unsatisfied. Instead, Deleuze and Guattari conceptualise the apparently incomplete, unstable aspects of subjectivity as the *positive* conditions of the connections and productive relations which can exist between people and each other, and between people and other aspects of the material world. I am offering my own interpretation here, but we might understand Deleuze and Guattari's conception of desire as follows: if we never left our mothers' breasts, we would never know all of the many and wonderful forms of love and other experience which we can know, we would never make any of the marvellous and beautiful things which people can make, and merely to see these as compensations for some deeper loss is both misguided and deeply oppressive. But Deleuze and Guattari do not think that psychoanalysis is simply mistaken. They think that 'Oedipal' culture *really does* turn us into subjects who experience ourselves in this way, who can never experience full joy because we only experience it as something always-already lost; we really do endlessly punish ourselves and our lovers for not giving us what we think we need; men really do live in fear of losing their phallic authority and women really do fear and resent men for possessing it. This situation, according to Deleuze and Guattari, is the outcome of a very long history of thought and practice in the West which can only be understood by analysing the social, economic, material, bio-physical and psychic patterns of life throughout the history of civilisation. We live in a culture whose psychic structures psychoanalysis understands very well. But for Deleuze and Guattari, understanding them is not enough: we have to understand where they have come from, and we have to change them or evade them if we can.

What emerges from the attempt is a whole new philosophical vocabulary which strives to avoid the problems which beset the Western tradition, and new ways to think about creativity, complexity, hegemony and power. Where other philosophers of their generation (Derrida, Irigaray, Foucault) pointed out the problems with the whole way in which Western culture conceptualises some of the most basic features of experience, it was Deleuze and Guattari who went furthest in developing a new set of alternative concepts, often drawing on the vocabularies of the physical and mathematical sciences. So, for example, *Anti-Oedipus* opens with an elaboration of the concept of 'desiring-machine'. This concept often confuses readers precisely because it is so abstract and so loose. Almost anything can be a desiring-machine—a person, a computer, an unconscious drive, a piece of genetic code, a hand holding a bat or weapon or tool or brush, a bird, a crowd, a demonstration, a novel, a dream, an idea, a factory, a piece of skin, a lung—because a desiring-machine is any conjunction of elements which somehow intervenes in the world (later, Deleuze and Guattari were to prefer the even more general term *agencement,* normally translated as 'assemblage', to mean much the same thing). The value of this formulation is that it makes it possible to think about a whole range of issues without recourse to some of the basic assumed categories of Western thought. For example, there are many reasons why thinkers from various traditions have been troubled by the Western emphasis on the single, conscious human subject as the basic unit of experience and agency: apart from anything else, some have argued that it is this idea which leads to the idea of man as fundamentally separate from nature, which man can then seek to dominate and exploit at will, with eventually disastrous consequences. One of the implications of Deleuze and Guattari's conceptual vocabulary is that it enables us to think about the relationships between humans and other parts of the material world in quite different terms, as a complex network of conjunctions and disjunctions between various material elements and mechanisms.

It would take an entire book to detail even a few of the novel concepts proposed in Deleuze and Guattari's work (e.g. Massumi 1992). What we need to concentrate on here is the general political character of their ideas, although this in itself is not a topic on which commentators agree with any consistency. Broadly speaking, we can say that Deleuze and Guattari's work is very much in the spirit of 1968 and indeed of the New Lefts, in that it tries to develop a position which is at once collectivist and libertarian in is implications. It is radically opposed to hierarchy and to all concentrations of power. It is suspicious of fixity of any kind. It valorises the nomadic rather than the sedentary, the mobile rather than the static, the productive rather than the destructive, invention rather than analysis.

This valorisation is never unqualified, however. For example, in *A Thousand Plateaus,* the second volume of *Capitalism and Schizophrenia,* Deleuze and Guattari draw their famous distinction between the rhizome and the tree. Rhizomes are plant stems which grow underground, with roots and shoots growing from their nodes to constitute a spreading horizontal network which often extends over a large area. Deleuze and Guattari compare rhizomes to trees, which are vertical in shape, with roots clearly defined at the bottom, a single trunk and branches and leaves at the top. They see this contrast as a way of distinguishing between different forms of organisation and even different modes of thinking. Tree-like or 'arborescent' systems are characterised by a tendency to hierarchy, order, and stability. 'Rhizomatic' systems are characterised by horizontality, by multiple, complex connections between different nodes and points. These distinctions can be applied to actual systems of social organisation, from highly ordered and authoritarian societies and institutions (such as, say, the Catholic Church) to more democratic or anarchic sets of social relations (such as those which obtain between internet users engaged in peer-to-peer file sharing). They can also be applied to systems of thought. So, a strong tendency in Western thought since Plato understands and judges things in the world in terms of how far they match up to a supposed ideal, and tends to consider material reality as a corrupt, incomplete or degraded version of the transcendental ideal. This is an issue with which Deleuze was preoccupied in some of his earlier philosophical writing, in which he also identified an alternative tradition which tries to see the material world as it is without imposing pre-conceived categories on it. We can see the distinction here as analogous to the distinction between the arborescent and the rhizomatic, with arborescent thought looking at the world from the transcendental position, taking a God's eye view of things, and rhizomatic thought looking at the world from the ground up. Subsequent commentators have linked this approach to the microsociology of Gabriel Tarde, to the development of social history in the twentieth century and to all kind of approaches which see social institutions, political events and even natural phenomena as the outcomes of smaller 'molecular' processes (Alliez 2001; Delanda 2006). This focus on the molecular is one of Deleuze and Guattari's most characteristic features (Guattari 1984).

Where commentators do not agree is on the question of how far Deleuze and Guattari see this as merely correcting the bias in the Western transcendentalist tradition, and how far they really value the rhizomatic over the arborescent. This ambiguity arises when we consider almost all of the conceptual oppositions which Deleuze and Guattari mobilize in their work. One of the best-known terms from *Capitalism and Schizophrenia* is 'deterritorialisation'. This terms designates in very general terms a process whereby something fixed and stable ceases to be so, as its boundaries are erased and its component parts are rendered mobile. Deterritorialisation could refer to the effects of erosion on soil and rock or to what happens to traditional rural farming communities when the enclosure and privatisation of land forces them to migrate in search of work, but Deleuze and Guattari *mainly* use it to refer to processes whereby some oppressive or ossified mode of thought or practice is destabilised, creating new and exciting possibilities (Deleuze & Guattari 1983: 311–22). The opposite of deterritorialisation is territorialisation or reterritorialisation, whereby a given set of elements or a given space is re-ordered, bounded and partially stabilised. A third key distinction for Deleuze and Guattari is between 'striated' space which is differentiated, hierarchical and difficult to traverse (like a great city), and 'smooth' space which is continuous, enabling mobility and flow (like the sea or the nomad steppes; Deleuze & Guattari 1988: 474–500).

On a first reading it is certainly easy to read Deleuze and Guattari as basically advocating an anarchistic politics, aesthetics and epistemology which is inherently suspicious of any stable, ordered system whatsoever and which sets up these oppositions merely in order to celebrate the rhizome, the smooth space and all forms of deterritorialisation, and this is how they are often read. This is a problematic reading for several reasons, however. Firstly, Deleuze and Guattari themselves frequently qualify their polemics to insist that it is never enough to be simply for rhizomes, smooth spaces or deterritorialisation. Instead, they imply or make explicit at various points that these conceptual distinctions are merely useful analytical abstractions: there are no pure rhizomes or smooth spaces, and, as they state themselves, every relative deterritorialisation also involves some kind of reterritorialisation (Deleuze & Guattari 1983: 316)[3]. They even warn against the dangers of excessive or too-rapid deterritorialisation, against the folly of believing that a smooth space is liberating as such. From this point of view, one might say that Deleuze and Guattari draw our attention to the fact that there is a rhizomatic infrastructure to all sets of social relations (just as the wood in a tree has a cell-structure which is more rhizomatic than arborescent), but that there is also an arborescent dimension to any set of relations which are even minimally organised at all, and that they produce a set of descriptive conceptual tools which do not lend themselves necessarily to any one political perspective or project. Indeed, they themselves assert that 'no political program will be elaborated within the framework of schizoanalysis.' (Deleuze & Guattari 1983: 380).

That doesn't mean that Deleuze and Guattari did not have particular political allegiances. Guattari, in particular, had a lifelong affinity and involvement with radical leftist political movements and projects. Furthermore, schizoanalysis clearly emerges from an engagement with a set of problems which are specifically problems *from the point of view* of such a politics: there's no need to invent new ways of conceptualising social relations if you don't think there's something wrong with existing ones. Although they rightly and understandably wished to avoid the dogmatism of their leftist predecessors, Deleuze and Guattari remain clearly within the same tradition as Marx and the militants of 1968 and the New Lefts, trying to find ways of reconciling a libertarian philosophy with a non-individualist view of politics and the human condition. How do we maximize human freedom without making the mistake of thinking that freedom is merely a condition appertaining to individuals and is merely a question of being as separate and isolated from all other individuals as possible? This is the question which the socialist tradition has been grappling with since it became apparent in the early-nineteenth century that the freedom of the new middle classes to enclose land, expropriate peasants, hire workers for starvation wages and employ small children in dangerous industrial occupations was severely curtailing the freedom of the poor to live a decent life. It is the question which Deleuze and Guattari are still grappling with in much of their work, even if they find it necessary to tackle it at a very high level of abstraction.

The implications of Deleuze and Guattari's ideas for the anti-capitalist movement are largely to valorize much of its existing practice. The decentred, leaderless, networked forms which much of the anti-capitalist movement takes is decidedly rhizomatic in character. The maintenance of the World Social Forum as an open space and a process, rather than the basis for a party with a manifesto, is clearly motivated by a suspicion of authoritarian structures and representative mechanisms which is closely allied to Deleuze and Guattari's emphasis on the molecular dimension of social and political life and the dangers of territorialisation. Deleuze and Guattari's eschewal of humanism in favour of a view which sees humans as only one form of life, indeed one form of matter, amongst many, with all of which we share certain properties and characteristics, is very close to the spirit of much of the ecology movement, as Guattari's own turn to 'ecosophy' made explicit (Guattari 2000), although it is also potentially at odds with the explicit humanism of the World Social Forum charter of principles. At the same time the complexity of their approach to capitalism can help shed some light on some of the issues facing the anti-capitalist movement. Is it a movement to replace capitalism with some other total system of social and economic relations? Or is it an aggregation of different forces and projects opposed to the imposition of neoliberalism in every part of the world? Perhaps, in fact, there can be no absolute answer to this question: following Deleuze and Guattari, we might say that the attempt to escape the territorial matrix of neoliberalism, with its insistent coding of all social relations and all material things in terms of the logic of the commodity, requires at least some provisional reterritorialisation in a new vision of the possibilities of the social, even while no such vision must ever be allowed to close off new possibilities and new potential connections. As such, the anti-capitalist movement can only progress by way of an uncertain oscillation between a 'molar' condition of coherence and internal stratification and a 'molecular' condition of mobile disaggregation, between the 'paranoiac pole', 'which subordinates desiring-production to the formation of sovereignty and to the gregariou. .ggregate that results from it', and the 'schizoid pole', which 'overthrows the established power, and subjects the gregarious aggregate to the molecular multiplicities of the productions of desire' (Deleuze & Guattari 1983: 376).

In terms of the key concepts of power, complexity, hegemony and creativity, we can see that Deleuze and Guattari place a fundamental importance on creativity as, to some extent, the essential quality of matter itself (a position they derive in part from readings of Spinoza, Nietzsche and Bergson). Desire is not lack, but creativity, and creativity is what repressive institutions must always work to block or 'overcode' (Deleuze & Guattari 1988: 41; Guattari 1972: 162). Power, within this frame of reference, is an index of the relative degrees of *stratification* within a given assemblage. That is to say that power is a function of the relative capacity of the component parts of an assemblage to liberate fluxes of creative desire; or to channel, block or limit such flows:

> Our only points of disagreement with Foucault are the following: (1) to us the assemblages seem fundamentally to be assemblages not of power but of desire (desire is always assembled), and power seems to be a stratified dimension of the assemblage; (2) the diagram and abstract machine have lines of flight that are primary, which are not phenomena of resistance or counterattack in an assemblage, but cutting edges of creation and deterritorialisation. (Deleuze & Guattari 1988: 531)

The geo-physical language deployed by Deleuze and Guattari is perhaps an indication of how relatively far they travel from a vocabulary which would contain concepts like hegemony. However, bear in mind that hegemony, as we have argued, is precisely the capacity to *stabilise* a particular situation of power and to determine the field of possibilities which it contains. From this point of view, Deleuze and Guattari do not represent a break with the analytics of hegemony, but a resource with which to understand the psycho-socio-physical complexity of its mechanics in a manner which is entirely in keeping with the spirit of cultural studies. In particular, what Deleuze and Guattari draw our attention to is the extent to which relations of relative stability and relative speed operate *at every level of existence,* from the sub-molecular to the galactic. From this point of view, the idea of hegemony can only make sense if it is assumed not to be the name only for the type of political leadership which is exercised by dominant class fractions in advanced capitalist societies but also for a type of social/discursive/material/abstract relation which can obtain between all kinds of terms (such as *ideas, institutions, groups, classes, molecules* or *affects*). In fact, this abstraction of the concept of hegemony has been precisely Laclau and Mouffe's key theoretical innovation.

Laclau and Mouffe

If Deleuze and Guattari generally emphasise the importance of the nomadic, molecular, rhizomatic dimension of politics, then our next two writers are perhaps their logical obverse. Ernesto Laclau and Chantal Mouffe are widely regarded as the leading theorists of recent times to have developed the crucial concept of hegemony. This is a key term in much political and cultural theory of recent decades, where it derives almost exclusively from the translated work of the Italian communist leader and philosopher, Antonio Gramsci.

Gramsci's best known work, his *Prison Notebooks,* was written during the last years of his life, which he spent in a fascist prison, one of the victims of Mussolini's political terror. The work covers a vast range of political, social, economic, cultural and philosophical topics (Gramsci 1971). However, his concept of hegemony is by far the most influential element to have been taken up by the anglophone left, and it is the single most characteristic piece of jargon in the whole lexicon of cultural studies. *Hegemony* is often mistakenly understood to mean merely 'dominance' or 'control'. A better understanding of the term would be 'leadership', as a brief account of the term's genealogy in Marxist political theory should make clear. The term first emerges importantly in the writing of Lenin, and it emerges in the context of Lenin's practical efforts to develop a theory of revolutionary practice, something which Marx and Engels had very little to say about. In particular, Lenin was trying to organize a proletarian socialist revolution in a country (Czarist Russia) which did not have very sizeable proletariat, but that did have large numbers of oppressed, hungry, increasingly dissatisfied peasants. Marxist theory had tended to assume that before a revolution could be organised by the working-class majority, a country would have to pass through the historical process of capitalist modernisation, which would lead to its full industrialisation, the disappearance of the peasantry and the transformation of a majority of the population into proletarian industrial labourers. Lenin's so-called Bolshevik faction of the Russian Social Democratic Party believed that it would be possible for a revolutionary force made up mainly of peasants to succeed if it was effectively led by a well-disciplined party based in the industrial proletariat of the great cities (Lenin 1947). The famous communist symbol, the hammer and sickle, represents a social coalition of workers and peasants, and it was this coalition which effectively succeeded in replacing Czarism with a workers state following the revolution of October 1917. The concept of hegemony therefore emerged in the context of a conception of politics which saw it in terms of the creation of coalitions between different social groups, coalitions which the most advanced political forces would have to lead.

Antonio Gramsci, a loyal communist operating under very different conditions from Lenin, was preoccupied in part with the question of how this conception of politics could be developed in a way which would be appropriate to different conditions, such as the conditions of a mass democracy with a developing media culture within a much more economically developed and socially variegated society than Russia. Perhaps Gramsci's most lastingly influential observation is that hegemony—leadership—is not only an issue for those trying to martial potentially revolutionary forces in an all-out assault on the ruling class. It is also an issue for those social groups who are already in power and want to stay there, *and* for those political forces who want to challenge those in power even if the aim is not immediate revolution. In the former case, the hegemonic group has to exercise a variety of means by which to persuade the subaltern (non-hegemonic) groups to accept their hegemony, be it by brute force or various forms of bribery and persuasion. In the latter case, any radical political project faces the very difficult task of persuading a large and usually heterogeneous set of social forces to accept their leadership over that of the currently hegemonic group. In either case, however, politics will be not merely a matter of elections or military actions: it is also a matter of either side trying to win the hearts and minds of various other social groups, through whatever means available.

> A social group dominates antagonistic groups, which it tends to "liquidate", or to subjugate perhaps even by armed force. A social group can, and indeed must, already exercise "leadership" before winning governmental power (this is indeed one of the principal conditions for the winning of such power); it subsequently becomes dominant when it exercises power, but even if holds it firmly in its grasp, it must continue to "lead" as well. (Gramsci 1971: 57–8)

The press, the churches, the theatre, literature, the cinema, the schools can all be seen as places where the battle of ideas, the battle between different ways of seeing the world, is fought out between different social forces, their partisans and their representatives. This is why the concept of hegemony has proved so crucial for cultural studies. In fact, Gramsci explicitly argued that it would be necessary for radicals to make a thorough and serious study of all the elements of the culture which they inhabited so as to be able effectively to constitute a counter-hegemonic force (1985: 41–3), and to a large extent this is how many cultural studies practitioners have understood their own role since the 1970s. Even where such practitioners have had no interest in contributing to some broader political projects, Gramsci's conception of culture as the site of the struggle for hegemony between different social forces and their political projects has proved immensely useful as a lens through which to view the dynamics of past and present cultures and the ways in which they interact with processes of social, economic and political change.

When Laclau and Mouffe published their landmark study *Hegemony and Socialist Strategy* (1985), Gramsci's ideas were at the peak of their prestige amongst an anglophone audience. Interpretations of Gramsci and his concept of hegemony vary, as with any such important thinker, and only one strand of interpretation has rendered his ideas at the highest possible level of abstraction (which may or may not be a good thing to do, depending on your point of view). *Hegemony and Socialist Strategy* marked both the high point and in some senses the end of this process, as arguably the most rigorous examination of the concept of hegemony and the one which most decisively detached it from the Marxist context of Gramsci's thought. The book is in part a genealogy of the term *hegemony* as it evolves through the writings of Second International Marxists, Lenin and then Gramsci. It is also, in some senses, an assessment of the entire communist theoretical tradition in the light of post-structuralist theory: most notably the ideas of Lacan and Derrida. Put very simply, the argument runs as follows. The concept of hegemony as it emerges in Gramsci's thought involves a move away from any conception of politics as merely the expression of an underlying struggle between distinct and definite social groups: the 'class struggle' as Marx calls it. Even Lenin's project for the hegemony of the Bolsheviks involves a radical break with the Marxist idea that the communist party would be merely a political expression of the social identity of the working class. Lenin came to the conclusion that the working class would probably never develop a full political identity, full 'class consciousness' by itself, and that it required political leadership to enable it to do so (Lenin 1947). In making this assessment, he shifted towards politics as an active process that *shapes* the identities of its participants rather than merely gives expression to pre-existing identities. Gramsci's conception of hegemony went much further, as he developed a new political vocabulary to talk about the types of group which engage in politics. Laclau and Mouffe argue that Gramsci's notion (borrowed in part from syndicalist thinker Georges Sorel) of the 'collective will', which would be expressed by a class, or a section of a class, or even a 'historic bloc' made up of sections of different classes, marked a profound break with the 'class essentialism' of earlier Marxism. Although they think that Gramsci himself remained stuck within a class essentialist framework, they argue that he developed the concept of hegemony to the point where it already implicitly undermines that framework and that the breakdown of this framework can be seen to do so most clearly when understood in the light of Lacanian and Derridean philosophy.

As discussed in Chapter 2, Laclau and Mouffe's fundamental philosophical aim is to dispense altogether with any vestige of 'essentialism' (1985: 91–145). *Essentialism* is a term widely used in cultural and political theory. It is most commonly used today to refer to any notion of racial, gendered, ethnic, national or sexual identity as essential rather than socially or historically determined. So the idea that women are all naturally caring and maternal or that black people are all good at sport are essentialist notions. This is true, but it does not quite get at the heart of the conceptual critique of essentialism which is fundamental to Laclau and Mouffe's approach. At its most abstract, their anti-essentialist approach depends upon the assumption that, in effect, *no* object—actual or conceptual—has any *fundamental* meaningful identity: rather, the social being of all objects is dependent upon their situation in a system of relative differences from which they derive their identity. So our ideas about what a man really is are entirely dependent upon our ideas of what a woman is, a child is, an animal is or a plant is, and it is only this network of ideas about what is not a man which creates for us a consistent concept of *man.*

Now, this conception itself derives from two main sources. One is Ferdinand de Saussure's conception of language (Saussure 1983), which was so immensely important to the great structuralist thinkers of the mid-twentieth century (Lacan, Lévi-Strauss, Althusser, the early Barthes). Put very simply, Saussure argued that a language is a system of differences and that every term in the system only has meaning by virtue of its differences from other terms. The word/concept *cat* only has meaning by virtue of its differences from other words (*hat, fat, can,* etc.) and by virtue of the fact that the English language differentiates the world of small mammals such that it conceives of one set of those animals as cats as distinct from other sets (mice, dogs, rabbits, etc). We know that other cultures use other words to refer to cats, and it's possible to imagine a culture which did not make a clear distinction between cats and dogs, so it is only the arbitrary fact of this particular set of differences which gives the word/concept *cat* its meaning. The word *cat does not* express or even name some essential 'catness' which exists invariably, outside of culture.

Assume for the time being that we accept this model of how language works. To understand Laclau and Mouffe's anti-essentialism, it is necessary to understand that they transcribe this model of how *language* works into a model of how the whole of social experience works. Now, it is important to appreciate that they are not alone in this. Philosophers at least since the early-twentieth century have been arguing that, in effect, we experience the whole of our reality through the categories of language which we use not just to communicate, but to think. As such, as Wittgenstein argued 'the *limits of my language* mean the limits of my world' (1961). The realisation by late-nineteenth-century and early-twentieth-century anthropologists that cultures around the world had radically different ways of looking at the world—ways inscribed in the words they had or did not have for different elements of it—also gave rise to the idea that a language constituted a whole world view. Anyone who has spent any time studying a second language will have some sense of this. In French, for example, the verb *aimer* can mean 'to like' and 'to love' such that the fine distinction made between these two emotional responses in English does not quite apply in an equivalent way. So in this sense the categories of language constitute the entire framework through which we experience social reality, to the extent that linguistic and social realities are effectively coextensive.

This is the second key source of Laclau and Mouffe's anti-essentialism: the assumption that if language is a system of differences lacking any positive terms, then social reality must be the same, because it is coextensive with language (1985: 110). Now this assumption obviously raises all kinds of philosophical problems, and it is worth taking a moment to think about them. Firstly, it's important to understand what is *not* necessarily implied by this notion. It does not necessarily imply that there is no real world of material things which is separate from the words we use to talk about them. It does not mean that truth is simply whatever people believe or say is true. There is a very widespread tendency in casual commentary to assume that thinkers such as Derrida, Foucault and Laclau, or followers of some imaginary school of thought called *post-modernism* or *deconstruction,* believe that 'there is no such things as truth' or 'everything is just discourse'. This is almost never a correct summary of the opinions being so described. Many thinkers believe that linguistic and discursive categories shape the way we *experience* reality, and that we can never have any access to the real material world other than through the categories of language, but this in itself is not a terribly controversial idea, even if we don't agree with it, and it is not at all the same thing as believing that there is no material reality at all. Laclau actually goes further, at times suggesting that the logic of language is simply identical to or co-terminous with the logic of social relations (Howarth 2004: 266), but this still does not equate to denying the existence of reality.

The precise nature of the relationship between experience, language and the material world is an endless source of philosophical debate, and not one to which we are going to find final solutions to here. To understand Laclau and Mouffe's unique theoretical contribution, what we need to understand is their deployment of another key term in contemporary political and cultural theory: *discourse.* This is a widely used, little-analysed term (Gilbert 2004b), which has been popularised in cultural and literary studies by the work of Foucault (1972), but is also an object of study in its own right by sociolinguists such as Norman Fairclough (2003). In the latter case, the word *discourse* is a general term for almost any kind of linguistic activity. In the former case, the term is used very loosely, sometimes referring to linguistic activity and sometimes referring to other kinds of activity which are also somehow meaningful in character (so wearing a kind of clothing that has particular symbolic value is seen as a form of discursive activity). In this context, the term *discourse* can be said to refer to any socially meaningful practice, or any relatively coherent set of ideas about a given topic and the practices which embody, reproduce and are informed by those ideas. This, generally, is how Laclau and Mouffe use the term, specifying that the 'totality which includes within itself the linguistic and the non-linguistic, is what we call discourse ... In our terminology, every identity or discursive object is constituted in the context of an action' (Laclau 1990: 100–2). Laclau and Mouffe use this terminology to further develop a certain tendency in Gramsci's thought away from its roots in Marxism. For the perspective developed by Laclau and Mouffe, politics is not a matter of struggle between social classes, but between complexes of meaningful social practice: in other words, between discourses.

Now, some critics see this as a wholly idealist revision of Gramsci, turning the theory of hegemony into an account of politics as a 'battle of ideas' which completely loses sight of the Marxist understanding that politics is always about struggles over material resources (Joseph 2002: 104). There are two main points to make in response to this. One is that, if we consider the implications of the concept of discourse given above, it becomes clear that a struggle between discourses is always a struggle between sets of practices, as much as between sets of ideas, or in Deleuze and Guattari's terminology, between 'assemblages'. This is given a further twist in Laclau's recent work (2005), where it is not simply discourses but *demands* which enter into various relations of struggle.

The other thing to say is that Laclau and Mouffe do indeed see the fundamental difference between their position and that of classical Marxism in terms of their attention to psychological issues which Marxism ignores. Put very simply, classical Marxism largely assumes that people are rational creatures who can be relied upon to act in their own best material interests as long as they are adequately informed as to what they are. In the final analysis, Marx expected the proletariat to unite in opposition to capitalism because it would be the best way to ensure a high standard of living for itself. Laclau and Mouffe are heavily influenced by psychoanalysis (in particular the work of Jacques Lacan) and by its assumption that human beings are at best only occasionally motivated by reason (Laclau & Mouffe 1990). One of the politically relevant observations of psychoanalysis is that people, especially in groups, will often fight to defend a sense of themselves and their place in the world—an identity, in other words—at least as hard as they would fight to defend their apparent material interests. This has been a problem which radical political theory has had to cope with at least since the First World War showed that millions of workers were prepared to die for their country even when cruelly exploited by that country's ruling elite and when fighting in the war meant killing fellow-workers who had never done them any harm. In the period leading up to the war, many socialists believed that this could never happen, that the workers of Europe would never fall upon each other at the command of their own oppressors, their national ruling elites (Sassoon 1997: 27–31). In some senses the long search by Marxists for an adequate theory of ideology—of the political power of beliefs—was provoked by the disappointment of this disaster. Working in this tradition, Laclau in particular has stressed the enormous power of a sense of identity, and of the need for a sense of identity, in all kinds of politics.[4]

Although this all sounds very abstract—and it often is—it does have roots in a specific set of historical experiences. Laclau's thinking has been shaped by his experience of left-wing politics in Argentina, which has historically been characterised by the importance of Peronist populism, a form of politics not easily understood in terms of the expression of class interests (Laclau 1977: 143–98). More broadly, Laclau and Mouffe's thinking is widely seen as deriving from the experience of the emergence of the 'new social movements' and the decline of organised labour and the forms of socialism associated with it (Nash 2000). One of the most striking features of the post-1968 political landscape for Laclau and Mouffe is the proliferation of new political demands from various groups, and the unlikelihood of any single project encompassing all of those demands. One of the questions which Laclau and Mouffe try to address in this context, is: what is that might link together as many as possible of the radical demands of women, non-white people, youth, workers and so forth (Laclau & Mouffe 1985: 149–93; Laclau 2005: 129–72). For the fundamental political implication of Laclau and Mouffe's anti-essentialism is that there are simply no inevitable, inherent, natural connections between different sets of political demands or between specific demands and specific social constituencies: so if we want to create political connections between different projects and different groups, then making those connections is an active process. Marxists had traditionally seen the process whereby sections of the working class became radicalised as one whereby they became class conscious, that is aware of their *true* social identity (Lukacs 1971). Many feminists thought of the politicisation of women in similar terms. The implication of Laclau and Mouffe's anti-essentialism is that there is no true working-class identity, no essential femininity: rather, a politicised working-class or feminine identity is only one possible outcome of a struggle in discourse to connect workers or women with broader political projects, and Laclau and Mouffe would like to see such a project take the form of a general drive to maximise autonomy.

A crucial feature of Laclau and Mouffe's work is their rejection of any understanding of social formations as fully knowable totalities, and their emphasis upon the importance of recognising the complexification of social relations within advanced capitalist societies as the necessary terrain of contemporary political struggle.

> Every attempt to establish a definitive suture and deny the radically open character of the social leads to what Lefort designates as 'totalitarianism'; that is to say, to a logic of construction of the political which consists of establishing a point of departure from which society can be perfectly mastered and known ...
>
> But if there is no doubt that one of the dangers which threatens democracy is the totalitarian attempt to pass beyond the constitutive character of antagonism and deny plurality in order to restore unity, there is also a symmetrically opposite danger of a lack of all reference to this unity. For, even though impossible, this remains a horizon which, given the absence of articulation between social relations, is necessary in order to prevent an implosion of the social and an absence of any common point of reference. (Laclau & Mouffe 1985: 187–8)

For classical Marxism, the possibility of transcending capitalist society depended on the simplification of social structure and the emergence of a privileged agent of social change, while for us, the possibility of a democratic transformation of society depends on a proliferation of new subjects of change. This is only possible if there is something in contemporary capitalism which really tends to multiply dislocations and thus create a plurality of new antagonisms. (Laclau 1990: 41)

From this perspective, complexity is the central feature of social relations which makes political struggle necessarily *hegemonic* in character. Now, here is it is necessary to clear up a common confusion. In arguing that all political struggle must be hegemonic in character, Laclau and Mouffe are not arguing that it must strive for the total domination of a social field or for ideological uniformity within. In fact they are making the opposite argument. For Laclau and Mouffe, there simply *are no* fundamental, self-contained historical agents who *could* successfully engage in such a project. There is no singular antagonism which divides the social field. Every political/cultural/social/identity is always already fragmented and criss-crossed by its complex relations to others. As such, those temporary stabilisations of the political field which we can call *hegemonic* can only be achieved through processes of *articulation.*

Articulation is probably the key concept to have been developed by Laclau and Mouffe and then taken up in some parts of cultural studies (Slack 1996). *Articulation* is a word which has more than one meaning in everyday speech, and their use of it is best understood if we *don't* think of articulation as a synonym for expression (as in the phrase 'he articulated his feelings well to her that evening'). Rather, we should think of articulation as in anatomy or in the phrase 'articulated truck': articulation in this sense is a synonym for connecting, in a physical sense. For Laclau and Mouffe, the basic operation of politics is the articulation of terms (ideas/concepts/images/signs) to each other in highly unpredictable sequences or 'chains'. In Laclau's most recent work, the issue of what kind of 'terms' are articulated is further clarified when he writes that 'the unity of the group is, in my view, the result of an articulation of demands' (Laclau 2005: ix). A typical example of an attempt to create such a unity, which we have already referred to elsewhere, would be the effort in France 1968 by radical students to articulate their demands for autonomy, self-expression and an end to hierarchy with the demands of industrial workers for better pay and conditions. It was the failure of this attempt, partly because not enough common terms of reference could be found, which foreclosed the possibility of revolution in France at that time. Indeed, we might observe that it was in the pursuit of such a common point of reference that the concept of *autonomy* became so important to libertarian communist militants in Italy in the 1970s. For Laclau and Mouffe, hegemonic struggle is precisely the search for such common terms of reference, and as such almost always involves some partial transformation of the identities of *all* groups who enter into articulatory coalitions. For example (to use one of Laclau's own illustrations), when a trade union starts to articulate its concerns with those of local anti-racist campaigns, trying to create a common front between workers and ethnic minorities, it in the process finds its own identity changing, from being a mere representative of workers' rights to being a more genuinely political agent. Both the strategic coalitions which seek to challenge established hegemonic relations *and* the practices by which powerful groups seek to articulate their concerns to those of others involve such shifts in identity. 'We will call *articulation* any practice establishing a relation among elements such that their identity is modified as a result of the articulatory practice' (Laclau & Mouffe 1985:105).

Nonetheless, it is clear that even in this last example, there are power relationships in play: how many times has an anti-racist group accused a trade union or socialist organisation of trying to 'take over' its campaign? What happens if radical socialists convince anti-racists to subsume their struggle into that of the workers, focussing energies on the long-term, unachievable goal of proletarian revolution, thereby ignoring immediate local problems of police harassment and racial violence? Isn't this precisely the danger of what Deleuze and Guattari call 'majority'?

Laclau and Mouffe would probably reply that this is indeed a danger, and it is one that can only be averted if we pay careful attention to the mechanics by which groups are formed. In their more recent work, both have turned in different ways to the issue of how it is that communities, democratic or otherwise, can hold together, if it is not because their members share some essential identity. In this they have both to some extent been influenced by the psychoanalytic strand of thought which sees groups as bound together by their members' common identification with some relatively arbitrary symbol, image, or name. This derives from Freud's account of group psychology, in which he argues that what holds together groups is their members' common identification with a leader (Freud 1985). Laclau has developed this observation into a rich account of the centrality of 'empty signifiers' to political discourse (1996). Empty signifiers are those symbols or terms shared by a community which come to mean literally nothing (or almost-nothing) because they simply signify the very idea of the community as a community. For example, in Freud's account of group psychology, a term can take the symbolic place of the leader. We might think of the American flag or the monarchy in the United Kingdom as symbols with so many different associations to different constituencies that they really mean nothing, instead standing in for the very possibility of the national community existing at all. Different political discourses will seek to link their projects to these empty signifiers, struggling to become the effective source of their content, but the more definite the meaning of such a signifier, the less empty it becomes and the less it can do the work of simply naming the collectivity of the collective. So in the United States, for example, were the religious right really to accomplish their goal of clearly establishing an unambiguous correlation between the US flag, Christian fundamentalism and residual white supremacism, the result would be hegemonic crisis in the United States and a complete breakdown of American nationhood. All of the other constituencies who can still see something of their own traditions as evoked by the flag—which is for some the symbol of liberal democracy, of anti-imperialist struggle, of Enlightenment, of secularism, of a Union of the States within which slavery has been abolished and the civil rights of blacks and women guaranteed by law—would find themselves excluded, unable to identify with the prime symbol of nationhood, and the nation would consequently cease to exist.

The question this leaves open is how radical democrats should relate to this situation. What kinds of empty signifiers should they identify with and what should they do about the fact that they *know* that these signifiers are merely empty? To some extent this has been the issue addressed by Mouffe in some of her recent work. Mouffe argues that what characterizes a democratic community is the fact that the emptiness at its centre is in fact publicly acknowledged and institutionalised. In place of a leader, or a single creed, democratic communities have an endless contest between different ideas about what they should be and where they should go (Mouffe 2000). It is this endless and unresolvable conflict in exactly the place where non-democratic communities have something fixed and stable which defines a democratic community. From this perspective (which is rather close, but not identical, to that of the postmodernist philosopher, Jean-François Lyotard: see Lyotard 1988), one of the worst things that can happen is for some ideal vision of the community and its future to become fixed, freezing out the possibility of contestation which is the very substance of democracy itself. This is a very interesting formulation, especially when thought of in the light of the shared histories of the anti-capitalists movement, the new social movement and cultural studies. For what all of these different projects have shared has been a determination to question some of the fundamental assumptions which their societies have regarded as beyond question, to open up for public debate issues which had been closed off or never open to such debate. As such, they can all be understood as radically democratic projects. Furthermore, there is a fascinating parallel between the analysis of Laclau and Mouffe and Subcomandante Marcos's deliberate effacement of his status as leader: his refusal to take a title that would clearly name him as leader, his refusal to be identified as a concrete individual, his deliberate evocation of 'Marcos' as merely a fictional stand-in for all of the various democratic constituencies of the world. Indeed, it seems almost impossible that Marcos should have been unaware of Laclau's and Mouffe's work on these issue when he took the name Delegado Zero, especially given that some of Laclau's more abstract writing on this topic has engaged directly with the concept of *zero* as the 'empty' place which makes the whole system of modern maths possible (Laclau 1998). Whether he was or not, the resonances between radical democracy and Zapatismo are more than striking.

Finally, in considering the affinities between Laclau and Mouffe's ideas and those which inform the anti-capitalist movement, it is worth considering Laclau's important contribution to the theorisation of universality in contemporary political philosophy. In that field, a universal project or belief-system is usually defined as one which aspires to encompass the entire human race. Christianity is a universalism because it aims to be a religion for everybody. Communism is a universal project because it aims to liberate all people from exploitation through the abolition of class society. In recent times, postmodernist thinkers such as Lyotard (1984; 1988) have tended to condemn all universalisms as inherently totalitarian, suppressing difference and dissent with their suffocating vision of truth. Figures such as Alain Badiou, on the other hand, have argued that all radical politics must be universalist in nature if they are to move beyond the mere defence of 'particularisms' (specific identities such as nationality or religion; Badiou 2003). Laclau offers a more complex take on this problem, pointing out that every form of universality is always contaminated by some particularity from which it derives, and that the elevation of one particularism into a universal is one of the fundamental hegemonic manoeuvres (Butler, Laclau & Žižek 2000). Now, it is important to understand that any one concrete human subject could be defined in terms of any number of different particularisms: that is, any one of a number of distinct identity-traits. I could identify myself as a man, as British, as a public-sector worker, as white, as right-handed and so forth. From Laclau's perspective, what a universalist political discourse such as communism does is to elevate one such trait to the status of the universal basis upon which a common political identity could be formed. So the discourse of class struggle which is central to communism identifies one aspect of a person—the fact that they happen to work for a wage or salary—and tries to make this the basis for a political identity which can be shared by all who possess that trait, identifying them all as members of the proletariat.

We might add that from this perspective, the discourse of class struggle was always a potentially very powerful one. It is certainly true that most human beings today survive only by selling their labour, and objectively it seems like a perfectly good idea to try to get them to unite for a more equal world on the basis of that shared particularism. Unfortunately, this has not turned out to be very effective in practice: historically the social and cultural differences between people who work and the pull of national and religious identities which cross class lines has been too great for it to prove effective. From this point of view, contemporary anti-capitalism might be understood as a very intelligent substitute for the discourse of class struggle, precisely because it offers scope for a common identification between all who suffer at the hands of neoliberalism without depending upon any more substantial particularity as the basis for that identification.

There is something of a problem with Laclau and Mouffe's formulations, however, at least from the perspective of contemporary anti-capitalism. The psychoanalytic tradition from which they draw their accounts of the mechanisms of community tends to have a decidedly negative conception of the social. Freud's account of group psychology, for example, has been criticised for its model of the group dependent entirely on a leader for its very existence. There is no room at all in Freud's model for any notion of real *solidarity* existing between members of a group, and this seems to be replicated in Laclau and Mouffe's understandings of community, which consistently insists on antagonism as not only inherent to but constitutive of all social life. Now, this is a particular problem from the perspective of the anti-capitalist movement, one of whose characteristic features is a preference for horizontal forms (i.e. forms of organisation without a clear hierarchy and clearly defined leadership) over vertical forms of organisation. Within the Freudian perspective, there are no horizontal, transversal social relations at all, or if there are then they are only a byproduct of the vertical relations between leaders and the led[5]. From an anti-capitalist perspective, it is not

enough merely to argue for the emptiness of the place of the leader: it is surely necessary to conceive of groups as at least potentially leaderless and as bound together
by horizontal relations of solidarity *between* their members (Gilbert 2004b, 2004c).
Laclau and Mouffe are famous for their assertions to the effect that there is no such
thing as society, because all such images of wholeness as that evoked by the idea of
society or community are effectively illusory: mere fantasies holding together a group
of variegated and incoherent individuals. But it is not this which is really the problem
here. From an anti-capitalist perspective we can easily accept that every group identity is a provisional and partial fiction. What is more problematic is the assumption
that it is *only* through such group identities, rather than through complex processes of
mutual interaction, that collectivities can come into being at all.

From the perspective of Deleuze and Guattari, Laclau and Mouffe's work remains
stuck within the psychoanalytic horizon and as such can only see one very limited
part of the broad spectrum of human experience. From this point of view, we can
say that of course some, perhaps most, groups function in the way that Laclau and
Mouffe describe. Perhaps we could even say that all groups function in this way
to an extent: which is exactly the same as saying that all social relations have an
arborescent dimension. But what Laclau and Mouffe's perspective ignores is the
rhizomatic dimension which all social relations also share, the horizontal, transversal
lateral relations between members of groups which make truly *mutual* becomings
possible (Deleuze & Guattari 1983: 348–9). From this point of view, there is little
attention in Laclau and Mouffe's work to the ways in which power relationships
emerge and crystallise from below. Now, this absence in Laclau and Mouffe's perspective has led some critics to see them as implicitly authoritarian in their perspective, as some anarchist-influenced thinkers tend to see *any* position which draws on
Gramsci or Lenin as necessarily authoritarian (Day 2005). This is a very problematic
critique, for two reasons. Firstly because it simply overlooks what it is that Laclau
and Mouffe are trying to do in much of their work. Laclau in particular rarely tries to
say much about how politics *should* work and is largely concerned with how it really
does work. This remains a very important corrective perspective for anyone working
within the radical tradition, which has historically been very good at understanding
how people *ought* to behave in order to make the world a better place, but rather bad
at understanding why they don't. Any democrat, however radical, has to have some
understanding of why democracy is so rarely found in real life, why it never quite
works the way people want it to and why authoritarian relations are so widespread.
Much of Laclau's work and Mouffe's work has been concerned with understanding
these issues, moving beyond the limitations of a naïve perspective which is constantly
surprised by these facts of political life.

Secondly, Laclau's approach to issues such as empty signifiers and hegemonic
universality *could* be read as stressing the extent to which the 'nodal points' (Laclau &
Mouffe 1985: 139) around which hegemonic formations crystallise are always relatively arbitrary points in a generalised network of power relations. In other words,

hegemonic relations can be understood as relations which *emerge* between terms which are not in any prior or essential relation of superiority or inferiority. In other words, vertical relations may emerge from horizontal ones; molecules may coagulate into molar formations. The analytics of hegemony is not a prescription, but a description of how such processes operate. So on this particular reading, we could argue that Laclau and Mouffe do not accord logical priority to vertical relations but merely describe the logic of their emergence. I am not entirely convinced that Laclau does not, in fact, accord logical priority to vertical relations, but we can see here that it is at least possible to interpret his work in terms which do not. On the basis of such a reading, the gulf between Laclau and Mouffe, and Deleuze and Guattari may not be so great after all.

However, where there is a clear difference between them is in their contrasting conceptions of desire. Laclau and Mouffe are rigourously committed to the Lacanian formulation which understands the human subject (collective or individual) as constituted by an inherent *lack*. For Laclau in particular, the assumption that political desire is organised by the quest to locate the absent fullness of the social, or of the self, is axiomatic. Even in his most recent work, where Laclau takes the radical step of seeing politics as a process of conflict and struggle between differently articulated sets of *demands,* there is a gap between this formulation and one which understands desire in positive terms, as a positive force of production. A demand is always for something that one lacks, and a demand is made upon something which might be able to fulfil it. For Deleuze and Guattari, by contrast, desire produces: it is production itself, in fact.

Now, this brings us to the one of our key themes which we have not dealt with at length in this treatment of Laclau and Mouffe: creativity. What is clear here is that the gap between Laclau and Mouffe's ideas and Deleuze and Guattari's ideas is partly a function of the latter's emphasis on the positive creative force of desiring-production-power. It would be easy to present this simply as a weakness with Laclau and Mouffe's position, but we should be wary of doing so. In fact, one of the most learned commentaries on Deleuze's philosophy to have appeared in English recently argued that it is this belief in groundless creativity that is precisely the *problem* with Deleuze. For Peter Hallward (2007), Deleuze's romantic faith in the creativity of matter amounts to nothing more than mysticism. The position that Hallward would probably share with Laclau and Mouffe emphasises that creativity never occurs in a vacuum. If it is always social, then it is always relational, emerging from the complex and unpredictable interactions between things and people. If we do not demand things that we lack, of institutions which might give them to us but do not yet, then what is politics all about? In the case of anti-capitalism, the difference between Laclau's articulated demands and Deleuze's creative desire might be the difference between organising a complex coalition to demand that the World Trade Organisation stop imposing neoliberal policies on third world countries and start assisting with progressive development programmes (a relational, counter-hegemonic articulation of *demands*), and running off into the Oregon wilderness to live in a teepee and meditate (pursuing a line of flight, an uninhibited becoming-other which liberates us from the limits of capitalism). This is probably a crude reading of the differences: let's remember that Félix Guattari was a lifelong militant who never actually did run away from direct political confrontation or the difficulties of counter-hegemonic organisation. But it is worth keeping in mind.

We cannot make an exhaustive exploration of differences or similarities between Laclau and Mouffe, and Deleuze and Guattari here, but we don't need to. Both pairs of writers furnish concepts and arguments which will prove invaluable for thinking through some of the issues which the final two chapters will address. However, it is striking that the issues that we have just touched on bear precisely upon the project of our final pair of theorists. For if Laclau and Mouffe—expert thinkers of complexity, hegemony and power—have little to say about the issue of creativity, then Michael Hardt and Tony Negri rarely seem to think about anything else.

Hardt and Negri

Before we get around to looking at strengths and weaknesses of Hardt and Negri's work, we need to know who its authors are. It is at first glance the product of an unusual collaboration. While Hardt has an admirable history as a political activist in his own right, it's as a professor of literature and philosophy at one of the most comfortably privileged academic institutions in the world—Duke University—that he's best known. Negri, on the other hand, is the last great hero of 1968. A leading radical intellectual in Italy in the 1960s and 70s, he fled to Paris at the end of the latter decade after being falsely accused by the Italian government of playing a leading roll in the terrorist activities of the Red Brigades: the heroic status which has been accorded to Negri since is hardly surprising.

On the other hand, it is perhaps only accident of history that their respective biographies look so different, as Negri himself has always earned his living as a philosopher, and his recent solo work is far more abstract than is that co-authored with Hardt. Indeed, it is Hardt's familiarity and sympathy with the political and intellectual traditions of English-language cultural studies (Hardt & Negri 2000: 137–50) which really makes their work different from comparable works from other philosophers. What makes Hardt and Negri's collaborative work refreshingly distinct from many other exercises in post-structuralist or neo-Marxist political philosophy is not just its passion and commitment but the welcome sense that the authors at least know of the existence of life outside the seminar room or the organisational headquarters. Hardt and Negri's commentary on *Buffy the Vampire Slayer* (2004: 193) may not be the most expert, but the world of popular culture is not a closed book to them, and in this particular aspect they are arguably more Gramscian in their approach than many of their contemporaries.

While Hardt and Negri's first book is an interesting but relatively overlooked work on the theory of the state (1994), it was their second, *Empire* (2000), which really caught the imagination of a wider public, becoming an international bestseller. In it, they argued that the nature of political power was radically changing in the new world of networked communications and global flows of people, money, ideas. Writing against those who saw the new world order as dominated by old-fashioned US imperialism, they argued that in fact there was no actual centre to world power any more, with advanced capitalism depending for its profitability on a fluid and multifarious set of relationships between economic and political institutions of all shapes and sizes. This seems to many like an odd idea at first, but Hardt and Negri draw our attention to the fact that historically the great empires—Rome, the British Empire—did not operate as highly centralised authoritarian regimes, but instead grew according to a logic of endless expansion which often left real power distributed throughout a complex network of institutional relationships, much like those between national governments, corporations and international bodies such as the United Nations and World Trade Organisation today.

The emergence of the neo-conservative hegemony in the United States shortly after *Empire* appeared was widely seen as undermining this hypothesis, and Hardt and Negri have had some trouble in explaining how Bush's militaristic nationalism could arise in such a context. At a conference at the Tate Britain gallery in London, in 2002, in conversation with Stuart Hall, Hardt suggested that the failure of Bush's military adventure would ultimately bear out the thesis of *Empire.* While subsequent events have certainly lent some retrospective credibility to this argument, at the time there was a widespread sense that America's naked imperialism disproved the core thesis of *Empire.* One of the key arguments of Hardt and Negri's third book, *Multitude: War and Democracy in the Age of Empire* (2004), wrestles with this problem. It does not deal with it particularly well, because Hardt and Negri, although often brilliant philosophers, are not very convincing theorists of international relations. In particular they tend to stretch metaphorical conceptual analogies well past breaking point. For example, the hypothetical schema by which this book divides up the world into a new 'aristocracy' (including the European elites so alienated by US unilateralism), an American 'monarchy' and so forth is rather clumsy and has no obvious analytic value (Hardt & Negri 2004: 320–4) and does not sit well with their characterisation of 'Empire' as a decentred network, a kind of enormous, malign rhizome. Nor does it sit well with their parallel argument that we have entered a period in which the 'global state of war'—on terror, on crime, on drugs, on the enemies of the United States, on everything that poses problems for Empire—has become the ordinary mode of politics (Hardt & Negri 2004: 12–18), because this understanding makes much more sense in the light of a more complex and disaggregated conception of contemporary geopolitical power relations. In fact, the former argument seems to be motivated primarily by an insistent desire to use Spinoza's work on politics—which is largely concerned with drawing up model constitutions for ideally conceived monarchies—as a template, even where it's patently inappropriate to do so, as opposed to being motivated from any serious attempt to map the specificities of power in the world today.

I would argue that there is a more persuasive defence of *Empire* available than that made by Hardt in person or in *Multitude,* in that it does offer a brilliant description of the type of international capitalism which Clinton and Blair were intent on implementing in the 1990s. Led by the software industry and the internet boom, infused with the Californian values of social liberalism and hedonistic creativity, committed to multilateral interventions in defence of its agendas (from GATT to the war in Kosovo), this was clearly a new and aggressively borderless form of capitalism. However, there was very little on offer here for the industrialists and oil barons of the American South and Midwest or those non-metropolitan US populations excluded from the new cosmopolitanism. It's they who went on to form the political alliance underpinning the Bush government and its project to secure access to Middle-Eastern oil reserves. The fact that such an analysis is missing from Hardt and Negri's work is not just incidental: their tendency is almost always to speak in terms of broad-brush metaphors and abstract generalisations, and in the process they can end up making analyses which are just not very political, in that they offer descriptions of social states and processes without paying much attention to the actual specific power struggles which underlie them, or which might change them. Nonetheless, from the perspective of the story told in Chapter 2, of the gradual disassociation of the New Left and mainstream cultural studies from any actual political projects, Hardt and Negri's analyses remain crucial. The moment of *Empire* is the moment of Clintonian capitalism, which I have suggested is exactly the moment at which the traditions and hopes of the New Left were finally politically neutralised. The task of charting the new terrain from that moment on, in a spirit of explicit solidarity with the anti-capitalist movement, is exactly the crucial task which Hardt and Negri have taken upon themselves. Their attempt to link up many of the traditions and tendencies described in this book is therefore surely to be welcomed, and as such I think that all criticisms should be addressed to them only in a spirit of solidarity: it is hardly surprising if the results of their experiment are at times uneven. To understand something of the strengths and weaknesses of those results thus far, we have to understand a bit more about Hardt and Negri's general project, and in particular their concept of 'Multitude'.

Marx showed long ago that even as capitalism concentrates wealth in the hands of a few, it ensures that the real work of production is done by the many, amongst whom ever-greater levels of real interdependence and silent cooperation are required (1992: 376–8). Today this means that at the level of global production, cooperative communication and networked social power are already a reality, a reality the left must learn to build on in the twenty-first century by building a movement for real global democracy. This is the basic argument made in *Multitude.* Hardt and Negri use the term *multitude* to name this vast creative collectivity to which we all now belong, as well as the general condition of creative sociality as a fundamental fact of existence. Crucially, Hardt and Negri deploy this concept in order to name a field of collectivity which is composed of singularities: unique points of intersection and potential self-invention which cannot be subsumed into any simple totality nor reduced to the status of individuals. I am a singularity, you are a singularity: but this singularity has nothing to do with our individual nature: it is a function of the unique position that each of us occupies in an infinite network of relations, of our specific modes of *dividuality* (Deleuze & Guattari 1988: 341).

The term *multitude,* which tries to capture this sense of singularity/collectivity, is derived from early modern political philosophy. As already mentioned, the authors claim particular inspiration from the writings of Spinoza. In this they follow Deleuze, who once declared Spinoza the 'Christ of philosophers'(Deleuze & Guattari 1994: 60). Within the Deleuzian philosophical current, Spinoza's rationalist pantheism is understood as an implicit radical materialism which refuses any separation between different levels of being: 'body', 'mind', 'God' and 'world' are all placed on the same plane and understood to share the same basic substance. It is highly debatable as to whether Spinoza would have recognised his philosophy in such terms, but it is surely significant that he was excommunicated from the Jewish community of Amsterdam because his contemporaries certainly *did* see materialist atheism as the logical implication of his philosophy. In developing the concept of multitude—about which Spinoza really wrote nothing in any detail—Hardt and Negri remain committed to the conceptually egalitarian approach implied by Spinoza's assertion that all that exists is composed of a single substance, at the most fundamental level. On the other hand, Hardt and Negri's ideal definition of democracy as 'the rule of everyone by everyone' really stretches the credibility of their claim to be followers of Spinoza: Spinoza was very clear that the multitude who should have power in a democracy did not include such irrational elements as criminals, children or women (Spinoza 1958; 2000: 441–5).

Nonetheless, it is this substantive ideal of democracy as 'rule of everyone by everyone' that sets Hardt and Negri apart from other post-structuralist, post-Marxist political philosophers. As we have seen, Laclau and Mouffe tend to stress the relationality and partiality of all social identities, and their dependence on the shifting web of relationships in which all identities are caught up and which always leaves them perpetually unstable[6]. By contrast Hardt and Negri, along with other members of the Italian Autonomist tradition to which Negri belongs (Wright 2002), stress the creative power of groups and individuals to constitute their own collective identities and material realities, of which they see true democracy as the ultimate expression. Now, while the strength of this vision is its sheer inspiring poetry, its weakness is its failure to consider the relational, negotiable nature of political identities, which leaves Hardt and Negri unable to say anything meaningful about the problem of formulating political *strategies* and specific coalitions in the new global context. Hardt and Negri's claims that Empire has no centre and that any attack on any part of it is consequently also an attack on its centre are very problematic: they imply, in effect, that there is no need to chose between, say, spending our time producing subvertisments (parodied or defaced advertisements with an anti-corporate message), engaging in national electoral politics or undertaking militant trade unionism because each are equally attacks on the overall system of power. This is great news for those anti-capitalists who don't want to have to worry about the fact that for the most part they have so far completely failed to persuade publics in the North of the need to actively resist neoliberalism, but it will not get us very far in terms of addressing that failure. Beyond shutting our eyes and wishing very hard, it's never clear how Hardt and Negri imagine that the prophetic character of their work is going to manifest itself in some new political reality.

Despite its problems, Hardt and Negri's work makes a major contribution to contemporary radical thought in the courage with which it seeks to 'name the enemy', as Amory Starr might put it (2000). Whether or not we agree that *Empire* is a useful name for the complex of social relations and institutions against which the movement of movements is ranged, the daring and imagination with which Hardt and Negri seek to move beyond the simplicity of simply identifying the corporations as the enemy (which is what Starr does in her landmark study) is clearly valuable. At the same time, in identifying the we who resists, or might resist, Empire or neoliberalism, as the multitude, they do a great service in recovering the powerful Marxist observation that it is the *irreducibly collective* creativity of humans and their machines which produces the world we inhabit. This is a hugely important observation for cultural studies: for one thing, it offers an interesting route through the old debate between cultural populists and their critics. From this perspective, populists are right to stress the potential agency of the multitude who produce popular culture even as they consume it. However, if a celebration of this popular creativity loses sight of its inherently collective dimension and becomes a mere celebration of individualised consumer sovereignty, then it has simply collapsed into complicity with neoliberal ideology. Along similar line, it is striking to note the affinities between the optimism, the faith in democracy and in the power of creativity, and even the implicit teleology of Hardt and Negri's approach, with the tone and argument of Williams's *The Long Revolution* (1961).

Turning to more recent work in cultural studies, Jason Toynbee's important concept of *social authorship* as the basis for musical creativity has strong affinities with Hardt and Negri's ideas (Toynbee 2000). We can develop this observation to suggest a clear demarcation between the complex networks of creativity by which the *multitude* of producers, musicians, consumers, bloggers, file-traders, and so forth bring global music culture into being, and the processes by which certain sections of *Empire*—record companies, large media outlets, commercial distributors—seek to impose norms of capitalist sovereignty on it, particularly through the courts which enforce intellectual property rights. However, as so often with Hardt and Negri, it is the very strength of their terminology—it's bold, polemical way of dividing the world into two clearly demarcated antagonists—which is also its greatest potential weakness. The question which really emerges if we try to compare Hardt and Negri's gestures of naming with other frames of reference, is whether these gestures do not go too far in simplifying the very complex and uneven terrain of contemporary capitalism and the antagonisms to which it gives rise.

We can see, then, that the strengths and weaknesses of Hardt and Negri's approach all pivot on our four key themes: power, creativity, complexity and hegemony. Its strength lies in its emphatic demonstration that power and creativity are inseparable, and in its investigation of the complexity of postmodern forms of sovereignty. It's danger lies in the possibility that it *reduces* the complexity of contemporary politics with its Manichean dualism, occluding any understanding of the mechanics of hegemony which keep Empire in place in multifarious locations. It might even be, from Deleuze and Guattari's perspective, that Hardt and Negri's emphasis on creativity leads them to fail to theorise adequately that dimension of power which is manifested in the capacity of repressive institutions to stratify, codify, block and constrict, for which one name is antiproduction. Empire seems to be a form of capital which is entirely parasitic upon the rhizomatic multitude but which does not any longer avail itself of those powers of stratification and territorialisation which secure hegemony in given contexts: this may be one tendency of current capitalism, but it is not at all clear that it is the only one.

Nonetheless, Hardt and Negri's work remains a tremendous resource: a diagrammatic map of current systems of power, if not an exhaustive enumeration. Even those elements which I have identified as problematic are defensible as strategic gestures. It is true that the global scene today presents us with a complex field of interrelated, overlapping and disconnected antagonisms. But it is also true that any movement, or any analytical perspective, that wants to plot a trajectory away from the hegemony of neoliberalism must find ways to identify the *common antagonism* which so many disparate struggles and demands share today. That which stands in the way of so many democratic demands, that which blocks so many lines of possible becoming today, deserves a name: and Empire is as good a name for it as any. And what better name do we have for the possibility that this common antagonism might be realisable in political projects for global democratisation, than

> the multitude that, as Spinoza says, through reason and passions, in the complex interplay of historical forces, creates a freedom that he calls absolute: throughout history humans have refused authority and command, expressed the irreducible difference of singularity, and sought freedom in innumerable revolts and revolutions. This freedom is not given by nature, of course; it comes about only by constantly overcoming obstacles and limits. Just as humans are born with no faculties written in their flesh, so too there are no final ends or teleological goals written in history. Human faculties and historical teleologies exist only because they are the result of human passions, reason and struggle. The faculty for freedom and the propensity to refuse authority, one might say, have become

the most healthy and the most noble human instincts, the real signs of eternity. Perhaps rather than eternity we should say more precisely that multitude acts always in the present, a perpetual present. The first multitude is ontological and we could not conceive our social being without it. The other is the historical multitude or, really, the not-yet multitude. This multitude has never existed. We have been tracking ... the emergence of the cultural, legal, economic and political conditions that make the multitude possible today. This second multitude is political; and it will require a political project to bring it into being on the basis of these emerging conditions. These two multitudes, however, although conceptually distinct, are not really separable. If the multitude were not already latent and implicit in our social being, we could not even imagine it as a political project; and similarly, we can only hope to realise it today because it already exists as a real potential. The multitude, then, when we put these two together, has a strange, double temporality: always-already and non-yet.

(Hardt & Negri 2004: 222–3)

In this passage, Hardt and Negri's evocation of the multitude as a *potential* evokes Deleuze's understanding of the virtual as the field of infinite potential, of relations without fixed terms, from which the actual is crystallised (Massumi 2002). And it also echoes obliquely some famous remarks of Jacque Derrida's[7].

Even beyond the regulating idea in its classic form, the idea, if that is still what it is, of democracy to come, its "idea" as event of a pledged injunction that orders one to summon the very thing that will never present itself in the form of full presence, is the opening of the gap between an infinite promise (always untenable at least for the reason that it calls for the infinite respect of the singularity *and* infinite alterity of the other as much as for the respect of the countable, calculable, subjectal equality between anonymous singularities) and the determined, necessary, but also necessarily inadequate forms of what has to be measured against this promise. To this extent, the effectivity or actuality of the democratic promise, like that of the communist promise, will always keep within it, and it must do, this absolutely undetermined messianic hope at its heart, this eschatological relation to the to-come of an event *and* of a singularity, of an alterity that cannot be anticipated.

(Derrida 1994: 65)

In Derrida's later work, the promise of democracy 'to come', the possibility of justice and the potential for new forms of collectivity inherent in all social relations was an important theme, animating his invocation of a 'new international' with which to confront neoliberal hegemony. In many ways, it seems that Hardt and Negri's multitude is a further elaboration of this concept.

What all of these, admittedly very abstract, ideas allude to is one fact. Neoliberal capitalism may appear, at present, to be unshakeably hegemonic across much of the globe, but the desire for forms of collective and singular forms of life which it cannot tolerate has not gone away. Wherever that desire can be heard or felt or witnessed, there is the potential for positive change. If cultural studies can do anything with these ideas, and with the various conceptual tools delineated in this chapter, then it will be to identify both the points at which such potential might be actualised, and the real obstacles to its actualisation in specific contexts. This is not something that one book, or one whole life's work could do alone. But it is something that the next chapter will in part attempt, at least for the contemporary British context.

Notes

1. The terms 'rhizomatics' is posited by Deleuze and Guattari as equivalent to 'schizoanalysis', which is the term I have stayed with for most of this chapter (Deleuze & Guattari 1988: 22).
2. In fact, Gibson argues with great intelligence that the idea of power as infusing all social relations has often been assumed or rehearsed in the field, without being conceptually interrogated: in other words, cultural studies has a lot to say about power, without ever putting the concept of power itself into question. Unfortunately, there is not the space or the opportunity here to engage with Gibson's argument: I merely signal its salience to the reader before repeating the very gesture which Gibson criticises.
3. We don't have space here to get into the distinction between 'relative' and 'absolute' deterritorialisation in Deleuze and Guattari, unfortunately.
4. A final point to make with regard to Laclau and Mouffe's philosophical position is that they make an acute and complex defence of their own commitment to philosophical materialism (Laclau 1990: 105-12), which critics such as Jonathan Joseph (2002) simply fail to engage with at all: we don't have space to take up this debate here, but put very briefly, Laclau and Mouffe would argue that a properly materialist perspective is not simply a question of believing that things really exist outside of discourse—which they do not dispute—but of recognising that the structure of material reality is not that of logical concepts (which is the assumption they attribute to pre-Marxist idealism).
5. In Guattari's terms, this means that psychoanalysis cannot think 'transversality', although 'transversality' should probably not be equated directly with horizontality as such (Guattari 1972: 72-85; 2000: 106-59).
6. This is in itself closely related to Derrida's concept of *différance,* the undecidable condition of im/possibility haunting the trace-network which is the infrastructure of all phenomena.
7. Not by chance, I think, because Derrida's spectral différance, a field of infinite relationality, neither fully here nor elsewhere at any given point, is perhaps very close to Deleuze's 'virtual'.

–6–

Mapping the Territory: Prospects for Resistance in the Neoliberal Conjuncture

What are the prospects for an anti-capitalist politics today, and how can a cultural studies analysis enable us to address this question in a positive way? In this chapter, we will address this question with particular, but not exclusive, attention to the British experience. In the process, we will hopefully get a sense of which of the conceptual tools available to us in the realm of contemporary cultural theory are of significant use in understanding the dynamics of current power.

The Abstract Machine of Neoliberalism

The first thing to say on this issue is that the possibilities for any *explicit* and systemic challenge to capitalism in the United Kingdom or elsewhere outside of Latin America, are virtually non-existent at the present time. Since the end of the cold war, no systematic challenge to capitalism so conceived has emerged. In fact, the anti-capitalist movement, for better or for worse, has been defined by its very lack of a common vision or coherent programme to implement a different set of socio-economic relationships. In Britain in particular, despite the successful popularisation of some radical ecological themes, these have yet to translate into any kind of substantial critique of capitalism or the forms of behaviour which sustain it: even those relatively militant sections of the ecology movement which are trying to oppose the expansion of aviation in the United Kingdom largely frame their arguments in terms of the polluting potential of particular technologies (in particular aircraft), rather than of the incessant drive to capital accumulation (see, for example www.planestupid.com).

This situation occurs within the context of the wider success of neoliberalism as capital's key strategy since the collapse of Fordism in the early 1970s. In the so-called developed world today, there is virtually no real political opposition to neoliberalism, but only a range of ways of manifesting, implementing and accommodating to it. Outside of the West and North of the planet, it is radical conservatism which offers the only substantial challenge to the culture of liberal capitalism. There are exceptions, as we have seen, particularly in Latin America; but conditions there are so different that it is difficult to see what Northern anti-capitalists could learn from the Latin experience. Although some radicals in Western Europe may look to

Hugo Chavez as a model of what a socialist government might still do, the conditions obtaining in Venezuela are unlikely to be replicated here: very valuable reserves of natural resources, a majority of the population suffering relative poverty and a high level of social and cultural homogeneity existing amongst that population, making mobilisation of that population against US capital relatively easy. The situation in no Northern country is ever likely to resemble this one again.

While there are various local reasons why this should be the case, there are also key shared factors shaping the political milieu in almost all of the so-called advanced capitalist countries today. To understand these factors, it is necessary to consider the historical moment which is widely accepted as, one way or another, marking the beginning of the present era: the collapse of the weakly social-democratic consensus which had informed Western politics in the decades following World War II. The post-war settlement combined industrial capitalism with a strong welfare state, full employment and a relatively stable and conformist culture: especially in the domestic sphere, where the norms of the nuclear family were rigidly enforced. This was the cultural-political complex which Gramsci had first seen emerging in the 1930s and to which he had given the resonant name Fordism. For Gramsci, this new form of capitalism was typified by the Ford motor company, with its assembly lines, its relatively high wages and its moralistic paternalism (Gramsci 1971: 279–318).

Fordism constituted the technical, cultural and economic context for the great social compromise of post-war period, whereby the governments of the capitalist powers undertook unprecedented reforms, involving themselves in the management of the industrial economy, maintaining full-employment, which in turn kept the price of labour relatively high, greatly empowering workers and their organisational representatives, the trade unions. Governments of every political hue pursued a broadly social democratic agenda during this period, diverting tax revenues from corporations and the wealthy to fund the new institutions of the welfare state and contributing to a general increase in social mobility and social equality. In return, the labour movement was expected to remain disciplined and moderate, ultimately supporting America and its allies in the cold war with Soviet communism.

Like any assemblage, this 'historic compromise' (Gramsci 1971: 168) was never fully stable, and there were always tensions and resistances from without and within; including the communists who always claimed that the achievements of social democracy would be short-lived without a world revolution, the beatnik refusers of Fordist conformity, or the right-wing economists who bemoaned the fate of entrepreneurial man in the era of the welfare state (Hayek 1944). During the period lasting roughly from the mid 1960s to the mid 1970s, the entire arrangement of forces and compromises unravelled. Militant challenges to the Fordist settlement came from a number of directions: from women who were tired of having all of their desires and potential trapped in the bottle of the nuclear family, housewife being the only social role available to them as adults; from youth, bored by the monotonous conformism of industrial culture; from workers, impatient with gradual reforms handed down by patrician bureaucrats and strongly desirous of greater autonomy at work; and from those populations—in particular the colonised of Africa and their once-enslaved descendants in the West—who were still deprived of full access to the means of political participation and self-determination. These challenges amounted to a set of demands which Fordist capital simply could not meet while remaining profitable[1].

At the same time, competition with Japanese and West German firms began to threaten the profits of American and British capital (Brenner 2005). However, the methods by which such firms were able to establish themselves would soon be available to their rivals too, and this as much as anything has subsequently transformed the material landscape of global politics. The emergence of electronic, digital, robotic and cybernetic technologies has made it possible for a new technical regime to emerge, within which it is possible for capital to evade many of the mechanisms created by governments and organised labour to contain and codify it during the middle decades of the last century. Global computer networks now enable corporations to shift their locations regularly in search of ever-cheaper labour, without any real cost to the ongoing operations of the company. Intensifying competition between firms in this new technical context led, in the 1970s, to the emergence of a new productive paradigm—a new post-Fordist 'regime of accumulation' (Harvey 1989: 121–2), dependent upon rapid, flexible responses to fluctuations in demand and therefore demanding ever-greater levels of flexibility and specialisation on the part of corporations. All kinds of consequences have ensued, including the disaggregation of large firms into networks of specialised providers occupying ever-shifting sets of complex relationships with each other, and the consequent imposition of short-term contract work on huge sections of the workforce (Sennett 2006).

This is the context which made possible the staged implementation of the full neoliberal project, beginning with a military coup in Chile. Latin America—the United States's 'back yard'—has often been the site of the most direct confrontations between US-led post-Fordist capitalism and its enemies, and perhaps the most notable historical example dates from the moment of the early 1970s. The US-backed coup of 1973 against Chile's socialist president, Salvador Allende, led not just to the military dictatorship of Augustus Pinochet, but also to his implementation of the world's first neoliberal economic programme, directly overseen by students of Milton Friedman (Harvey 2005). The enforced privatisation of large sections of the economy, the implementation of so-called free-market industrial policies and the ruthless attacks on organised labour all presaged the kind of policy regime which Washington would soon be trying to impose on countries all over the world. Now, as much as we may detest such policies and their forced implementation, it is worth noting that the relative economic success of this project—achieved only at the cost of massive social inequality and a long-terms suspension of Chilean democracy—was in stark contrast to the economic and cultural stagnation which overtook the Soviet bloc during the same period. Having crushed attempts at liberalisation and democratisation in Eastern Europe in the 1950s and 1960s, the Soviet command economy could not adopt systems analogous to those which constituted the post-Fordist regime of accumulation. While the USSR's last communist leader—Mikhail Gorbachev—seems to have well understood that some such programme would be necessary to save the communist project, his reforms came far too late. Sclerotic state socialism simply could not compete with post-Fordist capitalism in terms of the sheer volume, scale and range of production, not could it offer any alternative sources of inspiration for a population whose desires were increasingly pulled in the direction of Western consumerism. The resultant collapse of soviet communism in 1989 removed the greatest single obstacle to the power of US-led capital; the largest and most highly organised territory outside of the world market was smashed open in the early 1990s; and a potential source of military or economic support was lost to anti-neoliberal governments the world over. The consequence has been to leave a world in which the neoliberal project meets with only partial and localised resistance at any point.

At this point it is worth asking ourselves just what kind of an entity we think neoliberalism is. Neoliberalism is an excellent example of the type of phenomenon which political and cultural theorists struggle to name with absolute clarity, precisely because it functions across a number of spheres. On one level neoliberalism is simply a discourse or 'discursive formation' (Foucault 1972: 38)—an organised set of statements about human nature, economics and politics—which insists upon the desirability of market relations as the paradigmatic form of human interaction in almost all imaginable social contexts. Almost all commentators would agree that this is a discourse which is in some sense *ideological,* insofar as its implication is to fully legitimate an existing set of social relations, neutralising most prominent critiques thereof, thereby legitimating the power of ruling elites while occluding the historical contingency of existing social relations. However, these accounts tell us relatively little about the actual social *effects* of neoliberalism, which could be both a discourse and an ideology without having any success at actually re-modelling reality in its own terms. It is only when conceived as a political *programme* enacted in accordance with its core ideological assumptions that we can get a sense of neoliberalism's varying impacts. Nowhere in the world has neoliberalism been implemented in some absolutely pure form. Indeed, it's not entirely clear what it would look like if it was: presumably the kind of stateless anarcho-capitalist utopia dreamed-of by Murray Rothbard (2003), or the kind of society imagined by Schumpeter (1954), in which democracy is an occasional and largely ceremonial affair, actual governance remaining in the hands of a technocratic elite. If neoliberalism is a programme, it is not clear that it is one with any absolute objective.

Perhaps the most succinctly sophisticated account of neoliberalism is that offered by John Clarke. Clarke makes an important case 'for treating neo-liberalism as a hegemonic project (rather than a singular ideology)' (2004: 89). In other words, as Clarke goes on to show, neoliberalism deploys a complex range of tactics in various discursive and individual contexts in order to try to define social reality and political possibility entirely in its own terms. In fact, all of the most lucid commentators on this subject (Harvey 1989, 2005; Grossberg 2005; Giroux 2004) make use of a Gramscian frame of reference in order to explain the operation of this project. To put this matter very simply: how far neoliberalism can go, and what it can actually achieve, will vary dramatically according to the balance of forces and the available resources in specific political contexts. For example, in the United Kingdom, where organised labour completely failed to cope, organisationally or intellectually, with the shift to post-Fordism, while very strong traditions of liberal individualism and social conservatism created a hospitable climate for New Right thinking, neoliberalism has succeeded in almost entirely shaping the political agenda since the 1970s. In France, by contrast—just a few miles away from the United Kingdom—a very different social and political history has produced a context in which successive attempts by successive governments to implement a fully neoliberal programme have been met with resistance, anger and reluctance, eventually producing a general sense of national malaise (the country unable to accept neoliberalism or fully to resist it) leading up to the election of conservative president Nicolas Sarkozy.

In fact none of these descriptions of neoliberalism are mutually exclusive. Neoliberalism is clearly, on one level, a hegemonic project, asserting and reinforcing the hegemony of finance capital after a period when the latter was relatively subordinate to the alliance of industrial capital with industrial labour which defined the Fordist settlement. As David Harvey puts it, in classically Marxist terms, neoliberalism's aim is the re-assertion of class power by the most ruthless sections of the bourgeois class: ultimately, the goal of almost all neoliberal policies is to lower the price of labour, increase the rate of profit, and remove obstacles to the exploitation of workers. However, there are lots of ways in which this might be achieved: the specific hegemonic project of neoliberalism is only one such, and so it is necessary to consider its detailed features in order properly to understand it. In discursive and institutional terms, the mode of operation of this hegemonic project is to re-shape social relations according to market logics (Leys 2001). Crucially, this leads to a situation in which the project involves and is supported by various social groups with a direct interest in the realisation of its aims but not strictly sharing the class interests of finance capital: thus, management consultants and marketing specialists find themselves with particularly privileged roles to play in neoliberal culture, even though they do not enjoy anything like the wealth and authority of, say, private equity fund managers or merchant bankers. These are the groups particularly animated by what Boltanski and Chiapello call 'the new spirit of capitalism' (2005) but it crucial to note that the force of this new spirit is such that it sweeps up many in its wake: schoolteachers, students, criminals, artists, waitresses and surgeons are all enabled to feel powerful and free precisely to the extent that they adopt the creative, expressive, individualistic, competitive, manically networking mode of existence typical of those hegemonic fractions. Furthermore, there is clearly an ideological dimension to neoliberalism's programme, insofar as it will tend to promote a singular ideology—competitive individualism—as explicitly as it can under given political circumstances.

The most important dimension of this account, however, is clearly that which stresses neoliberalism as a hegemonic project. From this point of view, neoliberalism is a *strategy* for the coordination of different elements—ideological, institutional, material and social—in the pursuit of its objectives. Now, where this strategy is successful, it is so precisely by virtue both of what it makes possible and of which possibilities it closes off, what it destroys and what it creates. For example, British universities have recently seen a protracted struggle over the attempt to create a true market in higher education. This was clearly one of the objectives behind the raising of student tuition fees in 2003. However, universities have to date largely subverted this aim by simply refusing to set differential fees, instead charging the same fee for all courses at all institutions. University administrators, teaching staff and students have all protested these 'reforms' partly on the grounds that, if successful, they would make possible a market in higher education only by making impossible a truly collaborative relationship between staff and students. It seems unlikely that, given the low levels of political organisation amongst all of these groups, the long-term neoliberal objective will be thwarted, but to date the outcome of the attempt has been complex, uneven and partial: not a true win for either side. At the time of writing, both students and academics are aware of pressure to transform higher education into a marketable commodity, but as yet a true market in higher education courses has not emerged. The attempt to close off and render impossible the experience of education as a collaborative pursuit of a public good and to make possible its full commodification has not yet wholly succeeded.

Considering the hegemonic project of neoliberalism as uneven in its effects, defined by what it makes possible and what it closes off, brings our account of this hegemonic project close to another potential term with which to understand neoliberalism. Using a term of Deleuze and Guattari's, we might describe *neoliberalism* as a name for the 'abstract machine' of post-Fordist capitalism. An abstract machine is a functional diagram of the forces animating a concrete assemblage. Conceiving neoliberalism as an abstract machine allows us to avoid any charge of ignoring the unevenness and relative failures of the various policies and programmes which are generally grouped together under that name, perhaps even better than does conceiving it as a hegemonic project. Neoliberalism does not manifest itself everywhere in the same way, or anywhere in it absolutely pure form. Nonetheless, it has a discernible identity precisely by virtue of the similarity of the operations which it attempts across a range of spheres which offer varying degrees of resistance to its 'cutting edges'. The diagram of neoliberalism is easily sketched, delineated as it is by the will to generate lines of flight which are lines for capital and only for capital: all other routes are blocked, all other becomings delegitimated; mobility is only permitted precisely to the extent that the object, subject or agent in question (e.g. the student, education) can take on the form of capital or the commodity. Again, it is not a matter of choosing between terms here as much as recognising their different emphases and uses. (From this perspective, incidentally, we might say that every successful hegemonic project produces the abstract machine of an actual assemblage, although not every abstract machine is effectuated in the form of a hegemonic project.)

Deploying these two terms in tandem has the advantage of emphasising a number of interrelated aspects of neoliberalism and post-Fordism. On the one hand, the idea of the *hegemonic project* emphasises the extent to which political, cultural, social and economic changes do not just happen by accident: even though their outcomes are unpredictable and their contexts contingent, things like neoliberalism happen in part because someone, somewhere wants them to. On the other hand, emphasising both the *abstract* and *machinic* dimensions of neoliberalism importantly draws our attention to the ways in which neoliberalism works very much with the grain of capitalism's most abstract logics. Although capitalism should not be equated with commodity-exchange per se, there is no doubt that the creation of new markets and the transformation of raw materials, services, ideas and people into tradable commodities has been fundamental to all processes of capital accumulation. This is why, according to Deleuze and Guattari, capitalism is defined by the *generalised decoding of flows* (1983: 224): or, to make a more precise translation from the French, a generalised decoding of *fluxes* (1972: 265). Unregulated and unopposed, the drive to accumulation through commodification will destabilise all fixed forms, be they the natural forms of the material world (which must be re-shaped in manifold ways before they can become commodified) or the forms of life of settled communities, traditional or modern. In Laclau's terms, we can therefore say that capitalism tends towards the dislocation of all structures (1990: 41–5). More precisely, we might say that capitalism amplifies, intensifies and deploys the dislocatory potential—the dimension of immanent instability[2]—inherent in any structural situation: any form of social life, however apparently fixed and changeless, will find itself disrupted and destabilised by the deterritorialising power of capital, revealing its ultimately irreducible contingency. In fact this is very close to Schumpeter's famous account that described capitalism as a process of 'creative destruction' (1954).

Now, this is to some extent only an abstract tendency of capitalism. If left unchecked, its logical consequence is to destabilise all existing social relations, including those relations of power which guarantee the hegemony of powerful groups. There is nothing to ensure that today's successful firm will not be overtaken tomorrow by some new technological innovation, that the children of its chief executives will not next week find themselves penniless and without powerful connections. There is no certainty that the lifestyles of industrial workers will not be transformed by new working practices or by the complete disappearance of their industries. The comfortable residents of a suburb may find themselves forced to compete or collaborate with immigrant workers to whom the suburbanites used to consider themselves inherently superior. The very ecosystem which sustains life in a region or across a whole planet might be disrupted beyond repair by the rapacious exploitation of irreplaceable resources. As such, capital, and the many social groups and institutions which enter into relationships of various kinds with it, must create varying types of institutional, political and technological arrangement in order to try to stabilise the field of social relations, maximising profits, enabling capital accumulation to go on without its very conditions of possibility being completely undermined.

One of the most influential ways of understanding the resultant system was the idea of the 'regime of accumulation', proposed by the regulation school economists (but others would argue that this formulation over-emphasises the extent to which capital accumulation must be seen as the basis for the entire formation). A potential problem with this concept is that it downplays the full interdependence of the social, political and economic elements of a social formation (Laclau 1990). From a post-Marxist perspective—informed by Laclau and Mouffe, Deleuze and Guattari, or all four—we would have to insist on the importance of the desiring investments, identifications and counter-identifications of the various agencies involved. For example, it would be impossible to understand the ways in which British capitalism has evolved in relation to its key macro-institutional context—the European Union—without understanding the economically irrational attachment of British conservatives to the national currency; residue, relic and magical symbol of Britain's long-lost pre-eminence in the mercantile universe. Bearing this in mind, we might best understand contemporary post-Fordist capitalism as a complex set of overlapping concretes assemblages—contingent arrangements of forces—with neo-liberalism as their abstract machine, always working to pull everything in the direction of the frictionless market, even if that means pulling down whatever edifice is temporarily housing it. Much that we today think of as traditional—the nuclear family, the job-for-life, the suburban neighbourhood—is actually a product of the decades of Fordism, which created very stable conditions of capital accumulation but kept finance capital on a tight leash, restricting the range of forms of expression (compare the dazzling popular modernism of early cinema with the output of Hollywood under the Hayes code and the studio system). Neoliberalism has dislocated and destabilised the key sources of personal and social identity—family, national media, public institutions—which that earlier era consolidated, partly by entering into unstable alliances with the desires of many for new modes of becoming (feminists, hippies, jazz musicians, bloggers, etc.), while attempting to restrict all of those new modes to new types of commodifiable identity.

Neoliberalism: Concrete Assemblage

So at certain levels of abstraction and operation we may conceptualise neoliberalism as both abstract machine and hegemonic project. However, this will be an empty conceptualisation unless we attend to the specifics of its instantiation in particular contexts, so it is worth reflecting now on the specifics of how the neoliberal machine-project is implemented and actualised in Britain today. At the time of writing, the mood in the country is one of considerable anxiety, as fears rise that a very long period of economic prosperity—effectively unbroken since the recession of the early 1990s—might be coming to an end. The banking crises which have already shaken US confidence have been replicated on a (so far) smaller scale with the run on the Northern Rock bank provoked by the revelation that it was heavily exposed in the US sub-prime mortgage lending market. More significantly, a small fall in overall property prices is provoking fears that the substantial slide in property values witnessed in the United States over the past two years might also be replicated here.

The potential significance of this can hardly be overstated. While rates of home ownership in Britain have been steadily increasing since the Second World War, the Thatcher government's policy of deliberately selling off social housing stock to tenants at well below market values had the effect of vastly increasing the proportion of middle-income earners with property. This was a brilliant strategic move which effectively recruited a large section of the working class—in particular the aspirational skilled workers who had been the traditional backbone of the labour movement—to the property-owning classes, at no cost to the elite, and at the same time isolated those poorest sections of the population still confined to social housing. By the mid-1990s, population growth, changing patterns of occupation (such as households shrinking in size as more and more people live alone) and the impact of regulations which restricted building of both social and private housing stock all combined to produce a chronic housing shortage. As a result, average property values in the United Kingdom have tripled since 1997. Low interest rates and a much freer financial regime than that typifying earlier decades have made it easy for the majority of adults who own their home to borrow against the increasing value of their properties or use various financial instruments to convert the rising market value of those properties into cash. The result has been an unprecedented orgy of consumer spending, further enabled by the low price of manufactured goods coming from China. At the same time, a series of crises have revealed the unreliability and instability of pension schemes heavily invested in the stock market. An ageing population, unable to rely on secure occupational pensions or generous state provision, has increasingly come to see property investment as its only guarantee of security. In short, both the immediate spending power and the perceived security of most Britons has become largely dependent on the market value of their homes.

This is a fascinating shift in the class dynamics of British society. The property boom has created a situation in which, if only temporarily, whole trenches of the population have earned more cash income from increased market value of their homes (in particular insofar as this is treated as security against cash borrowing) than they have from work. Technically, this arguably makes them capitalists, *at least as long as the situation obtains,* which it almost certainly cannot do indefinitely. Even for those citizens to whom this formulation would not apply, the fact of being property-owners, with their incomes and their future security tied closely to property values and interest rates, clearly alters the social position of these workers in a fundamental way. This, it is worth reflecting, is what hegemony means in practice: subaltern groups are not merely dominated or duped into consent to the existing social relations, but rather they are differentially included in the overall assemblage, in a manner which both significantly affects the real dynamics of power within it and materially affects the situations of all of its constituent elements.

Of course, access to the new consumer economy is largely through mechanisms of so-called cheap credit. The progressive dematerialisation of currency which characterises the whole history of capitalism reaches a new level here, as credit is extended to consumers on the basis of the rising market value of a non-productive asset, and their willingness to take advantage of that credit in order to facilitate consumption is widely seen as necessary to the health of the entire economy. This is a crucial point to understand, because whilst it seems to be more-or-less only this extension of buying-power which has so far persuaded large section of the population to acquiesce to the wider neoliberal and post-Fordist regime, many aspects of it are highly unpopular. At the same time, despite the widespread perception that the market is now effectively closed to new entrants—with first-time buyers priced out—and that this is a social problem in which government should intervene, it is by no means clear that any section of the political elite is prepared for the actual possible consequences of a decline in property values. I suggest that such consequences could be dramatic, simply because on most indicators, it seems that the British people, like most Europeans, are not very happy with the way in which their society is evolving. My contention, is that it is more or less *only* the feeling of prosperity created by the ten-year property boom and the levels of consumer spending which it has enabled which has so far secured the effective acquiescence of the British public to the neoliberal policy regime implemented by successive governments for the past thirty years.

What are the signs of this generic discontent? Social research routinely shows a general sense of pessimism and discontent with features of life such as 'work/life balance' (http://www.guardian.co.uk/politics/2007/apr/08/tonyblair.labour3). There is no question that overall average workloads have increased significantly in the past twenty years, yet no opinion poll has ever shown a generalised desire for more time at the office. In February 2007 a widely covered UNICEF report found the United Kingdom to have the unhappiest children in the wealthy world (with the United States not far behind), despite the country's relative affluence: an outcome generally attributed to the culture of long working hours for parents, highly competitive forms of individualism and consumerism prevailing in the culture of young people, and to high levels of social inequality (http://news.bbc.co.uk/1/hi/uk/6359363.stm). Shopping, it seems, is the only consolation for an otherwise depressed and discontented population.

What about those who are not able to participate in the massive increase in consumer spending which has characterised this period? It is worth noting that while overall inequality continues to rise in the United Kingdom, this is partly a function of the massive increase in wealth enjoyed by those with the most valuable resources. This is typical of a property bubble. The proportion of the population living in relative poverty has declined slowly but markedly since the shift from the ruthless anti-welfarism of the Thatcher years to the more careful and marginally more egalitarian programme of New Labour. New Labour has placed a high priority on bringing the unemployed into the labour market and has improved pay and conditions for those at the very bottom end of that market. However, it is striking to note that job growth has been almost entirely in sectors with weak traditions of unionisation and high proportions of short-term contract work (retail, low-grade IT services, etc.). The most striking fact about poverty in the United Kingdom is perhaps the very high proportion of the poor who are working women or single parents, on whom the burden of childcare and other family responsibilities still largely falls. At the same time young men from the poorest backgrounds are suffering disproportionately, with high levels of unemployment, high likelihood of involvement in crime, violence, and rocketing rates of young male suicide. As in the United States, these factors seem to affect young men from ethnic minorities to a disproportionate degree. What these various observations show is precisely the extent to which the socially excluded of contemporary Britain are precisely those groups least able to adapt to the conditions of the highly competitive, highly individualised labour market, in which long years of very disciplined and specialised training are required, and dependence upon community or social institutions is likely to leave participants at a grave disadvantage. Such groups are either largely excluded from the consumer economy, or are enabled to participate only by subjecting themselves to the long-term penury of unsustainable debt, or else they construct a consumer economy of their own. Consider the persistence of gangsta culture, which is today the most visible manifestation of the collaborative capacities of black youth (once considered the very standard of radical collectivity). What is this but an assemblage for the short-circuiting of radical desire? It glorifies a criminal economy, focussed on the drugs markets, which leads many of its more innovative and entrepreneurial participants to incarceration. It is infused with an ethic of conspicuous consumption and ruthless competition which simply mimics in extreme form the official labour market. It strives to ensure that for the first time in several generations, the common sense of black youth is not informed by a critique of capitalism and racism, but by an acquiescence to the expectations of a racist capitalist culture. Given the power of its disjunctive synthesis with the wider assemblage of neoliberalism, it is remarkable and noteworthy that so many young black men continue to refuse its dictates (c.f. Penn 2007: 163–6).

So we have a situation in which a certain degree of prosperity and personal satisfaction for a majority of the population accompanies a general dissatisfaction with the current possibilities for personal and collective life *outside* the channels of consumer culture, and the general exclusion of those who cannot participate at all on its terms. Insofar as the desire of the British can be channelled, configured and coded into the commodity-form, it is enabled to develop, proliferate and produce almost whatever it will. Desire which cannot be manifested in this way—desire for public life, for forms of personal experience which depend either on stable forms of collectivity (the experience of community, conviviality and solidarity with one's neighbours, for example) or on freedom from the regime of work (learning to paint without having to be a professional artist, taking a stroll by a canal on a weekday afternoon)—is curtailed, codified or denied. This is the reality of the neoliberal regime.

The lineaments of this regime first began to appear in the 1970s, as both conservative and labour administrations took reluctant and haphazard steps towards the deregulation of labour and financial markets along with curbs on taxation, public-spending and union power. In the 1980s Margaret Thatcher managed to popularise the key elements of this policy agenda by linking council house sales and tax cuts to a programme of socially conservative authoritarianism which promised to restore 'law and order' and curb immigration, articulating a socially authoritarian set of demands to a general desire for self-improvement which was codified in wholly individualist terms (Hall 1988: 1–92). However, with the decline of so-called traditional social values and the success of a liberal agenda on issues such as gay rights and abortion, this was no longer a viable strategy, and its continued dependence on it doomed the Conservative party to at least twelve years in opposition from 1997. Tony Blair's New Labour government, having flirted with rhetorical appeals to collectivism, egalitarianism and community, in fact went on to intensify the neoliberal programme, in particular pursuing an agenda to hollow out the public sector, handing over more and more of its functions to private agencies, while actively promoting a re-modelling of the relationships between services users and service providers to resemble more closely relationships between consumers and service retailers. This programme has gone along with a continued resistance to any efforts to regulate the labour market beyond the implementation of very minimal wage standards, with British workers enjoying some of the lowest levels of protection and security in the developed world. The consequence, as we have already noted, has been the emergence of a culture of very intense workloads supporting consumption-heavy lifestyles for the affluent and a continued struggle for survival for the less so. While economic inequality and social stratification have increased, various indicators of personal happiness have declined across the board, suggesting a population which is overworked, insecure and dissatisfied. There has been no enthusiasm for the direction of reform in the public services, or for the government's Atlanticist foreign policy.

So what sustains this regime? This is perhaps the key cultural studies question to ask of this situation. Conventional political sociology can tell us a good deal. For one thing, it can tell us that the British electoral system creates a situation whereby the views of affluent property-owners working in the private sector and living in the South of England, far away from the industrial areas where the labour movement was traditionally strongest, are today disproportionately important to the outcomes of national elections. Conventional political sociology also reveals the almost entirely unregulated press sector is dominated by right-wing tycoons with a heavy stake in the persistence of a low-tax, low-wage neoliberal regime. What it cannot tell us so well, however, is why these comparatively small sections of the population are *allowed* to set the political agenda so decisively. This is where a distinctively cultural analysis is required to answer the age-old question: what leads so many sections of a population like that of the United Kingdom to acquiesce to a political regime of which they are not the main beneficiaries? In other words, what persuades them to accept a subaltern position in the power dynamics of the country?

This is a complex question requiring a multidimensional answer, part of which we have already begun to outline. At the material and affective level, the shift to neoliberal post-Fordism has been accompanied by a real alteration in the position of large sections of the population. To put it simply, many workers have got a great deal of what they wanted from this arrangement: their own homes, cars, foreign holidays, cheap clothes, good food from around the world. These are all things which were beyond the reach of most British people in 1973 and are now a normal part of majority life. The project to channel all desire through the commodity-cutting machine has produced a vast range of often innovative and exciting new commodities to which many are genuinely and understandably attached: people love their cars, their games consoles and their wardrobes. While radicals may tend to see these as poor substitutes for bigger dreams of collective liberation, we would do well not to overlook the sheer attractive force of these pleasures. If the cultural populist tendency in cultural studies has a message it is this: underestimate at your peril the real affective power, the particular forms of corporeal affirmation and non-corporeal transformation (Massumi 1992: 28–9, 98) made possible by Levis jeans, Barbie dolls and Nintendo consoles. They brought down communism, after all.

Now, at the same time as these real gains are offered to large sections of the public, it is clear that they must also be persuaded that this is the best offer available to them, that other pleasures could only be achieved at the expense of these ones and would not compensate, that 'there is no alternative' to neoliberalism that would not be worse. To some extent this is the logically necessary function of any discourse which animates a hegemonic project. The necessity, normality and inevitability of a given course of action and the entire frame of reference which justifies it must be asserted, at times explicitly and at time implicitly. However, against crude simplifications of hegemony theory, we should emphasise that it will not always be necessary to convince the majority of a population of a particular view of the world in order to prosecute such a project successfully. Given a particular balance of forces, it may only be necessary to persuade a relatively small section fully, as long as there is no clear majority behind any coherent counter-project and as long as institutions can be re-shaped successfully in order to determine the limits of behaviour of key social actors. To put this latter point more simply: it doesn't really matter if you agree with the discourse of neoliberalism or not, as long as the people running your company, school or government agree with it and you are not part of an organised movement against it. In such a situation, you will find yourself forced to follow the rules of behaviour laid down for you—competing with colleagues, submitting to appraisals, signing short-term contracts—whether you want to or not (this an important dimension of the ways in which both Althusser and Foucault have conceived institutionalised forms of social power). This is why it has been so crucial for managers and communications experts to be wholly recruited by the new spirit of capitalism.

However, this new spirit, as Boltanski and Chiapello (2005) convincingly argue, did not only come about as a way to enforce the norms of neoliberalism. In fact, they show that it has in part emerged as a real *concession* to the militant attacks on managerialism and conformism which characterised the bohemian radicalism of the counter-culture. This is a crucial point to consider. Boltanski and Chiapello are concerned primarily with the ways in which the discourse of management-theory in the 1990s adopted many of the emphases and affective resonances of the radical discourse of 1968: although the authors confine themselves to French examples, this is a phenomenon which is easily observed in equivalent anglophone literature. The virtues of untrammelled creativity, autonomous self-organisation and horizontal organisation were championed in cutting-edge management theory some time before *hortizonality* and *networks* became buzzwords for the global justice movement. However, where some might see this as proof that such ideas, along, in fact with the rhizomatic thought of Deleuze and Guattari, are nothing but the obverse of contemporary capitalist ideology, Boltanski and Chiapello insist that it has been necessary for capitalism to adapt itself in some ways to the demands of those creative, energetic sections of the working population who were in the forefront of the events of 1968. This chimes somewhat with Toni Negri's parallel insistence that post-Fordism be understood as a necessary response on the part of capital to the organisation of militant workers and other group-subjects against the discipline and regulation of Fordism and its assembly lines, and it is a persuasive line of argument to anyone who thinks that anything at all has improved for working people in the West since the 1960s. This is a crucial issue for contemporary anti-capitalist thought and action to take on board: the challenge before us is to hold onto what remains of the social democratic legacy of Fordism, even to extend it, without giving up the libertarian gains of the post-Fordist era. It will not be easy.

That it will not be easy is clearly indicated by the fact that the main opposition to neoliberal culture today comes not from egalitarian radicals but from various forms of authoritarian collectivism. However, this itself is indicative of the relative success of the general project of social liberalisation which began with the so-called permissive era of the 1960s. Both legal frameworks and wider social attitudes since that time have evolved to constitute a very different cultural climate to that of the previous era. In 1978, Margaret Thatcher could speak on British television of her sympathy with those native Britons who 'feared they might be rather swamped by people with a different culture' and go on to win a general election. In 2004, the right-wing Conservative party leader Michael Howard sacked a member of parliament for making a racist joke at a private dinner. Today there are out gay Members of Parliament representing not just the parties of the left, but the Conservative party as well: this would have been unthinkable even at the beginning of the 1990s. This radical shift in attitudes has been replicated across most of Western Europe, but it is perhaps one of the most striking differences between Europe and the United States that moves towards such liberalisation in some quarters there has provoked an extreme conservative reaction in others. The reasons for this liberalisation are complex, but the sheer success of social liberalism as a political discourse, which has clearly become the hegemonic common sense of Western European culture, is at least in part due to its affective resonance with the materially individualising processes of neoliberalism's abstract machine. The capitalist tendency towards generalised decoding surely makes it relatively easy, at least for the prosperous, to accept the relativisation of values and the proliferation of lifestyles which characterise so-called postmodern culture: why fight this tendency in defence of a system of fixed norms and social values which would require a great deal of work and desiring-investment to maintain?

Following this line of reasoning, we can see that the neoliberal regime has itself intensified a number of ongoing changes to British culture. In particular, the mobilisation of complex and unpredictable flows of people which open labour markets demand continues to promote the 'cosmopolitanisation' (Beck 2006) of the culture. Rates of immigration have been at a historic high, suppressing the price of labour at the lower end of the social scale and maintaining the high demand for housing. This has provoked some anxiety amongst the settled population and sections of the conservative press, although how substantial this anxiety is is very hard to judge. There is little political support for the far right, and the Conservative party only began to recover from its historic slump in opinion polls once it began to distance itself from the anti-immigration, 'law'n'order' rhetoric of its disastrous 2005 general election campaign. There is little evidence of actual racism or crude xenophobia amongst the British public outside of some highly marginal poor white communities, and most public discourse on the largest group of recent immigrants—Poles—has focussed on the *benefits* that a new supply of cheap, skilled manual labour has brought to sections of the economy (as would be expected within a vigourously neoliberal context; e.g. Barton 2006). Yet opinion polls routinely show immigration to be a key object of public concern. One can conjecture here, with reference to a long and well-established literature (e.g. Hall et. al. 1978), that in such circumstances immigration, like crime, is a often a metonym for a very general, amorphous set of social changes over which publics perceive themselves to have no control, rather than designating any specific fear of nameable groups or eventualities. The rhetoric of anti-immigration today tends to focus less than it once did on the perceived dangers to the racial purity of the nation, or on the inevitability of conflict between distinct ethnic groups, and more on the issue of whether governments are adequately in control of their borders. Surely, then, this is what is really at issue here: governments are clearly *not* in control of their borders as they were in an age of regulated markets, industrial technology and relatively slow-moving information, and anti-immigration discourse

today seems to function more as an expression of displaced nostalgia for the lost capacity of national governments—and hence, by extension, the national communities
to whom they were accountable—to determine their own destinies.

This is the reality of globalisation as it is lived by most people in the British
context, and it is bound up intimately with the individualising tendencies of capitalism in general and neoliberalism in particular. Capital's deterritorialising, decoding
force tends to disaggregate communities and codify human experience in terms of
individuals, consumers and competitors (Massumi 1992: 136). Of course, this need
not lead to libertarian or even liberal political outcomes: one of the consequences
of a world where people are increasingly mobile and feel less directly connected to
each other than in the past is that the general *fear* of strangers can increase, leading
to authoritarian and even fascistic attempts to contain cultural difference, protect majorities from minorities and to police the borders and interstices of countries, cities
and cultures. There are some signs of such attitudes gathering strength in the United
Kingdom, and they have certainly animated both restrictions on immigration and the
British governments participation in the so-called war on terror, which has led to,
amongst other things, draconian curbs on the right of habeas corpus. More fundamentally, however, globalisation and individualisation have combined fundamentally
to weaken almost all forms of social power other than finance capital. Industry, organised labour, national and local governments, community groups, churches, public
media outlets, schools, universities, hospitals: almost all have found their general capacity to act diminish in comparison to the deterritorialised might of finance capital,
whose speculative mobility enables it to decide the fate of national currencies, whole
populations of workers, global media institutions, and so forth. The consequence
is a general retreat from politics as such, as collective action—institutional or
otherwise—seems unable to have any significant bearing upon material outcomes.

Perhaps the most striking symbol of contemporary responses was the public reaction to the invasion of Iraq in 2003. The largest national protest demonstration in
British history might have been expected to lead to a sustained and vigourous campaign against the most unpopular war in living memory, but the campaign that carried
on after the February march in London involved few new recruits to oppositional
politics. The population which was mobilised for the first time in significant numbers,
Moslem youth, was quickly contained by that traditional neutraliser of British radicalism, the Socialist Workers Party. In a manoeuvre which was absolutely typical of its
thirty-year history, the Socialist Workers Party set up a new political organisation—
the Respect Party—in alliance with various Moslem groups. Having recruited most
of the newly radicalised groups into the ranks of the new organisation, the Socialist
Workers Party proceeded to wreck it with their obdurate (but absolutely characteristic) refusal to cooperate with other constituent elements. The result: like peace campaigners in 2004, socialists looking for a an effective electoral strategy for the 2001
general election, and two generations of anti-racist campaigners before that, a whole
cohort of young militants found their first experience of politics to be thoroughly

enervating, dispiriting and disillusioning, thanks to the counter-revolutionary genius of the Socialist Workers Party's antipolitics machine. The wider consequence of the anti-war movement's failure—a result of Tony Blair's self-evident concern to maintain the Atlantic alliance irrespective of public opinion—was to further deepen the sense of general despair amongst a wide cross section of the public at the possibilities of political action. It is no surprise that the holding of the European Social Forum in London in 2005, dominated as the organisation was by the Socialist Workers Party, has produced no long-lasting effects. If anything, it marked the end of any visible anti-capitalist movement in the United Kingdom at all.

Resistance—Opposition—Escape

This, then, is the parlous situation in which the radical left finds itself Britain today. Almost devoid of the kinds of institutional framework and alternative media networks which sustain even the American left, there are very little grounds to believe that any kind of anti-capitalist intervention will achieve anything for a generation to come. In Laclau's terms, we could say that the current British political scene is almost entirely dominated by 'institutionalist' forms of politics (Laclau 2005) which do not admit the possibility of real, visible political antagonisms, but instead simply offer to administer the social sphere according to a technocratic logic of differentiation. No major political party, no significant dissident *within* any such party, no mainstream media outlet, no major NGO and only a muted few voices from the labour movement makes any kind of explicit critique of neoliberal policy assumptions. The nearest thing to a public voice for a critical position is the internal Labour party pressure group Compass, which argues for a moralistic social democratic position that would have been considered mainstream, even relatively conservative, in 1975. We might add that this torpor and this prevalence of institutionalist politics is typical of a political situation in which, broadly speaking, one project is fully hegemonic, the political space almost entirely territorialised by a singular machine. This does not mean that there is no scope for resistance, escape, invention and disaffiliation, but it does mean that until something changes—until some kind of radical dislocation occurs—then such scope will be severely restricted. So how can one respond to such a situation?

There are a number of possible responses. One is simply to wait it out. As I have already suggested, the current situation is in many ways unstable, in particular given its dependence upon an arguably unsustainable property boom. But if a crisis in the property market, or a rapid increase in the cost of Chinese-manufactured consumer goods, or an intolerable intensification of the effects of climate change, were to dislocate the situation, then various political projects other than neoliberalism would be presented with an opportunity to assert themselves. Unfortunately, there can be little doubt that, given such an eventuality, it is some kind of authoritarian conservatism that would be the most likely victor. In any situation of political crisis (radical dislocation/deterritorialisation), various discourses compete to offer an account of the situation which can recruit enough of the population to win control of the political space (hegemonising/deterritorialising it). For example, the success of the Christian right in the United States in part must be understood as a consequence of evangelical Christianity's capacity to explain the various social changes which poor and middle-class rural whites were affected by in terms which were more appealing and no less convincing than any available alternative; offering an optimistic narrative which cast God-fearing Americans as the heroes of a simple struggle against evil. Up until the 1950s the American left might still have offered many of the rural poor a radical social explanation for their woes and fears, drawing on the history and vocabulary of agrarian populism, although evangelical Christianity and biblical literalism were already strong elements of vernacular culture at that time. With the final rout of the popular left in the 1950s, and in particular with the recruitment of leading evangelists to the cause of fanatical anti-communism, evangelical conservatism was simply left as the only explanatory narrative which differed at all from that originating with the urban elites; and the elite urban story simply told the rural citizenry that they were backwards and should learn to accept that modernisation meant liberalisation. This is a grossly simplified account (see Grossberg 2005 for a far more sophisticated one), but it should suffice to illustrate the fact that the conditions which enable a discourse such as evangelical conservatism to hegemonise a dislocated space are many and complex. They involve the possibilities for affective resonance between various subject-groups and various political assemblages, as well as the sheer strength of the physical resources available to the various competitors. In a post-neoliberal Britain, which discourses and affective assemblages would be the ones most likely to succeed in promoting and replicating themselves at the expense of their competitors? Surely the initial advantage would be with those variants of neo-conservatism which can resonate with the xenophobia (literally 'fear of strangers') which neoliberalism itself helps to generate, which are already inserted into the wider global assemblage of the US-led 'war on terror' and which would be widely supported by the conservative press. In such a case, the press and capital will almost always work in parallel to promote the success of an authoritarian and anti-democratic set of responses. At the same time, the materially produced reality of everyday life under neoliberalism generates an affective field which easily resonates with such responses, as it often compels its subjects to experience fear and isolation whether they want to or not. Under such circumstances, there can be little doubt that some form of conservatism would have the best chance of winning the struggle to hegemonise and territorialise the dislocated situation. If this is not to happen, then radical democrats and anti-capitalists will have to mobilise some other discourses, some alternative stories, which have greater affective pull for significant numbers of people than do those of authoritarian conservatism.

Of course, from one point of view, this might not matter at all. If we abjure any notion of a society as a totality, then can't we hope simply to evade capture by the capitalist or state machines, plotting our own lines of flight and becoming, living minoritarian in the margins and interstices of whatever assemblages we encounter? Well ... no. For it is precisely the fact that society does not amount to a coherent totality with a clear centre that makes it impossible to think in terms of margins. As Hardt and Negri point out, Empire has no outside (2000: xiv): but that also means that it has no perimeter. The abstract machine of neoliberalism cannot be simply evaded, because its cutting edges are not simplistically located in time or space, instead constituting a set of modes for the actualisation of specific potentials under specific circumstances, which will not allow for any such tactic of evasion. It can only be submitted-to or contested, although the nature of its contestation will always be local and specific to a situation. To put this another way: you can run and hide, in your commune, squat, art gallery, laboratory or university department, but neoliberalism will find you soon enough. If you don't want to be deterritorialised and recodified by it, then you had better start looking for allies with which to form a 'war-machine' against it (Deleuze & Guattari 1988: 351–423). From this perspective, then, the task will always be to try to identify points of potential convergence between the radical desire to break down all concentrations of power, in particular those manifested in the freedom and authority of corporations and financial institutions, and the more immediate desires, hopes and fears of those who do not spontaneously identify themselves with any radical political project.

There are at least two ways to conceptualise the analytical task which such a strategy demands. One, derived from Laclau's framework, is to think in terms of the need to identify potential points of antagonism between currently hegemonic projects and widely shared sets of popular aspiration and assumption. In other words, to ask the question, where in contemporary culture do we find hopes, fears and beliefs which can be brought into direct confrontation with the implicit assumptions of neoliberalism? How could they be articulated into a common front with radical ideas and movements, avoiding their articulation to conservative and authoritarian alternatives? How could contemporary desires and discontents be connected and translated into a coherent set of *democratic demands* (Laclau 2005: 125–8) which would present a positive alternative to neoliberalism? Now, there is a very important point to make here. From Laclau and Mouffe's perspective, *all* identities (political, social, cultural, physical) are constitutively relational: they depend upon the network of terms within which the given identity is just one position. Any alteration in this network of terms, this set of relations, will therefore alter the identity of every component, however marginally. This applies to the hegemonic components just as much as any others. So any alliance or coalition between different social groups, projects, individuals or ideas will partially alter the identity of all those involved, including the so-called leading elements. In short: those who want to organise counter-hegemonies must be prepared to lose their own identities in the process.

Another way to conceptualise this issue is in terms of Deleuze and Guattari's logic of *becoming*. Keep in mind that Deleuze and Guattari work from the assumption that everything that exists is always in a state of relative flux, that everything (people, nations, political organisations, buildings, oxygen, water, stars, cells) is only ever in a condition of relative stasis, and that understanding anything is in part a matter of understanding the precise level of stability of it and its various aggregate parts, relative to all the others and to their own current, past and potential-future states. They deploy the concept of *becoming* to denote a space of transition/undecidability between potential states. When two terms, groups or individuals enter into some kind of relation, from this point of view, an interference-pattern is set up between them which marks the real emergence of something new, something not defined solely by either term or by some predictable approximation or average of the two. So for Deleuze and Guattari, the question of how terms relate to each other is always also the question of what it means to move from one state to another:

A point is always a point of origin. But a line of becoming has neither beginning nor end, departure nor arrival, origin nor destination; to speak of the absence of an origin, to make the absence of an origin the origin, is a bad play on words. A line of becoming has only a middle. The middle is not an average; it is fast motion, it is the absolute speed of movement. A becoming is always in the middle; one can only get it by the middle. A becoming is neither one nor two, nor the relation of the two; it is the in-between, the border or line of flight or descent running perpendicular to both. If becoming is a block (a line-block), it is because it constitutes a zone of proximity and indiscernibility, a no-man's land, a non-localizable relation sweeping up the two distant or contiguous points, carrying one into the proximity of the other—and the border-proximity is indifferent to both contiguity and to distance. The line or block of becoming that unites the wasp and the orchid produces a shared deterritorialisation: of the wasp, in that it becomes a liberated piece of the orchid's reproductive system, but also of the orchid, in that it becomes the object of an orgasm in the wasp, also liberated from its own reproduction. (Deleuze & Guattari 1988: 293)

Famously, they undertake a consideration of these issues by imagining what it might mean to undertake the sorcerous enterprise of trying to become a dog:

An example: Do not imitate a dog, but make your organism enter into composition with *something else* in such a way that the particles emitted from the aggregate thus composed will be canine as a function of the relation of movement and rest, or of molecular proximity, into which they enter. (Deleuze & Guattari 1988: 274)

Brian Massumi offers an excellent and highly relevant reflection on this idea:

It rarely happens that becoming-other pivots on a single body. Most becoming-others are initiated by preexisting populations who develop a collective sensitivity to the molar constraints applied to them and join to counter-actualize them. Becoming can only proliferate with carefully formulated group strategies (whether the group is yet to come or is already here—and it is preferably both). Becoming-other is thoroughly political. The social movements of Blacks, aboriginals, feminists, gays and lesbians—of groups relegated to sub-Standard conditions—provide far better frames of reference than Standard Man alone. (Massumi 1992: 102–3)

What does all this abstraction mean for us? In effect, it means the following: any counter-hegemonic politics, which seeks ultimately to displace the hegemony of neoliberalism, must try to plot vectors of potential becoming which do not merely subsume one set of identities or demands into another. What must be sought are both affective resonances and potential points of symbolic and discursive articulation between existing groups, sentiments, ideas and discourses, but also processes of exploration and invention which might allow unpredictable new becomings to emerge. The question then, of course, is where might we find the resources with which to actualise such a project?

Resource of Hope: Political Ecology

Well, it is worth considering what successes radical politics has had in the past decade or so[3]. Since the early 1990s, arguably the only issues on which forces to the left of New Labour have achieved anything at all have been a series of ecological campaigns, the most notable success being the campaign against the production and marketing of genetically modified food in the first years of this decade. The most visible, and temporarily successful, manifestation of a coherent, original radical project was Reclaim the Streets's brief period of high-profile activism and widespread public sympathy in the mid 1990s (see Chapter 3). Now, these are important examples, because they point to a deep and not altogether surprising vein of popular sentiment in the United Kingdom, particularly in England, organised around a sentimental attachment to the pastoral ideal of the country as a green and pleasant land. Historically, of course, this is an almost entirely artificial artefact (Boyne 1993). The United Kingdom was the first country in the world to go through the industrial revolution, to see a majority of its population living in towns and cities, and to achieve the kinds of population density typical of urban modernity. The cliché of pastoral England was largely invented in the 1890s and 1900s and was always a politically polyvalent construction. Partly, it was part of the broader mobilisation of a conservative imperialist imaginary, portraying the English to themselves as a nation of rural quietists, against the threat of socialist radicalisation spreading from the industrial centres of Manchester, Sheffield and Leeds. Up until this time, the English had seen themselves, and been widely seen abroad, as in the vanguard of industrial, scientific, liberal modernity (Perkin 1969). So it was partly the need to win support for the project of the British Empire, which by this time was diverting a good portion of the national resources and manpower, and to stave off the threat posed by the new wave of trade-union militancy centred on the organisation of dock-workers, that led to the mobilisation of this stereotypical idea of Englishness. On the other hand, socialist romantics such as Ruskin and Morris were equally instrumental in articulating this structure of feeling, as an imagined pre-modern idyll became the standard against which the deprivations of modern urban life could be judged and found wanting.

This was, in Foucault's terms, a classic struggle over power-knowledge: those with the capacity to do so used newspapers, music-halls, popular and classical music, sentimental literature, public events and various national occasions to articulate competing definitions of normative 'Englishness' which were quiet different from that which had prevailed earlier and which necessarily shared certain key traits. These discourses worked to create what Laclau and Mouffe call 'chains of equivalence' between the idea of Englishness and an ideal of rurality, but they differed precisely as to whether they included social deference, bucolic conservatism and abject imperialism in this chain, or whether they instead linked English pastoralism to a romantic and utopian ideal of a society free of exploitation, with ideals of craft, beauty and naturalness at its heart. These discourses competed not just through what they said and depicted, but through the affects that they mobilised and the way that they organised bodies in space, and it was on this level that the conservative version won out. Sentimentality, self-righteousness and a romantic attachment to the understated southern English landscape were all present in older elements of English culture, going back to the early middle ages, but it was the power of this discourse/machine to assemble them and to discipline bodies to make them resonate with its particular harmony—through the new public rituals centred on the monarchy, the jingoism of the music hall and organisations such as the Boy Scouts and related reforms in the military and in education—which made it so successful, preparing the British working classes to be slaughtered en masse in the Great War that would soon follow.

As Foucault has argued, however, even conservative discourses can be reappropriated and mobilised against regimes of power under the right circumstances, and it seems that where a sentimental, conservationist aesthetic can be articulated to a militant project, it can also sometimes succeed in mobilising the British in unexpected ways. It is worth reflecting that the most popular work of fiction in the English language, by a very long way, is J.R.R. Tolkien's fantasy epic *The Lord of the Rings*. Taking into account the phenomenal sales of theses books along with the success of the recent film adaptations, one clearly has to see this as the kind of phenomenon that cultural studies must try to explain and to learn from. Anyone who takes the time to study these texts will find a curious phenomenon. Tolkien's tales of aristocratic intransigence and feudal loyalty in the face of undifferentiated evil are set in a mythical world which is more-or-less precisely what Northern Europe would have looked like if all technological and social change had simply stopped around 1100. One noticeable aspect of Tolkien's fantasy is the extraordinary longevity of the political and dynastic formations which compose Middle Earth. Blood lines and city states last not for decades or centuries but for centuries or millennia. The nature of the fantasy is clear: imagine if the very first glimmerings of modernity has never been seen in the mercantile cities of Italy, if instead, the technical and social forms of the early middle ages had simply remained more-or-less static ever since, what would the world be like? It would be like Tolkien's Middle Earth. Of course, his is a world peopled with elves, dwarves, goblins and wizards, but that is much how people in eleventh-century Northern Europe seem to have imagined their own universe. At the affective and experiential level, to live in Middle Earth is to live in England or Denmark some time *immediately* before the appearance of the *very first* signs of modernity-to-come, safe in the knowledge that it never will. The critic Patrick Curry has actually argued for *The Lord of the Rings* as an ecological fable, to be welcomed as largely progressive in an age when green thinking is the most radical form of opposition to remorseless post-industrial capitalism (1997). Certainly it is possible to read this into much of the imagery and language of the story (in particular when a race of sentient trees destroy the fortress-factory-barracks of the evil wizard Saruman). But it is also possible to read more sinister implications into the fact that the story is peopled with dark-skinned and 'swarthy' multitudes who are always harbingers of evil: the mute humans from the hated 'South' and sub-human, pseudo-proletarian 'Orcs' leave little room for positive interpretation. No wonder that the book was condemned by Michael Moorcock as implicitly fascist (1978) and is popular with members of the extreme Right. However, it is also popular with hippies and radical greens like Curry. The lesson would seem to be that this sentimental scepticism towards modernity in general, which tends to take on a conservationist and ecological hue, is a very powerful element of English culture, but that it can be articulated to, or territorialised and activated by, progressive or reactionary forces, depending on the circumstances and the outcomes of particular struggles. The question then is how to go about trying to set up such possibilities for the future, actualising the radical potential in English conservationism and counter-actualising its potential to translate into narrow-minded defensiveness.

The implication of this analysis is that the basic intuition of Reclaim the Streets—that the key to promoting an English anti-capitalism lay in articulating it to ecological conservatism, and to a critique of the logic of privatisation which the car culture embodies—remains a brilliant one. The project of Reclaim the Streets was precisely to create a discursive and affective link between resistance to the destruction of ancient woodlands, the explicitly social and public pleasures of carnival, critique of the wider logic of social privatisation, the desire for alternatives to the commodification and competition embodied in the individualised culture of 'automobility' (Featherstone, Thrift & Urry 2005), and a general critique of neoliberal capitalism as such. Perhaps the only mistake that Reclaim the Streets made was to move too fast, much too fast, on a line of flight that took it away from the counter-molarity that it was in the process of gathering against neoliberal hegemony. Perhaps if its rhizomatic network of localised, molecular connections to other sites—to campaigns against the privatisation of local services, for example—had been given time to grow denser, more fruitful, more dynamic, then it could have imparted some of this speed to a wider field of forces, creating a much more effective 'war machine' against its enemies. This would have involved what Gramsci calls a 'war of position' (1971): precisely, a rhizomatic extension of resistant conjunctive and disjunctive syntheses (Massumi 1992: 47–57), rather than a sudden rush for victory. But instead Reclaim the Streets limited its efforts to the attempt to detonate a spontaneous overflow of desire. This never works, precisely because, as Deleuze and Guattari themselves insist, desire is *always assembled.* Anti-capitalists need rhizomes, but they need them in the form of relatively rhizomatic *assemblages*—that is, networks of institutions—not just empty flows of utopian urgency.

In a purely speculative vein, we might suggest that the impending ecological crisis is the material factor most likely to render neoliberalism unsustainable in the long term. Unfortunately, there is no guarantee, nor even any great likelihood, that a post-neoliberal response to the crisis will produce a more desirable regime than the current one. The obvious solution to a situation of radical social *and* ecological dislocation might well be an authoritarian, centralising, militaristic extension of state power without any renewal of democratic control over/within/beyond/against state institutions. This is one reason why libertarians who are sceptical of the value of democracy and its 'majoritarian' politics (Deleuze & Guattari 1994: 108) should nonetheless wish to ally themselves to the project to extend, renew and proliferate forms of democratic engagement: the alternative will not be freedom-from-belonging, but domination at the hands of an eco-totalitarian state. From this point of view, the ongoing project to articulate English ecological sentiment with radically democratic politics will be an urgent task. Curry's Tolkien-as-eco-warrior reading-machine and Reclaim the Streets's simultaneous invocation of a public, a democracy, a people and a planet *to come* (Derrida 1994) might yet have much to teach us here.

Resource of Hope—The Cosmopolitan Vision

The attentive reader might have noticed the quiet sidestep from discussing the *British* situation to discussing the *English* one in the preceding pages. This is not an issue which we have time to dwell on in any detail, but it is worth reflecting on the multi-national nature of Britain and its political implications. In recent years, an ambivalent nationalism has made itself felt in the two main Celtic components of the United Kingdom: Wales and Scotland. In fact the Scottish Nationalist Party has recently taken control of Scotland's national parliament for the first time. I call this nationalism 'ambivalent' because, while commentators such as Tom Nairn have long predicted the eventual 'break-up of Britain' (1977), there is relatively little support for full national independence in Scotland and virtually none in Wales. Rather, the trend has been to greater federal autonomy for these regions, while retaining the structures of the union firmly intact. This is good news for the Labour party, which would be finished as a political entity if either of those countries did leave the United Kingdom: Scotland and Wales have long been key centres of support for it. Interestingly, both the Welsh and Scottish nationalist parties advocate and pursue policies well to the left of New Labour, and the national identities of these countries are strongly marked by the sense that they are more egalitarian and collectivist in their outlooks, more forward-thinking in their commitments to democracy, ecology and social liberalism than the stodgy, self-centred, slow-witted English. While there are those who argue that an equivalent, positive English nationalism is the only way for the left to move forward on the postmodern terrain of particularist identity politics (Bragg 2007), this seems to me to be an utterly utopian proposition, which ignores the very deep entrenchment of individualist thinking in English culture (Macfarlane 1978) and the historical dependence of the British labour movement on its 'Celtic' components, including the Irish immigrants who helped to make the English labour movement in cities like Manchester in the early nineteenth century (Thompson 1963). There surely seems to be a better chance of articulating a radical Britishness by generating a resonant field between the positive poles of the new Celtic nationalisms, the democratic elements of English pastoralism and the striking vernacular cosmopolitanism which has become central to the self-image of London, the nation's ever-expanding capital, in recent years. These might yet become the coordinates of a new 'mattering map' of Britain, to borrow a phrase from Lawrence Grossberg (1992: 398): a 'structure of feeling' (Williams 1977) which can subtly redefine the affective and political priorities of twenty-first-century British identity in a way which allows us as much as possible of its potential for proliferating, molecular invention and becoming to express itself, without simply deterritorialising the country entirely, dissolving it into the flows of transatlantic finance capital (which is certainly one of Britain's possible fates within the foreseeable future).

The sources of and evidence for this vernacular cosmopolitanism are easy to see. Explicit racism is rarely encountered in contemporary London, and an extraordinary range of communities live and mingle in the city (Nava 2007). The idea that this is explicitly something to be proud of is a powerful element of public and popular discourse. The office of the mayor of London has sponsored on ongoing campaign—'One London' (http://www.london.gov.uk/onelondon/campaign/index.jsp)—celebrating the idea of London as a city characterised by the productive and peaceful coexistence of multiple ethnic communities, and in 2007 two comedians undertook a campaign 'to prove that London is the most cosmopolitan city in the world and therefore we think the best city in the world' (http://news.bbc.co.uk/2/hi/uk_news/england/london/6705871.stm). While Stuart Hall has rightly pointed out that deep inequalities and complex forms of geo-cultural segregation continue to characterise life in the capital—disappointingly for those who hoped that vernacular cosmopolitanism might mean take a more egalitarian form (Hall 2004)—it is not clear that this means that vernacular cosmopolitanism has not arrived at all (Gilroy 2004a). Cosmopolitanism and egalitarianism do not necessarily imply each other as virtues. *Cosmopolitanism* implies a tolerance of diversity, and there is nothing in such tolerance to guarantee that social inequalities should be an object of concern. Rather, articulating cosmopolitanism with egalitarianism might be a precise political task facing radical democrats today.

Indeed, this is surely the aim of a number of key writers on these topics of recent times. Jacques Derrida evokes the world's many traditions of *hospitality*—the welcome extended to the stranger—in order to think through what a cosmopolitan ethic might mean today. Invoking a Levinasian ethic of infinite responsibility to the Other, Derrida calls for an ethics of unlimited hospitality to the strangers who might arrive on our shores and on our streets (2001). In a similar vein, Paul Gilroy calls for a 'planetary humanism' as the political ethic for the twenty-first century (Gilroy 2004b). Hardt and Negri go further, if anything, positing the removal of all border controls affecting freedom of movement for people as one of the key demands of their imagined global radicalism, expressive of the multitude's freedom and will to democracy (2000: 396–400; 2004: 268–358). This is an interesting position, manifested in the activities of the No Borders Network (http://www.noborder.org/) whose constituent members and groups campaign for freedom of movement and for the rights of refugees of asylum-seekers everywhere.

One objection which might be made to these libertarian positions is that the mobility of migrants is rarely chosen and rarely benefits their new neighbours. To put matters very crudely, immigration to the United Kingdom has been encouraged in recent years as a way to keep the price of labour low and the demand for accommodation (and hence the price of property) high, not because of any ethical imperative to welcome the stranger: the UK government has never had any qualms about brutalising those potential refugees unlikely to contribute significantly to the workforce. While this benefits property-owners secure enough to feel unthreatened by new neighbours—happy to employ the services of cheap and competent builders, plumbers and cleaners from Eastern Europe—and social groups comfortable enough to enjoy the proliferating range of new cuisines that immigrant groups almost always make available (where I live in North-East London, one can purchase West African, South African, Jamaican, North Indian, Keralan, Kashmiri, Nepalese, Turkish, Greek, Algerian, Japanese, Cantonese, Thai, Malaysian, Szechuan, Polish, Jamaican, Pakistani, Bangladeshi, Italian, American and English food, within a few minutes walk of home: this is by no means atypical), it brings less tangible benefits to those established populations who must compete for low-paid work and affordable accommodation with the new arrivals. Access to high-quality public services, especially schooling, is notoriously poor for the residents of those areas most heavily populated by poor immigrants. This does not mean that I am about to argue for immigration controls, merely that those of us who oppose them must keep in mind the full complexity of the situation.

Now, as I have already indicated, the public response to this is ambivalent: a mixture of growing unease with the apparently unplanned and uncontrolled nature of cultural change and an increasing sense that classical racism is a residual sentiment, inappropriate to the twenty-first century. Anxiety around immigration does not necessarily translate into antipathy towards minority ethnic groups who are well-established as neighbours and co-citizens, but rather tends to focus on the shadowy threats posed by 'immigration' (never 'immigrants'), 'asylum-seekers' and 'terrorism'. But I do not make these remarks in order to justify anti-immigration policies or rhetoric in any way. Rather, I think that the situation demonstrates the inadequacy of any simple appeal to cosmopolitan virtues of cultural tolerance if an authoritarian xenophobia is not to be allowed to flourish. Cosmopolitan virtues can easily articulate to a liberal individualism which quickly becomes defensive once strangers are perceived to be a threat rather than a resource for one's material prosperity. An egalitarian ethic of hospitality, a general recognition of the global right to mobility, can only be promoted on the basis of what we might call an ethic of *solidarity* which extends beyond the immediately known community. But cosmopolitan solidarity might not best be thought of as an *ethic* so much as an *aesthetic*. It's potential resources are to be found not in abstract notions of justice and responsibility but in the visceral *pleasures* which 'cosmopolitanisation' makes possible, from eating to dancing to lovemaking. That the British visibly do take such pleasure, as demonstrated by the continued vibrancy of Britain's contribution to the sonic culture of the 'Black Atlantic' (Gilroy 1993), by the popularity of Indian food (a bigger industry than steel in the United Kingdom) and by the relatively high rates of ethnic intermarriage in the United Kingdom, is one potential resource for any attempt to plot radical democratic futures for the United Kingdom.

Resource of Hope—The Creativity of the Multitude

Of course, such pleasures do not have any simple meaning or effect. They can easily be codified by the logic of consumerism, made the basis for a comfortable lifestyle in which so-called exotic pleasures distract from the reality of exploitation, in particular in those parts of the world where most actual production now takes place. On the other hand, the growing interest in fair trade and ethical consumption indicates the extent to which even such codification can itself become a site of contested politicisation (Littler 2008). At the same time, this double-potential seems to be manifested across a range of emergent sites in contemporary culture. For example, any idea that the current scene is simply characterised by the breaking of social bonds and the prevalence of individualised anomie is problematised by a range of other developments. Most strikingly, the exponential growth in social-networking services and autonomous media-distribution sites (MySpace, Facebook, YouTube) might well seem to mark a new era of collective creativity and global networking, of voluntarily communities not bounded by locality or even identity. In fact, Boltanski and Chiapello argue that the 'new spirit of capitalism' is not simply *individualistic* in nature, but rather promotes an ideal of personhood which emphasises the value of being multiply connected to as many different points, people and projects as possible, as long as those projects have some chance of success. This 'connexionist' ideology demands not simply individuality, but a particular kind of flexibility and openness, as well as a certain ruthlessness: the successful networker has to know where and when to make and substantiate connections, as well as where and when to cut and run from connections that will only absorb precious time and attention without profit (Boltanski & Chiapello 2005: 459–66). Boltanski and Chiapello wrote their fascinating study before the rise of Facebook and MySpace, but certain features of the culture around these sites seem to bear out their hypothesis perfectly. One of the most obvious features of these sites is the extent to which users are encouraged to compete to list the most 'friends' on their profile pages. This is surely the ideology of connectivity at its most obvious: a neurotic obsession with the *quantity* of connections with almost no regard to their quality.

Actually, it would be too glib to draw this analogy without further qualification. The management literature which Boltanski and Chiapello base their arguments on clearly does advise its readers to judge the quality of their connections and to eliminate the poor quality ones, although in this case quality is a function of the efficiency and profitability of the projects which connection can generate rather than the substantial quality of the relationships themselves. At the same time, Boltanski and Chiapello are only two amongst a number of recent commentators (Castells 1996; Terranova 2004) to observe that the morphology of networks is critical to the operation of contemporary power relationships. In post-Fordist global capitalism, so the argument goes, power differentials are precisely a function of the relative density of networks. Those nodes in the global web of relationships which have the most links to others—powerful governments, corporations such as Microsoft, and so forth—are the points where the most power is concentrated. Perhaps we might bring all of these observations together to observe that in the network society, multiple links are an immediate resources advantage for any individual or institution, and the emphasis on friends in the world of MySpace and Facebook manifests an implicit understanding of this reality, but the effective activation of those links requires a degree of skill, discretion, flexibility and ruthlessness which is typical of the post-Fordist capitalist, but not necessarily typical of the MySpace user.

What this discussion brings to our attention is the problem inherent in any simplistic valorisation of rhizomes. It's clear enough that today, not just radical movements, or creative networks, organise themselves through dispersed, de-centred, horizontal networks. Today capital organises itself this way too. Perhaps, to some extent, it always did (Braudel 1984). So there can be no question of simply preferring rhizomes to trees. From any kind of political perspective, it is necessary to distinguish between different types of rhizome, different deployments of rhizomatic technique. In fact, this is much what Hardt and Negri have undertaken to do with their account of 'Empire' confronting 'Multitude'. From their viewpoint, Empire is always parasitic upon the creativity of multitude. To put this another way, the rhizomes which capital has to create in order to remain competitive are only ever reactive, negative, attempts to 'capture' (Deleuze & Guattari 1988: 424–73), commodify and regulate the complex, unpredictable, unmappable creativity of the rhizomes which workers, artists—everyone, in fact—are always in the process of generating. Following this line, we might see the social-network universe as both an embodiment of the potential for new, dynamic forms of culture in which production (of music, films, ideas, subjectivities, etc.) is always clearly social and always initially outside of the circuits of commodity fetishism, and a site of struggle between multitude and the forces that will seek to codify its desire, activating neoliberalism's abstract machine wherever possible.

In November 2007, Facebook launched a new 'viral' marketing system whereby advertisers could make use of the detailed information which the site holds about users and their activities in order to target advertising directly at individual users. Having established a global community of users, many of whom are now highly dependent upon the site for their social lives, Facebook intends to make use of this captive market, segmenting it, classifying it, codifying its components according to a logic of identity which is amenable to neoliberal capitalism's logic of relentless commodification. This draws our attention to a very interesting question about the possibilities for collectivity, community and sociality in the new networked world. For while this context may offer us the opportunity to develop friends, contacts and allies all around the globe, it may at the same time encourage us *only* to make contact with those with whom we share some specific interest or belief. Consider the ancient ideal of the *cosmopolis,* the 'universal city' as a meeting point for all cultures and people's, promoting an attitude of worldly tolerance and urbanity (Donald 1996). Now, consider that this ideal is to some extent dependent on the assumption that the members of the city's multifarious communities will find themselves forced to share the space of the city. Some co-mingling, some substantial interaction would thereby be inevitable. What becomes possible in the world of the web—and perhaps also in a postmodern metropolis—is that this compulsion to share space is no longer in place: it can be escaped easily, and one is able simply to seek out those with whom one already feels a close affinity. Rather than a universal culture, the result might be a culture in which the particularistic logic of *identity* governs the entire field. We might see the emergence and dissemination of the most violent and paranoid forms of Islamic militancy in just these terms: the internet has allowed isolated individuals and communities to enter into a global community obsessed with the paranoid–suicidal defence of its own identity, cut off from all engagement with the diverse communities who make up the actual neighbourhoods that they inhabit. In such an instance, the network becomes a site at which becoming is shut down, or channelled along only the most murderous and futile line of flight: becoming-bomb. However, Hardt and Negri's gambit is to argue that such logics are really secondary to the virtual reality of Multitude, as are the logics of commodification, market-segmentation and individualisation. For Hardt and Negri the actualisation of Multitude's true potential would involve a certain becoming-universal of every singularity in the achievement of true democracy: 'the rule of everyone by everyone' (2004: 247).

Whether or not we think that this gambit is likely to succeed, we can see this conflict between rhizomatic creativity and imperial logic operating at other sites as well. Consider the enormous popularity of celebrity culture and reality TV. There can be little doubt that pop cultural histories of this decade will remember the rise of *Big Brother* and *American Idol* as emblematic of the times. The most obvious way to understand these phenomena is as dramatisations of the ideological norms of neoliberalism. The ideology of competitive individualism—the idea that the normal, desirable mode by which individuals relate to each other is as competitors rather than collaborators—is the core tenet of neoliberal discourse. The attempt to force all behaviour and all becoming to conform with this template is an axiomatic operation of the neoliberal machine. What is on offer for the victors of these game shows is nothing more or less than fame itself, or at least, a greatly enhanced opportunity to achieve 'celebrity' status. And what is a celebrity apart from the most individualised model of the successful networker? The celebrity is connected, is recognised, has privileged access to those who are even better connected; but unlike the ideal networker, they are fixed in the public eye, stereotyped, type-cast, locked in by the individualist logic of 'faciality' (Gilbert 2004c). However, there is another side to this story. Much of the public commentary on *Big Brother* in the United Kingdom dwells on the dubious ethics of the various stratagems which the producers of the show engage in in order to *generate* conflict and *intensify* competition between the house-mates. Often it seem that, left to their own devices the housemates would collaborate and cooperate throughout the run of the series (who wouldn't?). What is frequently evident, then, is how far the producers (those embodied representatives of the New Spirit of Capitalism) have to go in order to *impose* their model of the social as a spontaneous site of individualised, competitive conflict on an otherwise peaceful scene. Furthermore, surely a key reason for the popularity of shows like these is the opportunity they offer the audience to participate: to form opinions, to share opinions, to voice opinions, to engage in a democratic process which actually makes a difference to an outcome. Empire (Fox, Endemol, etc.) may keep working to over-code this desire, to articulate its terms to those of a purely neoliberal discourse, but the desire itself is a desire for democracy.

This then, might be another 'resource of hope' in contemporary culture. The desire for participation, for democracy, for collaboration and cooperation, for free exchange of ideas and expressions outside of the logic of the market, for connection and collective becoming: these are all part of what makes possible the popularity of social networking sites, even of *Big Brother.* Let's be clear what is being suggested here. There is no question of implying that Facebook and *Big Brother* are inherently democratic, or even potentially progressive. If anything, the opposite is true. My personal, instinctual responses to these phenomena are almost entirely negative, and the vacuity of celebrity culture and the reality shows at the heart of it depress me on a daily basis. I can't watch *Big Brother* and, in fact, I instinctively mistrust anyone who can. But it is also undeniable that their popularity indicates *in part* a certain desire for participation, for collective agency, which neoliberal culture renders increasingly unrealisable elsewhere. It is here, perhaps, that another glimmer of possible hope can be discerned.

The question which all of this leaves open is just how it might be possible for these positive potentialities to be actualised. What would have to happen for the conserving instincts, the taste for cosmopolitanism and the desire for participation of many sections of the British public to organise themselves into a radically democratic political alternative to neoliberalism? Well, a number of things would have to happen. Firstly, as has already been suggested, some kind of popular narrative would have to get into wider circulation, highlighting the connections between a drive for limitless capital accumulation and the various features of contemporary culture which worry people so much and which can be associated with it closely. It wouldn't be hard to connect anxieties about the failed socialisation of children (Grossberg 2005) with a critique of the culture of long working-hours and the competitive mentality celebrated by *Big Brother.* However, this is easy to say, and much harder to imagine actually happening on a popular level. Can we imagine, merely hypothetically, what might make possible such a development? Well, there is no point simply imagining what if scenarios here, but one thing is certain; such a politics could only emerge in conjunction with some mobilisation of the groups, institutions and individuals who still, in large numbers, remain attached to, invested in and organised by the history of social democracy and the labour movement. The trade unions, much of the public sector, much even of the Labour Party membership, clearly remain attached to the social democratic project to build institutions which can protect many areas of collective and personal life from the ravages of capital; from commodification and the forced imposition of market relations; from the demand for profit, competitiveness and efficiency at the expense of creativity, collaboration and experimentation. Indeed, it can well be argued that, as disorganised and uninspired as residual social democracy may be, there is simply no comparing its political significance in the United Kingdom to that of those utopian fragments who claim explicit allegiance to the global justice movement, anti-capitalism and the World Social Forum project. The latter simply have no current resonance with a wider public whatsoever. In 2007 the left-wing Labour member of parliament John McDonnell did actually stand for the leadership of the party under the explicitly anti-capitalist slogan 'Another World is Possible': despite a vigourous campaign, he ultimately failed to secure enough nominations from his fellow Members of Parliament even to appear on the ballot paper.

While the remnants of social democracy have no vision, and a very weak analysis of what has happened to them, the anti-capitalist movement has no base, but what it does have is a vision and an analysis of the current situation which is in many regards more realistic and more clear-sighted than that which informs much of the politics of residual social democracy. In the meantime, large sections of the British public, arguable a majority thereof, are expressly unhappy with most to all of the neoliberal agenda. If there were to be any moving on from this moment, then it would surely have to involve some reactivation of the forces of social democracy, but those forces could only be so activated if they could be persuaded to accept the extent to which the very success of neoliberalism has undermined their received assumptions. Let's expand upon this point briefly before going any further.

There is an implicit argument for the project of neoliberal governance advocated by the architects of New Labour, and the main advisors to Bill and Hilary Clinton (e.g. Penn 2007). The argument goes something like this: representative democracy, mass participatory politics and genuinely egalitarian social democracy are now historical artefacts. They belong, more-or-less exclusively, to the period of Fordist capitalism, which depended upon a higher level of social integration than any form of capitalism before or since. None of these institutions possesses the flexibility or dynamism to cope with the complexity of contemporary, postmodern societies or to withstand the pressure of globalising capitalism and its corrosive flows. In this context we must accept that the only effective form of democracy is the market. Hence, only the marketisation of public services can hope to make them subject to any form of effective democratic accountability. In this new context, government will inevitably fall to technocratic elites who, if they are benign, will use the most powerful consultation techniques available (namely, those by which corporations consult their customers: focus groups, market-research) to ensure that they give people more-or-less what they want, in so far as it in their power to do so. Beyond this, the most that government can do for its customer-citizens today is to equip them as best it can to survive in the harsh and competitive environment of the global labour-market. Old-fashioned ideas like holistic education or generous public pensions may exert a certain sentimental pull, but that only makes them all the more dangerous, as today they are untenable goals whose fruitless pursuit will only prevent us from adequately equipping our citizens to look after themselves in a world from which government cannot protect them. Students must follow degree programmes which make them attractive to employers. Citizens must save for their own futures, or perish. The private sector is the only possible source of investment in public services, given the impossibility of raising adequate funds through direct taxation. This is the core argument in favour of what Anthony Barnett has called 'corporate populism', and the basis of what Finlayson calls the 'Schumpeterian workfare regime' (Finlayson 2003).

The trouble with this argument is that it seems to be right. Nothing that has happened anywhere in the world since 1973 offers serious evidence with which to contradict it. As Colin Crouch argues in his book *Post-Democracy* (2004), we are now living in the era when voter turn-outs plummet as electorates, explicitly or implicitly, realise that democracy simply does not work any more. Governments do not merely pursue occasional unpopular policies: they pursue entire social agendas which their publics explicitly oppose. Even in Eastern Europe, where the euphoria of democratisation is still part of living memory, electoral participation rates are in free-fall. Taking all this into account, it now seems fair to say that effective representative democracy—which broadly forced governments to act in line with the express wishes of the electorate—was, like social democracy, a historical phenomenon specific to the moment of Fordist modernity. That era ended a generation ago. This is an analysis which is strikingly rigourous and consistent so far as it goes, but which can only retain its pessimism about the prospects for democracy only if it assumes that representative democracy on the twentieth-century model is the ultimate endpoint of the 'democratic revolution' (Lefort 1994). There is no logical reason at all to assume this.

So the argument of the global justice movement, particularly as manifested in the World Social Forum project, is that much of this analysis is correct. But the difference is that it proposes, as an alternative to the imposition of market relations on every sector of the social, a new wave of experiments in participatory democracy, a proliferation of new sites for democratic deliberation and for the invention of new forms of both representative and non-representative democracy. In this it is actually proposing nothing new. The New Left first made arguments along these lines at the very beginning of the 1960s. What the impasses of the current conjuncture suggest is that far from being relics of the utopian 1960s, such ideas are more relevant today than ever before. However, if those of us who share this view—and are inspired by it—are to have any chance of persuading our potential allies to feel likewise, then we are going to have to think carefully about how we go about doing that, about what kind of connections we can make with those who do not spontaneously share our feelings, our assumptions, or our identities. In short, contemporary anti-capitalists will have to consider much more than they are often inclined to do, the fundamental question of political *strategy*. This is the subject of the next chapter.

Notes

1. For a related analysis of the politics of social democracy and its challengers, in a more rigourously Deleuzo-Guetarrian vein, see Massumi (1992: 120-40).
2. The 'play', in Derrida's terminology.
3. I've lifted this phrase from Raymond Williams (1989).

Beyond the Activist Imaginary: Nomadic Strategies for the New Partisans

This book set out to initiate a kind of dialogue between cultural studies and contemporary anti-capitalism, and to the best of its ability this is what it has done. It could have stopped with the last chapter, perhaps. After all, that chapter tried to do what cultural studies has always done best, which is to offer an analysis of current power relationships which might prove useful to radical political forces. However, the title of this book is *Anticapitalism and Culture,* and while it has worked through the possible ramifications of this phrase from many different angles, there is one way of approaching it that has not yet been fully explored: to offer a critical consideration of the culture of anti-capitalism itself, both as it is and as it might be.

The Activist Imaginary

Partisans of the radical democratic, anti-capitalist left, residing in any part of the English-speaking world today (apart, arguably, from New Zealand), finds themselves in an awkward position. The enormous success of neoliberalism in the so-called Anglo-Saxon world has created a situation in which the likelihood of any serious political challenge to the prevailing order at home seems decidedly slim. While the painful dismantling of Western European social democracy still has far to go, and may yet meet with decisive resistance, publics in these countries have largely acquiesced to the neoliberal trade-off: an end to almost all forms of egalitarian or communitarian social provision and a return to very high workloads in return for historically unprecedented opportunities for personal consumption. In the United States and the United Kingdom particularly, this situation has obtained for long enough now that it is hard to imagine any event less cataclysmic than, say, the British experience of World War II provoking sufficient opposition to it to reverse the trend[1]. At the same time, the concomitant feelings of despondency on the left make little sense in a more global context. The palpable instability of American imperial hegemony and the emergence of new and dynamic forms of collectivist, democratic resistance to neoliberalism suggest that in the arena of world politics there is a great deal to play for, and much reason for cautious optimism on the part of democratic anti-capitalists. Those of us identifiable in such terms therefore find ourselves partisans of an emergent international political movement with relatively little chance of making a real impact on the domestic political scene.

This ambivalent situation can provoke a range of emotional, intellectual and political responses, but most typically leads to a recognisable set of reactions which are deeply problematic. Activist culture since the late 1990s has tended to take on a defensive or millenarian character which simply evades the difficulties which the historical circumstances engender. The particular way of conceiving political activity, those who engage in it, and their relationship to the wider culture they inhabit which emerges in the practices and literature of the movement constitutes what I will call here an 'activist imaginary': that is, a phantasmatic way of relating to the world typical of those who identify themselves primarily as activists. This is the basis for the ideology of those 'activismists' criticised so skilfully by Featherstone, Henwood and Parenti in their essay on 'Left Anti-Intellectualism and its Discontents' (2004). The assemblage which supports this imaginary, I would suggest, includes not only the writings and activities of self-styled activists but those of political theorists and philosophers organically or hypothetically connected to the movement of movements and to militant anti-capitalism of more classical varieties: writers such as Slavoj Žižek, Alain Badiou and, at times, Hardt and Negri. At the level of political discourse, this mentality is manifest in the valorisation by both Badiou (2003) and Hardt and Negri of the figure of 'the militant' (in other words, the ideal activist of the activist imaginary). As Nicholas Thoburn writes

> From feminist, countercultural, left communist, situationist perspective, the militant has been challenged as an ascetic model of political practice that forms through a fetishised mode of commitment to 'action'. It is a model immanent to the formation of what Camatte calls 'political rackets', where groups emerge in equivalence to political concepts and theories against those outside the group—those with a less 'militant' attitude—and are propelled by the motive force of commitment and action to ever-more self-certain and self-important activity. Rather than accelerate political change, militant forms tend to end up producing specialised roles, hostility to others, fears of models and struggles outside their own variety of political truth.

> (Thoburn 2003: 144)

Support for this analysis comes in part from a key piece of activist literature which has already, less than a decade after its initial publication, achieved the status of a minor classic. 'Give Up Activism', an essay published anonymously as one of the contributions to the 'Reflections on J18' document in 1999, warns against the adoption of what the authors term an 'activist mentality', arguing that radical activity should not be 'the affirmation of the separateness and distinctness of a particular group' and pointing out that the adoption of a sectional and sectarian identity by a political minority is a sure route to political inefficacy and irrelevance. Appearing less than a year before the publication of the movement's first key text—Naomi Klein's *No*

Logo—the essay was remarkable both for its prescience and for its completely atypical character as a piece of effective auto-critique. As the author of 'Give Up Activism' was later to point out (see http://www.eco-action.org/dod/no9/activism_postscript. htm), the publication in which it first appeared was full of routine denunciations of the destructive inequities of capitalism, rehearsing a perspective which was merely the starting point for that essay's reflexive considerations of the strategic limits of actually existing anti-capitalism at the time of its publication. As such, many of the articles in this document, which was supposed to constitute a set of reflections on the relative successes of the 18 June 1999 demonstrations against finance capital (the 'Carnival Against Capitalism'), simply restated the already shared presuppositions of all of its authors and all of its possible readership, without asking any serious questions about the political effectiveness of their consequent actions.

This criticism can be extended much more widely to the entire—now quite extensive—field of recent anti-capitalist literature. Since the publication of *No Logo* an entire publishing genre has emerged made up of books largely modelled on that work and largely undertaking similar tasks. The standard form which the literature of the movement takes is what we might call the anti-capitalist catalogue: a gazetteer surveying a disparate range of current organisations, movements and campaigns, with often no direct and very little indirect links between them beyond the imaginative assertions of their chroniclers that they do indeed add up to some kind of large-scale global movement (e.g. Klein 2000; 2002; Mertes 2003; Kingsnorth 2003; Notes from Nowhere 2003; Yuen, Katsiaficas & Burton 2004). Of course, the very act of writing about them as such might be understood as a performative act of political articulation, creating links and equivalences between otherwise disconnected strands of a potential movement. As we shall see below, however, some strands of political theory associated with the movement are positively hostile to any such interpretation of its politics. Leaving aside this theoretical debate for one moment, we can see that there is already an implicit resistance to such an understanding in these texts insofar as the question of *how* connections might be made between otherwise heterogeneous political actors, groups and traditions is in general conspicuously absent from them. Instead, it tends to be merely assumed that these phenomena already share a fundamental identity and that little more is needed for that common identity to be realised than for the general features of their struggles to be described. To be clear, I do not intend this as a criticism of these books in themselves. Works such as *We are Everywhere: The Irresistible Rise of Global Anticapitalism,* edited by the Notes from Nowhere collective (2003) and featuring contributions, reports and essays from a fabulous myriad of sources, from all over the world, form an invaluable resource. What's more, the editors of that exemplary volume, for one, conclude by quoting from 'Give up Activism' and commenting on the need for the movement to move beyond the stage of initial activist enthusiasm, much in the spirit of present work. It's in a spirit of solidarity with that gesture itself, and as part of the auto-critique of the movement, that I offer these reflections on the limitations of any merely descriptive account of disparate modes of hypothetically anti-capitalist activity.

The fact that such descriptions make no particular claims to objectivity, being almost entirely partisan celebrations of the mere existence of resistance in various quarters, does not alter the fact that all that is offered is straightforward description rather than any kind of strategic assessment of their relative potentials, weaknesses, strengths and problems. Importantly, this reliance on description shares key features with a longer-established mode of left discourse whose objects are different but whose political shortcomings are exactly the same. Perhaps the most notable and popular intellectual of the anglophone left in the world today (and for some time) is Noam Chomsky. There is no question that Chomsky is a great contributor to the field of linguistics, an innovative and effective publicist of major political issues (for example, the relationship between the US government and the repressive Israeli state in the 1980s: see Chomsky 1983) and a useful rallying point for a certain kind of left liberal sensibility in the United States. However, Chomsky's political writings and oratory function almost entirely in a declarative mode, listing and detailing the depredations wrought by American corporate power in collusion with the United States and other governments and supra-governmental bodies, without ever proposing possible political solutions to the basic problem that allows them to be wrought in the first place: the continued global hegemony of American capital. It might seem far-fetched to imply that Chomsky apparently believes that nothing more is required of effective political intervention than that the evils and iniquities of globalised capitalism be simply asserted and re-asserted as often as possible, but this certainly is an explicit belief held by some in the anti-capitalist movement. During their 2000 public appearance, sharing a platform at an event organised by the World Development Movement in London to launch its public campaign against GATS (General Agreement on Trade in Services—one of the series of multilateral treaties by which the World Trade Organisation has sought to outlaw the most basic forms of resistance to neo-liberalism—Naomi Klein and George Monbiot both responded to questions along the general lines of 'What is to be done?' in terms which were revealing, and troubling. Klein propounded what she termed the 'vampire theory': the idea that phenomena such as GATS, when exposed to the light of publicity, simply shrivel up and die. Monbiot likewise tends to imply (and sometimes assert) that *letting people know* about the extraordinary destructive effects of contemporary capitalism is the primary task of radical politics. The explicit discourse shared by both of these writers, and that implicit in their tendency to write detailed expositions of how bad things are, while paying little attention to the question of how they might be changed, amounts to a politics of *disclosure,* which assumes that informing an uninformed public about the evils of capitalism is the aim and end of political activity.

There are a number of issues to consider when reflecting upon the shortcomings of a politics of disclosure, all of which touch upon long-running debates on the nature and functioning of ideology in advanced societies. The 'vampire theory' rests on the crudest possible understanding of the relationship between power, information and knowledge, assuming as it does that hierarchies of power remain in place only so long as the majority are unaware of the facts. In this it makes two key assumptions. Firstly, it assumes a simplistic distinction between, on the one hand, knowing the truth and being able to act on that knowledge and, on the other hand, remaining acquiescent in passive ignorance. Secondly, it assumes that the acquiescence of the majority is conditional only upon their ignorance, which it also confidently assumes. It therefore makes no distinction between ideology and ignorance, and sits in the long philosophical tradition which has asserted since ancient times, despite all evidence to the contrary, that knowing the truth will automatically make the knower virtuous. These are all assumptions which any critical engagement with the issues at hand has to abandon.

The first of these assumptions that I want to take issue with is the most basically empirical: the assumption that people *en masse* do not act against the iniquities of liberal capitalism simply because they do not realise how bad it is. It is worth noting here that writers such as Monbiot, Klein and Chomsky are not, to their credit, just liberal journalists denouncing individual acts and policies carried out by corporations or governments. They invariably see such actions as symptomatic of an entire social system whose endemic barbarism they wish to expose. However, this observation draws attention to the fact that it is never simply ignorance of particular historical details which they seek to correct in their imagined audience, but ignorance of the entire system of social relationships in which they participate. It is such ignorance which they clearly assume in their readerships.

This is an assumption which was challenged some time ago by Abercrombie, Hill and Turner. In their book *The Dominant Ideology Thesis* (1980), the authors suggest that there is simply no need to postulate a 'dominant ideology' as effective in societies in which a highly differentiated and specialised division of labour leaves most people entirely dependent upon the existing set of economic relations for day-to-day subsistence, as a range of factors other than actual conscious concurrence with the belief-system of a ruling elite will prevent large numbers of people from engaging in sustained revolutionary activity most of the time (Abercrombie et al. 1980: 158–86). Put very simply: it is quite possible to be fully aware that one is, like most of one's fellow-citizens, a victim of exploitation by a minority, without being sufficiently motivated by the fact to try to do anything about it. The motivation to act is even weaker where the victim of direct injustice is another, or even, say, future generations. Importantly, material constraints on political action are likely to be strongest on the weakest members of society: if feeding one's children is a struggle, but nonetheless an achievable goal within the parameters of the prevailing social order, then one is likely to concentrate on it rather than on trying to change the parameters of social order. In more general terms, it might well be that very large numbers of the population of a country like the United Kingdom would not disagree with any of the basic beliefs of a Monbiot or a Michael Moore, and perhaps more importantly would not be surprised by anything he had to tell them even if they were not knowledgeable about the specific details of current neoliberal policy. In which case, supplying them with such details is, on its own, unlikely to change their outlook or behaviour.

Indeed—and this will bring me to my second key criticism of the politics of disclosure—it might have the opposite effect. What if the effect of simply providing endless quantities of evidence for the sheer awfulness of capitalism is ultimately to reinforce the feeling of those receiving it that capitalism is indeed, in many ways, awful, but that its continual and unabated awfulness simply demonstrates how un-alterable and unmovable it is, and thus how pointless it would be to act against it? What the politics of disclosure entirely fails to take account of is this: historically, people do not act against a given social order unless they believe that there is a good chance that it can be changed and that the likely benefit to them of changing it will outweigh the likely risks involved in the attempt. Simply telling people how bad the order is and why does nothing to convince them of this. To put this another way: the semantic effect of this discourse may be to build up evidence against capitalism, but its *affective* consequence may be to contribute to the stratification of those social re-lations which it criticises. To put this yet another way: revolutions only happen when the desire for revolution is strong enough, productive enough, wide enough. This discourse promotes fear, but it does not engender revolutionary desire.

There is still more to this. Recent theorisations of the political functioning of discourse have gone considerably beyond debates over the nature of ideology, domi-nant or otherwise. A number of theorists, most notably Judith Butler, have revis-ited J. L. Austin's concept of the performativity of language: that is, the capacity of language to act in the world rather than simply to describe it (Austin 1962). When combined with an approach which stresses the discursive-pragmatic constitution of social reality and the normalising function of discourse and power-knowledge (Fou-cault 1979), this perspective draws attention to the role that all discourse plays in normalising that which it describes. Incidentally, Butler's work on the 'performa-tivity' of gender-discourse has been widely and routinely misunderstood precisely because of a misunderstanding of the concept of performativity, which is often as-sumed to imply a voluntaristic conception of identity as a simple product of wil-ful self-creation (a 'performance'). This reading overlooks the normalising function which Butler attributes (following Foucault, Austin and Derrida) to the performative dimension of discourse, a function which is not limited to situations which involve, for example, the reinforcement of socially sanctioned gender roles. Sociolinguists have long pointed out the ways in which even the most minor elements of every-day discourse serve to reinforce the invisible norms of socially constituted reality (Berger & Luckmann 1966: 65–146).

Considered in this light, what is the performative function of a discourse which endlessly rehearses the gesture of discovering (as if for the first time) the true iniq-uities of capitalism? It may be—in those very few cases in which the audience is genuinely unaware not just that this particular government or corporation was guilty of this or that crime but that such things can possibly happen at all in a modern democracy—that the effect will be to shock the listener or reader out of their complacency. But if the audience in question already has any suspicion that modern democracies largely serve the interests of finance capital, then such disclosure is more likely to reinforce the existing views of the audience in relation to that situation while also reinforcing their suspicion that the speaker or writer, in their very outrage at this wholly unsurprising event, is a representative of a position and world view fundamentally more naïve, and hence probably less effectual, than their own. More fundamentally, simply to *describe* such a situation without doing anything to expose its historical contingency or its potential alterability (by suggesting what might done to change it), might be, in fact, rhetorically to reinforce the general assumption that such a state of affairs is normal and inevitable.

This, then, might be said to be the first key feature of the activist imaginary: its state of perpetual outrage and surprise at the exploitative and undemocratic character of capitalist society and its implicit assumption that the appropriate political response is to seek to engender this state in an audience it assumes to be naïvely ignorant of the facts. This outrage is a species of what Nietzsche calls *ressentiment*—the moralistic resentment of the weak—and it can never be the basis for the kind of joyous becoming-other which any democratic opposition to neoliberalism would require. This finds its culmination in the affective modes which activist discourse works to provoke in its audience: an anger and outrage which will be manifested in various forms of *protest*.

Now, this is, admittedly, a caricature which many activists would reject. We would surely have to distinguish between, say, the moralistic outrage of an anti-capitalist publication such as *New Internationalist* magazine and the wit of an activist-artist such as Reverend Billy of the Church of Stop-Shopping (whose invented persona mocks the didactic moralism of anti-consumerism even while it enacts it). Indeed, much of the language of the movement has tended to abjure the notion of protest against injustice in favour of an emphasis on direct action against forms of oppression. However, this latter concept has itself been expanded to the point where any clear distinction between direct action and symbolic protest has all but been erased. The conceptual and terminological slippage is worth unpacking here, as it reveals a great deal about the range of effects which derive from one of the activist imaginary's fundamental features: its constitutive blindness to questions of political *strategy*. As Featherstone and colleagues write, 'the real price of not thinking' amongst action-oriented activists 'is the reduction of strategy to mere tactics, to horrible effect' (2004: 310).

In Search of Strategy

We can get a sense of what is at stake in this blindness to questions of strategy by considering a slippage which seems to have occurred in the usage of certain terms within the anti-capitalist movement during the last twenty years.

One of the hallmarks of the so-called new oppositional politics which emerged in the United Kingdom in the 1990s was the extraordinary fetish that its participants made of the phrase *direct action*. Direct action was presented in the slogans and literature of the emergent movement as the antidote to the degraded banality of parliamentary politics and its self-evident failings, and in many sections of the so-called anti-capitalist movement this remains the case today. What direct action actually meant in almost all such cases was forms of highly theatrical and frequently destructive protest whose function was to draw media attention to particular issues of political concern. In the particular case of the anti-roads movement, the aim went further, insofar as at least some of the tactics of the radical ecologists were aimed at making road-building prohibitively expensive, by massively inflating the security costs for construction firms involved. However, only the most conservative section of the movement—that concerned with protecting ancient woodlands in what amounted to a politics of militant conservationism—actually deployed this kind of tactic with any regularity. Those sections concerned with wider social issues of urban planning, housing and economic inequality only ever resorted to forms of action which effectively had the status of, in the words of the political commentator and activist George Monbiot, 'political street theatre'. Even the great clashes with police at Prague, Genoa and Seattle were ultimately nothing more or less.

The conceptual and terminological elision which allowed all of these types of activism to go under the heading of direct action had a longer history, of course. The use of tactics aimed at making it physically impossible, or prohibitively expensive, for corporations to carry out certain kinds of environmental despoliation, has a long history in the environmental movement (Wall 1999). Similarly, certain strands of anarchist politics have always laid a stress on the importance of making sustained physical gains in the course of political struggle, as exemplified in the success of the squatting movement in some parts of Europe (although whether, after the apparent defeats inflicted on that movement in places such as the United Kingdom and Denmark, we can still refer to much of that as success, is not clear). When I was growing up near Liverpool in the 1980s, I was more impressed by the anarchists than by any other left group in the city because they put their energy into trying to organise social centres and support services for squatters as well as trying to provide certain kinds of social service for local pensioners, while the other left groups talked idly about proletarian revolution and the correct analysis of the Russian revolution. For that particular group of anarcho-syndicalists, direct-action meant low-key attempts to build alternative social infrastructures, not highly public acts of spectacular protest, for which they had nothing but contempt.

The contempt in which such activists have traditionally held the very concept of protest raises a number of interesting conceptual questions. What exactly is a protest? Or rather, what is implied, logically, in the very concept of a protest? On one level, any protest implies an appeal to a shared set of norms against which the injustice of some action or situation can be measured, or to a higher authority who can be called upon to adjudicate and to pronounce a verdict of injustice. If such an authority really does not exist, then there is little to be gained by appealing as if it did, and if those authorities that do exist—government, media, corporations—can be assumed to be hostile to the aims of the protestors, then what is the point of protesting to them?

This, of course, is the old revolutionary criticism of any kind of protest politics. In certain strands of anarchism, this has historically led to an emphasis on the value of direct action in the 'here and now' in order to solve social and political problems. Intriguingly, however, the concept of direct action which became central to the emergent anti-capitalist movement in the 1990s largely lost the critical edge which this perspective had given it in the past. The phrase *direct action* had in the past designated a range of activities which at their mildest were intended to make it impossible for corporations to carry out environmental destruction unnoticed and unhindered, and at their strongest were intended to constitute permanent gains for revolutionary forces (whether that meant merely the permanent occupation of unused buildings by autonomous collectives or the coordinated occupation of factories, railways and other key sites of production and distribution in a consciously pre-revolutionary manoeuvre). Over the course of the 1990s, the term came to be used to designate any form of public protest involving destruction of property or spectacular theatrics. Consequently, today many participants in the anti-capitalist movement confidently believe themselves to be engaging in direct action, which they construe as inherently more valuable than engaging in representative politics of any kind, despite the fact that their anarchist, communist or even militant Green forebears would have scoffed at this description at their activities and subjected it to the same critique to which they subjected other kinds of protest politics.

Of course, this does not mean that the critique of protest politics was itself unproblematic. For example, we might defend the idea of the protest by arguing that a protest made in the absence of any clear legitimate authority or set of shared norms can be understood as a conscious attempt performatively to *install* such a set of norms or imagined authority where one does not actually (and perhaps cannot really) exist[2]. However, a protest will only function effectively in this way if it is informed by some *strategic orientation* which takes account of the larger political context and the particular aims of a wider project to intervene in that context. But what does would it mean to have such strategic orientation in the present era? When political parties no longer function as the organisational mechanisms whereby a range of political activities can be coordinated into a coherent strategy, how can such organisation take place at all?

There is an argument that could be made today, and that some activists and theorists do make (although I've yet to find an example of anyone doing so convincingly in print), that strategy *as such* is simply a redundant concept in this age of micropolitics, molecular revolution and social invention. The recent revival of interest in the ideas of Gabriel Tarde led by Eric Alliez (2001; 2004) and Maurizio Lazaratto (2002), the implicit spontaneism of Hardt and Negri, and a particular current of thought which takes in a Guattarian/Deleuzian emphasis on the molecular dimension of political activity, converge with the culture and practice of much activist politics on a position which simply refuses any suggestion that the multiplicity of political tactics deployed by activists, artists and intellectuals should or could ever be disciplined by subordination to some overall strategic project. Ironically, this resistance mirrors the reluctance of many NGOs to engage in long-term strategic political campaigns rather than only lobbying for short-term technocratic reforms. This is entirely understandable in both cases. There is an obvious resistance amongst activists today to anything that looks like an attempt to revive the discredited practices of party politics, revolutionary or reformist, whilst NGOs do not wish to compromise their tactical efficiency and autonomy for the sake of making dangerous commitments to highly tenuous political campaigns. What's more, there is a widespread recognition that such strategic coordination is always constituted by hegemonic acts which create and stabilise power relations between different components of a group, organisation or movement. The emphasis on the value of multiplicity, minority and invention which shapes the rhetoric of most Deleuzian thought clearly tends to generate an allergy to anything like a strategic orientation, which it is easy to associate with the great transcendental ontologies of modernity which it wishes to escape from. Strategies, for this perspective, are things deployed by the state, the proto-state of the party machine, and the party-state assemblages of fascism and Stalinism. Nick Land sums up such a stance when he claims that 'Foucault delineates the contours of power as a strategy without a subject ... Its enemy is a tactics without a strategy, replacing the politico-territorial imagery of conquest and resistance with nomad-micromilitary sabotage and evasion, reinforcing intelligence' (2003).

Unlike Land, no serious political philosopher seems willing to defend such a position with any conviction. Deleuze and Guattari were quite explicit in refusing to advocate a simple politics of disaggregation, insisting that what they called the molar dimension of politics could never be avoided (1988: 276, 506, etc.). Negri has written explicitly of the need for the anti-capitalist movement to develop counter-hegemonic strategies in order to constitute 'counter-powers' to Empire. Similarly, the neo-Tardian position is not one which logically forecloses the possibility of strategic thought, and it is in fact Brian Massumi, Deleuze and Guattari's most important translator and expositor to the anglophone world, who has offered one of the most precise and useful definitions of the term *strategy* to date:

> "Strategies" is the best word for ways of becoming: they are less theories about becoming than pragmatic guidelines serving as landmarks to future movement. They have no value unless they are immanent to their "object": they must be verified by the collectivity concerned, in other words submitted to experimental evaluation and remapped as needed. (Massumi 1992: 103)

This account of 'strategies' gives us some important clues as to what any minimal definition of *strategy* might have to include: an emphasis on pragmatics—on the question of 'what is to be done'—and an orientation towards some at least partially determinant imagined future. At the same time, of course, Massumi reminds us that strategies must always be experimental and therefore provisional: that's the difference between strategy and dogma. But recognising this difference need not lead us to abandon the notion of strategy altogether. A rigourous Deleuzean like Massumi well understands that politics cannot be thought effectively without it.

However, there is at least one representative of a consistently and resolutely anti-strategic mode of thought on the contemporary philosophical scene. The French philosopher Alain Badiou, despite writing in French since the 1960s and being well-established as an academic and playwright in his native country, has only recently come to the widespread attention of anglophone readers. Badiou's is a notoriously abstract and difficult body of ideas in places, in particular because of his reliance on advanced mathematics (specifically, post-Cantorian set theory), to which he accords a special ontological status (Hallward 2003). We won't have space here to go into even the essentials of Badiou's philosophy in any detail, but we can at least consider some of its political implications. Broadly speaking, Badiou asserts a philosophical and political position which is in effect directly opposed to that which emerges from the work of thinkers such as Derrida and Laclau and which implicitly informs most cultural studies. In general terms, these writers tend to stress the impurity of philosophy as a discursive genre, and by extension to stress the interconnectedness of different modes of being and types of practice (politics, art, etc.) alongside the non-finality of any event, conclusion or process. Badiou, by contrast, is committed to an understanding of events, truths and subjects as absolutely singular and self-founding in nature: what makes an event authentic, a truth true, or a subject something more than just a person, is precisely the force with which it separates itself from what precedes and surrounds it. Badiou's distinctive approach is probably best summed up in his key concept of 'fidelity to an event' (Badiou 2003: 42): that keeping-faith with the singular specificity of an event which characterises subjective authenticity. Examples of the type of event under discussion here would be moments of religious conversion, political revolution or falling-in-love. Importantly, Badiou sees these types of events as actually occurring only rarely. Like many French philosophers of recent decades, Badiou is fascinated by the concept of the event: the moment when something truly new or permanently transformatory occurs in the world. This is an obvious issue of concern for anyone with an interest in the possibilities of political change in any context: how do we know when something has really changed? How do we induce such changes when we want them? How do we respond to them when they occur? For Badiou, true events are few and far between, and authenticity can only ever be achieved by way of a commitment on the part of individuals to following through the logic of events to their ultimate conclusion. Importantly, however, this commitment is not simply an emotional orientation on the part of a pre-existing subject, it is rather the very thing which brings the subject qua subject into being.

We can see from this brief summary that Badiou's philosophy is profoundly anti-processual in nature. Change in Badiou's world does not come about as a result of overlapping and complex tendencies interacting to create tipping points. It does not come about because of the patient work of long-term, broad-based political campaigns. Exactly how and why it *does* come about is never clear, and it may be that this question can simply never be answered. In this, we can see that Badiou's position is radically different from any politics or philosophy inspired by Gramsci. From this point of view, the 'war of position' does not even count as truly political activity and the idea of building counter-hegemonic coalitions is an anathema. Indeed, it follows from this perspective that even the kind of 'conjunctural analysis' called for by Gramsci and typical of the best cultural studies (e.g. Hall et al. 1978), a careful attempt to weigh up the balance of political forces in a given situation, is simply pointless because it is only an irruption which breaks the knowable limits of any given conjuncture that can actually achieve anything.

In fact, the logic of Badiou's position might well be understood as correlating precisely to the political practice of those far-left sects from which both the Gramscian New Left and the key strands of the anti-capitalist movement have always sought to distance themselves. Indeed Badiou was an explicitly committed Maoist for many years, a position so sectarian and ultra-leftist as to have had no real equivalent in the landscapes of post-war anglophone left politics or in any Western country today. Where Badiou's political thought and practice have subsequently broken with Maoism, however, it has done so in precisely such a way as to distance itself from this sectarian tradition, by asserting itself as a 'politics without party' (Hallward 2003: 43), and by its engagement with a range of social struggles (such as the struggle of illegal and undocumented immigrant workers in France) which it makes no effort to subsume into an overall narrative of progress or understand in terms of a simple logic of partisanship. It's worth noting that even while this position breaks with the stifling sectarianism of traditional leftism, it also marks out Badiou's philosophy as more clearly than ever anti-Gramscian in character, because Gramsci is usually understood to have advocated an expansive model of the political party as a necessary agent of social change, which is quite different from advocating a break with the notion of party altogether (Gramsci 1971: 147–57). In political terms, how far Gramsci seriously advocated something different from the Leninist model of the highly disciplined and centralised party remains a matter of dispute and competing interpretation, but that debate need not concern us here. What is more relevant is the extent to which this question of party marks a point of difference between Badiou and the contemporary thinker with whom he is most often linked in the minds of anglophone readers: Slavoj Žižek. Žižek, a fascinating and infuriating thinker (Gilbert 2007), who claims his main inspirations are from Hegel and Lacan. He is a noted admirer of Badiou and is particularly close to him in his belief that the subject is essentially self-founding (Žižek 1999: 159). While Žižek—who is generally contemptuous of both cultural studies and the anti-capitalist movement—shares an 'eventral' philosophy with Badiou and a commitment to the idea of revolution, he has in recent years vociferously advocated the Leninist ideal of the disciplined and 'intolerant' revolutionary party. We will come back to this issue shortly.

How far can we understand the anti-capitalist movement in something like Badiou's terms? Well, it would certainly be possible to do so. A number of key moments might be cited as 'events', 'fidelity' to which has constituted new political subjects since the early 1990s. Most notably, the Zapatista uprising of 1994 might be seen as such, and in many ways the history of the subsequent struggle in Chiapas makes it look much like a distinctive political 'series' (a sequence of happenings following on directly from a singular event) as conceptualised by Badiou. The Zapatistas emerged as a distinctive new form of politics which could not be assimilated by any of the pre-existing categories of politics discourse—class, party, etc.—and which were absolutely specific to the very situation—Mexico in 1994—whose pre-existing political limitations they exceeded. The fact that, while remaining an inspiration to the world, the Zapatistas have *not* formed any very significant lateral connections with other groups and organisations around the globe—even with the new wave of Latin American socialist governments—would further reinforce the idea that they are best understood in terms of their singularity rather than their exemplarity. The protests against the World Trade Organisation summit at Seattle in 1999 might be understood in similar terms, with the series of major summit protests which followed in subsequent years constituting a distinct series, although the fact that they do not seem to have had any impact at all on the functioning of neoliberal institutions would problematise such a reading. Finally, the convening of the first World Social Forum in 2001 might also be considered an event, although exactly the same criticism of such an understanding could be made. In fact, the further we progress through this list of potential Badiouean events, the less sustainable any such characterisation of them becomes. For example, the World Social Forum's explicit assertion that it is a 'process' rather than an event would seem to undermine any such characterisation, and the very project of the forum—to create a space for dialogue and possible linkage between different opponents of neoliberalism—is one which cannot be understood as authentically political or 'truthful' in Badiou's terms.

Badiou's perspective is interesting because it represents the limit-point and the most rigorous example of an 'anti-strategic' mode of political thought. For Badiou, it is the self-constitution of a political subject, brought into being by the event of a singular truth, which is the substance of real political activity. This may be a fascinating and at times inspiring perspective, but it is also one from which it would simply be impossible to understand the idea of the anti-capitalist movement as having any validity at all, because the very concept of such a movement is dependent, to some extent, on the assumption that the various struggles which make it up are not necessarily discontinuous from each other, but can and should work together as part of some broader coalition against neoliberalism. Without strategy, there might be struggles, but there can be no movement. We might put this another way, and say that if we conceptualise events such as the Zapatista uprising in Badiou's terms, then we can only understand them as generating a series of *tactics* directed at their enemies and at the unfolding of their own distinctive mode of being, but we cannot conceptualise them as even potentially bound together by any kind of a common strategy. The anti-capitalist movement as such, if it is to be anything more than a set of isolated and mutually irrelevant struggles deploying wholly localised tactics against their enemies, simply cannot dispense with strategic thought.

What Is a Strategy?

The question which this line of argument raises is that of how, if at all, we can recognise strategic thought when we see it. Ernesto Laclau has commented recently, in a review of *Empire,* on the relative instability of the frontier between strategies and tactics (Laclau 2001: 7), and it is clearly an aspect of any non-teleological politics that that frontier cannot be defined with absolute certainty, insofar as the long-term consequences of any action can never be known fully, if at all. In other words, we can never be wholly sure if what we are doing at the moment is really part of a long-term strategy or not, because we never really know what the long term will look like. Nonetheless I am going to argue that it is necessary to distinguish between strategic and tactical dimensions of political thought and action, and I am going to try to offer some schematic considerations of how that distinction can be made, however provisional and unstable such distinctions might always have to be.

Standard definitions of the distinction normally state that strategy is to be understood in terms of a long-term goal and that tactics is to be understood in terms of the short-term resolution of problems encountered or expected, either in reaching such goals or in defending an existing position. However, in the case of some general distinction between political strategies and tactics appropriate to the anti-capitalist movement, this distinction could only work in just these terms if there was a clear sense of an ultimate political objective: for example, the revolutionary overthrow of capitalism and its replacement with socialism, or a goal equally determinate. In the absence of any such clear goal (and it is clear that such an absence is one of the characteristic features of the movement as such), this particular way of formulating the distinction cannot hold. In its place we might merely make a distinction between making or aiming for potentially permanent and clearly temporary political gains. Take for example, the act of occupying a disused building and using it for some social purpose (an independent media centre, a social centre, a free crèche, etc.). If there is a real chance that the occupation might become permanent, that it might therefore constitute a permanent gain for the local community or wider democratic forces, then we can say that the action, however localised, has a strategic orientation towards the goal of a more equitable, social and democratic distribution of resources. If it is well known that the building is about to be demolished and there is no real chance of saving it, then this dimension is absent. Of course, there may still be a strategic element to the action if it is calculated that the eviction will cost the owners or the authorities so much that it will erode their commitment to carrying out such evictions in the future, or that the symbolic value of the occupation will be to effect a permanent consciousness-raising amongst at least some of those involved or some of those who learn about the event indirectly; but in any such case the strategic dimension is to be located in some effect of the occupation as a symbolic, economic or experiential event rather than as an action in itself. If the establishment of a 'temporary autonomous zone' (Bey 1985) with no likely permanent consequences is to be achieved, then what we have is a pure tactic, rather than an action with any strategic orientation at all.

Arguably this distinction is close to the classic account of the tactics versus strategy distinction offered by Michel de Certeau in *The Practice of Everyday Life:*

> I call a strategy the calculation (or manipulation) of power relationships that becomes possible as soon as a subject with will and power (a business, an army, a city) can be isolated. It postulates a place that can be delimited as its own and serve as the base from which relations with an exteriority composed of targets or threats (customers or competitors, enemies, the country surrounding the city) can be managed ...
>
> By contrast with a strategy ... a tactic is a calculated action determined by the absence of a proper locus. No delimitation of an exteriority, then, provides it with the condition necessary for autonomy. The space of a tactic is the space of the other. Thus it must play on and with a terrain imposed on it and organised by the law of a foreign power ...
>
> ... strategies are actions which, thanks to the establishment of a place of power (the property of a proper), elaborate theoretical places (systems and totalising discourses) capable of articulating an ensemble of physical places in which forces are distributed ... At the very least they attempt to reduce temporal relations to spatial ones through the analytical attribution of a proper place to each particular element and through the combinatory organisation of the movements specific to units or groups of units ... Tactics are procedures that gain validity in relation to the pertinence they lend to time—to the circumstances which the precise instant of an intervention transforms into a favourable situation, to the rapidity of the movements in that change the organisation of a space, to the relations among successive moments in an action, to the possible intersections of durations and heterogeneous rhythms, etc. In this respect, the difference corresponds to two historical options regarding action and security (options that moreover have more to do with constraints than with possibilities): strategies pin their hopes on the resistance that the establishment of a place offers to the erosion of time; tactics on a clever utilisation of time, of the opportunities it presents and also of the play that it introduces into the foundations of power. Even if the methods practiced by the everyday art of war never present themselves in such a clear form, it nevertheless remains the case that the two ways of acting can be distinguished according to whether they bet on place or on time ...
>
> In short, a tactic is an art of the weak.

(de Certeau 1984: 36–7)

de Certeau's characterisation of the tactic as 'an art of the weak' and of the strategy as an operation of the powerful has had a lasting impact, and clearly resonates with an important element of the activist imaginary even amongst those participants in it who may never have heard of de Certeau. The analytical strengths and weaknesses of de Certeau's account are easily lost sight of under the effect of his persuasive and subtly charged imagery, but as such it is important to understand the appeal and rhetorical effect of that imagery. Few of de Certeau's imaginable readers, and few self-identified anti-capitalist activists, are likely to identify themselves with armies, walled cities or corporations: the imagery of the artful, cunning, mobile guerrilla, which his account of 'tactics' evokes, is clearly far more appealing than that of the domineering and powerful institution defending and extending its territoriality. This imagery distinctly prefigures Deleuze and Guattari's celebration of the nomadic war machine, always escaping the boundaries of the state, although Deleuze and Guattari's analysis is actually far more subtle and complex (1988: 351–423). Note the appeal to a certain *identity* which is implicitly made here and the aestheticisation of the position of 'the weak' which results. It's this identification with the romantic position of the marginal which can be seen as one of the fundamental elements of the activist imaginary, and which is exactly what the author of 'Give up Activism' warned against.

The romantic rhetoric of this passage leads de Certeau into an analysis which is in certain respect very weak. Its most striking feature is its entirely static character: it makes sense only from a perspective within which the overall position of the strong vis-à-vis the weak is unchanging and unchangeable: strength and weakness are posited here as identity positions rather than as relational effect of contingent power relations. The strong are presented as defending and possibly extending a place of power, but there seems to be little sense that that space and the power which enables its constitution might themselves have to be reproduced, or to have been produced or won in the first place. The notion that the weak might want to try to stop being weak, to challenge and re-order the power relations which leave them weak, is not really on the agenda here at all. Logically, for such a desire to be entertained and acted on, it would be necessary for the weak to engage in just the sort of calculations as to what actions might lead to permanent advantage and might overcome threats to the realisation of such goals which de Certeau understands as strategies.

The fact that the analytics of power presented in this passage does not allow for any such possibility is telling. It is precisely this inability to conceptualise power in a way which is appropriate to the perspective both of those seeking to retain and extend concentrations of power and those seeking to dismantle them which is typical of the activist imaginary. In other words: that activist imaginary cannot think hegemony. The activist imaginary finds it very hard to conceptualise strategy *even* for the purpose of 'changing the world without taking power' (Holloway 2002). This is illustrated most clearly by the treatment of such ways of conceptualising power in literature which is exemplary of current activist thought. One recent work illustrates this trend perfectly: Richard Day's *Gramsci is Dead*. Day tries to articulate a contemporary postanarchism which is in many ways useful and interesting, but which can only distinguish itself from Laclau and Mouffe's radical democracy by offering a misleading and misinformed caricature of the latter. In fact, Day simply misses the entire point of the post-Marxist turn in Gramscian theory. Laclau and Mouffe's most radical innovations have been precisely to liberate the analysis of hegemonic relations from any assumption that those relations necessarily configure a singular social totality (93–127) and to predicate their analyses on the assumption that all identities are inherently relational, unstable and ultimately incomplete. Hegemony, for Laclau and Mouffe, is not a thing, or a structure, or a particular location in the topology of the social, but simply a type of *relationship* which can operate in many different kinds of context. Identity, for Laclau and Mouffe, is simply never really achieved as such: it is rather, in the words of Judith Butler, 'the lived scene of coalition's difficulty' (1993: 115). Yet Day writes under the assumption that to speak of hegemony is not just to speak of a particular type of relation but to assume that we can conceptualise society as a totality with a locatable centre of power.

Day entirely misses these core points in assuming that the logical conclusion of Gramscian political analysis can only be political projects which demand subservience to a singular ideology on the part of all their participants, projects which seek to 'integrate' minority elements into liberal society. The contradictions become absolutely stark when Day tries to conclude his flawed polemic. Day argues—correctly, if without any originality—that 'one of the basic problems of contemporary politics is figuring out how to get more people in more places to overcome not only their desire to dominate others, but their desire to be dominated' (2005: 203). However, he completely fails to recognise the extent to which any such process of 'getting more people to' do anything at all that we want them to do and they aren't spontaneously doing is, by definition, a calculated exercise of power and an attempt to get them to alter their identities, however minimally, in line with our desires: in other words, is a *hegemonising* act. Day goes on to warn against the politics of '*converting* others' while making the absurd claim that 'a hegemonic orientation ... sees only two possibilities: being the ones "on top" or one of the many "at the bottom"' (2005: 206). What's really instructive here is the precise blind spot which emerges in Day's thinking. He wants to imagine a politics in which the business of getting other people to change their behaviour, to bring it in line with his own, somehow just happens without anyone having to do anything to make it happen: in other words, he wants a politics in which the question of *strategy,* the question of *how you persuade others to agree with you,* is simply occluded. Day spends his entire book caricaturing any position which takes this issue seriously as wanting to practice a politics of absolute domination, but he is ultimately unable to distinguish his own politics—insofar as it is a politics at all—from that which he criticises.

It's worth spelling out in a bit more detail what a more accurate understanding of the 'strategic orientation' might involve. From its earliest beginnings, the tradition of theorisations of hegemony which includes Lenin, Gramsci and Laclau is concerned with the question of leadership, however abstractly we may wish to understand it. Any theory of hegemony is a theory of leadership: *not,* as contemporary commentators such as Day continue to assert to this day, a theory of domination as such, although domination may, and may not, come into it. It is a theory of the processes whereby distinct social groups persuade other social groups to acquiesce to their political agendas (even if those agendas only involve being left alone). Leadership so conceived does not necessarily imply the imposition of a singular will on others but any process by which the *direction of travel* of a group or individual is influenced. This may involve, rather than an imposition of identity, many different types of mechanics: seduction, imitation, persuasion or self-transformation, for example. The element which leads may well (as the Taoist classics emphasise) have to alter its own mode of self-composition in order to allow change to occur; it may even have to engage in a 'becoming-imperceptible' (Deleuze & Guattari 1988), a partial dissolution of itself. But still, as long as some change occurs which the leading element willed, or even which is only the outcome of a process which that element deliberately catalysed, then to some extent 'leadership'—persuasion, hegemony—has occurred. Any process which sets up an alteration in the direction or composition of a group or situation or any process which induces change which is anything other than absolutely autarchic in nature, involves some element of hegemony.

Let's be very clear here. To advocate a wholly posthegemonic or non-hegemonic conception of politics—as do Day or Scott Lash (2007) or Nicholas Thoburn (2007)—is to imply that relations of influence never occur between different elements in a political process (or that they should not). In practice, advocates of such a 'posthegemonic' or non-hegemonic position can only logically do so on condition that they regard it as matter of complete indifference whether anyone, anywhere, ever agrees with them or not. If such writers are confident that they are never going to suffer because someone somewhere does not agree with them (closing the department that they think should be kept open, refusing to collect the household refuse that they think should be collected, sending them to prison for an act that they do not think should be illegal, etc.), then so be it. Otherwise, this is nonsense.

Within the Gramscian tradition it is axiomatic that any theory of leadership (which, importantly, could just be a synonym for persuasion or influence) must account for the processes both by which power is maintained in hierarchical situations *and also* by which it can be challenged. At their most basic, all theories of hegemony have asserted that the success of any political project depends on the capacity of its proponents to persuade or influence diverse constituencies and to coordinate them for as long as it takes to realise its key goals (which might be only a moment, a singular point of convergence, just long enough to make something happen; or might be for a very long time). This holds for Lenin's assertion that the revolutionary proletariat must lead the peasantry in a united coalition, Gramsci's argument that any revolutionary class must widen its socio-political role such that it is seen to represent the interests of most people in society (rather than the corporate interests of a narrowly defined group) and Laclau's far more abstract formulation according to which hegemony relies upon the production of *equivalence* between otherwise disparate terms. Laclau's work is of particular relevance here, as it demonstrates convincingly that the type of operation described by de Certeau as strategies must be undertaken to some extent by *any* political project which aspires to *any* kind of demonstrable success at all: including the kinds of libertarian projects advocated by Day and Thoburn. Any political project which seeks either to change or to reinforce existing power relationships (and any project which does not seek either of these goals is clearly not political in any meaningful way) must *to some degree* seek to render itself, as de Certeau phrases it in the passage cited above, 'capable of articulating an ensemble of physical places in which forces are distributed' and to establish relations of exteriority between itself and that which it opposes or opposes it.

Laclau further emphasises the extent to which politics is always in part a question of making connections between otherwise unconnected elements of the socio-discursive field (which is always also the field of social practice) through the construction of 'chains of equivalence': for example, Thatcherism famously managed to create an equivalence between nationalist authoritarianism and free market economics, characterising both immigrants and native trade-unionists as enemies, which was by no means inevitable or even particularly logical (Hall 1988: 123–49). This process of articulation which creates horizontal connections between ideas or constituencies which would not otherwise have been articulated can be understood as one of the fundamental features of political strategy as such. Laclau has written extensively on the centrality to political projects of the process by which the *particular* meanings of key discursive terms are attenuated as they enter into ever-wider chains of equivalence, and we can follow him in arguing that at least the aspiration to such horizontal extension of a group's or idea's (a 'demand's' in Laclau's latest terminology) political affiliations is one of the features which characterises an action as having a strategic orientation. Put very simply, a strategic orientation involves trying to persuade other people who don't already agree with you to do so: persuading them to link their demands with yours (Laclau 2005: 67–83). A certain orientation towards a universalising horizon is therefore one of the characteristics of a strategic orientation. That also means taking account of those power formations, those assemblages of assemblages, which are *relatively* universal in their effects. This is not the same as saying that every hegemonic or counter-hegemonic project has to define fully the identity of every group and individual who participates in it. In the case of the anti-capitalist movement, for example, it is clear that many groups and individuals with diverse agendas can take part in it without subsuming their identities into it, but it is also clear that there must be some points of agreement, convergence or common antagonism between participants for a movement to exist at all (Starr 2000: 166–7).

Following this logic, we can develop another aspect of de Certeau's account. According to Laclau, the logic of equivalence which governs articulatory practices has a strict conceptual opposite (which is also its necessary complement and correlate): the logic of differentiation. The logic of differentiation is simply the logic which governs the emergence of all meanings (and hence all identities, all demands, and all political positions), following Saussure's observation that all signs within a system of meaning acquire their significance only from their position within a system of differences. According to Laclau's scheme, it is not possible for a number of particular political demands to be articulated with each other, overcoming the logic of differentiation which governs their emergence as specific demands, without the creation of a relation of exteriority—a 'dichotomic frontier'—between the resultant chain of equivalence and that with which it is in a relation of antagonism (Laclau 2005: 72–124). Thus de Certeau and Laclau would be in strict agreement that what I am calling a strategic orientation would involve the positing of a frontier between a given political project and its presumed antagonist/s. We can take this further and suggest that, by the same token, tactics work along the axis of differentiation rather than that of equivalence: this is precisely what would be meant by de Certeau's assertion that tactics are defined by the absence of a 'proper locus'. If we follow Laclau in seeing the proper locus as tendentially produced by articulatory practices which work along the axis of equivalence while producing a dichotomic frontier—a relation of exteriority—then the tactic can be conversely understood as that action which is *not* oriented towards the production of any such set of relations, but which rather furthers the logic which differentiates the particularity of a specific demand. To return to our hypothetical occupation of a building, we can now say that the action would possess a *strategic* dimension insofar as it aimed to create some relation of equivalence between otherwise particular demands (perhaps, for example, the demands of local residents for affordable housing and of local youth for relatively autonomous spaces in which to congregate), and a purely *tactical* dimension insofar as it simply foregrounded the particularity of one demand or group (for example, most social centres in London merely serve as public sites for the expression of a very homogenous and relatively exclusive anarchist bohemian identity). The kind of politics of minority or the act favoured by commentators such as Day might therefore be understood as purely tactical in nature.

Now, it might be asked how this notion of strategy could be thought of as compatible with Massumi's Deleuzian definition that was discussed above. Becoming is often understood as a purely 'immanent process, without reference to exterior terms or phenomena, and Deleuze famously equates difference and differing with creativity and becoming as such (1994: 222–261). However, it is worth considering that for Deleuze and Guattari, becoming is almost never simply a process in itself. Every becoming is a becoming-something: becoming-animal, becoming-child, becoming-woman, and so forth. Becoming always involves a destabilisation of an existent identity and a vector of travel, possibly just a *swerve*[3], in the direction of something else. It is therefore emphatically *not* a mere process of autarchic self-creation. At the same time, it must be emphasised that for Laclau and Mouffe, the hegemonic articulation of 'chains of equivalence' will always destabilise and transform the identities of *all* terms in the chain, including the hegemonic terms—hegemony is not merely a situation in which one group or individual or idea forces itself upon others, but one which alters the identities of all concerned—and this process of destabilisation is not entirely unlike Deleuze and Guattari's conception of becoming. Massumi empha- sises the pragmatic and future-oriented nature of strategies, and this again chimes nicely with the notion of strategy that has been elaborated here. Now, it would be pointless and impossible to deny that there are real philosophical and political dif- ferences between Deleuze, Guattari, Massumi, and Laclau and Mouffe, but there is more of a convergence and a greater degree of complementarity here than is often realised. Where the strategic question, from a neo-Gramscian perspective, might be 'how will we connect our project with others, without losing sight altogether of our original aims and identity', the strategic question from Massumi's perspective might be 'With *what* potential future-states will we try to enter into a relation of becom- ing, and how? In what direction should we move, and by what means?' This is not necessarily a question of identifying a *goal,* but of deciding upon or pointing towards a vector of travel *from where we are now:* not a plan, but an *orientation.* In other words, insofar as such an orientation emerges with any reference whatsoever to a wider horizon of the present/future than the narrow confines of the moment, and as long as it is the product of a decision rather than a wholly passive reaction, then it must have a *strategic* dimension. To refuse such a strategic dimension is to insist on staying exactly where we are. This is why there can be no purely tactical politics: pure tacticality can only be a refusal of politics in favour of a paranoid insistence upon an unchanging identity.

Having said this, let's now give Richard Day his due. He may not have succeeded in killing Gramsci, but he does draw our attention to an important issue: the history of the left is full of instances in which the commitment to some overarching strategy has been the pretext for the suppression of all difference, all becoming, all invention. The French Communist Party did not see the radical students of 1968 as part of its strategy for proletarian revolution. The Comintern's attempt to hegemonise the anti- fascist forces during the Spanish Civil War helped smother the emergent culture of collective libertarian experiment which was emerging there. Bill Clinton's strategy of 'triangulation' made it impossible to launch an effective attack on corporate privi- lege and so doomed his healthcare reforms to failure. The list could go on. I want to suggest two possible, complementary routes out of such traps, which can only work effectively if they work together: partisanship and nomadology.

Taking Sides: The Strategic Orientation of the Partisan War-Machine

The model of effective politics which emerges here is one which would have a num- ber of implications, many of which might be contested by the representatives of the activist imaginary, and all of which would problematise some of its most characteristic assumptions and habits. In the case of the anti-capitalist movement, for example, such a perspective would give rise to the observation that the emergence of a global movement of movements cannot be taken for granted and cannot be regarded as the simple result of a range of different groups and demands realising their fundamental identity. If a minimal political identity is to emerge which can make a coherent movement out of even a few of the many sets of demands which could can be understood as antagonistic to neoliberalism, then it will only be the result of difficult and deliberate political work. This can be contrasted to Hardt and Negri's claim that

> Faced as we are with a series of intense subversive social movements that attack the highest levels of imperial organisation, however, it may no longer be useful to insist on the old distinction between strategy and tactics. In the constitution of Empire there is no longer an "outside" to power and thus no longer weak links—if by weak link we mean an external point where the articulations of global power are vulnerable. To achieve significance, every struggle must attack at the heart of Empire, at its strength. That fact, however, does not give priority to any geographical regions, as if only social movements in Washington, Geneva or Tokyo could attack the heart of Empire. On the contrary, the construction of Empire, and the globalisation of economic and cultural relationships, means that the virtual centre of Empire can be attacked from any point. The tactical preoccupations of the old revolutionary school are thus completely irretrievable; the only strategy available to the struggles is that of a constituent counterpower that emerges from within Empire. (Hardt & Negri 2000: 59)[4]

Apart from the fact that the final conclusion is something of a non sequitur (one can agree with it without acceding to any of the paragraph's previous assertions, as one can accede to any one of them without acceding to the others), the passage poses some serious problems. In brief, it implies that capitalism has reached such a complete and terminal stage that the logic of combined and uneven development (Löwy 1982) no longer applies: capitalism is now so fully developed that there is an absolute consistency in its formation that renders strategic orientation unnecessary, as Empire can be attacked with equal success at any point. The response to this situation which the passage recommends is interesting. Essentially, it evokes the Gramscian distinction between 'war of position' and 'war of manoeuvre', only to assert—in a reversal of Gramsci's argument—that the only appropriate mode of politics now is the war of manoeuvre: the singular assault on the central locus of power, which can now be reached from anywhere[5]. The war of position—the 'trench warfare' whereby anti-capitalist forces must seek to extend their range by an uneven process of occupation, transformation and annexation of various parts of the complex terrain of contemporary societies—is no longer necessary, and nor are the complex strategic calculations which would go with it.

This is clearly an appealing conclusion for participants in the activist imaginary and has clear echoes of Badiou also, for its implication is that we no longer have to worry about the issues raised by the 'Give Up Activism' essay. We don't have to worry about whether our actions have any political efficacy. We don't have to worry about the question of whether we are connecting at all with people outside of our activist subcultures, because every action we undertake is always already making a successful direct hit against the very heart of Empire. How convenient.

The split between this conception of politics and that typical of the Gramscian tradition could not be more decisive. For Gramsci and his followers, the 'war of position' has always involved a difficult but necessary engagement with the popular: that is, with the lives, attitudes and priorities of people outside the immediate political milieu (Gramsci 1971: 229–39). The tradition of British cultural studies was profoundly shaped by two generations of intellectuals influenced by this perspective, implying as it does that the general field of popular culture and everyday life is a necessary terrain of political struggle. One of the characteristic features of the activist imaginary is precisely a refusal to make any such engagement. One of the striking features of activist media is the almost complete lack of engagement with any aspect of contemporary culture which does not constitute an immediately recognisable element of the milieu of activist subculture in anything other than censorious terms. As we have mentioned already, follow the culture links on most Indymedia sites, and you might find news about squatted punk gigs, samba classes and Earth First! gatherings (as is right), but there are few, if any, references to the world of music, TV, literature, fashion and food, in which most of the population of the North lives. Discussions of how supporters of the movement might go about the business of persuading non-supporters of the rightness of their cause are simply not on the agenda.

This draws attention to a further interesting element of the distinction between strategy and tactics: culture—the field of shared meanings and shared modes of experiential organisation (Williams 1961: 57–88; Gilbert 2006)—is, I would suggest, the field in which political strategies as such are deployed. Insofar as strategy works along the axis of equivalence and combination, it operates always in the sphere of commonality for which culture and the popular are synonyms: in the sphere of what Deleuze and Guattari call 'concrete assemblages'. To be precise, in the language of Deleuze and Guattari, cultures are 'constellations' of assemblages (Deleuze & Guattari 1988: 406). This is an observation with wide applicability. For example, in the domain of creative practice, we could characterise art as a site of tactical innovation, constantly developing new aesthetic, affective and communicational techniques, which can be articulated with and assembled into any number of possible strategic projects (from those of radical social movements to those of global corporations), and whose potential for such re-articulation is never limited by the nature of the tactics themselves.

From this perspective we could say that a lack of strategic thought, or even an active resistance to it, is common to the practice of much of the anti-capitalist movement and that of many intellectuals and artists today who might identify themselves as having a critical relationship to neoliberal culture. Like much contemporary theory and art practice, the spectacular tactics of the movement try to provoke its audience into a problematic relationship with its situation, to promote a certain reflexivity with regard to accepted cultural norms and socio-economic arrangements, but without prescribing any predetermined solutions to the problems which it invites us to acknowledge. In the process, these fields of practice all generate what amounts to an ever-proliferating array of *tactical* innovations without any strategic orientation. Thus the development of new organisational techniques, new uses for various technologies, new concepts or new modes of perception is carried on without any view to the uses to which they might or should be put; and inevitably such invention is almost entirely appropriated and exploited to its fullest by capital, all in a manner largely analogous to the workings of experimental science. In this sense, we might say that the various avant-gardes of art practice, philosophy and political activism amount to *tactical laboratories* existing in relative isolation from any wider political project which might protect their inventions from exploitation by capital. Groups like the Space Hijackers, who organise 'spontaneous' parties on the London Underground train system are a case in point—while they see their activities as inherently anti-capitalist in nature, their tactics and methods have already been borrowed by cutting-edge corporate marketers, while they themselves have had no discernible impact on neoliberal culture in the United Kingdom (http://www.spacehijackers.co.uk).

Now, let me clarify what I am saying here and what I am not. I am not saying that all these awful people are just frivolous time-wasters, bourgeois dupes of corporate hegemony. I am not saying that they are morally weak or politically untrustworthy or anything of that nature. All I am saying is the following. Capital clearly acts on a strategic plane. Neoliberalism is the name we give to the current hegemonic strategy of capital's leading sections, and it is clearly manifested in initiatives such as the General Agreement on Trade in Services (Whitfield 2001) and the project for the European Union constitution and their various equivalents at the national, regional and municipal level the world over. Even in the absence of anything resembling a political strategy, the power of post-Fordist capital to deploy its abstract machine is undeniable: its capacity to propagate its social logic is unmatched by that of any organisational or economic rival in the world today. As such, isolated tactical innovations lacking any kind of protection or any capacity to organise themselves into what Deleuze and Guattari call a 'war machine' will always find themselves re-captured by more powerful agencies.

It's no doubt a recognition of this weakness which provokes much of the hostility aimed at activist politics and radical theory by figures such as Slavoj Žižek. At the other end of the scale from anarchist-inspired thinkers such as Day, implicitly refusing any notion of strategy as inherently totalitarian, Žižek calls for a return to Lenin as the great strategist of revolutionary communism and the great advocate of the party form as the means by which political strategy should be formulated and implemented. Žižek suggests that we should return to Lenin while acknowledging that the specific content of his project in 1917 is no longer relevant to our situation today.

Pursuing a line of argument partly borrowed from Badiou, Žižek insists that Lenin's great contribution is to assert both the irreducible value of the all-transforming revolutionary act, and the necessity of disciplined, dogmatic 'intolerance', for any effective revolutionary organisation (Žižek 2002).

Žižek is certainly right to discern a chronic and disabling lack of strategic thinking on much of the contemporary radical scene, and a similarly disabling distaste for militancy amongst so-called radical intellectuals, and he is right that no attempt to get past the resulting impasse can avoid an encounter with Lenin. Žižek is impressed by Lenin's willingness to break with Marxist orthodoxy, according to which Russia was nowhere remotely close to being ready for a proletarian communist revolution in 1917, and thereby to take advantage of a historically unprecedented situation of socio-political crisis in order to transform the historical scene in which he found himself (Žižek 2001; Žižek 2002: 7–12). He is also impressed by Lenin's willingness to abjure the niceties of consensual liberalism in order to defend a militant position of revolutionary anti-capitalism (Žižek 2001; Žižek 2002: 167–78).

However, while it is clearly true that Lenin's break with Marxist orthodoxy was in some senses exemplary, both theoretically and pragmatically, Žižek's characterisation of the nature of this break is both reductive and counter-productive in its implications. Žižek almost invariably presents Lenin's break an example of pure volition, unmediated will, a fundamental act in the most metaphysical and individualistic sense (Žižek 2001: 26). By contrast, I would argue that Lenin's decision to push the revolution to its logical conclusion was not some miraculous accession to grace, but the product of a careful strategic calculation and a willingness to recalibrate the terms of that calculation in the face of emergent events. Far from being the singular intervention which changed everything, Lenin's decision was the product of a willingness to accept that he could not control events and that no theoretical dogma could predict them. Lenin had to accept the fact that the revolution was not unfolding according to the classical Marxist scheme and hence to take political opportunities as they arose. It was therefore an openness to the incalculability of the future which characterised Lenin's perspective and distinguished it from later Stalinist dogmatism. It was a willingness to accept the fact that his actions were always already caught up in a destabilising network of causes and effects which forced Lenin to act as he did, not some pure moment of revelation. In fact Žižek does seem to acknowledge this much when he describes Lenin's attitude as one of 'authentic historical openness' (2001). Furthermore, when Žižek writes against the notion of 'politics without parties', he does so in a register which seem to assume that everyone who has ever questioned the organisational appropriateness of Bolshevism in the twenty-first century has advocated a complete renunciation of all party organisation whatsoever. In fact, much of Žižek's substantial point on the need for parties and intolerance in politics can be boiled down to his insistence on the need to take sides in politics, a position which can just as well be derived from Chantal Mouffe's reading of Schmitt, amongst other sources (Mouffe 2000). While these two writers would clearly disagree on fundamental issues—most notably the centrality and viability of the concept of re-volution to radical democratic struggle—they can both be read as arguing that there can be no effective politics without contestation.

Which brings us back, once again, to the question of strategy; and of how to coordinate a disparate and dispersed array of political actors and actions against a common enemy as vast and powerful as neoliberalism and in favour of—if not a singular vision of the future—at least a range of visions which are not mutually exclusive and which are generally democratic in character. In this sense, there is a clear need for some kinds of political practice to do the work of connecting a dis-parate range of political tactics (from demonstrations to media interventions, from strikes to factory occupations, from election campaigns to government lobbying) with some kind of overall set of social objectives informed by a broadly coherent set of ethics and values. This is exactly what the political party used to try to do, and Gramsci's 'The Modern Prince' remains the classic vision of this whole gamut of functions being carried out by a single organisation. The reasons why such a vision has become untenable today are well-known. Postmodern societies are too complex, too differentiated and too porous for any one organisation to carry out this range of functions effectively and with any kind of legitimacy, unless it were to be the vehicle of some new kind of fascism. More than this, many of us may well be suspi-cious that the twentieth-century party form was always too fascistic in its tendencies. However, this only leaves us in a trickier position than ever. If we recognise that we need something like the kind of strategic coordination which the political party used to provide, but we reject Žižek's calls for a return to vanguardism, and the even the whole history of centralised party organisation, what, then, is to be done?

One answer—partly inspired by Hardt and Negri's turn to early modern phi-losophy—might be to return to a pre-twentieth-century concept of party, meaning not a tightly structured membership organisation, but a more diffuse assemblage of mutually resonant opinions and goals. In English at least, the notion of *party* is as old as political democracy, and for most of its history the term simply designated a common body of opinion oriented towards a shared set of political goals, short and long term. It might seem simple enough, even completely banal, to suggest reviving this usage in order for anti-capitalists to recognise themselves as 'a party'. It might well be argued that the concept of the movement of movements is one which already serves just this function. But I think that we have identified a number of problems with current thinking on the nature of political identity and strategy which indicate that making such concepts effective will prove to something of a challenge, and will require a very subtle, but very specific understanding of the relationship between tactics and strategies. For what is required for tactical interventions against neolib-eral hegemony—from street protests to academic journal articles, policy propos-als to film reviews—to be effective, is a certain *strategic orientation,* which is *not* the same thing as saying that they need to be informed by a singular ideology or oriented towards a singular imagined goal. A deliberate orientation away from the normativity of neoliberal assumptions and practices, toward the possibility of their democratic transcendence, but without a singular political identity or ultimate goal, would be quite different from either the strategyless tactics of the avant-gardes or the totalitarian intolerance of the Žižeko-Leninist vanguard. It would be an orientation made in the spirit that Amory Starr so eloquently evokes when she observes that 'The international invitation to be a Zapatista mirrors the invitation to be queer—it is a moral solidarity around a political economic critique, not any kind of claim around interiority or essence' (2000: 167).

In practice, this would mean that the current task for those us seeking to move beyond the spectacular protests of the post-Seattle period towards some more substantial project to remake democracy for the twenty-first century might be to work on making possible the productive synthesis of new specific connections between the already vast, but hugely dispersed range of opinions and social actors opposed to the hegemony of neoliberalism and to its authoritarian opponents. Making this possible would depend more than anything on the opening, and intensifying, of spaces in which the unpredictable self- coordination of multiple elements might become possible, allowing new practices of democracy and collective self-invention to emerge. This touches on a very important point. There exists already in much of the West a large number of groups and individuals—arguably a clear majority—who are dissatisfied and displeased with the hegemonic persistence of neoliberalism and its social, political and cultural consequences, who value much of the social democratic legacy and who do not wish to forego the liberal social and cultural gains of the past 40 years. These range from the militant activist to the Christian Aid volunteer; from the Italian garment-industry worker to the disillusioned French voter, voting against the incumbent government in every election in living memory; from the conceptual artists and independent film-makers to the public-service broadcasters and the Archbishop of Canterbury. It's in the facilitation of connection and the creation of opportunities for common strategising between actors and thinkers from a range of social sectors that the possibility of democratic transformation must lie. To be clear then, this is not a matter of unification, homogenisation or centralisation, but of the creation and intensification of relays, the actualisation of potential nodes and points of concentration, the active production of 'commons'.

This is why the emergence of the social forums is so important, but, importantly, large-scale social forums are not the only form which this kind of politics can take. On some level, the social forum is the model for the type of space of engagement that we need at almost every scale, from the global to the micro-institutional. From the school to the nation-state and the supra-national state, anti-neoliberal radical democratic forces will need to keep working to create spaces of engagement wherein the strategic orientation of a vast range of political and potentially political activities can be sharpened, adjusted, amplified and problematised, in a process which practically manifests what Laclau has called the 'multiplication of public spaces' (1990: xv). Žižek is right, I think, to remind us that *simply* constituting democratic spaces would be insufficient: these spaces will only be politically effective if they are, like the social forums, constituted on the basis of a shared understanding that, at the very least *something is happening* (globalisation, neoliberalism) which none of us asked for—in which we are all nonetheless implicated—and which it behoves us to name as some kind of an enemy (Starr 2000); and on the basis of a willingness to at least countenance the possibility of a definitive militancy in countering it. But it is in the constitution of such opportunities to *strategise,* and not simply in the heroic declaration of a new vanguard, that the possibility lies of effective strategies emerging. Deleuze and Guattari's evocation of the rhizome comes here to be entirely relevant: *rhizomatic* is precisely what the nature of the connections so created should be, and what the nature of such strategising will have to be.

I have already hinted, and would like now to suggest explicitly, that the social forums thus conceived must have something of the quality of the 'war machine'. This is a key phrase from Deleuze and Guattari which does not necessarily designate a military organisation at all. The war machine is a particular type of assemblage which is definitively distinguishable from the State and which '*in no way has war as its object,* but rather the emission of quanta of deterritorialisation, the passage of mutant flows (in this sense, every creation is brought about by a war machine)' (Deleuze & Guattari 1988: 229–30). War machines are those mobile, transformatory, 'nomadic' sites of innovation which might be partially captured by State institutions but which are never wholly inside them, their abstract nature as war machines being defined by their radical exteriority to the State (Patton 2000: 109–15).

Now, from this point of view, it is important for us to bear in mind that there is nothing inherently progressive about war machines. Neoliberalism is, as much as anything, an assault by the war machines of finance capital on the social-democratic institutions of the State. 'A commercial organisation is also a band of pillage, or piracy' (Deleuze & Guattari 1988: 360): just think of all those corporations profiting from the privatisation of education services and water supplies. Perhaps it is too simple to pose capital against the State here. Rather we should say that the institutions of the welfare state were always themselves composite assemblages with cutting edges that could go either way: potentially engines of collective self-empowerment for the subject-groups of workers, refugees, women, and so forth who used them, but also potentially institutions of discipline and control. A school can be a place where a community finds new ways to think and be, beyond the mere demands of the labour market and elite culture. It can also be an oppressive institution for the imposition of conformity. In its former aspect, a school or any public institution can take on the character of a war machine, but in the latter instance it always becomes an instrument of the State. This follows as long as we remain within Deleuze and Guattari's frame of reference, of course: from other perspectives the very idea of the State might be crude and simplistic (Foucault 2004: 79). But let's stick with Deleuze and Guattari for now, because they provide us with a remarkably productive way of thinking through these issues. For example: Raymond Williams's pioneering New Left analysis of post-war capitalism was precisely focussed on the issue of how to amplify a certain potential in the reformed and newly invented institutions of the welfare state and public education, a potential which could carry them along a vector of transformation that would make them part of the 'Long Revolution' (Williams 1961) *against* capital and discipline, towards a radically democratic horizon. From this perspective, we can see that neoliberalism is, precisely the counter-revolution against Williams's Long Revolution'. Neoliberalism is characterised by a specific mode of interaction between certain institutions of the State (government, central banks, public-sector management) and the war machines of finance capital *against* the radical possibilities inherent in some of the institutions of social democracy, an alliance between the pirates of finance and the new managerial technocracy (see Clarke & Newman 1997; Bewes & Gilbert 2000), against the multitude and its war machines.

> It is thus proper to State deterritorialisation to moderate the superior deterritorialisation of capital and to provide the latter with compensatory reterritorialisations …
>
> States are not at all transcendent paradigms of an overcoding but immanent models of realisation for an axiomatic of decoding flows. (Deleuze and Guattari 1988: 455)

The New Left always dreamed of a radical democratisation of these institutions from a perspective which tended to see democracy as a force that was always working *against* the State, as Miguel Abensour would have it (Abensour 2004). This is one reason why so many former radicals have become agents of neoliberalism's war on the social democratic state (most New Labour ministers have espoused radical socialism at some point in their youth). The difference between a radical democratic deterritorialisation of the welfare state and its capture by neoliberal capital can sometimes be very hard to discern, at first.

So what are the implications of all this? Simply that the social forum should be conceptualised not as a model of an alternative State or a reformed State but as a mutant assemblage, and that the social forums should be seen not as potential political committees of some uniform political movement. Rather they should be seen as points of relay, democratic research labs, communicating junctures in a networked assemblage which would aim to let loose war machines against the power of neoliberalism and its institutions to codify and territorialise, rather than becoming defensive guardians of the State. In practice, this would have some serious and mundane implications. The repeated calls for social forums to take up positions, to become themselves proto-parties, would have to be resisted. The loose anti-capitalist party, the new international, might be an assemblage of war machines, but to try to turn each forum-machine into a party would kill it. Any temptation on the part of anti-capitalist forces to fall back on nationalism, parochialism, protectionism, or authoritarianism would have to be resisted. This might sound obvious, but it would be all too easy for all opponents of neoliberalism to follow the path which has already led many to religious fundamentalism, looking for security, stability and safety from the decoded flows of capital by hiding behind God and holy books (Gordon Brown recently promised 'British jobs for British workers', although the fact that this is widely regarded as having been a serious faux pas is some grounds for hope ...).

Let's emphasise here again that the value of the social forum model is not only to be derived from the success or failure of the actual social forums to date. Rather the value of the social forum model can be derived from the virtual social forum expressed in the World 'Social Forum' charter of principles, which is a kind of diagram of a political space which would work to actualise the radical democratic potential of the multitude which passes through it. Social forum could be a name for any kind of institutional experiment which tries to open such a space: a student council, a works committee, a community centre. That such experiments are initiated all the time, all over the place, can hardly be doubted. The aim of anti-capitalism as a movement would be to create some field of resonance between each of these points (on a different frequency to that of the State. See Deleuze & Guattari 1988: 433).

So, we want to proliferate ... public spaces, social forums, war machines ... but in practice, in the concrete assemblage of British culture that we examined in the last chapter, what hopes is there of doing this? In the particular situation of the British cultural context and the British political experience, the problem of how to imagine anti-capitalism as anything more than a politically irrelevant subculture is particularly stark. Arguably, the move from anti-roads protests to self-defined anti-capitalism at the end of the 1990s involved a shift away from a politics whose primary function was to politicise previously taken-for-granted aspects of everyday life and to widen out the zone of that politicisation (a political war machine), and its substitution with a politics of self-definition (a paranoid tactic of identity). During this period, the implicit policing of the boundaries of activist subculture became much more intense—excluding, for the most part, anyone not committed to full-time struggle—just as the targets against which it is ranged became at once narrower and less accessible (the entire edifice of global capitalism, no less). The question this leaves us with is this—what other kinds of political practice could do the opposite? What would be needed to help spread and deepen a sense of affiliation, however loose, between all those who feel some dissatisfaction with the neoliberal project and its consequences, to make possible a common *swerving* of this abstract swarm away from the neoliberal attractor and towards another?

Well, all kinds of things would have to happen, but let's reflect on what a few of them might be. For one thing—and this is crucially important—there would have to be some notions, some ideas, images and affects in circulation concerning what it might mean to be a partisan of anti-capitalism but not a full-time activist. Partisanship without identity would be the necessary possibility here. Now, this is a proposal that would shock many who themselves identify with the activist imaginary. They would no doubt see this as symptomatic of the kind of authoritarian thinking that they have always opposed, implying as it does that some people should be really politically active and others should be just passive supporters of the movement, an idea which at its worse implies the split between the professional revolutionary elite and the ordinary masses of Leninist theory.

There are several responses to make to this. One is that it is a position which is entirely utopian and refuses to learn anything from history. There has never been a radical movement which mobilised an entire population for any length of time, and those movements which change things invariably do so by winning large-scale support amongst a diverse public, not all of whom *can* be full-time activists: altering the affective orientation, the molecular composition, of a range of different subjects/ groups/singularities without demanding conformity to a model. Which comes to our second point. As discussed earlier in this chapter, there are all kinds of pragmatic reasons as to why many people cannot involve themselves heavily in direct political activity at a given moment, except in moments of absolute social crisis. A political movement which really wants to effect any kind of social change has to find a way to include, to attract, to resonate with such people. Inclusion in this sense does not necessarily involve taking a direct part in political activity, but a more general sharing of attitudes, assumptions and responses—an affective exchange—which can translate into active political support at times of real crisis and can become a basis for a generalised militancy which does not depend upon the presence of militants for its success. For such a shared collection of ideas and affects to become effective, however, it has to have some bearing on aspects of people's lives which are not usually thought of as directly the provenance of politics.

In fact this is precisely how the most successful of the new social movements have achieved what they have. The diffusion of feminist, anti-racist, and green ideas has been dependent on just such a rhizomatic process of cultural dissemination, rather than on the recruitment of ever-larger numbers to the ranks of activist militancy. How exactly this might happen today is not a question I could answer without lapsing into prescriptive dogma. Let these remarks stand rather as an invitation to artists, philosophers, journalists, media critics, students, teachers, political inactivists and anyone else who's interested: what might enable a radically democratic critique of neoliberalism and the ideal of the social forum to proliferate? What new forms and contents might we invent for that purpose (if only ever partly or that purpose)?

And what role might cultural studies or cultural theory play? Well, since the 1970s, cultural studies and the spread of cultural theory throughout the humanities and social sciences have clearly played a role in this process. In particular, generations of graduates, including politicians, policy-makers, journalists and broadcasters have clearly been influenced by the attention to issues of class, gender, race and sexuality in the study of literature, media and visual culture which cultural studies helped to popularise. This is not to say that it was cultural studies which *caused* this shift, nor can it be said to have been merely a passive result of some broader cultural shift in which it played no part. Rather, we can say that the spread of cultural theory, especially via the influence of cultural studies, has played a small but important role in disseminating a set of political perspectives which have had a decisive impact in re-shaping cultural attitudes and the broad political climate. This is one of the reasons that the 'new spirit of capitalism' has had to include a real belief in the value of personal freedom and unlimited creativity, why even conservative politicians today cannot publicly espouse racist views. Despite the habitual hostility of Oxbridge-educated journalists to cultural studies, cultural theory, literary theory and media studies, despite the relative success of the reactionary myth of political correctness, we can still say that such reactions would be entirely superfluous were it not for the fact that these phenomena *have* been successful in contributing to changes in attitudes, behaviours and realities.

Reflecting on this process tells us a lot about the way in which ideas are disseminated through a culture, and in particular about the possible relationships between academic work and political movements. Both activist and academic culture are often suffused with a certain anxiety about these relationships. Academics often worry that they do not write for a broad public, whereas activists often condemn academics for not producing books which are easy for non-specialists to read. These anxieties only make sense if we imagine, mistakenly, that the only way for academic ideas to relate to political movements is for them to constitute the basis for manifestos which are then enacted directly by the movement, 'on the streets'. In truth the processes by which ideas circulate is much more complex. An academic work may only be read by a few hundred people, but those few hundred may all be university teachers who will carry some of the work's ideas into their teaching, which may involve communications with hundreds of students each. Those students may in turn carry some of those idea into other spheres of life, and so on. Furthermore, the job of politically informed academic work in the humanities (of which cultural studies is exemplary) is not usually to inspire activists at all, but either to influence and change the academic milieu itself in line with the long-term objectives of the political movement, or to generate analyses which might of use to general sympathisers of the movement. In other words, the point of producing a complex feminist analysis of a play by Shakespeare might be to contribute to the women's movement's understanding of Shakespeare (and hence, presumably, many other things), but it might also be to recruit scholars and students of Shakespeare to the broad attitudes of the women's movement. This might seem like a very small victory. So it is. But without such small victories, there can be no great ones: this is precisely the point on which both Gramsci's notion of the 'war of position' and Guattari's emphasis on 'molecular politics' converge. Committed cultural criticism (feminist studies, of Shakespeare, for example) can play a very useful role in helping to think through what it might mean to think from a partisan perspective without having to carry a party card[6]. At the same time of course, generating a committed critical position is not the most important role for intellectual work in relation to political projects: even more important is its critical capacity to offer some space for reflection upon the assumptions, reflexes, successes and failures of a radical movement, reflection that the everyday pace of political activism doesn't always allow. Even more than this, however, the historic aim of cultural studies has been to make the best possible analyses of contemporary configurations of power which might help to plot routes towards more democratic futures.

From this point of view, we might say that radical cultural theory is and always has been asking the same question: what does it mean to study culture from a radical democratic perspective? Cultural studies has always had the same job: to analyse the shifting patterns of contemporary culture, identifying those surfaces of emergence which might offer scope for an intensification of democracy and the proliferation of difference, keeping a watch on those new forms of stratification and control which work to reinforce hierarchy and compulsory individualisation. While this task may often be carried out in sympathy with radical movements, they must also involve taking those movements themselves as objects of critical reflection, as well as considering how their best innovations might be carried forward into other areas. This is what this chapter has tried to do.

Notes

1. Of course, we should not rule out the possibility of both the consequences of climate change and the need drastically to reduce carbon emissions provoking such a crisis before too long.
2. The entire Lacanian critique of militancy since 1968 could be activated here, but that is not a critique which I wish to endorse.
3. A clinamen.
4. Whether Hardt and Negri would now stand by this argument, in the light of some of the qualifications that they have made in *Multitude,* is not entirely clear.
5. This should not be confused with the nomadic mode of operation of Deleuze and Guattari's 'war machines'. Gramsci uses the term 'war of manoeuvre' specifically to designate a conflict in which there is only one central site of contestation.
6. What might a radical-democratic cultural criticism involve? I've reflected on this elsewhere (Gilbert 2001, 2004c, 2006), but others might do it much better.

Conclusion
Liberating the Collective

> If it wants to live up to its potential, cultural studies has to be as proudly, loudly political as philosophy is glowingly useless.
>
> Brian Massumi *Parables for the Virtual*

What can it mean to rise to Massumi's challenge? On one level, it must always mean to put the idea of the political itself into question, as cultural studies and cultural theory practitioners are so often so good at doing. And yet, on another level, destabilising concepts like 'the political' is the job of philosophy. The question of 'what the political is' is a crucial one that we can never stop asking: but at the moment when we ask it, we're doing metapolitics, micropolitics, deconstruction, philosophy. This is something to be done in hushed voices, deliberately, uncertainly, *stammering* (Deleuze & Parnet 1996: 11, 73). To be proudly, loudly political is something different. It must involve a certain partisanship; not an adoption of identity, not a Jacobin assumption of a binarised world-view, but a sense that there are, whether we like it or not, conflicts which we are touched by and which we touch, unavoidably. We don't choose them. It matters (literally), sometimes, to which sides in these conflicts we lend our strength, talents, insights and inventions, our proud, loud voices.

Of course, without dogma to guide us, we cannot know in advance, before we start to look, what those conflicts are; between which parties or for what stakes. This is why the first task of cultural studies is always an analytical one; to analyse conjunctures, to measure the balances of force, to figure out what the stakes are. Sometimes they will be small and sometimes large. But even if we reject any notion of totality (and we do), it remains the case that there will be some conflicts so large, involving such extensive constellations of assemblages, that they make themselves immanent to countless situations on every conceivable scale. The conflict between neoliberalism and its multiple opponents—many of them willing something at once freer and more egalitarian than it can allow—is one such conflict. It is played out in so many innumerable locations (from patented genes to wrecked continental ecosystems) that we cannot help but encounter it and become caught up in it. If we don't think we are, it's only because we don't know we are. If we don't know we are, it's only because we haven't looked. Looking is part of the point of cultural studies.

What have we learned? The book set out with the aim of staging a dialogue between cultural studies and the anti-capitalist movement. As promised, this dialogue could often take place only at a high level of abstraction, and if nothing else I hope this has produced some useful insights into the relative valencies of important currents in recent cultural and political theory. But along the way we have also developed a number of claims about the nature of contemporary capitalism and its intersections with particular formations of power and desire: making such claims is always an integral task of practicing cultural studies. What has come up a number of times in several chapters—although it has not been previously highlighted as a key theme—is something about the nature of the current conjuncture and the specific role of culture in it. That noticeable something is this: the remarkable proximity between those zones of innovation and emergence from which alternatives to neoliberal capitalism might emerge and the leading edges of that capitalism itself; the remarkable proximity between those defensive enclaves which might be transformed into war machines and those which are merely apparatuses of control. There is a difference, a real difference, and yet a very fine line, between the rhizomatic politics of the social forums and the connexionist rhetoric of the New Spirit of Capitalism. There is a difference, a real difference, and yet a very fine line, between the Zapatistas' defence of their homeland and the defensiveness of a British xenophobe.

The difference isn't that hard to discern. It's about radical democracy on the one hand, capital accumulation on the other; becoming-Zapatista on the one hand, England-belongs-to-me on the other. But discerning it and naming it is the job of cultural studies.

Is this just stating the obvious? Is this simply apparent to everyone? Has it always been like this?

I don't think it has always been like this. I'm hardly the first person to observe that the relationship between capitalism and culture has changed in recent decades, as culture has itself become the main site for the production of value. This is the phenomenon theorised in different ways as the rise of 'immaterial labour' (Lazzarato 1996), the emergence of the knowledge economy, the rise of the creative industries or postmodernity. There may have been other points in history when it was like this. To some extent, capitalism has always been dependent on the very creative energy which could best be turned against it. But that creativity was not always exercised primarily in the field of culture, and the cultural machines which capitalism was connected to (the churches, the old universities, the mass media) were once very far from those of the workers. Richard Hoggart's *The Uses of Literacy,* the very first book in cultural studies, was in part telling the story of a closing gap, a closing gap between the workers' culture and that of the mass (state/capital) media. That gap has continued to close, but it has also mutated, and cultural studies still has the job, fifty years on, of thinking about the consequences. Let's say we've learned this much: this new situation, as these various theorists have described it, is real, and really different, and demands a certain political attention in conceptual terms that we have tried to draw out.

Is it obvious? It certainly isn't obvious to everyone. A certain vein of Marxist anti-capitalist critique, best represented right now by Slavoj Žižek, assumes that anything so proximate to capitalism must be similar to capitalism, and so denounces all of the most radical lines-of-flight of the day (cultural studies, post-Marxism, postmodernism, deconstruction, *Anti-Oedipus,* queers, feminists, Marcos … the list goes on and on) in the name of God-knows-what-alternative to capitalism (Gilbert 2007; Laclau 2005: 232–9). Similarly, a vein of libertarian futurist pseudo-Taoist nihilism denounces any strategy of defence as merely conservative, majoritarian, communitarian, clinging onto the past. This attitude surfaces in its pure form very rarely: much more frequently it takes the form of a nonchalant assertion that anti-consumerism, egalitarian politics, or the suggestion that artistic or theoretical practices might sometimes reflect on their own politics, are manifestations of an old-fashioned left moralism.

Of course we don't want moralism, we loud, proud, joyful, radically democratic anti-capitalists. We just don't want to be trapped. Artists, scientists, architects, philosophers, media theorists, cultural critics, policy specialists; we may think ourselves safe in our workshops, galleries, laboratories, seminar rooms, offices, libraries, in our spaces of tactical invention. But to what use will the techniques and tactics that we invent be put? Do we even want to have a say in this? Do we even care?

If, on some level, however abstract, you are never strategising against Empire, capital or the state, then you can be sure that they are strategising against you. You may comfort yourself that 'there is no hegemony', but Washington knows that there is hegemony, and News International knows that there is hegemony. What's more: they don't care that you don't believe in their hegemony. They don't need to hegemonise you to get you cornered: they've got enough on their side already. They don't need you to believe in them to capture you. All they need to do is to organise the space you move in. If you don't coordinate your singular points of resistance/escape/becoming with those of others, then you won't have a chance. All of your key coordinates will be determined for you. No line of flight will take you far enough to escape: the world is round, in case you hadn't heard.

Let's go to social forums, publish online for free, organise public workshops, give away art, refuse to sign recording contracts, turn down jobs in marketing, build houses for co-ops, research collaboratively. Many are doing this already of course: let's salute the heroes of open source, peer-to-peer, and so forth, and see what the rest of us can learn from them. Let's liberate the collective from the trap of commodity-career-celebrity-mine.

I'm no hero. I'm not doing much of this. But I think we should keep trying. Don't you?

The way lies ahead, in taking the inventive potential released by capitalism so far that we become so other so as no longer to act in the perceived "private" interests of a separate Self that we have in any case already ceased to be (if we ever were it). We must embrace our collectivity. This requires a global perception of the capitalist relation as the constraint that it is, the development of a systematic sensitivity to its axiomatic, and shared strategies of resistance to it and its symbiotic despotisms, in a world-wide resonation of desires. The aim would be less to overthrow neoconservatism than to counter-actualize its residually molar individuals as local-global correlation of becomings-other. We are in this together, and the only way out is together, into a supermolecularity where no quasicause can follow: a collective ethics beyond good and evil. But most of all, beyond greed.

(Massumi 1992: 140–1)

Bibliography

Abensour, Miguel (2004), *La Democratie contre l'Etat,* Paris: Éditions de Félin.

Abercrombie, Nicholas, Stephen Hill and Bryan S. Turner (1980), *The Dominant Ideology Thesis,* London: George Allen Unwin.

Adorno, Theodor (1973), *Negative Dialectics,* trans. E. B. Ashton. London: Routledge.

Adorno, Theodor, and Max Horkheimer (1944), *Dialectic of Enlightenment,* trans. John Cumming. London: Verso.

Albert, Michael (2003), *Parecon: Life After Capitalism,* London: Verso.

Alliez, Eric (2001), 'The Difference and Repetition of Gabriel Tarde', http://www.goldsmiths.ac.uk/csisp/papers/tarde/alliez.pdf (accessed January 15, 2008).

Alliez, Eric (2004), 'Anti Oedipus: 30 Years On' in *Radical Philosophy* March/April 2004. London: Radical Philosophy.

Althusser, Louis (1971), *Lenin and Philosophy,* trans. Ben Brewster. New York: Monthly Review Press.

Amin, Ash (1994), *Post-Fordism: A Reader,* Oxford: Blackwell.

Anderson, Benedict (1983), *Imagined Communities,* London: Verso.

Anderson, Perry (1964), 'Divide and Conquer', (editorial) in *New Left Review November-December 1964.* London: Verso.

Anderson, Perry (2000), 'Renewals', in *New Left Review* (second series) 1. London: Verso.

Andrews, Geoff (2003), *Endgames and New Times: The Final Years of British Communism 1964–1991,* London: Lawrence & Wishart.

Andrews, Geoff (2005), *Not a Normal Country: Italy After Berlusconi,* London: Pluto Press.

Ang, Ien (1985), *Watching Dallas,* London: Methuen.

Angelis, Massimo de (2001), 'Marx and primitive accumulation: The continuous character of capital's "enclosures"' http://www.commoner.org.uk/02deangelis.pdf (accessed January 15, 2008).

Angelis, Massimo de (2006), *The Beginning of History: Value Struggles and Global Capital,* London: Pluto.

Arnold, Matthew (1960), *Culture and Anarchy,* Cambridge: Cambridge University Press.

Austin, J. L. (1962), *How to Do Things With Words,* Oxford: Oxford University Press.

Badiou, Alain (1993), *Ethics: An Essay on the Understanding of Evil,* trans. Peter Hallward. London: Verso.

Badiou, Alain (2003), *Saint Paul: The Foundation of Universalism,* trans. Ray Brassier. Stanford: Stanford University Press.

Barry, Andrew, Thomas Osborne and Nikolas Rose (eds), *Foucault and Political Reason: Liberalism, Neo-liberalism and Rationalities of Government,* London: Routledge.

Barthes, Roland (1972), *Mythologies,* trans. Annette Lavers. London: Jonathan Cape.

Barthes, Roland (1973), *The Pleasure of the Text,* trans. Richard Miller. New York: Hill & Wang.

Barton, Fiona (2006), 'The New Britons', *The Daily Mail* 18 May 2006.

Baudrillard, Jean (1988a), *The Ecstasy of Communication,* trans. Bernard and Caroline Schutze. New York: Semiotext(e).

Baudrillard, Jean (1988b), *Selected Writings,* Mark Poster (ed.). Cambridge: Polity.

Bauman, Zygmunt (2001), *The Individualised Society,* Cambridge: Polity.

Beck, Ulrich (2006), *The Cosmopolitan Vision,* trans. Ciarin Conin. Cambridge: Polity.

Beck, Ulrich, and Elisabeth Beck-Gernsheim (2001), *Individualisation: Institutionalised Individualism and Its Social and Political Consequences,* London: Sage.

Beck, Ulrich, Anthony Giddens and Scott Lash (1994), *Reflexive Modernisation,* Cambridge: Polity.

Bennett, Tony (1979), *Formalism and Marxism,* London: Methuen.

Bennett, Tony (1998), *Culture: A Reformer's Science,* London: Sage.

Berger, Peter L., and Thomas Luckmann (1966), *The Social Construction of Reality,* London: Penguin.

Bewes, Timothy (2002), *Reification: Or the Anxiety of Late Capitalism,* London: Verso.

Bewes, Timothy, and Jeremy Gilbert (eds) (2000), *Cultural Capitalism: Politics After New Labour,* London: Lawrence & Wishart.

Bey, Hakim (1985), *T.A.Z. The Temporary Autonomous Zone, Ontological Anarchy, Poetic Terrorism,* Brooklyn: Autonomedia.

Bhabha, Homi (1994), *The Location of Culture,* London: Routledge.

Bird, Tessa, and Tim Jordan (1999), 'Sounding Out New Social Movements and the Left: Interview with Stuart Hall, Doreen Massey and Michael Rustin', in Tim Jordan and Adam Lent (eds) *Storming the Millennium.* London: Lawrence & Wishart.

Bobbio, Noberto (1989), 'The Upturned Utopia', in *New Left Review* 177. London: Verso.

Boltanski, Luc, and Eve Chiapello (2005), *The New Spirit of Capitalism,* trans. Gregory Elliott. London: Verso.

Bookchin, Murray (1991), *The Ecology of Freedom,* New York: Black Rose Books.

Bookchin, Murray (1988), 'The Crisis in the Ecology Movement' in *Green Perspectives* 6, [Online], http://www.social-ecology.org/article.php?story=20031117103 040124 (accessed January 15, 2008).

Bourdieu, Pierre (1986), *Distinction: A Social Critique of the Judgement of Taste,* trans. Richard Nice. London: Routledge.

Bové, José, and François Dufour (2001), *The World is Not For Sale: Farmers Against Junk Food,* trans. Anna de Casparis. London, Verso.

Bowman, Paul (2007), *Post-Marxism Vs. Cultural Studies,* Edinburgh: Edinburgh University Press.

Boyne, Georgina (1993), *The Imagined Village: Culture, Ideology and the English Folk Revival,* Manchester: Manchester University Press.

Bragg, Billy (2007), *The Progressive Patriot: A Search for Belonging,* London: Black Swan.

Branford, Sue, and Bernardo Kucinski (2003), *Politics Transformed: Lula and the Workers Party in Brazil,* London: Latin American Bureau.

Braudel, Fernand (1984), *Civilisation and Capitalism Vol. 3: The Perspective of the World,* trans. Sian Reynolds. London: Collins.

Brenner, Robert (2005), *The Economics of Global Turbulence,* London: Verso.

Burbach, Roger, Bill Robinson and Fiona Jeffries (2001), *Globalisation and Post-modern Politics: From Zapatistas to High-tech Robber Barons,* London: Pluto.

Butler, Judith (1990), *Gender Trouble,* London: Routledge.

Butler, Judith (1993), *Bodies that Matter,* New York: Routledge.

Butler, Judith, Ernesto Laclau and Slavoj Žižek (2000), *Contingency, Hegemony, Universality,* London: Verso.

Byrne, E., and Martin McQuillan (1998), *Deconstructing Disney,* London: Pluto.

Callinicos, Alex (2003), *An Anti-Capitalist Manifesto,* Cambridge: Polity.

Cassen, Bernard (2004), 'Inventing *ATTAC*', in Tom Mertes (ed.), *A Movement of Movements,* London: Verso.

Castells, Manuel (1997), *The Power of Identity,* Oxford: Blackwell.

Centre for Contemporary Cultural Studies Race and Politics Group (1982), *The Empire Strikes Back: Race and Racism in 70s Britain.* London: Hutchinson in association with the Centre for Contemporary Cultural Studies.

Centre for Contemporary Cultural Studies Women's Studies Group (1978), *Women Take Issue,* Birmingham: Centre for Contemporary Cultural Studies, University of Birmingham.

Certeau, Michel de (1984), *The Practice of Everyday Life,* trans. Steven Rendell. Berkeley: University of California Press.

Chomsky, Noam (1983), *The Fateful Triangle: United States, Israel and the Palestinians,* Boston: South End Press.

Clarke, John (2004), *Changing Welfare, Changing States,* London: Sage.

Clarke, John, and Janet Newman (1997), *The Managerial State,* London: Sage.

Cohen, Stan (1972), *Folk Devils and Moral Panics,* London: MacGibbon & Kee.

Couldry, Nick (1999), *The Place of Media Power: Pilgrims and Witnesses of the Media Age,* London: Routledge.

Couldry, Nick (2000), *Inside Culture: Re-imagining the Method of Cultural Studies,* London: Sage.

Crouch, Colin (2004), *Post-Democracy,* Cambridge: Polity.

Curry, Patrick (1997), *Defending Middle Earth: Tolkien, Myth and Modernity,* London: Palgrave.

Day, Richard J. F. (2005), *Gramsci is Dead: Anarchist Currents in the Newest Social Movements,* London: Pluto.

Debord, Guy (1994), *The Society of the Spectacle,* trans. Donald Nicholson-Smith. New York: Zone Books.

Debord, Guy (1959), 'Detournement as Negation and Prelude', in Ken Knabb (ed.) (1981) *Situationist International Anthology.* Berkeley: Bureau of Public Secrets.

Delanda, Manuel (1996), 'Markets, Antimarkets and Network Economics', http://www.cddc.vt.edu/host/delanda/pages/markets.htm (accessed January 15, 2008).

Delanda, Manuel (1997), *A Thousand Years of Non-Linear History,* New York: Zone Books.

Delanda, Manuel (2002), *Intensive Science and Virtual Philosophy,* London: Continuum.

Delanda, Manuel (2003), '1000 Years of War: CTHEORY Interview with Manuel Delanda', http://ctheory.net/articles.aspx?id=383 (accessed January 15, 2008).

Delanda, Manuel (2006), *A New Philosophy of Society,* London: Continuum.

Deleuze, Gilles (1990), *The Logic of Sense,* trans. Mark Lester and Charles Stivale. New York: Columbia University Press.

Deleuze, Gilles (1994), *Difference and Repetition,* trans. Paul Patton. New York: Columbia University Press.

Deleuze, Gilles, and Félix Guattari (1972), *L'Anti-Oedipe,* Paris: Editions Minuit.

Deleuze, Gilles, and Félix Guattari (1983), *Anti-Oedipus,* trans. Robert Hurley, Mark Seem and Helen R. Lane. Minneapolis: University of Minnesota Press.

Deleuze, Gilles, and Félix Guattari (1988), *A Thousand Plateaus,* trans. Brian Massumi. London: Athlone.

Deleuze, Gilles and Félix Guattari (1994), *What is Philosophy?,* London: Verso.

Deleuze, Gilles and Claire Parnet (1996), *Dialogues,* Paris: Flammarion.

D'Emilio, John (1992), 'Foreword' in Jay and Young (eds) *Out of the Closet: Voices of Gay Liberations,* Twentieth Anniversary Edition, London: Gay Men's Press.

Derrida, Jacques (1982), *Margins of Philosophy,* trans. Alan Bass. Hemel Hempstead: Harvester.

Derrida, Jacques (1991), 'Choreographies', in Peggy Kamuf (ed.) *Between the Blinds: A Derrida Reader,* Hemel Hempstead: Harvester Wheatsheaf.

Derrida, Jacques (1994), *Spectres of Marx,* trans. Peggy Kamuf. London, Routledge.

Derrida, Jacques (2001), *On Cosmopolitanism and Forgiveness,* trans. Mark Dooley and Michael Hughes. London: Routledge.

Donald, James (1996), 'The Citizen and the Man About Town', in Stuart Hall and Paul du Gay (eds) *Questions of Cultural Identity.* London: Sage.

Doyle, Timothy and Doug McEachern (1998), *Environment and Politics,* London: Routledge.

Dworkin, Dennis (1997), *Cultural Marxism in Postwar Britain: History, the New Left, and the Origins of Cultural Studies,* Durham: Duke University Press.

Eagleton, Terry (2000), *The Idea of Culture,* Oxford: Blackwell.

Fairclough, Norman (2003), *Analysing Discourse: Textual Analysis for Social Research,* London: Routledge.

Featherstone, Liza, Doug Henwood and Christian Parenti (2004), 'Left Anti-Intellectualism and its Discontents', in Eddie Yuen, George Katsiaficas and Daniel Burton Rose (eds), *Confronting Capitalism: Dispatches from a Global Movement,* New York: Soft Skull Press.

Featherstone, Mike (1991), *Consumer Culture and Postmodernism,* London: Sage.

Featherstone, Mike, Nigel Thrift and John Urry (eds) (2005), *Automobilities,* London: Sage.

Finlayson, Alan (2003), *Making Sense of New Labour,* London: Lawrence & Wishart.

Fiske, John (1987), *Television Culture,* New York: Routledge.

Ford, Simon (ed.) (2005), *The Situationist International: A User's Guide,* London: Black Dog Publishing.

Foucault, Michel (1972), *The Archaeology of Knowledge,* trans. A. M. Sheridan Smith. London: Tavistock.

Foucault, Michel (1979), *The History of Sexuality Volume 1,* trans. Robert Hurley, London, Penguin.

Foucault, Michel (1983), 'Preface', to Gilles Deleuze and Félix Guattari *Anti-Oedipus,* trans. Robert Hurley, Mark Seem and Helen R. Lane. Minneapolis: University of Minnesota Press.

Foucault, Michel (1991), *Remarks on Marx:* Conversations with Duccio Trombadori. trans. R. James Goldstein and James Cascaito. New York: Semiotext(e).

Foucault, Michel (2004), *Naissance de la Biopolitique,* Paris: Gallimard Seuil.

Foucault, Michel (2005), *History of Madness,* ed. Jean Khalfa. London: Routledge.

Frank, Thomas (2002), *New Consensus for Old: Cultural Studies From Left to Right,* Chicago: Prickly Paradigm Press.

Freud, Sigmund (1985), 'Group Psychology and the Analysis of the Ego in Group Psychology and the Analysis of the Ego', in *Civilisation, Society and Religion,* London: Penguin.

Frow, John (1995), *Cultural Studies & Cultural Value,* Oxford: Oxford University Press.

Fuller, Matthew (2005), *Media Ecologies,* Cambridge: The MIT Press.

Genosko, Gary (2003), *The Party Without Bosses: Lessons on Anti-Capitalism from Félix Guattari and Luís Inácio 'Lula' da Silva,* Winnipeg: Arbeiter Ring Publishing.

George, Susan (2004), *Another World is Possible If . . . ,* London: Verso.

Gibson, Mark (2007), *Culture and Power,* London: Berg.

Giddens, Anthony (1998), *The Third Way,* Cambridge: Polity.

Gilbert, Jeremy (1999), 'White Light/White Heat; *Jouissance* Beyond Gender in the Velvet Underground', in Andrew Blake (ed.) *Living Through Pop,* London: Routledge.

Gilbert, Jeremy (2001), 'A Certain Ethics of Openness: Radical Democratic Cultural Studies', in *Strategies* November 2001.

Gilbert, Jeremy (2004a), 'The Second Wave: the specificity of New Labour neo-liberalism', in *Soundings.* London: Lawrence & Wishart.

Gilbert, Jeremy (2004b), 'Signifying Nothing: "Culture", "Discourse" and the Sociality of Affect', in *Culture Machine* 6, http://culturemachine.tees.ac.uk/frm_f1.htm (accessed January 15, 2008).

Gilbert, Jeremy (2004c), 'Small Faces: The Tyranny of Celebrity in post-Oedipal Culture', in *Mediactive* 2, London: Lawrence & Wishart.

Gilbert, Jeremy (2006), 'Dyer and Deleuze: Post-Structuralist Cultural Criticism', *New Formations* 58. London: Lawrence & Wishart.

Gilbert, Jeremy (2007), 'All the Right Questions, All the Wrong Answers', in Paul Bowman and Richard Stamp (eds) *The Truth of Žižek,* London: Continuum.

Gilroy, Paul (1987), *There Ain't No Black in the Union Jack,* London: Routledge.

Gilroy, Paul (1993), *The Black Atlantic,* London: Verso.

Gilroy, Paul (2004a), *After Empire: Melancholia or Convivial Culture?,* London: Routledge.

Gilroy, Paul (2004b), *Between Camps: Nations, Culture and the Allure of Race,* London: Routledge.

Giroux, Henry (2004), *The Terror of Neoliberalism: Authoritarianism and the Eclipse of Democracy,* Boulder: Paradigm Publishers.

Gitlin, Todd (1987), *The Sixties: Years of Hope, Days of Rage,* New York: Bantam.

Gitlin Todd (1995), *The Twilight of Common Dreams: Why America is Wracked by Culture Wars,* New York: Henry Holt.

Gopal, Priyamvada and Neil Lazarus (eds) (2006), *New Formations 59—After Iraq: Reframing Postcolonial Studies,* London: Lawrence & Wishart.

Gramsci, Antonio (1971), *Selections from the Prison Notebooks,* trans. Quentin Hoare and Geoffrey Nowell Smith. London, Lawrence & Wishart.

Gramsci, Antonio (1985), 'Questions of Culture', in Antonio Gramsci *Selections from Cultural Writings,* David Forgacs and Geoffrey Nowell-Smith (eds). trans. William Boelhower. London: Lawrence & Wishart.

Grossberg, Lawrence (1982), 'Experience, Signification, Reality', in Lawrence Grossberg (1997) *Bringing it all Back Home: Essays on Cultural Studies,* Durham: Duke University Press.

Grossberg, Lawrence (1992), *We Gotta Get Out of This Place: Popular Conservatism and Popular Culture,* New York: Routledge.

Grossberg, Lawrence (1995), Cultural 'Studies: What's In a Name?', in Lawrence Grossberg (1997) *Bringing it all Back Home: Essays on Cultural Studies,* Durham: Duke University Press.

Grossberg, Lawrence (2005), *Caught in the Crossfire: Kids, Politics and America's Future,* Boulder: Paradigm.

Grossberg, Lawrence, Cary Nelson and Paula Treichler (eds) (1992), *Cultural Studies,* New York, Routledge.

Guattari, Félix (1972), *Psychanalyse et Transversalité,* Paris: François Maspero.

Guattari, Félix (1984), *Molecular Revolution: Psychiatry and Politics,* trans. R. Steed. London: Penguin.

Guattari, Félix (2000), *The Three Ecologies,* trans. Paul Sutton. London: Athlone.

Hall, Gary (2002), *Culture in Bits,* London: Continuum.

Hall, Stuart (1988), *The Hard Road to Renewal: Thatcherism and the Crisis of the Left,* London: Verso.

Hall, Stuart (1992), 'The Rest and the West: Discourse and Power', in Stuart Hall and Bram Gieben (eds), *Formations of Modernity,* Cambridge: Polity.

Hall, Stuart (1996), 'The problem of ideology: Marxism without guarantees', in Morley, David and Kuan-Hsing Chen (eds), *Stuart Hall: Critical Dialogues in Cultural Studies,* London: Verso.

Hall, Stuart (1997), 'Culture and Power', interview in *Radical Philosophy* 86, London: Radical Philosophy.

Hall, Stuart (2004), 'Divided City: The Crisis of London', http://www.opendemo cracy.net/arts-multiculturalism/article_2191.jsp (accessed January 15, 2008).

Hall, Stuart, Charles Critcher, Tony Jefferson and John Clarke (1978), *Policing The Crisis,* London: Macmillan.

Hall, Stuart, Dorothy Hobson, Andrew Lowe and Paul Willis (eds) (1980), *Culture, Media, Language: Working Papers in Cultural Studies, 1972–79,* London: Routledge.

Hall, Stuart and Martin Jacques (eds) (1989), *New Times: The Changing Face of Politics in the 1990s,* London: Lawrence & Wishart.

Hall, Stuart, and Tony Jefferson (eds) (1976), *Resistance Through Rituals: Youth Sub-cultures in Post-war Britain,* London: Hutchinson.

Hall, Stuart, and Paddy Whannel (1964), *The Popular Arts,* London: Hutchinson Educational.

Hallward, Peter (2003), *Badiou: A Subject to Truth,* Minneapolis: University of Minnesota Press.

Hallward, Peter (2007), *Out of this World: Deleuze and the Philosophy of Creation,* London: Verso.

Hardt, Michael and Antonio Negri (1994), *Labor of Dionysus: A Critique of the State Form,* Minneapolis: University of Minnesota Press.

Hardt, Michael and Antonio Negri (2000), *Empire,* Cambridge: Harvard University Press.

Hardt, Michael and Antonio Negri (2004), *Multitude: War and Democracy in the Age of Empire,* New York: The Penguin Press.

Harraway, Donna (1991), 'A Cyborg Manifesto: Science, Technology, and Socialist-Feminism in the Late Twentieth Century', in *Simians, Cyborgs and Women: The Reinvention of Nature,* 149–81, New York: Routledge.

Harris, David (1992), *From Class Struggle to the Politics of Pleasure,* London: Routledge.

Harvey, David (1989), *The Condition of Postmodernity,* Oxford: Blackwell.

Harvey, David (2005), *A Brief History of Neoliberalism,* Oxford: Oxford University Press.

Hayden, Tom (ed.) (2001), *The Zapatista Reader,* New York: Nation Books.

Hayek, Friedrich (1944), *The Road to Serfdom,* London: Routledge.

Hebdige, Dick (1979), *Subculture: The Meaning of Style,* London: Methuen.

Hermes, Joke (1996), *Reading Women's Magazines,* Cambridge: Polity Press.

Hesmondhalgh, David (2002), *The Cultural Industries,* London: Sage.

Hills, Matt (2002), *Fan Cultures,* London: Routledge.

Hindess, Barry, and Paul Hirst (1975), *Pre-Capitalist Modes of Production,* London: Routledge & Kegan Paul.

Hindess, Barry, and Paul Hirst (1977), *Mode of Production and Social Formation,* London: Macmillan.

Hoggart, Richard (1957) *The Uses of Literacy,* London: Chatto & Windus.

Holloway, John (2002), *Change the World Without Taking Power: The Meaning of Revolution Today,* London: Pluto.

Hoppe, Hans-Herman (1989), *A Theory of Socialism and Capitalism,* Norwell: Kluwe Academic Publishers.

Howarth, David R. (2004), 'Hegemony, Subjectivity, Democracy' in Simon Critchley and Oliver Marchart (eds), *Laclau: A Critical Reader,* London: Routledge.

James, C.L.R. (1989), *The Black Jacobins: Toussaint L'Ouverture and the San Domingo Revolution,* New York: Vintage Books.

Jameson, Frederic (1991), *Postmodernism or, The Cultural Logic of Late Capitalism,* London: Verso.

Jardim, Anne (1970), *The First Henry Ford: A Study in Personality and Business Leadership,* Cambridge: The MIT Press.

Joseph, Jonathan (2002), *Hegemony: A Realist Analysis,* London: Routledge.

Katsiaficas, George (1987), *The Imagination of the New Left: A Global Analysis of 1968,* Boston, Mass.: South End Press.

Kidd, Dorothy (2003), 'From Carnival to Commons: the Global IMC Network', in Eddie Yuen, George Katsiaficas and Daniel Burton Rose (eds), *Confronting Capitalism: Dispatches from a Global Movement,* New York: Soft Skull Press.

Kingsnorth, Paul (2003), *One No, Many Yeses: A Journey to the Heart of the Global Resistance Movement,* London: Free Press.

Klein, Naomi (2000), *No Logo,* London: Flamingo.

Klein, Naomi (2002), *Fences and Window: Dispatches from the Anti-globalisation Debate,* London: Flamingo.

Kristeva, Julia (1984), *Revolution in Poetic Language,* trans. Margaret Waller. New York: Columbia.

Lacan, Jacques (1977), *Écrits,* trans. Alan Sheridan. London, Routledge.

Laclau, Ernesto (1977), *Politics and Ideology in Marxist Theory,* London: New Left Books.

Laclau, Ernesto (1990), *New Reflections on the Revolution of Our Time,* London, Verso.

Laclau, Ernesto (1996), 'Why Do Empty Signifiers Matter to Politics', in Ernesto Laclau *Emancipation(s),* London: Verso.

Laclau, Ernesto (1998), 'The Politics of Rhetoric', Essex Papers in Politics and Government. Colchester: University of Essex.

Laclau, Ernesto (2001), 'Can Immanence Explain Social Struggles?', *Diacritics* Winter 2001. Ithaca: The John Hopkins University Press.

Laclau, Ernesto (2005), *The Populist Reason,* London: Verso.

Laclau, Ernesto and Chantal Mouffe (1985), *Hegemony and Socialist Strategy: Towards a Radical Democratic Politics,* London: Verso.

Laclau, Ernesto and Chantal Mouffe (1990), 'Post-Marxism Without Apologies' in Ernesto Laclau (ed.), *New Reflections on the Revolution of Our Time,* London, Verso.

Land, Nick (1992), *The Thirst for Annihilation: Georges Bataille and Virulent Nihilism,* London: Routledge.

Land, Nick (2003), 'Meltdown', http://www.ccru.net/swarm1/1_melt.htm (accessed January 15, 2008).

Lash, Scott (2007), 'Power after Hegemony: Cultural Studies in Mutation?', *Theory, Culture, and Society,* 24(3): 55–78.

Lash, Scott and John Urry (1987), *The End of Organised Capitalism,* Cambridge: Polity.

Lasn, Kalle (1999), *Culture Jam: How to Reverse America's Suicidal Consumer Binge—And Why We Must,* New York: William Morrow & Company.

Lazzarato, Maurizio (1996), 'Immaterial Labour', http://www.generation-online. org/c/fcimmateriallabour3.htm (accessed January 15, 2008).

Lazzarato, Maurizio (2002), *Puissances de L'invention: La Psychologie Économique de Gabriel Tarde Contre L'Économie Politique,* Paris: Le Empêcheurs de Penser En Rond.

Leavis, F. R. (1948), *The Great Tradition,* London: Chatto & Windus.

Lee, Richard E. (2003), *Life and Times of Cultural Studies,* Durham: Duke University Press.

Lefort, Claude (1994), *L'Invention Démocratique,* Paris: Fayard.

Lenin, V. I. (1947), *What Is To Be Done?,* Moscow: Progress Publishers.

Lenin, V. I. (1975), *Imperialism, the Highest Stage of Capitalism,* Moscow: Progress Publishers.

Leys, Colin (2001), *Market Driven Politics,* London: Verso.

Littler, Jo (2005), 'Putting the Shoe on the Other Foot', http://www.signsofthetimes. org.uk/(accessed January 15, 2008).

Littler, Jo (2008), *Radical Consumption in Contemporary Culture,* Milton Keynes: Open University Press.

Löwy, Michael (1982), *The Politics of Combined and Uneven Development,* London: Routledge.

Lukacs, Georg (1971), *History and Class Consciousness,* trans. Rodney Livingstone. London: The Merlin Press Ltd.

Lyotard, Jean François (1984), *The Postmodern Condition: A Report on Knowledge,* trans. Geoffrey Bennington and Brian Massumi. Manchester: Manchester University Press.

Lyotard, Jean-François (1988), *The Differend: Phrases in Dispute,* trans. Georges Van Den Abbeele. Manchester: Manchester University Press.

Lyotard, Jean-François (2004), *The Libidinal Economy,* trans. Ian Hamilton Grant. London: Continuum.

Macfarlane, Alan (1978), *The Origins of English Individualism,* Oxford: Blackwell.

Marcos, Subcomandante Insurgente (2001), *Our Word Is Our Weapon: Selected Writings of Subcomandante Insurgente Marcos,* New York: Seven Stories Press.

Marlow, Alan and Barry Loveday (eds.) (2000), *After MacPherson: Reflections on Race and Policing After the Stephen Lawrence Enquiry.* London: Russell House Publishing.

Marx, Karl (1934), *The Eighteenth Brumaire of Louis Napoleon* [Online], Progress Publishers: Moscow. http://www.marxists.org/archive/marx/works/1852/18th-brumaire/ ch01.htm (accessed January 15, 2008).

Marx, Karl (1992), *Marx's Capital: A Student Edition,* London: Lawrence & Wishart.

Marx, Karl and Friedrich Engels (1998), *The Communist Manifesto,* London: Verso.

Massumi, Brian (1992), *A User's Guide to Capitalism and Schizophrenia: Deviations from Deleuze & Guattari,* Cambridge: Massachusetts Institute of Technology Press.

Massumi, Brian (2002), *Parables for the Virtual: Movement, Affect, Sensation,* Durham: Duke University Press.

McGuigan, Jim (1992), *Cultural Populism,* London: Routledge.

Mckay, George (1996), *Senseless Acts of Beauty: Cultures of Resistance Since the Sixties,* London, Verso.

Mckay, George (ed.) (1998), *DiY Culture: Party & Protest in Nineties Britain,* London: Verso.

McMillan, John, and Paul Buhle (2003), *The New Left Revisited,* Philadelphia: Temple University Press.

McRobbie, Angela (1990), *Feminism and Youth Culture: From 'Jackie' to 'Just Seventeen',* Basingstoke: Macmillan.

McRobbie, Angela (1992), 'Post-Marxism and Cultural Studies', in Lawrence Grossberg, Nelson, Cary and Treichler, Paula (eds), *Cultural Studies,* New York, Routledge.

McRobbie, Angela (1994), *Postmodernism and Popular Culture,* London: Routledge.

McRobbie, Angela (1998), *British Fashion Design: Rag Trade or Image Industry,* London: Routledge.

McRobbie, Angela (2005), *The Uses of Cultural Studies: A Textbook,* London: Sage.

Mercer, Kobena (1994), *Welcome to the Jungle,* London: Routledge.

Mertes, Tom (ed.) (2003), *The Movement of Movements: A Reader,* London, Verso.

Miami Theory Collective (1991), *Community at Loose Ends,* Minneapolis: University of Minnesota Press.

Middleton, Richard (1990), *Studying Popular Music,* Milton Keynes: Open University Press.

Miller, Daniel (1987), *Material Culture and Mass Consumption,* Oxford: Blackwell.

Mitchell, Juliet (1974), *Psychoanalysis and Feminism,* London: Allen Lane.

Moorcock, Michael (1978), 'Starship Stormtroopers', http://flag.blackened.net/liberty/moorcock.html (accessed January 15, 2008).

Moore, Michael (2003), *Dude, Where's My Country?,* London: Penguin.

Morley, David & Kuan-Hsing Chen (eds) (1996), *Stuart Hall: Critical Dialogues in Cultural Studies,* London: Routledge.

Mort, Frank (1996), *Cultures of Consumption,* London: Routledge.

Morton, Donald (ed) (1996), *The Material Queer: A LesBiGay Cultural Studies Reader,* Boulder: Westview Press.

Mouffe, Chantal (2000), *The Democratic Paradox,* London: Verso.

Mulhern, Francis (2000), *Culture/Metaculture,* London: Routledge.

Mulvey, Laura (1989), *Visual and Other Pleasures,* Basingstoke: Macmillan.

Nairn, Tom (1977), *The Break-Up of Britain,* London: New Left Books.

Nash, Kate (2000), *Contemporary Political Sociology,* Oxford: Blackwell.

Nava, Mica (1992), *Changing Cultures: Feminism, Youth and Consumerism,* London: Sage.

Nava, Mica (2007), *Visceral Cosmopolitanism: Gender, Culture and the Normalisation of Difference,* Oxford: Berg.

Negri, Toni (1988), *Revolution Retrieved: Writings on Marx, Keynes, Capitalist Crisis and New Social Subjects 1967–83,* London: Red Notes.

Nietzsche, Friedrich (1968), *The Will to Power,* trans. Walter Kaufman and R. J. Hollingdale. New York: Vintage.

Nixon, Sean (1996), *Hard Looks: Masculinities, Spectatorship and Contemporary Consumption,* London: UCL Press.

Notes from Nowhere (2003), *We Are Everywhere: The Irresistible Rise of Global Anticapitalism,* London: Verso.

Parisi, Luciana (2004), *Abstract Sex,* London: Continuum.

Patton, Paul (2000), *Deleuze and the Political,* London: Routledge.

Penn, Mark (2007), *Microtrends,* London: Allen Lane.

Perkin, Harold (1969), *The Origins of Modern English Society,* London: Routledge.

Plant, Sadie (1992), *The Most Radical Gesture: The Situationist International in a Postmodern Age,* London: Routledge.

Polanyi, Karl (1944), *The Great Transformation: The Political and Economic Origins of our Time,* Boston: Beacon Press.

Prigogine, Ilya and Isabelle Stengers (1984), *Order Out of Chaos: Man's New Dialogue with Nature,* New York: Bantam.

Raby, Diana (2006), *Democracy and Revolution: Latin American and Socialism Today,* London: Pluto.

Retort (2005), *Afflicted Powers,* London: Verso.

Ross, Andrew (ed.) (1997), *No Sweat: Fashion, Free Trade and the Rights of Garment Workers,* London: Verso.

Rothbard, Murray (2003), *The Ethics of Liberty,* New York: New York University Press.

Rutherford, Jonathan (2003), *Mediactive 1: Knowledge/Culture,* London: Lawrence & Wishart.

Sassoon, Donald (1997), *One Hundred Years of Socialism: The Western European Left in the Twentieth Century,* London: Fontana.

Saussure, Ferdinand de (1983), *Course in General Linguistics,* trans. Roy Harris. London: Duckworth.

Schumpeter, Josef A. (1954), *Capitalism, Socialism and Democracy,* London: Allen & Unwin.

Sen, Jai, Anita Anand, Arturo Escobar and Peter Waterman (eds) (2003), *The World Social Forum: Challenging Empires,* New Delhi: Viveka Foundation. [Online] http://www.choike.org/nuevo_eng/informes/1557.html (accessed January 15, 2008).

Sennett, Richard (2006), *The Culture of the New Capitalism,* New Haven: Yale University Press.

Shepard, Benjamin and Benjamin Hduk (eds) *From Act Up to the WTO: Urban Protest and Community Building in the Era of Globalisation,* London: Verso.

Shiva, Vandana (1997), *Biopiracy: The Plunder of Nature and Knowledge,* Cambridge: South End Press.

Slack, Jennifer Daryl (1996), 'The theory and method of articulation in cultural studies', in Kuan-Hsing Chen and David Morley (eds), *Stuart Hall: Critical Dialogues in Cultural Studies,* London, Routledge.

Slater, Don (1997), *Consumer Culture and Modernity,* Cambridge: Polity.

Smith. A. C. (1975), *Paper Voices: The popular press and social change 1935–65,* London: Chatto & Windus.

Smith, Paul (1997), *Millennial Dreams: Contemporary Culture and Capital in the North,* London: Verso.

Spinoza, Benedict De (1958), *Tractaus Philosophicus* in *The Political Works,* trans. A. G. Wernham. Oxford: The Clarendon Press.

Spinoza, B. (2000), *Ethics,* trans. G.H.R. Parkinson. Oxford: Oxford University Press.

Starr, Amory (2000), *Naming the Enemy: Anti-Corporate Movements Confront Globalisation,* London: Zed Books.

Steele, Tom (1997), *The Emergence of Cultural Studies: Cultural Politics, Adult Education and the English Question,* London: Lawrence & Wishart.

Taylor, Richard (1988), *Against the Bomb: The British Peace Movement 1958–65,* Oxford, Clarendon Press.

Terranova, Tiziana (2004), *Network Culture,* London: Pluto.

Thoburn, Nicholas (2003), *Deleuze, Marx and Politics,* London: Routledge.

Thompson, E. P. (1963), *The Making of the English Working Class,* London: Gollancz.

Tormey, Simon (2005), *Anti-Capitalism: A Beginner's Guide,* Oxford: Oneworld.

Toynbee, Jason (2000), *Making Popular Music: Musician, Aesthetics and the Manufacture of Popular Music,* London: Hodder Arnold.

Unger, Roberto Mangabeira (1998), *Democracy Realised,* London: Verso.

Urry, John (2004), 'The System of Automobility', *Theory, Culture and Society,* Volume 21, Number 4–5. London: Sage.

Vaneigem, Raoul (1983), *The Revolution of Everyday Life,* London: Left Bank Books/Rebel Press.

Vaneigem, Raoul (2003), *A Declaration of Human Rights: On the Sovereignty of Life as Surpassing the Rights of Man,* trans. Liz Heron. London: Pluto.

Vico, Giambattista (1999), *New Science: Principles of the New Science Concerning the Common Nature of Nations,* trans. David Marsh. London: Penguin.

Wainwright, Hilary (2003), *Reclaim the State: Experiments in Popular Democracy,* London, Verso.

Wall, Derek (1999), *Earth First! and the Anti-Roads Movement,* London: Routledge.

Weber, Max (1947), *The Theory of Social and Economic Organisation,* ed. and trans. Talcott Parsons. New York: The Free Press.

Weber, Max (1968), *Max Weber on Law in Economy and Society,* ed. Max Rheinstein, trans. Edward Shils and Max Rheinstein. New York: Simon and Schuster.

Wheeler, Wendy (2006), *The Whole Creature: Complexity, Biosemiotics and the Evolution of Culture,* London: Lawrence & Wishart.

Whitfield, Dexter (2001), *Public Services or Corporate Welfare,* London, Pluto Press.

Williams, Raymond (1961), *The Long Revolution,* London: Chatto & Windus.

Williams, Raymond (1966), *Communications,* London: Chatto & Windus.

Williams, Raymond (ed.), (1968), *The May Day Manifesto 1968,* London: Penguin.

Williams, Raymond (1973), *The Country and the City in the Modern Novel,* Oxford: Oxford University Press.

Williams, Raymond (1977), *Marxism and Literature,* Oxford, Oxford University Press.

Williams, Raymond (1982), *Culture and Society,* London: Hogarth Press.

Williams, Raymond (1989), *Resources of Hope,* London, Verso.

Williamson, Judith (1978), *Decoding Advertisements,* London: Boyars.

Willis, Paul (1977), *Learning to Labour,* Farnborough: Saxon House.

Winship, Janice (1981), *Woman Becomes an 'Individual',* Birmingham: Centre for Contemporary Cultural Studies.

Winship, Janice (1987), *Inside Women's Magazines,* London: Pandora.

Wittgenstein, Ludwig (1961), *Tractatus Logic-Philosophicus,* trans. D. F. Pears and B. F. McGuinness. London: Routledge & Kegan Paul.

World Social Forum (2002), 'Charter of Principles of the World Social Forum', http://www.forumsocialmundial.org.br/(accessed January 15, 2008).

Wright, Steve (2002), *Storming Heaven: Class Composition and Struggle in Italian Autonomist Marxism,* London: Pluto Press.

Yuen, Eddie, George Katsiaficas and Daniel Burton Rose (2004), *Confronting Capitalism: Dispatches from a Global Movement,* New York: Soft Skull Press.

Yuen, Eddie, George Katsiaficas and Daniel Burton Rose (eds) (2002), *The Battle of Seattle: The New Challenge to Capitalist Organisation,* New York: Soft Skull Press.

Žižek, Slavoj (2001), *Did Somebody Say Totalitarianism?,* London: Verso.

Žižek, Slavoj (2002), 'Afterword: Lenin's Choice', in Žižek (ed.) *Revolution at the Gates: Selected Writings of Lenin from 1917,* London: Verso.

Zylinska, Joanna (2005), *The Ethics of Cultural Studies,* London: Continuum.

Index